'Behrman has produced a fascinating, ambitious and wide-ranging book that explores sanctuary and asylum from various perspectives. At a moment when asylum seems under threat, this timely analysis reminds us of the importance of history but, crucially, challenges the role of law in protecting forced migrants and providing solutions.'

Dallal Stevens,
University of Warwick, UK

'Refugee law as protection? Think again. Taking us through Agamben and Rancière and from the Antiquity to the development of Christian thought to the sanctuary movement in the US and Sans-Papiers resistance in France, the author demonstrates how the legal paradigm threatens or even erases the practice of asylum. Erudite, clear and compelling.'

Marie-Bénédicte Dembour,
University of Brighton, UK

'Why are refugees so often seen as intruders into societies in which they seek safety and security? This book provides important insights into the role of law in the ideology and practice of exclusion. It is a valuable resource for those who wish to understand the predicaments of refugees in the 21st century.'

Philip Marfleet,
University of East London, UK

Law and Asylum

In contrast to the claim that refugee law has been a key in guaranteeing a space of protection for refugees, this book argues that law has been instrumental in eliminating spaces of protection, not just from one's persecutors but also from the grasp of sovereign power. By uncovering certain fundamental aspects of asylum as practised in the past and in present day social movements, namely its concern with defining space rather than people and its role as a space of resistance or otherness to sovereign law, this book demonstrates that asylum has historically been antagonistic to law and vice versa. In contrast, twentieth-century refugee law was constructed precisely to ensure the effective management and control over the movements of forced migrants. To illustrate the complex ways in which these two paradigms – asylum and refugee law – interact with one another, this book examines their historical development and concludes with in-depth studies of the Sanctuary Movement in the United States and the Sans-Papiers of France.

The book will appeal to researchers and students of refugee law and refugee studies; legal and political philosophy; ancient, medieval and modern legal history; and sociology of political movements.

Simon Behrman is lecturer in law at Royal Holloway, University of London.

Law and Migration

Series Editor: Satvinder S. Juss, *King's College London, UK*

Migration and its subsets of refugee and asylum policy are raising up the policy agenda at national and international level. Current controversies underline the need for rational and informed debate of this widely misrepresented and little understood area. *Law and Migration* contributes to this debate by establishing a monograph series to encourage discussion and help inform policy in this area. The series provides a forum for leading new research principally from the law and legal studies area but also from related social sciences. The series is broad in scope, covering a wide range of subjects and perspectives.

Other titles in this series:

Immigration, Integration and the Law
The Intersection of Domestic, EU and International Legal Regimes
Clíodhna Murphy

Regional Approaches to the Protection of Asylum Seekers
An International Legal Perspective
Edited by Ademola Abass and Francesca Ippolito

Asylum – A Right Denied
A Critical Analysis of European Asylum Policy
Helen O'Nions

The Integration and Protection of Immigrants
Canadian and Scandinavian Critiques
Edited by Paul Van Aerschot and Patricia Daenzer

Towards a Refugee Oriented Right of Asylum
Laura Westra, Satvinder Juss and Tullio Scovazzi

Gender and Migration in Italy
A Multilayered Perspective
Edited by Elisa Olivito

Bureaucracy, Law and Dystopia in the United Kingdom's Asylum System
John R. Campbell

Children's Rights and Refugee Law
Conceptualising Children within the Refugee Convention
Samantha Arnold

Law and Asylum
Space, Subject, Resistance
Simon Behrman

For more information about this series, please visit www.routledge.com/Law-and-Migration/book-series/LAWANDMIG.

Law and Asylum
Space, Subject, Resistance

Simon Behrman

Routledge
Taylor & Francis Group

LONDON AND NEW YORK

First published 2018
by Routledge
2 Park Square, Milton Park, Abingdon, Oxon OX14 4RN

and by Routledge
711 Third Avenue, New York, NY 10017

Routledge is an imprint of the Taylor & Francis Group, an informa business

© 2018 Simon Behrman

British Library Cataloguing-in-Publication Data
A catalogue record for this book is available from the British Library

Library of Congress Cataloging-in-Publication Data
Names: Behrman, Simon, author.
Title: Law and asylum: space, subject, resistance/Simon Behrman.
Description: Abingdon, Oxon [UK]; New York, NY: Routledge, 2018. |
Series: Law and migration | Includes bibliographical references and index.
Identifiers: LCCN 2018001442 | ISBN 9781138304178 (hardback)
Subjects: LCSH: Asylum, Right of. | Refugees – Legal status, laws, etc. |
Freedom of movement (International law) | Illegal aliens.
Classification: LCC K3268.3.B44 2018 | DDC 342.08/3—dc23
LC record available at https://lccn.loc.gov/2018001442

ISBN: 978-1-138-30417-8 (hbk)
ISBN: 978-0-203-73034-8 (ebk)

Typeset in Galliard
by Florence Production Ltd, Stoodleigh, Devon, UK

Printed in the United Kingdom
by Henry Ling Limited

Dedicated to the memory of Bernard Behrman
(1931–2013)

Contents

x *Contents*

Acknowledgements

First and foremost, I must thank Patricia Tuitt and Thanos Zartaloudis. They have been excellent teachers, guides and critics from the first germ of this project. It is not an exaggeration to say that without their support this book would never have taken shape in the first place. They helped me avoid numerous errors and dead-ends and opened up pathways for my research.

The School of Law at Birbeck, where I carried out most of the research and writing, provided the most stimulating research environment that I could have hoped for. They, together with the Arts and Humanities Research Council (AHRC), provided me with research funding, and I thank them for their faith in this project when it consisted of just a short research proposal and some promises.

The bulk of the work on the US Sanctuary Movement was done during my stay at the John W Kluge Center at the Library of Congress. This was made possible by generous funding from them as well as the AHRC. My 5-month residency at the Kluge Center was one of the happiest periods of my work on this book. In particular, I must thank Mary Lou Reker who was so welcoming and helpful and who shared with me her own experiences of providing sanctuary to a Vietnam War draft-resister in the early 1970s. Evey Luther also provided much needed research assistance, which she did with grace and humour, despite the often tedious nature of the work.

The staff and volunteers at the following were all enormously helpful in locating material: Dumbarton Methodist Church, Washington, DC; History Library, US Citizenship and Immigration Services, Washington, DC; First United Methodist Church of Germantown, Philadelphia (where they also provided me with coffee, biscuits and lunch, as well as friendly encouragement in my work – the tradition of hospitality is very strong there!); Swarthmore College Peace Collection, Philadelphia; Graduate Theological Union Archives, Berkeley; and the library of the Wisconsin Historical Society, Madison.

As well as being an often lonely task, research and writing can also make a person rather self-absorbed. For those closest to me, I know that work on this book often made me irritable and distant. Yet in spite of that, I have always felt supported by them. In particular, I must thank Asuka who took on the lion's share of household responsibilities at various crunch points and was always encouraging when I experienced a crisis of confidence in my writing. Dimitri and Bruno had to put up with a father who was often distracted, surrounded by books and papers and a computer that was, to their annoyance, not available for cartoons. To Hannah and Mum my apologies for not being around to help out much. I thank you all for your patience and understanding, and your love.

My father, Bernard Behrman, died in the middle of work on this book. It is one of my greatest regrets that he did not live long enough to read it and to offer his own critical comments. He was himself an exile, having originally left his native South Africa in the late 1950s to pursue graduate studies in England. When increased repression of the anti-Apartheid movement, of which he was an active member, culminated in the infamous Rivonia trials, he found himself unable to return to South Africa for the next three decades. So, at various moments, he was, in the jargon, an economic migrant, a refugee *sur place* and an exile. The fact that he was never firmly categorised as one or any of these things was largely down to the politics and the conditions that prevailed then, before immigration and refugee law became as restrictive and obsessed with categorisation as it has in recent decades. Thanks to him I grew up surrounded by politics and other activists, many of whom had become refugees. That experience, perhaps more than anything else, has been the most important education I have ever had. My dad, as well as being a loving father, was also one of my best teachers, and my hero. This book is dedicated to his memory.

A note on terminology

This is a book about asylum and refugees, written from a legal perspective. Some readers, who share a similar disciplinary background to me, will be bothered that I use words such as 'refugee' and 'migrant' in ways that do not conform to their usual legal meaning. Indeed, it is one of my main arguments that such categories should be much more flexible than their legal formulations allow. As such, use of the word 'refugee' throughout this book does not imply accordance with the definition given in the 1951 Refugee Convention and other legal texts. There are occasions where I have used formulations such as 'refugees/migrants' (notably in relation to the Sans-Papiers) or 'forced migrants' to indicate that the people being discussed will encompass multiple concepts at the same time.

Introduction

How to explain the contemporary downfall of the refugee and the degradation of asylum? What strategies can be effective in resisting this phenomenon which appears to worsen by the day, and re-establish meaningful protection for people forced to leave their homes? These are the central questions that drive this book. My argument is essentially that we need to orientate ourselves away from a persistent reliance on law, specifically refugee law, as a means to overcome the crisis facing refugees. In my view, activists, lawyers and most especially refugees themselves have become trapped within a legal paradigm that offers a pretence of protection, when in fact it provides all the necessary tools for states to restrict access to asylum. How has that happened? The short answer is that asylum has been confused with the regime of refugee law, and that in turn the 'refugee' has become subsumed into a legal category. Indeed, my argument can be boiled down still further into the proposition that there is a fundamental antagonism between asylum and law, which expresses itself as a conflict between focussing on the *space of asylum* and *delineating a refugee subject* in fixed terms.

As this book shows, asylum – or 'sanctuary' as it became known in medieval Europe – was historically characterised as a space beyond the law where people could find protection, whereas refugee law, at both national and international levels, was created with the primary aim of rigidly defining and controlling the refugee subject. Asylum was about escaping the grasp of the sovereign order, whereas refugee law is framed as a burden-sharing mechanism between sovereign orders. The rules of asylum were concerned with bounding space; refugee law, by contrast, fixes its gaze on defining the contours of the refugee themselves, and controlling their movements. The origins of phenomena such as detention centres and camps, of the 'bogus' or 'failed' asylum-claimant, therefore lie not in a corruption of refugee law but in its very essence. As such, refugee law is itself a corruption of asylum.

Yet, refugee law is presented to us as a branch of human rights law, as itself a guarantor of protection for the refugee.[1] This argument is hard to square with

---

1 Chakrabarti S, 'Rights and Rhetoric: The Politics of Asylum and Human Rights Culture in the United Kingdom' (2005), 32, *Journal of Law and Society*, 131; Schoenholtz AI and Bernstein H, 'Improving Immigration Adjudications Through

some basic statistics. Of the three top hosting states for refugees in the world at the time of writing, two – Pakistan and Lebanon – are not parties to the major refugee treaties, and the third – Turkey – while a party to the 1951 Refugee Convention, maintains a reservation excluding non-Europeans, i.e. almost all refugees in the world today, from eligibility for refugee status under that treaty. In contrast, many states that were founding signatories to the Convention, such as the United Kingdom, Australia and France, have some of the smallest numbers of refugees, together with the tightest controls over refugee admissions.[2] These figures are not anomalous, but represent long-standing trends. The existence of a regime of international refugee law therefore does not equal access to protection. Indeed, one might almost suggest the opposite is the case. However tempting as it is to surmise this, it represents a basic logical fallacy. To simply point out a correlation between two things – in this case statistics on refugees and the existence or otherwise of a refugee law regime – does not in itself prove a link between them. One purpose of this book is, therefore, to establish that causal link.

This book contains an argument in three parts. First, I interrogate what exactly has formed the basis of asylum historically. My aim here is try to uncover the origins and substance of asylum. In particular, I have attempted to uncover those points at which law and asylum have encountered each other, and what the outcome of those meetings has been. Second, in order to challenge the narrative that asserts that contemporary refugee law is grounded in humanitarian concerns and the principle of protection for the refugee, it has also been necessary to uncover the threads that, woven together, have created the fabric of the current legal regime of asylum. This has resulted in an extensive discussion of the history of asylum and refugee law that begins in antiquity and ends with the 1951 Convention and even more recent national legislation such as the US Refugee Act of 1980. I make no apologies for attempting a discussion of this scope. It is precisely the myopia of most discussions of refugee law, which look no further back than its most recent manifestations, typically the 1951 Convention and its precursors following World War I, which I believe has led to a set of false assumptions, namely that refugee law follows the groove of asylum, and that its foundations are humanitarian in nature. By taking the (much) longer view, I believe that a clearer perspective on the question can be reached.

Asylum as a widespread and established practice came to an end with the dawn of modernity and the ensuing hegemony of the nation-state and law. Yet, asylum

Competent Counsel' (2008), 21, *Georgetown Journal of Legal Ethics*, 55; Joly D, 'A new asylum regime in Europe' in Frances Nicholson and Patrick Twomey (eds), *Refugee Rights and Realities: Evolving International Concepts and Regimes* (Cambridge University, 1999); Webber F, *Borderline Justice: The Fight for Refugee and Migrant Rights* (Pluto, 2012); McAdam J, 'The Enduring Relevance of the 1951 Convention' (2017), 29, *International Journal of Refugee Law*, 1.

2   *Convention Relating to the Status of Refugees*, 28 July 1951, United Nations, Treaty Series, 189. For the most up-to-date statistics, see the UNHCR website: www.unhcr. org/uk/figures-at-a-glance.html.

survived on the basis of religious and political solidarity, providing protection to people in need, who presented themselves at their door. For example, following the restoration of the English monarchy in the 1660s, regicides found sanctuary among colonists in New England[3]; in ante-bellum United States, escaped slaves from the South were hidden in a network of houses, farms and churches, known as the Underground Railroad[4]; during World War II, almost the entire town of Le Chambon in southern France organised to hide and protect people threatened by the Nazi occupiers[5]; again, in the United States, Vietnam War draft-resisters were given sanctuary in churches during the 1960s[6]; and since the 1970s, there have been a series of movements in various countries in Europe and North and Central America, which have provided protection for refugees, from both violence in their home states and the authorities in the receiving state who have sought to deport them. These are all examples of what I call 'grassroots asylum', by which I mean that they have reconstituted asylum from the bottom-up as spaces beyond and resistant to law and the sovereign order. Thus, the third part of this book examines two highly significant examples of 'grassroots asylum' – the US Sanctuary Movement and the French Sans-Papiers. These chapters should hopefully illuminate the extent to which law, especially refugee law, ends up corrupting rather than underpinning the reappearance of asylum in its modern guise.

The argument of this book is framed within a mainly genealogical methodology in which I attempt to uncover the developments of asylum and refugee law. A genealogical approach, as defined by Michel Foucault, is one that seeks to uncover the hidden histories of ideas and practices and of conflicts over meanings, of rival paradigms that have sought supremacy at various points, and that attempts to relentlessly historicise rather than accepting a single linear and impliedly inevitable development.[7] Law is a prime example of an apparatus that claims to have no history, to have always already existed. Refugee law, which has existed for less than a century, cannot get away with such a conceit. However, it still claims to be founded upon the idea of a single more or less unchanging refugee subject – one who is persecuted for his opinions whether political or religious or for certain inherent characteristics and one who has moved beyond the borders of their

---

3   Osterweis RG, *Three Centuries of New Haven* (Yale University, 1964), 55–64.
4   Siebert WH, 'A Quaker Section of the Underground Railroad in Northern Ohio' (1930), 39, *Ohio Archaeological and Historical Quarterly*, 53; Siebert WH, *The Mysteries of Ohio's Underground Railroads* (Long's College Book Company, 1951); Siebert WH, *The Underground Railroad: From Slavery to Freedom: A Comprehensive History* (Dover Publications, 2006).
5   Hallie PP, *Lest Innocent Blood Be Shed: The Story of the Village of Le Chambon, and How Goodness Happened There* (Harper and Row, 1979).
6   Willigan JD, 'Sanctuary: A Communitarian Form of Counter-Culture' (1970), 25, *Union Seminary Quarterly Review*, 517; Foley MS, 'Sanctuary! A bridge between civilian and GI protest against the Vietnam War' in Marilyn B Young and Robert Buzzanco (eds), *A Companion to the Vietnam War* (Blackwell Publishers, 2002).
7   Foucault M, 'Nietzsche, genealogy, history' in DF Bouchard (ed), *Language, Counter-Memory, Practice: Selected Essays and Interviews* (Cornell University, 1977).

country of origin – and represents the continuation of the tradition of 'asylum'. What follows in this book, therefore, does not claim to be, nor does it aim at, a complete or an objective history of asylum or refugee law. Instead it seeks to pinpoint and elucidate competing strands of history, of turning points, of threads dropped and picked up. As Foucault writes:

> The isolation of different points of emergence does not conform to the successive configurations of an identical meaning; rather, they result from substitutions, displacements, disguised conquests, and systematic reversals.[8]

As such, this book will challenge the narrative that posits some continuity between asylum and refugee law, presenting instead a set of parallel but antagonistic histories, in which concepts such as 'asylum' and 'refugee' have been subject to 'invasions, struggles, plundering, disguises, ploys'.[9]

The word 'asylum' is derived from the Greek word *asulon*, meaning 'without right of seizure'.[10] The question that then arises is: freedom from seizure by whom or by what? In broad terms we can say, freedom from seizure by one's pursuers. Even today asylum for refugees in law can be correctly understood in this way. Even if a refugee is locked up in detention, or confined to a specified dispersal or reception area, they are still beyond the reach of those persecuting them in their home country. However, in its original usage, and in terms of its practice up until the modern age, it meant freedom from seizure by the secular authorities and/or exemption from the law. This notion is the central theme that runs right through this book. For law has repeatedly laid claim to the space of asylum, to judgement over who should be granted it, and, most perniciously, it has captured the minds even of those who would be the firmest advocates of asylum, from elements within the medieval church to contemporary refugee activists, by inculcating a way of thinking and acting which replicates the legal paradigm that they are apparently resisting.

I share the conclusion reached by others that the nation-state and capitalism have been key elements in the erosion of asylum and the downfall of the refugee.[11] But in my view, it has been primarily law that has acted as the vehicle for establishing and normalising the quantification and control of the refugee. Moreover, as we reach further back into history, we find that at various points,

---

8   Ibid 151.
9   Ibid 139.
10 Kirby LJ, 'Sanctuary: The Right of Asylum in the Corpus Iuris Canonici' (Masters Thesis, Catholic University of America, 1986), 1.
11 For example, Arendt H, *The Origins of Totalitarianism* (Schocken, 2004); Marfleet, *Refugees in a Global Era* (n 10); Bauman Z, 'Who is Seeking Asylum – and from What?' (2005), 4, *Mediactive*, 90. Atle Grahl-Madsen also makes the point that once states were established based on 'the principle of the Sovereignty of the People . . . it was considered necessary to determine as precisely as possible who belonged to "The People"'. Grahl-Madsen A, 'The European Tradition of Asylum and the Development of Refugee Law' (1966), 3, *Journal of Peace Research*, 278, 280.

the legal paradigm has threatened or actually erased the practice of asylum. What is new in the modern period is the universalising grasp of capitalist relations and the totalising effect of the nation-state, along with the biopolitical control over the subject. As such, the idea that law in the form of rights such as those contained in the 1951 Refugee Convention can protect the refugee from the effects of capitalism and the sovereign state is thoroughly misguided. Law is in fact a function of these socio-economic structures and power relations. The problem for the refugee is, in short, not too little but too much law. The argument of this book, therefore, rests crucially on certain understanding of what law is. My approach is to recognise the legal form as one that facilitates the norms of capitalism, through a hollowing out and placing of the subject within a set of paradigms governed by biopolitics and the commodity form. Therefore, before I launch into a long and detailed description of the historical confrontation between asylum and law, it is necessary to explain how I understand the legal form and its problematic nature in relation to asylum and the refugee. Many of the themes introduced here will become reference points throughout the book.

Some preliminary notes on the nature of law

Biopolitics

One of the most striking aspects of law's encounters with asylum is the persistent attempt to measure, categorise and control the refugee. Perhaps the best way of understanding this process is through the concept of *biopolitics* as described by Foucault.[12] He identifies how the focus of sovereign power shifted from being concerned primarily with territory or space to one directed at human beings as objects of sovereign control. On the one hand, the liberal ideology of capitalism insists on letting things follow their course; crises will happen.[13] On the other hand, for the sake of the security of the polity overall, the population must be managed and disciplined in such a way that order remains. For a long time the question of the refugee was intimately bound up with seeking to engage with the circumstances that gave rise to refugee movements in the first place. Hence, reception of the Huguenots was framed within a wider struggle against Catholic Europe, and in the nineteenth century, asylum for republicans and nationalists was underpinned by solidarity against the old monarchies of Austria, Italy, etc.

---

12 Although Foucault is often thought to have relegated law to merely one of the disciplines [cf. Alan Hunt and Gary Wickham, *Foucault and Law* (Pluto, 1994)], at various points, he appears to argue that the key to disciplinary power lies in the judgement of truth versus falsity, which in turn is inextricably tied to the legal paradigm, e.g. Foucault M, 'Truth and juridical forms' in James D Faubion (ed), *Power: Essential Works of Foucault 1954–1984, Volume Three* (Robert Hurley tr, Penguin, 2002); Foucault M, *The Birth of Biopolitics: Lectures at the Collège de France 1978–1979* (Graham Burchell tr, Picador, 2010), 34–38.

13 Foucault M, *Security, Territory, Population: Lectures at the Collège de France 1977–1978* (Graham Burchell tr, Palgrave Macmillan, 2007), 48.

Today, mass forced migration is rarely addressed at its source – instead it is perceived to be an inevitable outcome of the natural course of things, an unfortunate consequence of market forces or simply the result of backward uncivilised conditions elsewhere. As Michel Rocard, then prime minister of France, stated in 1989: 'We cannot accommodate all the misery of the world' (*Nous ne pouvons pas accueillir toute la misère du monde*). From the point of view of states, the key point is to create the legal and physical borders to prevent that disorder from disrupting the home front. And so, Foucault writes:

> [T]he law prohibits and discipline prescribes, but possibly making use of some instruments of prescription and prohibition, to respond to a reality in such a way that this response cancels out the reality to which it responds – nullifies it, or limits, checks, or regulates it.[14]

Today, the apparatus of refugee law prescribes what a refugee is and how she should behave or respond to the circumstances in which she finds herself, e.g. leave her home country, present herself and her narrative in good order and with proof. Those who fail to do so are then prohibited from being granted asylum. As we shall see in Part II, refugee law emerged precisely out of the concern to bring 'order' to the 'chaos' of mass forced migration. Implicit in Rocard's statement above is the idea that severe disruption to people's lives will occur – such is life and the vagaries of economics and politics – but at the point at which the effects reach our borders, a legal process to filter and control that phenomenon must be in place.

Further, biopolitics is a form of power whose goal is the maintenance of the population, as a singular object, as the source of the state's wealth. In a dialectical fashion, the management of the population as a singular object requires the most detailed monitoring, measuring and recording of each individual human subject. Hence, politics becomes ever more concerned with the person, right down to their physical being, ergo *bio-politics*. Foucault's schema would have the various modern apparatuses of power bound together by the principle of *governmentality*. Whereas biopolitics establishes the norms by which power is exercised, governmentality operates at a somewhat higher level. It is grounded within the fundamental notion that society can only function under circumstances where the population becomes the object of managerial control.[15] Proper government becomes inextricably tied to the ability to enforce security and to enable a proper accounting of the population. The biopolitical paradigm thus becomes the *sine qua non* for sovereign power to operate effectively. So engrained is the presumption that society can only function where subjects are governed, that it is not merely a strategy of power but a way of thinking about the world itself, hence *govern-mentality*.

14 Ibid 47.
15 Ibid 108, and generally.

As we will see later when excavating the origins of modern refugee law, the primary concern driving its development has indeed been precisely to judge the refugee subject, to apply rules and techniques that can efficiently manage their movements and that can construct an objective universal standard of the 'refugee' against which each individual forced migrant can be measured. Refugees, who by their nature as people who cross borders irregularly, bringing with them the scars and trauma of violence and instability, trouble the trinity of security, territory, population; they present a challenge to the order of things. This, more than any concern for the refugee or the origins of their plight, has come to predominate in the age of refugee law.

The security paradigm/state of exception

For Giorgio Agamben, the 'state of exception', which, along with refugee law, has for the first time achieved its most fully developed form over the course of the twentieth century, is a key illustration of the way in which biopolitics has become the reigning paradigm of power, for it dissolves any remaining distinction between law and life:

> Law that becomes indistinguishable from life in a real state of exception is confronted by life that, in a symmetrical but inverse gesture, is entirely transformed into law.[16]

The refugee is a key instance in Agamben's conception of this phenomenon. This is because sovereignty is grounded in the notion of those who properly belong within the polis; those who do not; and especially those such as refugees who enter the space of this or that sovereign order irregularly, present a challenge to this nexus and thus become subjects who must be held at a distance, yet at the same time must fall squarely within the scope of law so as to be controlled and accounted for. This apparent contradiction can be explained in the context of what Agamben identifies as the central feature of the sovereign order today: the state of exception has become increasingly indistinguishable from its supposed antinomy, law. The effect has been that what were once moments of exception have now become the norm. Although Agamben first began discussing this phenomenon in the mid-1990s, our world post-9/11 has arguably confirmed his thesis time and time again. One of the fields in which the state of exception as the norm has become most evident is in regard to the treatment of refugees. The archetype of this grey zone in which law is both absent and all-encompassing is in the spaces of refugee camps, detention centres and the like, which have become the standard means by which to manage refugee movements across the globe over recent decades, long predating the 'war on terror'.

---

16 Agamben G, *Homo Sacer: Sovereign Power and Bare Life* (Daniel Heller-Roazen tr, Stanford University Press, 1998), 55.

According to Agamben, the sovereign state of exception is one where the law is in *'force* but does not *signify'*.[17] He goes on to describe the contemporary scene as one where:

> Everywhere on earth men live today in the ban of a law and a tradition that are maintained solely as the 'zero point' of its own content, and that include men within them in the form of a pure relation of abandonment.[18]

High on the list of subjects of this form of abandonment must be found refugees. Yet, I would argue, this emptiness of content with the law, epitomised in our reigning state of exception, necessarily leaves open a space for the law to be applied or decided in some concrete manner. I would also question Agamben's argument that in the state of exception, the law relinquishes completely the force of application in favour of abandonment. Rather, the law is left open as a pure form of force, the content of which must be filled by reference to something outside itself. This external reference can be a number of things – economics, politics, religion, etc. In refugee law, the 1951 Convention bestows certain rights and duties on states and refugees. But the definite content of the provision – who is a genuine asylum-seeker/refugee? – requires a reference to political and religious frameworks in order to determine whether or not the person has been perse-cuted for political or religious reasons, as stipulated in Article 1(A). And yet, law obscures this subjective contestable aspect through its claim to universality as mere form. Abandonment suggests being simply left outside of the law. But there is no genuine 'outside the law' in a state of exception. Thus, abandonment can be experienced as such – refugees, for example, being left outside of the protection of human rights, civil law, etc. – but the state of exception in fact leaves no-one outside, as law collapses into life and vice versa. So, while refugees are stripped of rights and denied access to legal representation, they are not expelled from the realm of law: quite the opposite, in fact. In order for the refugee 'problem' to be managed effectively, they must become ever more subjected to law. In the discussion of the evolution of international refugee law in Part II, this theme will be evidenced in a more concrete manner.

The erasure of the political

The erasure of distinctions between law and life has a further effect: the subsuming of political questions by legal judgement. Alain Badiou has identified the problem by which a spurious ethics of universalism and humanitarianism, codified in law, has denied its own origins and precludes a space for contesting the norms that result from this framework. He writes:

17 Ibid 51.
18 Ibid.

The Law (human rights, etc.) is always *already there*. It regulates judgements and opinions concerning the evil that happens in some variable elsewhere. But there is no question of reconsidering the foundation of this 'Law', of going right back to the conservative identity that sustains it.[19]

Instead, we need to assert against a totalising and universalising ethics the primacy of politics, of contestability, of what Jacques Rancière calls 'dissensus', where the part of society that has no part asserts its right to be, against those who would deny them their place in that society.[20] Indeed, when we come to look at the long history of asylum in Part I of this book, it becomes clear that solidarity stemming from partisan positions has been an essential and often determining aspect of its practice, and crucial in guaranteeing asylum worthy of the name for refugees. It was what set the stage for the asylum offered to the Greeks of antiquity fleeing from this or that city-state order, for the early Christians sheltering people involved in resistance to Rome, of a theologically informed alternative to legal space in the Middle Ages, of safety for the partisans in various ideological schisms from the Reformation to the revolutions of the twentieth century. But what should become clearer as the book progresses is the way in which law operates to close down the political space that asylum facilitates. The Sanctuary Movement and the Sans-Papiers – discussed in Part III – illustrate the attempt to reopen such a space, but also its effective closing down again once legal criteria to distinguish between 'deserving' and 'undeserving' refugees re-assert themselves at the heart of these movements.

Rancière poses politics as 'dissensus' against the notion of politics as the commonality of a *polis* that in reality is riven by disparities of wealth and power.[21] Just as Marx polemicised against abstract universal rights as forms that concealed and perpetuated real inequalities, so Rancière identifies a similar process at work in our contemporary concept of politics.[22] The 'political', as commonly understood today, becomes the means by which states come to speak 'for the people' and identify its goals as synonymous with the people; consensus thus becomes the guiding principle. Dissensus, however, is a politics concerned 'with what can be argued, the presence or absence of a common object between X and Y'.[23] Rancière identifies those who are victims of injustice, those who are excluded, among whom we can of course include the refugee, as that part of society which has 'no part in anything'. He goes on to argue that,

---

19 Badiou A, *Ethics: An Essay on the Understanding of Evil* (Peter Hallward tr, Verso, 2001), 33.

20 Rancière J, *Disagreement: Politics and Philosophy* (University of Minnesota, 1999), 9.

21 Ibid, generally.

22 Marx K, 'On the Jewish Question' in *Early Writings* (Rodney Livingstone and Gregor Benton trs, Penguin, 1975).

23 Rancière (n 20) xii.

it is through the existence of this part of those who have no part, of this nothing that is all, that the community exists as a political community – that is, as divided by a fundamental dispute, by a dispute to do with the counting of the community's parts even more than of their 'rights'.[24]

The reality of this dispute, one that is irreconcilable under conditions where society is divided by class, race, citizens/foreigners, indeed by any form of privilege or oppressive power, is obscured by talk of equality under the law and of politics as the coming together of subjects whose interests cannot in fact be reconciled; the typical form of this type of politics is humanitarianism. Real politics only 'exists when the natural order of domination is interrupted by the institution of a part of those who have no part'.[25] Thus, between the demand for protection by the refugee and the response of the putative host community, there cannot be any finality, for politics 'is the sphere of activity of a common that can only ever be contentious, the relationship between parts that are only parties . . . whose sum never equals the whole'.[26] So, for the refugee to make a claim for a place within the *polis* is not the same as seeking some kind of superficial consensus among the various parts of the host community. Rather it is a claim to *establish themselves* as being at least a part within that *polis*.

In the discussion of the Sanctuary Movement and the Sans-Papiers in Part III, one of the key themes that emerges is the tension between those who recognise that asylum is fundamentally geared towards the political, as a site of contestation with sovereign power, and those who wish to shoehorn asylum into a depoliticised humanitarianism. This latter group, moreover, in seeking a legitimising universalism, finds themselves pulled towards accepting the restrictive practices of refugee law, indeed going so far as to actually perform many of the more obnoxious aspects of the law. In contrast, the claims of the refugees are framed in terms, not merely of their own suffering but of the responsibilities of the host states for the conditions that have led them there in the first place. Such arguments, about modern-day imperialism, the legacy of empire and post-colonial exploitation and oppression, exceed the bounds of law; they can only be expressed in terms of Rancièrian politics.

Capitalism and law

Zygmunt Bauman's concept of refugees as waste suggests a similar way of understanding refugee law as a mechanism for the ever-greater control and management of the subject, and of the effective management of population as a source of the nation's wealth.[27] Waste is an inevitable product of capitalism,

24 Ibid 9.
25 Ibid 11.
26 Ibid 14.
27 Bauman (n 11).

a problem growing exponentially as the search for profit chases the bourgeoisie across the globe in the search for new markets.[28] Bauman is right that the characterisation of asylum-seekers as 'waste' accurately reflects the dominant discourse, one that sees forced migrants as a burden on the 'public interest', a cost without benefit. It might be thought that to be conceived of as 'waste' is antithetical to qualification as a legal subject with rights, particularly the right of access to justice – except that waste must be disposed of in an orderly way if it is not to 'pollute' and thus disrupt 'normal' life. Patricia Tuitt describes the 1951 Convention and other instruments of international refugee law as operating 'at [their] inception' to reduce 'the external costs of refugee-producing phenomena'; refugee law thus operates 'as a mechanism within which such costs can be spread, distributed or shifted to other states'.[29] These costs can be counted in pure financial terms. Indeed, much of the discourse today which seeks to argue for ever further reductions in the right to protection is couched precisely in this language.[30] In retrospect, perhaps the 'Golden Age' of refugee protection in the decades following World War II was more a function of the long economic boom together with the politics of the Cold War, than the coming of refugee law.[31] States in a period of plenty were able to pay the 'cost' of refugees, and in a period of post-war reconstruction in Europe and a labour shortage, newcomers were always useful.[32] Also, politically, refugees from the 'other side' carried with them significant propaganda value. Therefore, insofar as there was a post-war Golden Age of refugeehood, it was primarily a result of political economy, not law. Moreover, in the context of a generalised labour shortage in the West,

28 Marx K, 'The communist manifesto' in Max Eastman (ed and tr), *Capital, The Communist Manifesto and Other Writings* (The Modern Library, 1959), 321.
29 Tuitt P, *False Images: The Law's Construction of the Refugee* (Pluto, 1996), 7.
30 For example, the UK government's rationale for fast-tracking asylum applications and expanding detention of asylum-seekers as being driven at least partly by cost-effectiveness. 'Controlling Our Borders: Making Migration Work for Britain – Five Year Strategy for Asylum and Immigration' (2005), available at www.gov.uk/govern ment/uploads/system/uploads/attachment_data/file/251091/6472.pdf, accessed 16 December 2017; equally the Australian government's policy known as Operation Sovereign Borders, which increases the military operation to prevent refugee arrivals by sea, is heavily backed by reference to the cost of 'managing illegal boat arrivals'. The Coalition's Operation Sovereign Borders Policy – July 2013, available at lpaweb-static.s3.amazonaws.com/Policies/OperationSovereignBorders_Policy.pdf, accessed 16 December 2017; more recently, the agreement between the EU and Turkey in March 2016 was effectively a €3 billion bribe by the former in return for the latter acting as a buffer zone for Syrian refugees attempting to reach Europe. EU-Turkey statement, 18 March 2016, www.consilium.europa.eu/en/press/press-releases/2016/03/18/eu-turkey-statement/, accessed 16 December 2017.
31 Joly (n 1). Although Joly argues that Article 33, the principle of non-refoulement, is the exception to this, the one right in the Convention addressed directly to refugees, rather than to states.
32 Marfleet (n 11), 172–174.

refugee law as a valve for relieving the economic pressure on states was superfluous. This explains why in many states, the reception of refugees continued to operate on a relatively informal or discretionary basis throughout the years of the post-war boom. In France, for example, irregular migration was effectively encouraged by the state as a way of dealing with a persistent labour shortage during the *trente glorieuses*. But if we go a little deeper into the relationship between capitalism and law, we find that the legal form necessarily produces subjects based on the norms of commodity exchange. It is here that the work of Evgeny Pashukanis becomes key.

Pashukanis argues that just as the relations of capital are formed around the commodity, which becomes such only when it enters into relations with another in the form of exchange, so also law essentially grows out of the inter-relationships between subjects who barter their respective bundles of rights.[33] And so, concepts of agency that are central to commodity exchange *ipso facto* become those that define agency in law. For Pashukanis, therefore, the bearer of rights is not prior to the law, nor is he the product of law or the liberal state. Instead, the legal subject is the necessary outgrowth of the commodity owner:

> At the same time . . . that the product of labour becomes a commodity and a bearer of a value, man acquires the capacity to be a legal subject and a bearer of rights.[34]

The legal subject is nothing more than an abstraction from real human beings already alienated, through the process of capitalist production, from their relationship to nature, and their fellow human beings. In this, the reification of commodity production, and of legalism, serves one and the same function: to facilitate relations of capital. The ruthless calculation of value, the necessity for strict rules in the marketplace, the egoistic competition between individuals, the primacy of relationships based on contract represent, in short, a social form saturated in the 'icy water of egotistical calculation'.[35]

While law is obviously not specific to societies based on commodity exchange, it reaches its highest and most generalised form under such a system. The universal claim of law leads to what Bernard Edelman has described as an 'anthropological illusion', in 'which the law has in its belief that it holds an eternal discourse on eternal man. In this way, the law [takes] on its true dimensions. It [fills] the political space . . . it [sanctions] political power in order to sanctify private property'.[36] It follows, then, that in order to transcend the subjectivity imposed

---

33 Pashukanis EB, *Marxism and Law: A General Theory* (Barbara Einhorn tr, Pluto, 1989).
34 Ibid 112.
35 Marx (n 28), 323.
36 Edelman B, *Ownership of the Image: Elements for a Marxist Theory of Law* (Elizabeth Kingdom tr, Routledge & Kegan Paul, 1979), 22.

by the law/capital nexus, one must break the bounds of law and reclaim a space for a politics that lies beyond. Of course, this brings us back to some of the concerns expressed by Badiou and Rancière, and the problems that are identified in the discussion of the Sanctuary Movement and the Sans-Papiers in Part III.

The legal subject for Pashukanis functions in a dehumanising way, not merely by reducing the individual to a commodity owner but in the same way that capital eyes up every resource or product, so too law insists on measuring, categorising and defining the subject. Here, one can see a correlation with the biopolitical paradigm identified by Foucault, where the focus of power is on the person rather than on the territory or space more generally. Indeed, as I have already mentioned, one of the major paradigm shifts identified in this book between the tradition of asylum and refugee law is from a concern with spaces of protection to a concern with the character and person of the refugee. The price of legal subjectivity is a categorisation lacking the human dimension. Instead, we are faced with a subject who 'attains the significance of a mathematical point, a centre in which a certain number of rights is concentrated',[37] or put another way, 'a unit of displacement'.[38] The flip side of this is that when one falls outside of a recognised legal category, as is the case with many of the people who have crossed the Mexico-US border or ended up as undocumented migrants in France, their whole identity is framed in public discourse solely in terms of their illegality, e.g. 'illegal aliens', '*clandestins*'. One of the defining features of the Sactuary Movement and especially the Sans-Papiers has been the attempt to remake their identities in ways that resist legal categories.

The imposition of tropes of bourgeois subjectivity can be seen in refugee law in other ways too: e.g., in the fact that claims must be based on the *individual* experience of persecution. The refugee is forced to perform a type of agency judged on the basis of choice: *choosing* to adhere to or proselytise a political or religious belief, *choosing* to cross a border, *choosing* to make a claim, etc. Political violence that does not fit the 'rational' or 'enlightened' norms of liberal democracy – anarchism, Islamism, or any struggle that does not seek state power or whose organisational form is disparate – is not considered political.[39] In all these ways, the prism of law filters out so many of the complexities of the refugee experience. An inverse relationship exists between the legal and the political space open to refugees to make their claim for asylum; while one opens out, the other closes.

A common feature found in all these perspectives – the biopolitical management of population, the collapsing of life into law, the subsuming of the political, the refugee as waste, the commodity form of law – is the impulse to colonise

---

37 Pashukanis (n 33), 115.
38 Goodwin-Gill G, 'Refugee identity and protection's fading prospect' in Frances Nicholson and Patrick Twomey (eds), *Refugee Rights and Realities: Evolving International Concepts and Regimes* (Cambridge University, 1999), 246.
39 For a detailed discussion of how bourgeois notions of agency find their expression in refugee law, see Behrman S, 'Accidents, Agency and Asylum: Constructing the Refugee Subject' (2014), 25, *Law and Critique*, 249.

and hegemonise to the exclusion of other methods of defining the subject. Two alternatives which have been edged out by law and have a central place in the historical narrative of asylum are religion and politics. The crisis faced by the refugee today is thus not only the immediate cause of her flight, nor just the arduous nature of moving across borders and claiming asylum, but the fact that there is no escape from the law that seeks to subjectivise her in the way in which I have described. In short, the refugee is no longer able *not* to be a legal subject.

What I hope to have demonstrated so far is that the narrative that argues for more legal rights for the refugee misses the essential reason for their degraded place in society over recent years. This is not to say that they, their lawyers and those who campaign on their behalf should not demand that refugees should have this or that legal right: the right not to be imprisoned or deported and the right of access to housing and other means of support are necessary and sorely lacking for many forced migrants today. But making demands *of* law is not the same thing as demanding recognition *by* law; seeking the latter entails placing oneself in a reciprocal relationship with a structural form which has systematically stripped the refugee of their role as a complex active subject. The price has been the depoliticisation of both the refugee subject and the question of asylum itself. For forced migrants, it is not legal subjectivity that needs reclaiming but it is political subjectivity – the ability to assert one's own identity and needs in ways that do not fit the paradigm of nation-state-capital, a construct that gains its normative power through law. Globally today, there is, in truth, no real space of asylum as it had previously existed, only an unbroken sphere of law. And the further the law reaches into the space of refugeehood, the more refugees as human beings are being erased by it. This violence is a problem immanent to the legal form itself. It therefore cannot be a question of a better or fairer system of refugee law. The imperium of law and the space of asylum cannot co-exist. This key point should, I hope, become increasingly evident over the course of this book.

Part I
The space of asylum

Introduction to Part I

SANCTUARY. A place of refuge where the process of the law cannot be executed.[1]

At the close of the fifteenth century, in a court case concerned with a violation of sanctuary, the right of asylum was pleaded for as one which reached back to the Old Testament and Romulus.[2] There is evidence that sanctuary cities described in the Bible influenced the creation of sanctuaries set up in various English towns in the 1540s.[3] But this stream is all but submerged during the period of the rise of the nation-state, capitalism and the hegemony of law from the sixteenth century onwards. Mere trickles of this tradition are only just visible by the end of the nineteenth century, before disappearing altogether.

Yet, notions of exile and asylum are a foundation stone of Western culture. Exile is central to the narrative of the Old Testament from the Fall, through to the wanderings of Jacob as described in Genesis, the Jewish diaspora and the exodus of the Israelites from Egypt and the Babylonian exile.[4] Moreover, there are a number of references in the Bible to sanctuary for the oppressed and needy.[5] The reference above to sanctuary cities is found in chapter 35 of Numbers, and the concept has survived even into the modern age with Sanctuary Cities in the United States, where undocumented migrants are free from harassment by municipal authorities over their legal status.

While this book focuses on what might be termed the Western tradition of asylum, it has existed as an ancient practice throughout the world. There is some

1   Bouvier J, *Bouvier's Law Dictionary: Volume II* (Francis Rawle ed, rev edn, Boston Book Co., 1897).
2   Baker JH, 'The English Law of Sanctuary' (1990), 2, *Ecclesiastical Law Journal*, 8, 10.
3   Field T, 'Biblical Influences on the Medieval and Early Modern English Law of Sanctuary' (1991), 2, *Ecclesiastical Law Journal*, 222
4   Carroll RP, 'Exile! What exile? Deportation and the discourses of diaspora' in Lester L Grabbe (ed), *Leading Captivity Captive: 'The Exile' as History and Ideology* (Sheffield Academic Press, 1998), 63.
5   Deuteronomy 10:19, 19:1–13, 23:16–17, 24:17–18; Exodus 21:12–14, 22:21, 23:9; Leviticus 19:33–34; Numbers 35:9–34.

evidence – vague, it must be said – of asylum in India and China before the Christian era.[6] Some have argued that the Southern African philosophy of *Ubuntu*, which emphasises a collective approach to human rights and which focusses on the needs of the most vulnerable in society, contains a principle of hospitality to the stranger above and beyond the notion of asylum as commonly understood in the Global North.[7] Islam has a particularly rich tradition of asylum that both dovetails with and goes beyond that of the Judeo-Christian one that dominates in the West. Indeed, the Islamic tradition of sanctuary has much in common with that of Judaism and Christianity, and the concept of hospitality to the person fleeing danger (*hijrah*) is taken from similar notions in the Old and New testaments.[8] Just as Judaism and Christianity have exilic narratives at the core of their founding texts, so too Islam dates its birth to the exile of the Prophet Mohammad to Medina.[9] Following his conquest of Mecca, Muhammad declared two sites as sanctuaries for those who had opposed him.[10] As we will see, Christianity inherited much of its tradition of sanctuary from the pagan practices that preceded it. Equally Islam also continued older traditions of asylum from the Arab civilisations that existed prior to the seventh century.[11] However, Khadija Elmadmad makes the interesting point that what distinguishes Islam from the other monotheistic religions is that the former never codified asylum into law.[12] Perhaps this might be why, as Elmadmad describes, the Islamic tradition on asylum has tended to be more comprehensive and all-embracing than its rivals. For example, the Quran places a duty on Muslims to offer asylum to all, regardless of whether or not they are co-religionists, whereas Christianity and Judaism have tended to be more sectarian and restrictive in their approach.[13]

When the ancient tradition of asylum re-emerges during the post-World War II period, it is qualitatively different. Rather than regulating spaces of refuge, it defines the person and movements of the refugee; the tradition of sanctuary as a space within the polis, yet where the writ of the sovereign power does not run, is turned inside out. Instead, sanctuary involves moving beyond the borders of the polis altogether – only, of course, to be forced to seek protection from another polis, another law. The literatures on the ancient practices of sanctuary and asylum on the one hand and contemporary refugee law on the other are vast. Yet, very rarely are the two ever discussed together. What I hope to show is that,

---

6 Bassiouni MC, *International Extradition and World Public Order* (AW Sijthoff, 1974), 88.
7 Mokgoro JY, 'Ubuntu, the Consitution and the Rights of Non-Citizens' (2010), 21, *Stellenbosch Law Review*, 221.
8 Elmadmad K, 'Asylum in Islam and Modern Refugee Law' (2008), 27, *Refugee Survey Quarterly*, 51, 52–53.
9 Ibid 53.
10 Bassiouni (n 6), 87.
11 Ibid 55. Arnaout GM, *Asylum in the Arab-Islamic Tradition* (UNHCR, 1987).
12 Elmadmad (n 8), 53.
13 Ibid 54. Abou-El Wafa A, *The Right to Asylum between Islamic Shari'ah and International Refugee Law A Comparative Study* (UNHCR, 2009), 43.

ancient though it is, asylum has always had to fight a battle of survival against law. Following the French Revolution, the Convention abolished all sanctuaries by declaring, 'The right of asylum is being abolished in France, for it's now the law being the asylum of all people'.[14] The dominant ideology of modernity, of autonomous and equal subjects before the law, is often invoked to denounce sanctuary as a relic of a 'barbaric' past, ill-suited to our 'civilised' societies today.[15] Yet, as we shall see, the treatment of petty criminals, traitors, subversives and other 'undesirables' was frequently more humane and more contested than is the case with today's asylum-seekers. Moreover, it is precisely the loss of spaces within the polis, yet without the grasp of the sovereign power, which has led us to the complete hegemony of the law. It would not be true to say that asylum has mainly, or indeed ever, been a place without sovereign authority. The priest-hood, whether pagan or monotheistic, or the local lord, have always asserted sovereign power over the space either on their own terms or on the basis of dogma, but rarely have they asserted such power over the asylees themselves. For sure there were rules about use of the space of asylum and conduct within it, but this tended to be guided either by respect for the sacred space, i.e. not impinging upon the altar, or for practical reasons, i.e. not carrying weapons. A test for admission was either perfunctory or non-existent. In this sense, asylum remained for most of the period under discussion as a place free from seizure by the legal paradigm, one founded upon a rigid delineation and judgement of the subject. What follows is not, and does not aim to be, an exhaustive discussion of the history of asylum: that would require several volumes at least, and indeed the many elements are well covered in the available literature, which I have drawn upon here. Instead I have focussed on certain texts and moments in which asylum is defined, and on highlighting encounters between law and asylum.

14 Quoted in Bianchi H, *Justice as Sanctuary: Toward a New System of Crime Control* (Indiana University, 1994), 144.
15 For example, Stanley A, *Historical Memorials of Westminster Abbey* (John Murray, 1886), 414; de' Mazzinghi TJ, *Sanctuaries* (Halden & Son, 1887), 101; Trenholme N, 'The Right of Sanctuary in England: A Study in Institutional History' (1903), 1, University of Missouri Studies, 1, 96; Thornley ID, 'The destruction of Sanctuary' in RW Seton-Watson (ed), *Tudor Studies* (Longmans, 1924), 185; West EH, 'The Right of Asylum in New Mexico in the Seventeenth and Eighteenth Centuries' (1928), 8, *The Hispanic American Historical Review*, 357, 359; de Martin PTD, *Le Droit d'Asile* (Librarie du Recueil Sirey, 1939), 453; Carro JL, 'Sanctuary: The Resurgence of an Age-Old Right or a Dangerous Misinterpretation of an Abandoned Ancient Privilege?' (1986), 54, *University of Cincinnati Law Review*, 747, 767.

1 The rise and fall of asylum in antiquity

Ancient Greece

In terms of specific recorded instances of asylum, we begin with a failed coup at Athens in 632 BC.[1] The leader of the rebellion, Cylon, along with some of his allies, sought refuge in the Temple of Athena on the Acropolis. They had to be persuaded to leave by the archon Megacles with the promise that their lives would be spared. Custom and religious belief decreed that they could not be removed by force of arms. Some accounts describe the refugees leaving the temple with a rope tied to the statue of the goddess, suggesting a belief that the merest physical connection with the temple from the outside granted a form of protection. It was only when the rope snapped, or perhaps was deliberately cut, that Megacles allowed many of his supporters to set upon and kill the suppliants. Although Cylon's attempted coup had not received much popular support, Megacles was heaped with opprobrium by his fellow Athenians for violating the principle of asylum: 'He had polluted himself and his clan [the Alcmaeonids] by violating the right of asylum'.[2] The entire family were for a time exiled from the city, along with the dug-up bones of the clan's ancestors.[3] Two hundred years later, Pericles, an Alcmaeonid, was taunted for being part of a 'polluted' clan.[4] Such was the power of asylum as a belief and as an institution during the immediate pre-classical period. It is notable that this recorded instance of asylum, as a place exempt from the civil power, occurs shortly before the coming of Solon's reforms and the birth of law in the modern sense. It is perhaps telling that, following the coming of a properly juridical order, this is the only such example of asylum as a space within the territory of a secular authority that is recorded in Greece for almost 400 years.

---

1   This story is recounted in Plutarch's essay on 'Solon'. Plutarch, *The Rise and Fall of Athens* (Ian Scott-Kilvert tr, Penguin, 1960), 52.
2   Balogh E, *Political Refugees in Ancient Greece* (Witwatersrand University, 1943), 6.
3   Plutarch (n 1), 53.
4   Thucydides, *History of the Peloponnesian War* (Rex Warner tr, Penguin, 1972), 110.

On becoming archon, Solon instituted an amnesty for all Athenian refugees.[5] Well, almost all: those convicted of murder, manslaughter and the attempt to set up a tyranny were excluded. Elemér Balogh comments that this was evidence of a 'socio-political' measure designed to 'win back all the really useful citizens' who had earlier fled, and by implication to continue to keep out those considered undesirable.[6] There were three classes of person who were granted citizenship under Solon's law: exiles, permanent settlers and 'benefactors of the state'.[7] This was in contrast to the pre-Solonian period when citizenship was granted freely, particularly to those Greeks who had been exiled from other Greek states and were permanently resident in Athens. However, Solon's law allowed citizenship *only* to exiles permanently resident in Athens and to those who came 'to practise a trade'.[8] Hence, Solon's law represented a narrowing of the 'circle of eligible persons'.[9] Cynthia Patterson suggests that this law was negative, i.e. it did not allow *other* sorts of foreigners access to citizenship.[10] Whatever the precise effects of the law, the key point in this instance is that the formation of a legal code involved categorising and restricting the right of strangers to enter the sovereign space.

Following Solon, the stories of refuge and asylum fall into two main categories, both of which are governed by principles of political solidarity. First, the accommodation of fellow citizens or those from allied states in wartime; the reception in Athens of those from the Attican countryside fleeing the advancing Spartan army at the beginning of the Peloponnesian War is one such example.[11] The second type of refugee was the political or military leader who had fallen out of favour among his own people, and who had therefore fled to another city-state for safety. Balogh writes of these cases: 'The exiled usually had no difficulty in finding refuge with neighbouring states, who very often were the enemies of the exiling one'.[12] Perhaps the most striking example of this is Alcibiades, the Athenian *strategos* who, following the debacle of the Sicilian campaign, fled to the arch-enemy Sparta. After subsequently falling out with the Spartans, he then sought refuge in Persia, the historic enemy of all Hellas. It was only when his

5 Plutarch (n 1), 61.
6 Balogh (n 2), 58.
7 Billheimer A, 'Naturalization in Athenian Law and Practice' (PhD Thesis, Princeton University, 1922), 24.
8 Plutarch (n 1), 67. Plutarch reports claims that Solon felt that only those who had been exiled from their home country could be trusted to remain loyal to their new home.
9 Billheimer (n 7), 26. Billheimer suggests that there is evidence that this circle was widened to include those engaged in 'permanent settlement to practice a trade'. Billheimer (n 7), 28.
10 Patterson C, *Pericles' Citizenship Law of 451–50 B.C.* (The Ayer Company, 1981), 18–19.
11 Thucydides (n 4), 135.
12 Balogh E, 'World Peace and the Refugee Problem' (1949), 75, *The Hague Academy of International Law*, 363, 379–380.

faction in Athens returned to power that he was able to return, and again serve as *stategos*.[13] In the case of Themistocles, who also fled into exile to Persia, Balogh comments: 'Only with the hereditary enemy could the outlaw find safety'.[14] Thus, the political element of asylum remained key in Athens during the fourth-century BC when refugees were only granted citizenship by the general assembly of the *demos*, 'when the persons concerned had been especially helpful to Athens and when their banishment was the result of their pro-Athenian attitude'.[15] The key point in all these instances of refuge is that they are primarily about political alliances and solidarity, and not about legal categories of asylum or of the refugee. These may indeed have been the most viable criteria for claiming asylum, following Solon's confining of formal asylum within legal parameters.

Asylia

As an institution, *asylia* develops in the Greek world from around the beginning of the third-century BC.[16] In the period of struggles and wars between Alexander's successors, certain towns and cities were decreed to be 'sacred and inviolable', earning the epithet, *asylia*, literally *a* (not) *sylia* (subject to seizure).[17] In *Asylia: Territorial Inviolability in the Hellenistic World*, Kent J. Rigsby has put together a comprehensive survey of the evidence for all places deemed 'inviolable' in the Hellenistic world from the third-century BC to the early first-century AD. They were places deemed neutral as between the rival Greek states. As 'sacred and inviolable' spaces, they were off limits to any military attack from other Greeks. *Asylia* were also exempted from paying certain taxes to authorities that at various times sought to extend their control over territories. One example is the city and country of Alabanda which was granted *asylia* around 202 BC by Antiochus III. In his decree, Antiochus sums up the benefits of *asylia* by emphasising 'peace and tax relief' as the effects of the grant.[18]

Although the benefits of *asylia* were rather prosaic, they were founded upon religious belief. Claims for *asylia* were commonly made on the basis of some link with a particular god. They might be the site of oracles, or of shrines to some deity. Often *asylia* was granted on the promise that the town concerned would host Pan-Hellenic games, which were of course religious festivals. For example, Magnesia attempted to gain recognition of *asylia* in 221/220 BC by offering to

---

13 His remarkable career is described by both Thucydides (n 4) Books Six–Eight and Plutarch (n 1), 245–285.
14 Balogh (n 2), 22.
15 Ibid 51.
16 de Martin PTD, *Le Droit d'Asile* (Librarie du Recueil Sirey, 1939), 18.
17 Scott MC, 'Asylia' in Roger S Bagnall and others (eds), *The Encyclopedia of Ancient History* (Wiley-Blackwell, 2012).
18 Rigsby KJ, *Asylia: Territorial Inviolability in the Hellenistic World* (University of California, 1996), 333.

host a competition for the Greeks of Asia. This application was ignored and they made a new claim some 10 years later, this time offering to host quadrennial Pan-Hellenic games; only then was *asylia* granted to them.[19]

The granting of *asylia* to a particular city, temple, etc., was bestowed by a recognised Pan-Hellenic authority such as the Amphytronic Council at Delphi, by kings, or they were granted by a series of states after lobbying by those places wishing to claim the status of *asylia*. Originally, *asylia* was granted to representatives of the Amphictyonic Council travelling to meetings around the Greek world. It was also used to cover those travelling to Pan-Hellenic festivals.[20] These people were immune from being interfered with during their travels. Thus, we find in *asylia* the origins of an aspect of asylum that would be fundamental right through to the late middle ages, one we will encounter many times: immunity or freedom from seizure. The first known grant of *asylia* for a city, rather than just a temple, is Smyrna in the 240s BC. An oracle was received from Apollo, demanding honour to the goddess Aphrodite, whose temple lay in the city. Following this, King Seleucus II declared Smyrna to be 'inviolable' and exempt from paying tribute. Seleucus also wrote a letter asking the rest of the Greek world to join him in recognising *asylia* at Smyrna. Ambassadors then toured the Greek world, using the oracle and the letter from Seleucus, asking for recognition of *asylia*.[21] The process of granting *asylia* thus demonstrates its function as one of diplomacy between the various Greek city-states.[22] To make a claim for *asylia* was effectively to declare neutrality in the many internecine wars of the Greeks.

Thus far *asylia* is defined mainly in terms of a set of benefits or a sense of reverence accorded to a specific place. In other words, their starting point was a definition of space, not of a subject who may or may not have access to it. Their role was not primarily one of refuge. Nonetheless, their inviolable status, along with the notion of spiritual protection given by the relevant deity, meant that they were often used as places of asylum, as we would understand it. According to legend, Apollo received refugees at Delphi such as Orestes and Ion.[23] This legend undoubtedly contributed to the enormous veneration held by all Greeks for this particular temple. The Temple of Artemis at Ephesus was one of the most famous *asylia* in Greece.[24] It was, possibly, founded by the Amazons who took

---

19 Ibid 180. There is some dispute over the fact that in the surviving responses to the second Magnesian campaign, not all other states explicitly recognise asylia. But Rigsby suggests several quite mundane reasons for this, which do not necessarily mean that asylia was not in fact granted, e.g. careless writing of the decrees, the previous granting of asylia by those city states or the subsuming of asylia into grants to Magnesia in terms of 'what they request, in keeping with the oracle'. Ibid 182–183.
20 Ibid 108.
21 Ibid 95.
22 Ibid 4–5.
23 Ibid 44.
24 de' Mazzinghi TJ, *Sanctuaries* (Halden & Son, 1887), 6.

refuge there. There is no surviving evidence for the original grant of *asylia* for this great temple. We only have confirmation of its sacred and inviolable nature from the Romans. Rigsby suggests the possibility that the 'Ephesians invoked older traditions about refuge to persuade the Romans that the Artemisium was an asylum'.[25] The legend of Artemis portrayed her as a protector of refugees, and there were many stories found in both historical and mythical accounts of fugitives seeking sanctuary in her temple. In the only surviving work of Achilles Tatius, he sets a scene in this Temple 'of an elaborate proceeding to determine whether a suppliant had just claim on the goddess's protection'.[26] This juridical process of admittance is anomalous, however, and may be because Tatius is writing many centuries later from the perspective of the Roman Empire at its height: a period and a place obsessed with legal procedure. The key point is that the *asylia* were spaces of refuge outside the law.

We also possess a number of recorded instances of popular reverence for *asylia* as places of refuge. For example, when royal agents seized a fugitive from the temple of Demeter in Alexandria, the local population protested.[27] As early as 242 BC, King Leonidas and his daughter took refuge in the temple of Athena Chalcioecus, remaining there in safety until new ephors took office.[28] In around 170 BC, a Jewish High Priest, Onias, sought refuge in the temple of Apollo at Antioch. He was lured outside and killed on the orders of Antiochus IV, which again led to a major outcry in the city.[29] The fact that Onias had to be enticed from sanctuary before being seized shows that even kings were hesitant to violate the temples. It is also worth noting that even though this was a pagan space, reverence for asylum could extend sanctuary to a Jew. Thus, it is clear that the question of delineating spaces of asylum was more important than the question of delineating the subject of it. In 168 BC, King Perseus of Macedonia sought refuge in the temple at Samothrace. The Romans, besieging the temple, demanded the surrender of the king, but did not seize him themselves. Here again a powerful force, the Romans, was forced to respect the inviolability of the temple as a refuge. Perseus later surrendered to the Romans of his own volition.[30]

There is, therefore, significant evidence of *asylia* as refuge. As widespread and as available as *asylia* was to refugees, what was involved was the transfer of an ancient custom/right of asylum which belonged to the fugitives themselves, which was then transmogrified into a right bestowed upon the cities and towns of *asylia* to offer sanctuary to them.[31] This was a product, Gunther Plaut argues, of attempts by the amalgam of Greek states to create some stability in the midst of almost perpetual warfare. More bluntly, Norman Trenholme notes:

25 Rigsby (n 18), 385–386.
26 Ibid 386–387. The work of Tatius is *The Adventures of Leucippe and Clitophon*.
27 Polybius, *The Histories: Volume Four* (WR Patton tr, Heinemann, 1925), 533–534.
28 Plutarch, *Plutarch on Sparta* (Richard JA Talbert tr, Penguin, 1988), 62–63.
29 Rigsby (n 18), 497.
30 Ibid 397–398.
31 Plaut WG, *Asylum: A Moral Dilemma* (Praeger, 1995), 37–38; Timbal (n 16), 17.

'It is said that in time of war the Greek asylums were crowded with suppliants, while in time of peace they were often deserted'.[32] William C. Ryan asserts that 'this was the principle purpose of asylum in classical times: to save the lives of those defeated in war'[33]; whereas for Bulmerincq, 'A feeling of humanity gave birth to the Asyla of the Greeks'. [34] Rigsby's exhaustive study of the institution leads him to conclude:

> Our inscriptions leave no doubt that these declarations [of *asylia*] were first and foremost a religious gesture, increasing the honor of the god. In strict logic, they do not seem necessary: all temples were supposed to be inviolable, and for a city the option of military neutrality was always there, without the need of someone else's declaration.[35]

The answer to this conundrum, Rigsby suggests, is that a juridical process stepped in to perform what had once been a spiritual or communal sense of duty. One could see this as a positive parallel with modern refugee law, upholding human rights in a world of total wars and genocide. Yet, the transfer of the right from the refugee to the place of refuge had unfortunate implications. In terms of places of sanctuary for refugees, the Greek *asylia* were, in certain respects, quite restrictive:

> In practice . . . escaping to a temple was not enough for a fugitive from the law: the god or the god's priest could refuse him . . . Commonly, one who took refuge in a temple was required by the temple to undergo a kind of trial to determine whether his flight was 'just'.[36]

Moreover, the Romans, in their attacks on the institution, exploited the juridical paradigm, already latent in the system of *asylia*. If a place was inviolable mainly due to a legal grant, rather than divinely ordained, then it could equally be revoked under secular authority. Following the revolt of Mithridates against the occupation, the Romans moved to strip many of the *asylia* of their inviolable status. After many years of violating the sanctuary, the Romans finally revoked the Temple of Artemis of its sacred and inviolable status in 88 BC. Stories about supposed 'lawless behaviour' in the temple 'entered Roman legal lore as a grave objection to the right of asylum'.[37] The city of Miletus' grant of *asylia* was also

---

32 Trenholme N, 'The Right of Sanctuary in England: A Study in Institutional History' (1903), 1, *University of Missouri Studies*, 1, 5.
33 Ryan WC, 'The Historical Case for Sanctuary' (1987), 29, *Journal of Church and State*, 209, 213.
34 Bulmerinq A, *Das Asylrecht in seiner geschlichtlichen Entwicklung* (Martin Sandig, 1853), paraphrased in Mazzinghi (n 24), 108.
35 Rigsby (n 18), 14.
36 Ibid 10.
37 Ibid 393.

removed by the Romans around the same time, after they had supported Mithridates' rebellion. Instead, the sacred and inviolable status was restricted to the precinct of the temple within the city. This dovetails with the general Roman thinking on *asylum*, that it applied only to places of religious worship and not to cities, towns, etc.[38] At this stage, the Romans moved only to reduce *asylia* to temples and other places of religious veneration. One can speculate that this was either because it was all that was necessary to establish complete sovereign authority over Greece or because, in the wake of Mithridates' rebellion, attempting to attack the status of the most revered sites of the Greeks would have been a provocation too far. However, a century later, even the temples would have to submit themselves to a juridical process in order to maintain their historical role as asylums, places inviolable in which individuals would be free from seizure.

The nineteenth-century historian of asylum, August von Bulmerincq, echoes the prejudices of the Romans when he writes:

> More generally in Greece however, the characteristic was the perpetuation of a state of lawlessness, by the consecration of a caprice, and the protection of crime, so their law of Asylum hurt the law itself, and they even sought to justify it; whereas the more enlightened amongst them, where society had attained higher development, as at Athens, recognized the misuse and sought to limit it. Abolish it they dared not; for it was a divine law.[39]

While Bulmerincq is guilty of grossly telescoping the history of *asylia* in Ancient Greece, this passage is more instructive in shedding light on a particularly legalistic view of asylum, one that we will repeatedly encounter in the history of asylum, and of its treatment by historians: namely, that it is a product of backward or primitive societies, an institution to be overcome with the dawn of a rule of law. For Bulmerincq, the Romans' emasculation of *asylia* represented through their 'general system of jurisprudence . . . a higher development'.[40] Or, as Rigsby suggests: 'It may be that what truly undermined the ancient Greek usage of religious refuge was the availability of more reliable alternatives: the layered system of the Roman Empire and the spread of Roman citizenship with its peculiar advantages and protections'.[41] This sense of the superiority of law over asylum was certainly one adhered to by the Romans themselves as they proceeded to all but eradicate the *asylia* and the concept of sanctuary from the civil authority.

Rome

Rome was a society whose self-identity was famously defined by its attachment to law. Perhaps no other society prior to the modern age was so bound by a legal

---

38 Ibid 177.
39 Bulmerincq (n 34), paraphrased in Mazzinghi (n 24), 108.
40 Ibid 110.
41 Rigsby (n 18), 586.

structure and rationality. The notion of a unitary sovereign order and the rule of
law all but excluded the possibility of asylum as it had been understood before
then. With the conquest of Greece in the second-century BC, and particularly
following the quelling of Mithridates' rebellion a century later, the *asylia* were
increasingly restricted by the Romans. Another century later, the Emperor
Tiberius enacted legislation, which effectively regulated them out of existence.
The Roman period witnesses the effective erasure of asylum by law; the legal
paradigm of Rome simply could not accommodate the existence of spaces beyond
the authority of the state and its law. As Pierre Timbal notes: 'The rigorous
justice of Rome, inspired by the principle of the public interest, could not allow
for *asyla*', which would have entailed a failure to punish the guilty. The republican
ideology of Rome was founded upon the idea of a state based on a system of
laws, perfected through legislation that would 'assure the complete security of
all its citizens'.[42] We can see the extent to which the concept of asylum was
completely alien to the Romans in the fact that they did not possess a word for
it. Instead, they were forced to use various circumlocutions or borrow words
from the Greek.[43] In a relatively recent work, Karl Shoemaker has argued that
sanctuary was a more consistent practice during the Roman Empire than is
commonly argued.[44] However, even he acknowledges that this remained restricted
to forms of intercessions during trials, and to very temporary protections offered
when clasping the feet of certain revered statues in Rome. In other words, the
existence of spaces that existed permanently outside the law and sovereign rule
were not a feature in the Roman period. Some of the old *asylia* remained in
conquered Greece, but they were tolerated, rather than revered. And as we shall
see, eventually they were effectively abolished during the rule of Tiberius early
in the first-entury AD. The re-emergence of asylum, or sanctuary as it would
become known, was as a form of resistance to Roman rule. Indeed, as we shall
see in Part III, asylum/sanctuary has been asserted in our times also as a form
of resistance. The story of asylum in Rome is of a concentrated battle between
law and asylum in two phases. The first takes place in the context of the rise of
the Empire and the consequent destruction of asylum and the second occurs
around four centuries later as the Western Empire crumbles, and so asylum once
more has a space in which to take root.

Asylum in the Roman imagination

In 42 BC, 2 years after the assassination of Julius Caesar, the Roman Senate
ordered a temple to be built in the Forum, dedicated to his cult. The Temple of
Divus Julius was an asylum open to all seeking refuge.[45] This was unique, as we

---

42 Timbal (n 16), 25–26.
43 Ibid 26.
44 Shoemaker K, *Sanctuary and Crime in the Middle Ages 400–1500* (Fordham University
    Press, 2011), 29–34.
45 Dio C, *Dio's Roman History: Volume 5* (Earnest Cary tr, Heinemann, 1969), 155.

know of no other instance where the central power of either the Republic or the Empire created or licensed a new asylum.[46] There was just one problem with this temple of refuge, located in the heart of the city, open to all without prejudice. It was built with a huge wall surrounding it and thus it was, in all practical terms, inaccessible. As Cassius Dio puts it, the temple 'had inviolability in name only'.[47] And so a pastiche of asylum was created in place of the real thing. I would argue that increasingly modern refugee law presents a reflection of the Divis Julius: we have a similar promise of asylum, but for the vast majority of the forcibly displaced they are faced with almost impregneable walls of sovereign borders and legal processes.

While the Divus Julius was a real temple with a fake claim to sanctuary, its inspiration was a genuinely open, if mythical, asylum – a myth, nonetheless, that 'is certainly one of the noblest that survives from classical antiquity'.[48] The famed sanctuary of Romulus on the Capitolium, whose function was to accumulate the founding population of Rome, was largely made up of runaway slaves and criminals. This space remained, as Plutarch described it, 'a place of refuge for fugitives, which they called the Temple of the Asylaean God. Here they received all that came . . . declaring that they were directed by the oracle of Apollo to preserve the asylum from all violation'.[49] Rigsby points out the problematic aspect of Romulus' asylum for Roman concepts of space and law:

> In Rome, sacred space supplied no precedent or analogy for the right of sanctuary – hence the lack of a Latin word for this function . . . this place [the asylum on the Capitolium] 'between two groves' seems rather conceived of as negative space, no-man's land, subject to no law.[50]

Dench points out another problematic aspect for the Romans: having a tale of mixed races and criminals as the founding myth of Rome conflicted with the high-flown and noble claim of Roman civilisation.[51] The aristocratic Cicero once casually referred to these refugees as the 'crap of Romulus'.[52] For criminals and vagabonds to be founders of Rome would also have offended against the Romans' pride in their society of laws and due process. Juvenal mocked the

---

46 Dench E, *Romulus' Asylum: Roman Identities from the Age of Alexander to the Age of Hadrian* (OUP, 2005), 17.
47 Dio (n 45), 155.
48 Dench (n 46), 2.
49 Plutarch, *Plutarch's Lives* (John Langhorne and William Langhorne trs, William Tegg, 1862), 16.
50 Rigsby (n 18), 577.
51 Dench (n 46), 16.
52 Cicero, *Letters to Atticus: Volume One* (DR Shackleton Bailey tr, Harvard University, 1999), 133. Shackleton Bailey translates the phrase 'Romuli faece' as 'Romulus' cesspool'. But Dench's rendering, which I have used here, conveys a greater sense, I think, of Cicero's attitude to the original inhabitants of Rome. Dench (n 46), 16.

obsession among the Roman upper classes for attempting to trace their ancestry as far back as possible. They would, he pointed out, end up discovering their origins among the dregs of society who made up the arrivals at Romulus' asylum.[53] It is certainly understandable, therefore, that arguments among Roman historians about the nature of Romulus' asylum should persist well into the time of the Empire. For example, Dionysius of Halicarnassus' description is worth quoting for the light it sheds on the prejudices during the early period of the Roman Empire:

> [F]inding that many of the cities in Italy were very badly governed, both by tyrannies and by oligarchies, [Romulus] undertook to welcome and attract to himself the fugitives from these cities, who were very numerous, paying no regard either to their calamities or to their fortunes, provided only they were free men . . . but he invented a specious pretext for his course, making it appear that he was showing honour to a god.[54]

Note first the nobility Dionysius attaches to the asylum by painting the fugitives in the colours of political refugees, fleeing backward dictatorships for 'civilised' Rome. And then there is his rationalist disparaging of any religious basis of asylum. Livy's description of the refugees as 'rag-tag-and-bobtail' is far more dismissive and condescending. He also attempts to explain away the ignoble founding of Rome as of a piece with the founding of many other cities at the time who would 'shark up a lot of homeless and destitute folk and pretend that they were "born of earth"' to be founders of the new city.[55] As far back as the late Roman Republic, it seems a distinction was being made between deserving political fugitives and unworthy economic migrants.

Rome and the Greek asylia

From fake temples and troublesome myth, we turn to the actual history of Rome's engagement with asylum in the form of the *asylia* inherited from the Greeks. With the triumph of the Roman over the Greek world, *asylia* was latinised into *asylum*. The word 'asylum' first appears during the reign of Augustus, a period which saw a great interest in antiquarianism and foreign words in Roman literature. Thus, the Romans would have been keenly aware of the fact that 'asylum' came from

53 Juvenal, *The Sixteen Satires* (Peter Green tr, 3rd edn, Penguin, 1998), 69–70.
54 Dionysius of Halicarnassus, *The Roman Antiquities of Dionysius of Halicarnassus: Volume One* (Earnest Cary tr, Heinemann, 1937), 355.
55 Livy, *The Early History of Rome* (Aubrey de Selincourt tr, Penguin, 1971), 42. Cicero, with the exception of the casual remark made in a letter to a friend that is quoted earlier, when describing the founding of Rome either just mentions the refugees in passing [Cicero, *De Oratore: Volume One* (EW Sutton tr, Heinemann, 1942), 27–29] or fails to refer to them at all [Cicero, *De Res Publica, De Legibus* (Clinton Walker Keyes tr, Heinemann, 1928), 115–123].

the Greeks.[56] However, the Romans understood asylum to mean a space within the *polis* where the writ of civil law did not run: a space of non-law to which fugitives could escape. For the Greeks, on the other hand, *asylia* meant a neutral space existing between the various polities, not within them. This, of course, reflected the patchwork nature of sovereignty in Ancient Greece. For the Romans, whose state was unified and centralised and based on what we would recognise as a 'rule of law', such spaces were either inconceivable or simply could not be tolerated. It is no wonder that the Romans were 'uneasy' about asylum.[57] A similar resistance to exemptions from the writ of secular law holds today in modern Western states. Indeed, the scandal of contemporary sanctuary movements is evidence of this, as discussed in Part III. The sacredness of holy places and their separation from the secular law was a feature of the Church in the medieval period, as we shall see in Chapter 2, but this distinction was abolished by the modern state, as it was by the Romans some fifteen centuries earlier.

First, and in an *ad hoc* manner, the Romans simply violated *asylia* and removed suppliants. But this was risky, as it frequently provoked a popular reaction to what was perceived by the locals as sacrilege. Any attempt at simply abolishing a privilege with ancient roots might well have caused an even worse reaction. Therefore, instead, the Romans progressively starved the institution of *asylia* through legal regulation and restrictions. Once again, this dynamic bears many of the hallmarks of the contest between law and those seeking sanctuary from its grasp, as will be evident in the discussion of the US Sanctuary Movement and the Sans-Papiers in Part III. Rigsby notes: 'The Greek people claimed no authority concerning whether some temple might receive refugees, but the Roman government did'.[58] They began by dispensing with places of *asylia* and refuge based solely on custom rather than any formal grant. As early as the second-century BC, the Romans acknowledged *only* the temple at Delphi as *asylia* and not the surrounding city and country. At this stage, the Romans were already 'groping toward the application of their own notion of an asylum', one that was far more restrictive, and more symbolic than real.[59]

But the real turning point came in AD 22, when the Emperor Tiberius ordered a review of all Greek *asylia*.[60] They had to reapply to the Roman authorities for their 'inviolable' status by providing proof of the original grant and/or evidence of divine associations, often an impossible task; on this basis, about 70% of the applications were rejected by Rome. In addition, the Romans instituted what *they* conceived of as asylum on the same principle as that already applied to Delphi: restricted solely to temples and not to cities or towns. Also, henceforth,

56 Dench (n 46), 16. See also Livy, *Rome and the Mediterranean* (Henry Bettenson tr, Penguin, 1976), 231.
57 Rigsby (n 18), 417.
58 Ibid 22.
59 Ibid 49.
60 Tacitus, *The Annales of Imperial Rome* (Michael Grant tr, Penguin, 1973), 148–149, 164.

the Romans granted no new asylums. The space of asylum was therefore not exactly prohibited by law, merely regulated by law slowly out of existence. Within two centuries, *asylia/asylum* had all but vanished in the Roman world. Anne Ducloux writes: '[F]rom Tiberius to Antoninus Pius, [the Empire] had endeavoured to erase, progressively, those places of asylum that had been rooted within the recently conquered Greek world'.[61] Contemporary accounts emphasise that erasure of asylum was bound up with ensuring the integrity of law. Tacitus describes the review of AD 22 as ensuring public order. It is worth quoting him at length here, because it is the only source that we have for this legal vandalism of *asylia*; it also gives us a valuable insight into the Roman prejudice towards asylum, one which was to be closely mirrored 1,500 years later with the abolition of Church Sanctuary in Western Europe:

> In Greek cities criminals were increasingly escaping punishment owing to over-lavish rights of sanctuary. Delinquent slaves filled temples. Asylum was granted indiscriminately – to debtors escaping their creditors, even to men suspected of capital offences. Protecting religious observance, these communities were protecting crime itself; and interventions provoked outbreaks which no authority could control. So the cities were requested to submit their charters and their representatives to investigation at Rome. Some cities then voluntarily abandoned their unfounded claims. Many however persisted, on the strength of ancient religious myths or their services to Rome. It was a splendid sight, that day, to see the senate investigating privileges conferred by its ancestors, treaties with allies, edicts of kings who had reigned before Rome was a power, even divine cults; and it was free, as of old, to confirm or amend.[62]

A further two centuries later, a 'right of asylum' would appear in Roman law. This, as is discussed below, was in response to resistance to the decaying Empire, and a reflection of the growing power of the Christian church. While many scholars have considered Hellenistic *asylia* as refracted back through this Roman 'right of asylum', Rigsby points out that:

> Tacitus leaves no doubt about the substance, logic, and legal source of the [Roman] privilege: it was the 'right of asylum' of a temple, immunity of sacred space from civil law, and it was granted by that sovereign who controlled the city.[63]

The key distinction is that the Romans saw asylum not as the result of something above or beyond the sovereign power but as a privilege granted by it.

---

61 Ducloux A, *Ad ecclesiam confugere: Naissance du droit d'asile dans les églises* (De Boccard, 1994), 254.
62 Tacitus (n 60), 148.
63 Rigsby (n 18), 286.

This legalistic view of asylum has far more in common with the modern concept of the right of asylum as essentially vested in the state – i.e. its right to grant asylum – rather than the tradition of the Greeks which saw asylum as spiritually ordained and thus *supra legem*.

The Early Church

The resurrection – the word is apt in this context – of asylum comes with the rise of the Christian Church and the terminal crisis of the Roman Empire that took hold in the fourth-century AD. These two phenomena are closely linked. Examples of refusal to pay taxes, assassinations of local officials of the Empire and other forms of sabotage proliferated, and increasingly the perpetrators of these acts then sought refuge and protection in churches. With the integration of the Church and the Roman state following the adoption of Christianity as the state religion during the closing decades of the century, it became necessary that the rules concerning the 'taking of sanctuary had to be sorted out'.[64] But it would be a mistake to assume that this was a natural process, pre-determined by the prevailing socio-political circumstances. The establishment of Church asylum, an institution that would last for over a millennium, was a product of struggle by a significant proportion of the population, led by Church fathers such as St. Augustine, St. Ambrose and St. John Chrysostom, who called upon Christians to defend their churches as sanctuaries from those, including the Roman authorities, who attempted to remove suppliants. The Roman statutes of 21 November 419 and 23 March 431 have long been considered the earliest laws on the right of asylum, and as such mark the origins of asylum in the modern sense. But this is not quite true. There had already been a growing movement from the people and from the Church in various parts of the Empire, which only later culminated in these two seminal laws.[65]

In early Christianity, all of its sacred places of worship were places of asylum. This is in contrast to the religious places of the Greeks, only some of which were deemed to be refuges. Ducloux suggests that the granting of asylum was for the Greeks primarily based on 'political opportunism'.[66] I suspect that she is focussing rather too narrowly on the later institution of *asylia*, and, as such, misses on its strong religious origins in places such as Delphi. Nonetheless, I think she has a point. As we saw earlier, asylum in the broader sense played an important political role in the various interstate and civil wars of the fifth- and fourth-century BC. But it would also be incorrect to say that the Church conceived of asylum purely in religious terms, to the exclusion of politics. The assertion of Church supremacy against the secular Roman law was, of course, by its nature a political stance. In any case, to try and draw too rigid a distinction between religion and politics in any context is a fruitless task. However, Ducloux is undoubtedly correct in

---

64 Harris J, *Law and Empire in Late Antiquity* (Cambridge University, 1999), 151.
65 Ducloux (n 61), 6.
66 Ibid 7.

how she conceives of the relationship between asylum and law during the twilight of the Empire:

> What emerges clearly is that law did not give birth to the right of asylum . . . it was regarded by all as a religious principle higher than the secular law, a kind of right born of a divine spirit.[67]

The right of asylum already existed for the Church as something granted by God, irrespective of the domain of temporal law. The principle of asylum in the Christian Church was founded upon the idea that the refugee could pay penitence in the house of God.[68] The laws promulgated in 419 and 431 were, therefore, not about *granting* the right of asylum in Church spaces, rather it was a matter of fixing 'the necessary legal penalties to ensure its respect by everyone, and, with the aim of protecting the purity of the sanctuary but also to ameliorate the conditions of life for the refugees'.[69] By contrast, the granting of *asylia* in Greece was not guaranteed by any legislative text, 'its only value was religious',[70] and, I would add, political. So long as the religious superstructure of belief held, the inviolability of asylum was respected. With the subsuming of Greece into the Roman Empire, so the edifice that underpinned asylum collapsed. From the moment Christianity became the state religion in 380, the customary right of asylum took on a greater significance for non-Christians such as Jews and Pagans: 'For them the juridical consequences of a custom, where traditionally all customs had the force of law so long as they were not *contra legem*, was invested with great importance'.[71] This, no doubt, gave an impetus to conversion. Thus, it was in the interests of the Church to fight for the inviolability of its places of sanctuary so as to prove in practice that the house of God was able to offer all the divine protection that such a place was meant to provide. This perhaps demonstrates the value of law in protecting asylum. But when examined in detail, the role of law will be seen as, on balance, negative.

Early Christian theology and asylum

One of the reasons for the perseverance of the institution of asylum, in spite of its almost complete erasure following the Tiberian laws of AD 22, is that ordinary people would have continued to look for places to seek protection from cruel masters and the severities of the law. Now, however, they looked to the new temples that were replacing the old pagan ones: the Christian churches.[72]

---

67 Ibid 7.
68 Ibid 59.
69 Ibid 8–9.
70 Ibid 110.
71 Ibid 87.
72 Ryan (n 33), 216. Often this was literally the case, with old pagan places of worship being appropriated by the church.

It was through this continuous popular usage that the institution was able to be reborn from the fourth century onwards.[73] We have the testimony of St. Ambrose, St. Gregory Nazianzen and Ammianus Marcellinus that there existed from the fourth century the practice of seeking asylum in churches.[74] According to J. Charles Cox, Constantine's Edict of Toleration in 303 would have likely begun the process of Churches being widely recognised as places of asylum.[75] Surviving evidence shows that during the first three quarters of the fourth century, asylum existed as a religious principle adhered to by many Christians. This is all in the century before the laws of 419 and 431. There is also an obscure reference to a 10-year-old boy seeking refuge in a church in the town of Pavia, possibly in 326, thus making it the earliest evidence for the Christian Church as a place of asylum. For Ducloux, the evidence is too vague and, in places, too contradictory to accurately date this event, or to ascertain the exact nature of his reception in the church.[76] The source of this story, Sulpicius Severus, does not, in any case, refer to the boy as having been granted shelter in *a* church, but instead in *the* Church (*confugit ad Ecclesiam*), in contrast to the widely used phrase for asylum in the following decades: *ad ecclesiam confugere* (to seek refuge in a church). In other words, the boy may have come under the protection of the institution rather than a specific place.[77] Nevertheless, this demonstrates that already the Church was viewed as offering shelter from the secular world around it.

At the Council of Sardica in 343, the Church leaders turned the notion of the mercy of the Church into a positive obligation on the clerics. The eighth canon issued by the council stated that those suffering from some injustice, or sentenced to exile, could seek refuge in the 'mercy of the Church'.[78] This could have been a purely spiritual form of refuge as perhaps was the case with the boy of Pavia. However, this canon was interpreted by many local priests as meaning that legal penalties could not be carried out until the church had had a chance to consider the case for mercy. In this was born a popular practice of seeking physical refuge in a church so as to claim mercy, and to gain succour for so long as it took for the request to be considered. As a result, the law's hand was expected to be stayed until the Church had made its judgement.[79] Ducloux suggests that the practice of seeking mercy from the Church was already something of a popular practice encouraged by certain local churches. The aim was to prevent punishment that would result in the loss of life or limb. This intercession was at least partly driven by the early Christian Church's opposition in principle to the 'shedding

73 Ducloux (n 61), 254.
74 Vauchez A, Dobson B and Lapidge M (eds), *Encyclopedia of the Middle Ages: Volume Two* (James Clark & Co., 2000), 126.
75 Cox JC, *The Sanctuaries and Sanctuary Seekers of Mediaeval England* (George Allen & Sons, 1911), 2.
76 Ducloux (n 61), 23.
77 Ibid 24–25.
78 Ibid 27, 32.
79 Ibid 31–32.

of blood'.[80] Clerics therefore took it upon themselves to act as 'ambassadors of mercy before the throne of justice'.[81] It is for this reason, Timbal argues, that asylum was effectively 'recreated through the practice of intercession by the clerics'.[82] In particular, the clerics could rest their practice on theological grounds, the prophets of the Old Testament and Jesus in the New Testament having all acted as intermediaries between the faithful and their god.[83] John P. Sexton, in discussing Anglo-Saxon church sanctuary, places the same emphasis on intercession as 'a balm to sooth the sting of institutional justice'.[84] As such, there developed the idea of a separate jurisdiction before which the imperial law was made to pause. And indeed, reverence for the Church as a place of divine sanctuary and refuge extended later to the 'barbarians' as they took over territory formerly belonging to Rome. Theodoric I, for example, commuted the sentence of a man convicted of homicide from death to exile, solely on the basis that the condemned man had sought sanctuary in a church. Indeed, it became a law under the Visigoths that those who gained asylum in a church would have their death sentence commuted.[85]

It was only in the last two decades of the fourth century, particularly after the final establishment of Christianity as the state religion in 380, that the seeking of asylum in churches evolved from being merely an *ad hoc* tool into a custom adhered to by the popular, and increasingly Christianised, will.[86] It would also have guaranteed the respect from the secular authorities necessary for the principle of intercession to work.[87] Moreover, mass popular support for resistance to imperial agents was increasingly widespread and so attempts by the authorities to remove refugees from churches often provoked riots. An attempt in 399 by the consul Eutropius to enact a law banning recognition of church asylum was defeated: testimony to the growing power of the Church. In an ironic twist, shortly afterwards, Eutropius was himself forced to seek asylum in the church of St. John Chrysostom at Constantinople after his fall from power.[88] Chrysostom attempted to intercede on his behalf, but on this occasion, his intervention was unsuccessful and Eutropius was executed. This was likely due to popular hatred towards this notoriously corrupt consul.

---

80 Shoemaker, citing Mommsen, points out that intercession was also a feature of Roman penal law. Following conviction by a magistrate, the guilty could seek *intercessio* from another magistrate to mitigate their sentence. Shoemaker (n 44), 30. However, the crisis of the Empire reduced the scope of such leniency.
81 Trenholme (n 32), 8.
82 Timbal (n 16), 32.
83 Ibid 36.
84 Sexton JP, 'Saint's Law: Anglo-Saxon Sanctuary Protection in the Translatio et Meracula S. Swithuni' (2006), 23, *Florilegium*, 61, 78.
85 Ducloux (n 61), 88.
86 Ibid 60.
87 Timbal (n 16), 43.
88 Ibid 71; Thurman WS, 'A Law of Justinian Concerning the Right of Asylum' (1969), 100, *Transactions of the American Philological Association*, 593, 595.

The phrase used by the early Christians for asylum was *ad ecclesiam confugere* (to seek refuge in a church). It was this term – or variants of it – which was used in the imperial legislation that came later.[89] The complete avoidance of any mention of terms such as 'asylum' or '*asylia*' was almost certainly due to the prejudice held by the Romans towards the old Greek institution, and by the Church towards a relic of paganism; but also, as the bishops were well aware, they could not guarantee the inviolability that the term 'asylum' denoted. Thus, they always referred instead to the 'seeking of refuge', in Latin *confugere* or in Greek *kataphugein*.[90]

The struggle between Christian mercy and law

Under pressure, the imperial authorities initially sought to repeat Tiberius' trick of recognising in law the institution of asylum, and in so doing defining it and legislating it out of existence. The first statute to actually refer to asylum (*confugiendum ad ecclesias*) is that of 18 October 392. Here, the law decreed that those fleeing debts owed to the state would not be allowed to seek refuge in churches unless the bishop was prepared to make good the money owed.[91] This is likely to have been an attempt to clamp down on tax avoidance, a common form of resistance to the authorities at the time. Moreover, as Cox points out, this law was only 'done in order to explain and regulate a privilege already recognised and well established'.[92] There is no mention of other categories of refugees other than public debtors. Therefore, on the principle that 'all that is not prohibited is permitted', it is possible that the imperial authorities might have tolerated all other types of refugees. Yet, as Ducloux points out: 'the belief that the temple of God is inviolable and sacred is not yet sufficiently rooted for the emperor to adhere to it without restrictions'.[93] And indeed, this law must be seen in the context of other legislation enacted by Theodosius I just 7 months previously, which introduced severe penalties for magistrates who failed to ensure that those convicted of the most serious crimes were punished.[94] At a time of intense crisis for the Empire, Theodosius was trading off limited recognition of asylum for stability through obedience to the law. In 398, a new law barred those guilty of capital crimes, along with public debtors, from claiming asylum. Another law, enacted a year earlier, was more pernicious in its effects, closing off asylum to Jews who had opportunistically converted to Christianity so as to take

---

89 The Imperial constitution of 18 October 392 refers to confugiendum ad ecclesias; that of 17 June 397 describes refugees as ad ecclesias confugientes. See Ducloux (n 61), 15.
90 Ducloux (n 61), 33–34.
91 Ibid 57.
92 Cox (n 75), 3.
93 Ducloux (n 61), 59.
94 Law of 13 March 392; Timbal (n 16), 61.

advantage of asylum in churches. One of the effects of the law of 397 was that it 'transformed bishops into inquisitors' by putting the onus on them to enquire of all who sought sanctuary if they were 'genuine' Christians, or if they were 'illegal' refugees.[95] At the same time, the law now placed a burden upon the suppliant to prove that they were genuine converts. The resonance for our own time with its discourses of 'illegal', 'genuine' or 'bogus' refugees is inescapable. Moreover, it turned the custodians of the asylum, the clerics, into its gatekeepers. This was resisted by some of the leading bishops of the time, notably Augustine of Hippo.

Ducloux describes St. Augustine as the 'theoretician' of asylum in the early Church.[96] In one of his sermons, he declares that the church is a 'common refuge', open to all who seek sanctuary. He speaks of three kinds of refugees: 'the unjust who flee the just, or the just who flee the unjust, or the unjust fleeing the unjust'. He goes on to argue that it is not for the Church to distinguish which is which. If 'we had wanted that the guilty could be removed from [the church], then it would not be a place to which the innocent would flee . . . Thus, it is better that the guilty should have shelter in the church than the innocent should be snatched from it'.[97] As Ducloux argues, Augustine was appealing to his flock that at any time one of them might require asylum. If they were to demand judgement on those who sought sanctuary today, what would happen when they would be judged by others as worthy or not of being granted asylum?[98] Augustine's declaration that asylum was open to all was a rejection of the laws of the last decade of the fourth century, which sought to distinguish between deserving and undeserving fugitives.[99] It was also, in my opinion, a rejection of law as a method of regulating asylum. Instead of laws demarcating the deserving from the undeserving refugee, Augustine was in favour of the church as the City of God, to be open to all, an approach much more in tune with hospitality than law, of delineating a space of asylum rather than a subject, as the law sought to do.[100] Augustine's view was that no matter how heinous the crime committed, or how far from the church's teachings the fugitive was, Christians must always love the sinner, and recognise their duty to help them avoid eternal damnation in the hereafter.[101] In this, he was following the words of St. Paul. In an extraordinary passage in his first letter to the Corinthians, Paul condemns those Christians who would seek justice through the law.[102] They should, he insists, leave it to God to pass judgement on a person's character. In everyday matters

95 Ducloux (n 61), 63.
96 Ibid 170.
97 Quoted in Ibid 172–173.
98 Ibid 181.
99 Ibid 182.
100 Augustine, *The City of God* (Henry Bettenson tr, Penguin, 1984), Book 1.
101 Timbal (n 16), 47.
102 I Corinthians 6.

of conflict, he advises seeking an honest broker from within the community 'who will be able to decide between his brethren'.[103]

So, by the close of the fourth century, asylum had re-emerged, first as a practice and then as custom based on belief in divine authority, in the context of a rapidly waning secular authority. As such, the imperial law could no longer ignore or deny such a right; it rather attempted on several occasions to regulate and normalise asylum by restricting its application. Yet, during this period, imperial agents seeking out fugitives frequently violated churches. The inviolability of asylum, an idea gaining momentum within the Church and among the populace, was not yet an established fact. However, during the final decade of the fourth century, according to Ducloux, 'the violation of the sacred refuge is increasingly felt to be a form of sacrilege'.[104] For Timbal, the combination of respect for the sacred space of the church together with the already established practice of clerical intercession with the authorities created a viable institution of asylum for the first time in the Roman world in spite of, not because of, the law.[105]

The question then arises as to how a custom could arise that trumped the law. This would have been a particularly difficult problem in the context of an authority as legalistic as the Roman Empire. But, as Ducloux shows, asylum was not an 'ordinary custom'.[106] It had the force of popular will symbiotically reinforced by the claim by certain bishops that the sanctuary of the church was also the will of God. Thus, the custom of asylum began to have the force of 'a right *supra legem*, which cannot be contradicted by temporal law'.[107] Furthermore, the church possessed the legitimacy of being the established religion. Ducloux, summarising the first couple of decades of the fifth century, argues that it was due to the propagation of the right of asylum to all by charismatic bishops such as St. Augustine and others that popular belief and practice developed. Eventually, 'the legislature had no choice. It *had* to regulate the conditions for the application of the right of asylum to conform to the rules established by the Fathers of the Church'.[108]

There are examples from the early decades of the fifth century to show how widespread respect for church asylum had become. In 408, Stilicon, a Roman governor accused of collaboration with the Visigoths, was hunted down by the authorities and took asylum in a church in Ravenna. Imperial soldiers entered the church and assured the bishop that the Emperor Honorius would not have him killed. Stilicon then left the church. Once outside, the soldiers announced to him that he had been condemned to death for crimes against the state, and he was taken away under arrest to his execution. Although by deceit the suppliant

---

103   I Corinthians 6:5.
104   Ducloux (n 61), 85.
105   Timbal (n 16), 55.
106   Ducloux (n 61), 91.
107   Ibid.
108   Ibid 205 (emphasis in original).

had been lured outside of the place of sanctuary, Honorius, as a Christian, 'could neither ignore the religious basis nor the custom of asylum'.[109] Thus, Stilicon could not be killed or arrested in the church itself. To do so would have 'provoked popular anger that would be certain to manifest itself if the asylum had been openly violated'.[110] Ducloux suggests that 'the imperial agents hesitated to execute an act which appeared to them to be sacrilegious'.[111] During the sack of Rome 2 years later, Alaric respected the churches as inviolable places of refuge, and the refugees within them, both pagan and Christian, were not seized. Could this have been based on political calculation?[112] In other words, could even a 'barbarian' leader have realised that violating the asylum would be a step too far? Might he have feared provoking too great a response from the populace and Christians in Rome and elsewhere? We simply do not know, but the fact remains that the roots of asylum were sufficiently strong that even a new occupying power was forced to respect it. And in yet another instance, in 411–412, Bishop Synesius of Cyrene felt confident enough to launch a public attack on the Roman governor of Libya, citing, among other things, the posting up of 'edicts to the doors of the church illegally denying suppliants the right of sanctuary'.[113] But perhaps the decisive turning point came in 419 when large numbers of people in Carthage sought refuge in the churches there, as a result of widespread refusals to pay taxes and the assassination of a despised and corrupt tax official. For several months, they refused to come out, and they were supported by the local bishop, Augustine. Further, as Ducloux puts it:

> The custom of asylum had become so implanted in their attitudes that, despite the gravity of their crimes, the African authorities made no attempt to seize the fugitives ... the time had come for the legislature to decide officially if the churches constituted places where the temporal law remained suspended.[114]

These events, therefore, forced the enactment in the Western Empire on 21 November 419 of what was the first law to grant the right of asylum. This law was followed by similar legislation in 431, which applied to the Eastern Empire. These laws made the violation of asylum a criminal offence. Whereas the laws of 392 and 398 explicitly defined who could *not* gain asylum, these laws, in particular the one of 431, were 'sufficiently vague to include all possible categories of refugees as benefiting from asylum'.[115] In addition, whereas custom had restricted the asylum to the space within the walls of the building (that is the sacred space

---

109   Ibid 120.
110   Ibid.
111   Timbal (n 16), 74.
112   Ducloux (n 61), 134.
113   Harris (n 64), 156.
114   Ducloux (n 61), 163.
115   Ibid 226.

of the church) so as to prevent any refugees being apprehended from the outside, the law of 419 extended the space of the asylum to a perimeter 50 paces (75 m) beyond the church. And in 450, Roman law extended the boundaries of the asylum as far as the perimeter of the 'churchyard or precincts, including the houses of bishops and clergy, cloisters, courts, and cemeteries'.[116] This allowed the refugees access to fresh air and daylight. The effect of extending the space of asylum by law was also to extend the sacred space of the church. At a stroke, the church gained in power and status via the law's extension of its sacred domain beyond the church building itself. At this stage, a comingling of law and asylum had certainly some immediate benefits for both the Church and those who sought asylum within its precincts. There were also factors at work which facilitated a greater control by the Church authorities over church space itself. For example, the law of 431 made clear that the enlargement of the space of asylum also meant that there was sufficient room so that refugees would be able to obey the ban on defiling the sacred altar.

However, the law, in recognising and bringing asylum within its domain, had also 'defined the conditions for its application'.[117] In this manner, the laws of 419 and 431 sought to regulate the behaviour of the refugees within the sanctuary. Although they placed no restrictions on who could seek asylum, the laws instructed on refugee behaviour and where they could reside within the sanctuary. The law of 431 prohibited the carrying of arms into the sanctuary, demanding that the refugee place all faith in the divine power of the Church to protect them. To carry arms for protection was thus a demonstration of a lack of faith on the part of the refugee, and therefore made them unworthy of gaining asylum.[118] Thus, even this most liberal of asylum laws defines, orders and restricts. Yet, until 419–420, the safety of the asylum remained a matter of chance. The question of whether refugees would remain safe there depended on various things, not the least of which was the support of the local population and the bishop.[119] But there is no evidence to establish whether or not the imposition of a law vitiated the need for political or popular support. The Church was led, through its partnership with law, to play a role in controlling and policing asylum according to the legal paradigm. So also, in 431, the Council of Ephesus issued its own decree delimiting the spaces *within* a church which could be deemed sanctuaries. The net effect of these laws is described by Harris: 'The result . . . was a set of regulations which, taken as a group, laid greater stress on restrictions imposed on the privilege than on the importance of the right as a refuge'.[120]

Of course, once the law establishes its right to control an institution or practice, even on the most benign terms, it legitimises its right to then later alter the terms on a more restrictive basis. An example of this occurred just a year after the liberal

116   Cox (n 75), 3.
117   Ducloux (n 61), 207.
118   Ibid 228.
119   Ibid 163.
120   Harris (n 64), 151.

legislation of 431. The law of 28 March 432 'considerably reduced' access to sanctuary for slaves.[121] This law instructed that the slave's master had to be notified where he had taken asylum, but the master was then obliged to guarantee that the slave would not suffer 'afflictive punishment' on being returned to him.[122] However, the master was permitted to use force if necessary to remove his slave and take him back. There was therefore a contradiction in that, on the one hand, refugees – especially slaves – were prohibited from carrying arms into the church, yet on the other hand, the master was permitted by the law of 432 to use arms to remove his slave if necessary. In short, according to Ducloux, the principles of asylum open to all in the law of 431 were 'mocked' (*bafoués*) by the law passed a year later.[123]

The Church struggled to marry its commitment to asylum available to all who were prepared to accept Christ, while at the same time respecting the institution of slavery as an example of property rights. Paragraph 9 of the law of 28 February 466 made clear that, as a slave was the property of his master, for him to run away was a form of theft. This law clearly followed in the same spirit of that of 432.[124] The compromise devised by the Council of Orange in 511 was that flight to sanctuary could not vitiate the rights of ownership, but it was up to the clergy rather than the slave owners or the secular authorities to decide on the terms of the slave's access to sanctuary or their expulsion from it.[125] In other words, the Church had internalised the juridical process, rather than continuing to resist, as Augustine had done, its secular form. In doing so, the church had accepted a shift from a theological form of hospitality to a set of legal restrictions.

The transmission of Church asylum into the Middle Ages

As a custom, the principle of sanctuary was remarkably inclusive, allowing the guilty as well as the innocent, Christians as well as Jews and pagans, to use the church as a place of safety.[126] The Roman governments in both east and west were forced to recognise asylum in law in a series of pieces of legislation beginning in the late fourth century and culminating in the seminal laws of 419 and 431. Therefore to say, as Michel Lauwers does, that 'the Roman law was a Christian law' is to miss the point that Christian faith, theology and custom were at several points in direct conflict with the law.[127] Nevertheless, as Rome was forced to

---

121 Ducloux (n 61), 164.
122 Carro JL, 'Sanctuary: The Resurgence of an Age-Old Right or a Dangerous Misinterpretation of an Abandoned Ancient Privilege?' (1986), 54, *University of Cincinnati Law Review* 747, 752.
123 Ducloux (n 61), 242.
124 Ibid 243.
125 Mazzinghi (n 24), 90.
126 Ducloux (n 61), 174.
127 Lauwers M, 'Le cimetière dans le Moyen Age latin: Lieu sacré, saint et religieux' (1999), 54, *Annales*, 1047, 1056.

bend to the will of the Church, its laws were heavily coloured by Christian concepts. What the Justinian Code defines as a sacred space protected from incursion simply follows from the Christian idea that all, whether saint or sinner, had the right of asylum within the church's perimeters.[128] However, by the time of Justinian, the law regulating church asylum required that all refugees had to be registered and formally declare their reasons for seeking asylum.[129] Moreover, clerics were legally bound to receive legal summonses directed at any fugitives remaining within the sanctuary.[130] The Justinian Code also prohibited murderers, adulterers, rapists, heretics and those guilty of *lèse majesté* from the right of sanctuary.[131] In Novel 17 of the year 535, Justinian justified this exclusion on the basis that 'the security of the holy precincts is accorded not to those who commit injustice but to those who are the victims of injustice'.[132] Once again we have law distinguishing between the deserving and the undeserving based on 'objective' criteria. As William S. Thurman states: 'Imperial regulations and exceptions affecting asylum became so numerous that its availability was greatly diminished'.[133] The attempt by Justinian to re-establish order within and to defeat enemies without came partly at the expense of asylum.[134] Nonetheless, and this is a crucial point, just as in Greece, violators of asylum were liable to 'popular odium' and the perception that they had 'pollut[ed] themselves'.[135] As such, asylum was a valuable tool in at least staying the hand of the pursuer, whether private or state.

The restrictiveness of the Justinian Code is evidenced by problems in Byzantium regarding asylum. There was an apparent contradiction between the law of Justinian, prohibiting murderers from taking asylum in churches, and the grant that he gave to the Hagia Sophia in Constantinople, which allowed murderers asylum in that particular church. As a result of this anomaly, Church leaders exerted pressure on Constantine VII some four centuries later to adopt a more liberal law regarding asylum. Constantine's compromise was to allow those who had committed intentional murders the right of asylum on condition that they had voluntarily gone to the church to confess their crime.[136] Effectively, therefore, by the later half of the twelfth century, the Hagia Sophia had assumed jurisdiction over the treatment of murderers, and by extension over much of the dispensation of criminal justice.[137] The Church justified this on the basis that secular

---

128   Ibid.
129   Watson A (tr), *The Digest of Justinian* (University of Pennsylvania, 1985), 1.12.6.10.
130   Ibid 1.12.6.1–2.
131   Cox (n 75), 4; Timbal (n 16), 92.
132   Novel 17.7 and 37 [535], cited in Macrides RJ, 'Killing, Asylum, and the Law in Byzantium' (1988), 63, *Speculum*, 509, 510.
133   Thurman (n 88), 595.
134   Timbal (n 16), 89.
135   Thurman (n 88), 596.
136   Macrides (n 132), 511.
137   Ibid 514.

punishments were insufficient to expiate the sin of the suppliant. Only confession and 'the conscientious observance of penitential acts' were enough to redress the sinful act in the eyes of God.[138] But in the twelfth century, Emperor Manuel I decreed that the law be restored to the original Justinian formula: that asylum be only available for the 'innocent', i.e. those whose crime was not intentional.[139] On the other hand, as R.J. Macrides shows, certain clerics had always kept to the more restrictive criteria of Justinian when judging asylum claims, whereas others were more liberal and followed Constantine VII's ruling.[140]

Macrides paints a picture of a weak central authority where laws were regularly promulgated and with equal regularity were ignored. As a result, when accused persons fell into the hands of the civil authorities, they were often the victims of rough or overzealous punishment, particularly if they were poor or powerless. So for many accused perpetrators of crime, intentional in nature or not, whether they were guilty or innocent, 'If they fell into [the hands of the civil authority] they were finished, but with the church they had a future'.[141] But the Justinian Code, if followed to the letter, would have effectively erased any possibility for those at or near the bottom of society to mitigate the harsh punishments of the medieval world. In the West, on the other hand, where, commensurate with the decline of state authority, the power of the Church increased, ecclesiastical protection was a valuable commodity and ensured that the institution of sanctuary grew from strength to strength. In bold terms, where the state was strong, asylum was compromised, and where the state and its law withered, asylum retained its status.

But the reach of the Digest of Justinian was to be long. A thousand years after its creation, the secular authorities, in their successful struggle to suppress church sanctuary, would invoke it repeatedly.[142] Yet, the Justinian Code came too late to influence the already developing legal codes of the Anglo-Saxon and Frankish societies in the West. For them, the earlier Theodosian Code, containing the more liberal legislation of 419 and 431, provided the template for asylum.[143] And so it was these laws that formed the model on which asylum law was based within Western Christendom throughout the fifth and sixth centuries.[144] In particular, the law of 431 was incorporated into the Breviary of Alaric II of 506, which was instrumental in preserving much of Roman law in Western Europe into the middle ages.[145] Indeed, sanctuary was known and practised not only by the Visigoths but also by many other tribes throughout the Teutonic world,

---

138 Ibid 534.
139 Ibid 513.
140 Ibid 532.
141 Ibid 538.
142 Timbal (n 16), 92.
143 Schoemaker (n 17). See also Timbal (n 16), 96–137, for a detailed exposition of this development.
144 Ducloux (n 61), 258.
145 Lauwers (n 127), 1057.

although these were largely a result of the growing influence of the Church.[146] In 620, Pope Boniface V declared that the privilege of sanctuary was 'valid throughout Christendom'.[147] But the Church very early on confirmed the Theodosian Code, during the time of Pope Leo I (440–461). This Code prohibited public debtors – those who had in some way financially defrauded the state – from taking asylum.[148] Yet, the provision was added that it would be for the Church to examine those seeking asylum and to judge whether or not they would be granted sanctuary.[149] In this way, the Church again ignored St. Augustine's warnings on clerics becoming judges. Yet, while the transmission of asylum into the Middle Ages owed something to its incorporation into late Roman law, for much of the period in the West from the sixth century until the eleventh century, while secular law withered on the vine, sanctuary was a more or less autonomous institution. Indeed, as Timbal argues, it was precisely in the context of the 'crumbling' (*émiettement*) of secular authority that asylum enjoyed a significantly expansive development.[150] The extent to which the practice of asylum/sanctuary broke free of the legal paradigm during those six centuries is evidenced by the struggle that was waged by the new class of lawyers from the twelfth century onwards, in order to re-establish the legal framework of this ancient and persistent tradition.

146   Shoemaker (n 44), 57.
147   Pope S, 'Sanctuary: The Legal Institution in England' (1987), 10, *University of Puget Sound Law Review*, 677, 680.
148   Cox (n 75), 4.
149   Carro (n 122), 753.
150   Timbal (n 16), 95.

2 Sanctuary in England

Elements of medieval sanctuary

Ecclesiastical asylum existed throughout Western Europe during the Middle Ages.[1] But perhaps the longest unbroken tradition of asylum in recorded history is that of England, which began, at the latest, in the sixth century and lasted around 1,100 years until the early seventeenth century.[2] It has been estimated that by the thirteenth century, there were around 30,000 sanctuaries of various sorts throughout the Norman kingdom of England and Northern France.[3] Some medieval chroniclers claim that the right of sanctuary dates from as early as the second century when, according to legend, King Lucius introduced Christianity to England.[4] Even if this story is merely the stuff of myth, Cox suggests that it is at least 'highly probable' that church asylum was practised during the closing decades of the Roman occupation, which ended in 410.[5] However, the first recorded evidence of asylum in England dates from the very end of the sixth century. Following his conversion to Christianity around 597, King Ethelbert of Kent drew up the earliest surviving Anglo-Saxon laws, the first of which establishes the inviolability of churches.[6] The punishment for breach of church peace (*frith*,

1   de Martin PTD, *Le Droit d'Asile* (Librarie du Recueil Sirey, 1939); Shoemaker K, *Sanctuary and Crime in the Middle Ages 400–1500* (Fordham University Press, 2011).
2   Sanctuary also existed in Wales, Scotland and Ireland. See Cox JC, *The Sanctuaries and Sanctuary Seekers of Mediaeval England* (George Allen & Sons, 1911), chapter 15. In Wales, the laws of Hywel Dda dating from the tenth century refer to sanctuaries. Curiously, these describe fleeing to sanctuary as 'a legal act of disobedience'. At least some of the Welsh sanctuaries were very large. One at Amroth encompassed an area of 50 acres. Ibid 309.
3   Jordan WC, 'A fresh look at medieval sanctuary' in Ruth Mazo Karras, Joel Kaye and E Ann Matter (eds), *Law and the Illicit in Medieval Europe* (University of Pennsylvania, 2008), 18–19.
4   Trenholme N, 'The Right of Sanctuary in England: A Study in Institutional History' (1903), 1, *University of Missouri Studies*, 1, 10.
5   Cox (n 2), 5.
6   See Simpson AWB, 'The laws of Ethelbert' in Morris S Arnold and others (eds), *On the Laws and Customs of England* (University of North Carolina, 1981), for a detailed and subtle evaluation of the place of Ethelbert's laws in English legal history, and in particular their relationship to the early church and Roman law.

fryth or *gryth*) was to be double that for breach of the king's peace.[7] These Germanic terms, *fryth* and *gryth*, appear to share an etymological root as a term for 'wood'. The Saxons often declared certain woods to be sacred and, therefore, places of sanctuary.[8] Indeed, Tacitus in his *Germania* describes the Teutons' holding sacred various woods.[9] The recognition of woods as sacred, and thus as places of sanctuary, can also be found in Ancient Greece and Rome.[10] Throughout the Anglo-Saxon period, there were two kinds of peace to be kept: the peace of the king and the peace of the Church. The king's peace was *de jure*, but it was the Church's peace which was *de facto*. This is because fugitives relied mainly on church rather than king's peace.[11] Presumably, this was due to the Church's superior power and command of respect during this period.

In 680, King Ine of Wessex enacted a legal code that includes the following article:

> If anyone be guilty of death, and he flee to a church, let him have his life, and make *bot* (satisfaction or fine) as the law may direct him. If anyone put his hide in peril [i.e. commit a crime punishable by flogging], and flee to a church, be the scourging forgiven him.[12]

Jorge L. Carro would have Ine's sanctuary laws 'work[ing] in conjunction with a legal compensation system to protect the accused from the custom of bloodfeud'.[13] But this would be to project onto this period of English history a developed system of legal relations that it simply did not possess. Instead, the Christian reverence for the saints and holy relics played the key role in upholding spaces of sanctuary. The decisive influence upon the development of sanctuary in the north of England, for example, was the cult of St. Cuthbert. A seventh-century monk and Bishop of Lindisfarne, he reportedly stated on his deathbed that he wished his tomb to be a place of refuge for others. In the face of the Viking invasion of Lindisfarne, his remains were moved to various places on the mainland before being interred at Durham. In the late ninth century, it was claimed that a vision of the saint had appeared calling for the entire area lying between the rivers Tyne and Wear to be granted by the Northumbrian king as a sanctuary for all, including homicides, for a period of 37 days.[14] The strength of

---

7 de' Mazzinghi TJ, *Sanctuaries* (Halden & Son, 1887), 11; Cox (n 2), 6.
8 Mazzinghi (n 7), 7.
9 Tacitus, *Germania* (JB Rives tr, Clarendon Press, 1999), 80–81.
10 Timbal (n 1), 19; Dionysius of Halicarnassus, *The Roman Antiquities of Dionysius of Halicarnassus: Volume One* (Earnest Cary tr, Heinemann, 1937), 355.
11 Trenholme (n 4), 13.
12 Quoted in Cox (n 2), 7.
13 Carro JL, 'Sanctuary: The Resurgence of an Age-Old Right or a Dangerous Misinterpretation of an Abandoned Ancient Privilege?' (1986), 54, *University of Cincinnati Law Review*, 747, 754.
14 Cox (n 2), 96.

belief in the shrine of St. Cuthbert led to tales being told as late as the twelfth century of even wild beasts respecting the sanctuary precinct.[15] The records at Durham list the place of origin for most of the sanctuary-seekers. Large numbers arrived from places very far away, including London, Essex, Surrey and Somerset. Many of these will have fled there because of the generous scope of sanctuary afforded at Durham. But, in addition, a number of fugitives came from Yorkshire, close to the sanctuary of Beverley, whose privileges 'were greater than any other sanctuary in the kingdom'.[16] One can surmise that, in those cases, the only reason to go to Durham would be the enormous reverence for the cult of St. Cuthbert as a guarantor of asylum. The association with saints, particularly with relics connected to them, was often a cornerstone of places of sanctuary, in much the same way as the Greek *asylia*.[17]

A twelfth-century clerk, Garnier of Pont-Sainte-Maxence, referring to the circumstances of Thomas à Becket's murder, states that, on seeing his assailants approaching, Becket made his way to the vicinity of Canterbury's holy relics as that alone would save him from his would-be murderers.[18] At Winchester, the sanctuary was linked to tales of St. Swithun's protection of criminals, slaves and other fugitives. 'In the resulting confrontations between the harshness of legal punishment and Swithun's merciful intercession, Swithun is placed in opposition to the zealous promulgation and enforcement of law that characterised late Anglo-Saxon England'.[19] As late as the mid-fifteenth century, a monk at Westminster defended the offer of sanctuary to debtors because of the presence of holy relics within the sanctuary precinct, as this gave them the authority to defend and protect those in poverty who were 'unable to wield the tools of influence in a corrupt judicial system'.[20] Thus, sanctuary was predicated on being separate from, and perhaps actually antagonistic to, the law. Justice was grounded in a theological rather than a legal framework, for it was based on being able to rescue men's souls, which would be lost forever if the temporal law succeeded in executing criminals. Placing oneself in sanctuary would not have been seen, therefore, as escaping the consequences of one's actions, but was a way of facing up to them and repairing one's relationship with God. As John P. Sexton writes:

---

15 Ibid 103.

16 Ibid 118.

17 The great sanctuaries that arose in France around the same time were also associated with important saints, including St. Martin de Tours, St. Denis de Paris, St. Aignan d'Orléans, St. Médard de Soissons, St. Marcel de Châlons, St. Germain d'Auxerre, St. Hilaire de Poitiers, St. Martial de Limoges and St. Sernin de Toulouse. Timbal (n 1), 128.

18 Hayes DM, *Body and Sacred Space in Medieval Europe, 1100–1389* (Routledge, 2003), 21.

19 Sexton JP, 'Saint's Law: Anglo-Saxon Sanctuary Protection in the Translatio et Meracula S. Swithuni' (2006), 23, *Florilegium*, 61, 62.

20 McSheffrey S, 'Sanctuary and the Legal Topography of Pre-Reformation London' (2009), 27, *Law and History Review*, 483, 513.

'The privileges and protections of the church were commensurate with the respect due to God and his immediate subordinates, the saints'.[21]

Alfred the Great promulgated another set of laws in 887 which begin to give a more detailed picture of the practice of church sanctuary. Three articles of this code mention church *frith*, within which it is stated that those claiming asylum were allowed to remain in sanctuary for up to 7 days or, in special cases, up to 30 days. Again, special penalties for violation of church sanctuary are mentioned.[22] Alfred also explicitly cited the biblical sanctuary cities as a source for his laws.[23] These laws mark a significant development, for they were a secular intervention in the evolution of sanctuary. The king was not only granting sanctuary but also laying down some of the basic procedures for its operation.[24] The insistence on the inviolability of the church can be found in the laws of King Athelstan in 930, King Ethelred in 1014 and Ethelred's successor King Cnut. During the period of up to 30 days in which the suppliant was in sanctuary, the clergy would act as negotiators between the fugitive and his pursuers. This could result in *wergeld* redemption or debt slavery where the suppliant placed himself in service to his pursuer for a certain time.[25] Again, we see the crucial role in interceding that was adopted by the clergy, and which provided a practical role and thus respect for the institution of sanctuary. On the other hand, the intervention of the law involved placing restrictions on the practice by limiting the amount of time that could be spent in sanctuary, and formalising the procedures in such a way that eventually the suppliant would be forced to fulfil his legal responsibilities.

During an invasion by the Danes in the tenth century, during which Abingdon Abbey in Oxfordshire was destroyed, the sanctuary of Culham which was attached to the abbey was left untouched. It is reasonable to speculate, as Cox does, that this was out of respect for the sanctuary rights it possessed.[26] Certainly by the time of the Norman invasion, the principle and practice of seeking asylum in a church was well established. But we also have a recorded instance of a quite disturbing violation of sanctuary. On St. Brice's Day (13 November) 1002, a pogrom against the Danes in England was ordered by Ethelred. Some Danes took sanctuary in St. Frideswide monastery in Oxford. The response of the rioters was to burn the entire monastery down, killing all who had sought safety within it. According to Trenholme, however, this was a very rare example of the violation of sanctuary during the Anglo-Saxon period.[27]

21 Sexton (n 19), 62.
22 Cox (n 2), 7.
23 Shoemaker (n 1), 55.
24 Ryan WC, 'The Historical Case for Sanctuary' (1987), 29, *Journal of Church and State*, 209, 218.
25 Pope S, 'Sanctuary: The Legal Institution in England' (1987), 10, *University of Puget Sound Law Review*, 677, 682.
26 Cox (n 2), 206.
27 Trenholme (n 4), 16.

William the Conqueror's laws contained within the *Textus Roffensis* make no mention of sanctuary. But they do contain a chapter confirming the Anglo-Saxon laws, which presumably included the right of church sanctuary.[28] Moreover, William was responsible for the building of Battle Abbey and the conferring upon it of significant immunities. The Abbey was given absolute control over all land within a mile and a half of its centre. This entire space, spreading over three miles in diameter, was deemed a sanctuary where 'any person guilty of theft, manslaughter, or any other crime . . . [could] take refuge . . . receive no injury, but depart entirely free'.[29] But the immunities afforded were even more generous than this. The Abbot had the right to pardon anyone convicted of a capital offence that he should meet anywhere within the realm.[30] As such, the immunity was not restricted just to the large precinct of the Abbey itself. Moreover, the Abbey was allowed to hold its own court and to have full jurisdiction in the execution of justice within its precincts.

But Battle Abbey, as generous as its grant was, was not an exception. It was part of a class of sanctuaries that operated on different terms from that of regular church sanctuary. These were known as chartered sanctuaries. All consecrated churches automatically possessed the right of sanctuary that gave suppliants the right to remain there for a certain number of days, on performance of certain formalities and for certain crimes. Certainly no legal proof was required for these sanctuaries because of their general character.[31] But in addition, the king could, and did, confer on certain places a wider set of immunities beyond that of the churches. Most of the time, these places were themselves consecrated spaces, but occasionally they were not. Some of these chartered sanctuaries existed before the Norman invasion, including those at Beverley, Durham and Westminster[32]; the one at St. Martin le Grand, located 'in the very bowels' of the city of London,[33] had proof of charter from William the Conqueror, although it is likely that it possessed this status even earlier.[34] The sanctuary at Beverley extended for a circumference of a mile and a half, with no less than six boundaries located at various distances within it, from the outer boundary at its edge through to the

---

28 Cox (n 2), 9.
29 Ibid 196–197.
30 There is at least one recorded instance of this privilege being exercised. '[In] 1364 the abbot of Battle (Robert de Bello) going towards London, met a felon condemned to the gallows in the king's marshalsea, and in virtue of his prerogative, liberated him from death. And although the king and other magistrates took much offence at the act, yet, upon plea, he had his charter confirmed'. *Lower's Battle Abbey Chronicle*, 204, quoted in Cox (n 2), 197.
31 Baker JH, 'The English Law of Sanctuary' (1990), 2, *Ecclesiastical Law Journal*, 8, 9.
32 Cox (n 2), 6, 50, 126. The others were Abingdon, Armethwaite, Battle Abbey, Beaulieu, Colchester, Derby, Dover, Hexham, Lancaster, St. Mary Le Bow, St. Martin le Grand, Merton Priory, Northampton, Norwich, Ripon, Ramsey, Wells, Winchester and York. Shoemaker (n 1), 216, footnote 68.
33 Duke of Buckingham, quoted in Cox (n 2), 66.
34 Ibid 80.

sixth which encompassed the high altar of the church itself. A similar system of boundaries existed for the chartered sanctuary at Hexham. The penalties for violating the sanctuary increased with each boundary crossed. So, a fine of £8 (an enormous sum for the tenth century) was levied for violating the outer boundary, while forcibly removing a suppliant from within the fifth boundary incurred a penalty of £144; violating sanctuary within the sixth and holiest boundary was deemed to be an offence for which no monetary payment was sufficient (*botalaus*), the penalty for which was instead death.[35] The reasons given for this last and drastic penalty were three-fold: contempt for the Reserved Sacrament, for the Lord's Table, and, most of all, for the sacred remains of St. John of Beverley contained within. Just as with St. Cuthbert in Durham, the presence of saintly relics was of crucial importance to the sacredness of sanctuary. These chartered sanctuaries were therefore examples of spaces in which the church's peace and the king's peace overlapped. It is possible to speculate that perhaps the granting of these immunities by the king was an attempt to associate himself with the greater purchase afforded by those claimed by the church. In any case, the spaces claimed by the chartered sanctuaries in some cases extended over huge areas. A letter addressed to Thomas Cromwell in 1534 refers to 'two great sanctuaries in Yorkshire . . . [that] have a least one hundred miles compass'.[36]

In an echo of the ancient right of sanctuary at the foot of statues of deities or emperors in Ancient Greece and Rome, King Athelstan's grant of sanctuary status at Beverley (early tenth century) decreed that anyone merely touching one of the boundary crosses of the precinct was immune from the law; the penalty for violating this was excommunication.[37] Dawn Marie Hayes describes the magical aspect of the theology that underpinned this kind of reverence: 'In the Middle Ages any person, place or object that came into contact with a source of sacredness had the opportunity to appropriate its energy'.[38] In some cases, just reaching the door of the church and grasping the knocker was sufficient to place one in sanctuary.[39] The right of sanctuary merely through touching a cross that had been erected by the church along the roads was recognised by the Council of Clermont in 1095.[40] Medieval sanctuary even extended, in parts of Europe, to plows and plowmen. This was due to the absolute importance of food production, and to the relative vulnerability of plowmen who often worked isolated in the fields some distance from their home.[41] This practice is recorded as lasting from at least the late eleventh century to the late fourteenth century,

---

35 Ibid 126–127.
36 Trenholme (n 4), 59.
37 Cox (n 2), 143.
38 Hayes (n 18), 5.
39 Baker (n 31), 9.
40 Timbal (n 1), 202.
41 Morey JH, 'Plows, Laws, and Sanctuary in Medieval England and in the Wakefield "Mactacio Abel"' (1998), 95, *Studies in Philology*, 41, 44–45.

and shows the extent to which immunities existed that fell even outside the religious sphere.

Whereas ordinary church sanctuary came within the church's peace, the chartered sanctuary came under the protection of the king's peace. Yet, once these charters had been granted the extent of their independence from the king was such that, as late as 1474, Edward IV was forced to *request* the archdeacon of Westminster to deal with certain 'abominable vices' that had been committed within its precincts. The king was evidently not able to impose order directly in this corner of his kingdom. From around the beginning of the fifteenth century, complaints began to be made officially to the crown that the chartered sanctuaries, particularly that of St. Martin le Grand, had become effectively 'nests of corruption', where criminals were allowed to live with impunity not only from the crime for which they had sought sanctuary but also from ongoing acts committed while they were there. One complaint made in 1403 alleged that stolen goods were being brought to St. Martin le Grand from all over London to be fenced.[42] And yet, although the king would listen to these complaints, no action was taken. However, some of the chartered sanctuaries such as Beaulieu, St. John of Colchester and at Abingdon were ordered to provide proof of their franchise, which apparently they were able to do.[43] Here we see an attempt to repeat the strategy of Tiberius: asking for the impossible-to-produce evidence of the original grants of *asylia*. But this time their immunities proved too strong for the secular authority to countenance any violation. In short, chartered sanctuaries were spaces where the king's writ did not run. The question this begs is why the king would grant such immunities in the first place. The simple and most common answer is that the secular authorities were just too weak in the face of competing sources of power. But the reality was somewhat more complicated.

Configuring church space

In her study of sacred spaces during the Middle Ages, Hayes argues that such spaces were configured through a specifically Christian understanding of the link between sacred space and the reverence for the Christian body.[44] Emile Durkheim's description of a world scrupulously delineated between the sacred and the profane does not fit either the worldview or the practice of medieval European peoples. For them, 'the physical world was at one and the same time sacred and profane – sacred as God's creation, profane as a place of human exile'.[45] This dialectical unity was further reinforced with the figure of Christ as

---

42 3 Parliamentary Roll, 503b. 4 Henry 4, cited in Mazzinghi (n 7), 45; Cox (n 2), 80–81.
43 Ryan (n 24), 223.
44 Hayes (n 18).
45 Ibid xxi.

both human and divine. Therefore, the modern attempt to exclude the every-day and the profane from sacred spaces is one that does not fit the medieval period.[46]

On the other hand, the importance of church buildings was that they provided safe spaces in a world in which the forces of good and evil were both present and in constant war with one another.[47] Medieval sanctuary was mostly attached to consecrated space, which could include not only the church itself but also cemeteries, monasteries and sometimes the residences of clergy. Consecration of space meant the effective divorcing of it from the world around it. As the thirteenth-century canonist Guillaume Durandus puts it, consecration 'appropriates the material church to God . . . in consecration it is endowed and becomes the proper spouse of Christ, which it is a sacrilege to violate adulterously for it ceases to be a place of demons . . .'[48]; or, as the ninth-century Archbishop Hincmar of Reims wrote: 'Christ is the head . . . of the Church, which is the body of Christ'.[49] One can see why violation of church sanctuary would have been held to be as sacrilegious as it was. The right of church sanctuary was thus nothing more than the 'legal acknowledgement of the specialness of sacred places'.[50]

Yet at the same time, the unity of space, which recognised that in a world in which both God and Satan were ever-present there could never be a strict division between the sacred and the profane, allowed churches – the dominant presence in almost every town and city – to perform a multiplicity of functions: lodging for pilgrims, trading of goods, social exchange and of course sanctuary, as well as the liturgy. The later effort to cleave the Church from the rest of society also affected how the nature of church space was perceived. As Hayes shows in the case of Chartres Cathedral and elsewhere, from about the mid-fourteenth century, there was a growing tendency within the Church to 'delaicize' consecrated space.[51] In doing so, the Church laid the basis for the expulsion of all practices that involved the presence of non-clergy for any purpose other than receiving religious instruction or blessing. This led more generally to the strict separation between the sacred and the mundane that has become a hallmark of modernity.[52] The church building thus became more alienated as a public space, less open to all as a protection from the violence and uncertainty that lay outside. From a different angle, the Protestant Reformation speeded up this process by devaluing the church and the clergy as *the* mediators with God, which in turn

---

46 Ibid xxi.
47 Ibid 5.
48 Quoted in Ibid 12.
49 Lauwers M, 'Le cimetière dans le Moyen Age latin: Lieu sacré, saint et religieux' (1999), 54, *Annales*, 1047, 1050.
50 Hayes (n 18), 19.
51 Ibid 69.
52 Agamben G, 'In praise of profanation' in *Profanations* (Jeff Fort tr, Zone Books, 2007).

also led to a decline in respect for church space.[53] This then became a factor undermining the ideological underpinnings of sanctuary.

Immunities

Barbara H. Rosenwein places medieval asylum within the framework of the more general context of immunities.[54] These were widespread during the period, and could apply to private lands and buildings as well as churches. Usually they allowed exemptions from taxes and/or incursions by the king's agents. In this respect, immunities resemble the *asylia* of Ancient Greece. For most historians, immunities demonstrated the weakness of medieval kings and states. But Rosenwein argues that the granting of immunities was fundamentally about defining spaces within the realm, and of '[accommodating] political power to a new sensibility about religious space'.[55] Because grants were solely within the king's gift, their very existence was in fact testimony to his power. This power demonstrated three things: 'first, it is a declaration of self-control; second, it is an affirmation of royal control over public agents and their jurisdiction; third, it is an announcement of control over the configuration of space'. [56]

Sanctuary, like other immunities, might also have been 'a practical tool . . . used to help keep the peace'.[57] This is evidenced by the development of some of the chartered sanctuaries in which the king sought to associate his *de jure* peace with that of the church's more concrete *de facto* immunity. This would have been especially important for the post-Conquest kings as they sought to establish, with some difficulty, their legitimacy as sovereign rulers over the land. In reference to this period, Trenholme notes: 'It was to harmonize [the] right of churches to afford personal protection with the right of the state to punish offenders that certain definite rules of procedure came in to being'.[58] This would lead to a greater paraphernalia of oaths, regulations and restrictions on the use of sanctuary, which will be discussed further below.

In the early medieval period, kings might also have extended immunities so as to offer more effective protection against raids by creating buffer zones. Such was the case with Charlemagne's grandson, Louis the German, who issued a *sub regia immunitatis* in 847 for the protection of churches within his realm.[59] But space, or spacialisation, was also closely linked to the maintenance of social stability. The sacred space of the church was, in the Middle Ages, a pole of

---

53 Hayes (n 18), 99–100.
54 Rosenwein BH, *Negotiating Space: Power, Restraint, and the Privileges of Immunity in Early Medieval Europe* (Manchester University 1999). See also Helmholz RH, *The Ius Commune in England: Four Studies* (OUP, 2001).
55 Rosenwein (n 54), 212.
56 Ibid 7.
57 Pope (n 25), 681.
58 Trenholme (n 4), 22.
59 Timbal (n 1), 151.

security for small and isolated communities. Without respect for sacred space, church protection would have been meaningless.[60] One immunity, of a completely secular nature, which stands out is that of Chester. The Earls of Chester claimed an immunity, dating back possibly to the reign of Edward II or earlier, which covered the entire county. Because of this they were able to offer sanctuary to fugitives, and allowed them to live anywhere within the county indefinitely. This sanctuary was open to all including, remarkably, Jews and heretics, who according to canon law were excluded from sanctuary.[61] There was self-interest involved here, for the Earls charged a fee for anyone seeking sanctuary and, where the sanctuary-seekers died intestate, all their goods were bequeathed to the Earl. This immunity was abolished during the reign of Henry IV, with all existing sanctuary men and women in Chester forced to leave the country in a process known as abjuring the realm, a practice that is described below.[62]

Nonetheless, the example of Chester allows us a window on a world in which sovereignty had a far more dispersed character than we are used to in the modern world. The fact is that not only churches or even whole towns but, indeed, whole swathes of the country could both be part of the king's realm, yet beyond the writ of his law. The immunity enjoyed by the county of Chester was shared by other earldoms such as those of Hoole Heath, Overmarsh and Rudheath, as well as Tynedale, Redesdale, the marcher lordships of Wales and the so-called 'palatine counties' such as Durham and Lancashire. According to John Bellamy: 'To live [in these places] was as effective as fleeing to a foreign land'.[63] In continental Europe, sanctuary towns were also widespread.[64] From at least the middle of the eleventh century, sanctuary villages were set up in south-western France. In each case, a ceremony presided over by local clergy, bishops and abbots involved the placing of crosses in the ground, signifying the boundaries of the sanctuary.[65] These villages were often set up in the middle of forests, and were open to all seeking refuge. There is perhaps a link here to the association of woods and sacredness that Tacitus describes among the Teutons.[66] Possibly, following the example of Romulus, they were created as forms of defence through rapid population increases, particularly in border areas such as the Pyrenees.[67] There were similar sanctuary villages in Normandy and Catalonia.[68] But with the

60 Lauwers (n 49), 1049.
61 Mazzinghi (n 7), 77. Bellamy J, *Crime and Public Order in England in the Later Middle Ages* (Routledge and Kegan Paul, and University of Toronto, 1973), 106.
62 Trenholme (n 4), 85–86; Mazzinghi (n 7), 16–17.
63 Bellamy (n 61), 106.
64 Reyerson KL, 'Flight from Prosecution: The Search for Religious Asylum in Medieval Montpellier' (1992), 17, *French Historical Studies*, 603, 604.
65 Ourliac P, 'Les villages de la région toulousaine: au XIIe siécle' (1949), 4, *Annales*, 268, 269.
66 Tacitus (n 9), 80–81.
67 Ourliac (n 65), 270.
68 Ibid 271.

encroachment of feudal relations and feudal power, these sanctuaries were all but extinguished a century later.[69] However, elsewhere the right of asylum and general immunities enjoyed by the churches led, from around the seventh century, to the founding and growth of villages in the areas next to them.[70] In addition, we have one example, although it seems likely that there would have been others, where the right of sanctuary was claimed on the basis of a claim to municipal freedom. Trenholme describes this claim made by the town of Bury St. Edmonds as late as 1327: 'the right of sanctuary was much prized by the burgesses as being a right and privilege belonging to the people and not merely to the Church and under ecclesiastical control'.[71] In short, the polities of medieval Europe were a collage of separate and overlapping, complementary and conflicting sovereignties, within which sanctuary was able to flourish.

Another type of immunity, which existed for a short time and could have received fugitives and offered them safety, was within the residences and offices of ambassadors. This privilege was abolished in Rome by the Pope in 1682. Where the supreme ecclesiastical authority led, secular sovereigns followed. One after another other European states followed suit to the point that, by the mid-eighteenth century, embassies as sanctuaries were effectively abolished[72] – although this tradition has, in recent times, been resurrected in a number of famous cases.[73]

Archbishop Pecham, in a letter written in November 1289, justified the church's immunities as follows:

> To the crown belongs not only severity and rigor of justice, but still more mercy and pity. By which Holy Church, by the king's will, saves evildoers by sanctuary, by orders, and by the religious habit, as appears in the north country, where murderers, after their crime, betake themselves as converts to the great abbeys of the Cistercians and are safe.[74]

The Cistercian monasteries prided themselves upon welcoming all converts, regardless of their crime. The fugitive, in return, pledged 'to lifelong labour for the good of the convent'.[75] The real point, as Pecham states, is two-fold. First, it reinforces Rosenwein's point that the granting of immunities was as much about asserting the monarch's power as it was about ceding jurisdiction to a powerful Church. Second, the value of sanctuary as a means of winning converts

---

69 Ibid 277.
70 Timbal (n 1), 170.
71 Trenholme (n 4), 87.
72 Mazzinghi (n 7), 92–93.
73 Crawford C, 'Embassy Confrontations and Diplomatic Asylum' (2009), 18 December, Diplomat www.diplomatmagazine.com/index.php?option=com_content&view=article &id=161&Itemi, accessed 24 January 2015.
74 Quoted in Cox (n 2), 191.
75 Ibid.

to the Church, and of enforcing penitence upon sinners, and thus ensuring the Christian order, outweighed any scruples about the deleterious effect it may have upon the temporal law.

Immunities effectively created 'a patchwork quilt of legal jurisdictions' even within the heart of the capital city.[76] The fifteenth-century dean of St. Martin Le Grand, Richard Caudray, described his sanctuary as 'in and yet not of the city'.[77] The borders for these immunities were sometime vague. As Shannon McSheffrey shows in the case of St. Martin's, the dividing lines, instead of being marked by sturdy walls, could be identified simply by certain customs as to where the sanctuary men habitually walked or drank,[78] and the boundary was easily crossed in either direction, with many citizens coming and going to either buy goods from the sanctuary men or to sell various supplies to them.[79] The fact that a pub, which was outside the sanctuary precinct, had a back room that lay over the boundary and was therefore frequented by sanctuary men, and that even a house was split so that one half was within the precinct and the other outside it, is testimony to the often haphazard and malleable nature of the boundaries of sanctuary, and of immunities in general. But it also points to the fact that spaces of sanctuary were often as much defined by custom and practice as by law.

Procedure

It is clear from many sources that people could, and did, spend years living in the chartered sanctuaries. A record from 1532, very shortly before the suppression of these sanctuaries, shows that fifty sanctuary men and women were residing within Westminster for 'life', with one of them having lived there already for 20 years. These included fugitives responsible for murder, robbery, debt and sacrilege.[80] The details varied between the different chartered sanctuaries; at Beverley, sanctuary was granted for 30 days, during which the canons of the church endeavoured to secure a pardon for the fugitive or other similar settlement with his pursuers. After this time, the suppliant was escorted to the boundary and handed over to the coroner. Any individual was allowed to seek sanctuary at Beverley up to three times. On the third occasion, he had to submit to a lifetime of service to the church, always remaining within the parish. However, a twelfth-century chronicler alludes to the fact that anyone guilty of a serious offence involving loss of life or limb was granted the right to lifetime sanctuary at the first claim. R.H. Helmholz writes: 'This fit the assumption of the canon law, since the purpose of its law of immunity was limited to saving the sanctuary seeker's life and limb'.[81] Thus, a lifetime term of sanctuary was possible there. Of these lifetime sanctuary men at

---

76 McSheffrey (n 20), 484.
77 Quoted in Ibid 487.
78 Ibid 488.
79 Ibid 494.
80 Cox (n 2), 72.
81 Helmholz (n 54), 58.

Beverley, records dating from the period 1478–1539 show there to be an average of eight new entrants each year. This does not include the many others who would have sought sanctuary for limited periods. At Beverley, there was even an absolute prohibition on coroners, sheriffs or any other secular official entering the church precincts in matters pertaining to sanctuary.[82]

At Durham Cathedral, there were always at least two people in place by the north door of the church waiting to receive fugitives seeking sanctuary at any time of the day or night. The sanctuary-seeker was to rap using the large door knockers, and he would be immediately received and would then take the oath of sanctuary. He would be given a black tunic adorned with a yellow cross so that 'every one might se that there was a prelige graunted by God and Sancte Cuthbert'[83]: again, evidence of the spiritual basis of sanctuary. Once a fugitive had been admitted to an ordinary church sanctuary, the four neighbouring parishes were duty bound to provide watchers to keep guard on the church. This was to ensure that the suppliant did not escape, and once the 40 days were passed, to ensure that no food or water could be passed to him. As Cox notes, this no doubt placed a certain burden on local communities whenever someone sought sanctuary within their local church.[84] Of course, a question naturally arises: what happened to fugitives once the allotted sanctuary time was up? If they had simply been handed over to their pursuers, this would have come into conflict with some of the basic principles of sanctuary such as preventing blood-letting or the application of harsh laws. The remedy available to suppliants in such circumstances was known as *abjuratio regni* (abjuration of the realm). Essentially, this involved the individual agreeing to leave the kingdom altogether, and to never return. Were they to come back, they would not have the protection of the law, but could be killed with impunity. In short, once they abjured the realm, they were civilly dead.[85]

Popular support for sanctuary

Referring to the great chartered sanctuary at Durham, Cox writes: 'So great was the general reverence for sanctuary, that in the enormous majority of cases the fugitive was absolutely safe as soon as he passed the churchyard gates'.[86] In response to demands from the sheriffs for restricting the rights of the chartered sanctuaries, Henry VI stated that the populace were likely to be highly supportive of the sanctuaries given the numbers who had sought protection there for debts and other crimes.[87] At Durham, surviving records show that a minimum of six

---

82 Cox (n 2), 134–136.
83 Rites of Durham (1593), quoted in Cox (n 2), 119.
84 Cox (n 2), 238.
85 For a detailed discussion of the practice of abjuring the realm, see Réville A, 'L'"Abjuratio Regni"' (1892), 50, *Revue Historique*, 1.
86 Cox (n 2), 125.
87 Ibid 85.

people sought sanctuary there every year, mostly homicides, although the actual figure is likely to have been much higher.[88] Beverley, with its reputation as the premier sanctuary in England, received over just one 60-year period fugitives from every county in the country – from Devon to Northumberland – with the exception of just four.[89] In Staffordshire, one of the least populous counties in England, twenty people sought sanctuary in a single year (1271). As Mazzinghi notes, if one were to extrapolate from that number throughout the entire country (and bearing in mind the total size of the population, between 4 million and 6 million),[90] a significant number of people took sanctuary each year.[91] Indeed, the total number of people seeking sanctuary in either churches or chartered sanctuaries is estimated to have averaged around 1,000 per year.[92]

Most of those who sought sanctuary came from the poorer sections of society.[93] This would accord with Macrides' point in relation to Byzantium: in general, the rich and powerful would have nothing to fear from the law or from private vengeance.[94] Surviving records from the sanctuary at Durham note only a small proportion of the suppliants' occupations. Of those that are recorded, most (about 60%) are labourers, peasants and artisans. Over a period of 60 years, just one knight and four 'gentlemen' are listed as having sought sanctuary.[95] Moreover, when one considers that the overwhelming number of sanctuary-seekers who did not have their occupations recorded would have come from the lower orders of society, then these numbers are put into even starker relief. A similar record covering almost exactly the same period at Beverley gives similar proportions: some sixty-nine labourers and poor peasants as compared with thirty-six 'gentlemen' and yeomen.[96] There is only a handful of recorded cases of women taking sanctuary. This may have been largely due to the greater difficulty they faced in getting away from the supervision of their fathers and husbands; their overall lack of independence is also likely to have been a contributing factor. However, a fascinating example of how sanctuary could work to a woman's advantage is evidenced by a case in 1225, in which an un-named woman made a false claim to having committed a felony just so that she could legitimately leave her husband by seeking sanctuary and then abjuring the realm. In other words, sanctuary could lay the basis, in Trenholme's words, for a 'mediaeval method of divorce'.[97]

---

88 Ibid 107.
89 Ibid 142.
90 Jefferies J, *The U.K. Population: Past, Present and Future* (Office of National Statistics, 2005), 2.
91 Mazzinghi (n 7), 41.
92 Pope (n 25), 677, footnote 2.
93 Trenholme (n 4), 66–67.
94 Macrides RJ, 'Killing, Asylum, and the Law in Byzantium' (1988), 63, *Speculum*, 509.
95 Cox (n 2), 108–109.
96 Ibid 137.
97 Trenholme (n 4), 69.

One indication of popular reverence for sanctuary involves the scandal of William de Lay from 1279. Having sought sanctuary at the Church of St. Philip and St. James in Bristol, he was forcibly dragged out by the constables and summarily beheaded. Part of the constables' defence was that de Lay had been a known petty criminal, often in prison. Yet, even so, the punishment meted out to the violators of sanctuary involved public scourging and being forced to join the crusades. But what is most striking about this incident is that, following de Lay's reburial within the consecrated ground of the church in which he had taken sanctuary, many local people began to treat his grave as they would that of a saint, regarding him as a martyr.[98] In the large chartered sanctuaries, so integrated within the economic and social fabric of the town were the sanctuary men and women, that even after the dissolution of the monastery of Beaulieu, local citizens petitioned Thomas Cromwell for the abbey's immunities to be extended. Peter Iver Kaufman writes: 'Integration with guiltless neighbours seems to have been the rule and isolation the exception'.[99] Where sanctuary-seekers were part of the community, they tended not to be seen as outsiders, nor as dangerous to others.

A major exception to the general respect and reverence for sanctuary is found in the attitude of Londoners to the great chartered sanctuary of St. Martin le Grand. From the beginning of the fourteenth century, regular complaints were made to the authorities, both ecclesiastical and secular, about the 'satellites of Satan', as the sanctuary men were known in the city.[100] The complaints seemed largely based on the apparent impunity enjoyed by criminals carrying out their trade and living their lives with their families within the large precincts of St. Martin le Grand. There were also reports that they would, on occasion, leave the sanctuary to commit further crimes, only to return and remain safe within the walls of the sanctuary. McSheffrey has identified most of those living in sanctuary at St. Martin le Grand as probably being foreign artisans.[101] And she suggests that many of them may have been there, not because they were criminal fugitives but because, excluded from the guilds, it was a way for them to engage in trade legitimately.[102] One wonders if the persistent hatred and venom directed at the sanctuary men there was largely due to xenophobia, given that there appears to be little evidence of similar levels of resentment about other sanctuaries, including St. Martin le Grand's London twin sanctuary at Westminster. Anti-foreigner prejudice is also evidenced by the fact that the alien traders in St. Martin le Grand were often the victims of raids by the city sheriffs for breaking the law against foreigners engaging in trade.[103] The infamous xenophobic violence of the

98　Cox (n 2), 246.
99　Kaufman PI, 'Henry VII and Sanctuary' (1984), 53, *Church History*, 465, 467.
100　Thornley I, 'Sanctuary in Medieval London' (1932), 38, *Journal of the British Archaeological Association*, 293, 298.
101　McSheffrey (n 20), 484.
102　Ibid 494.
103　Ibid 489.

Evil May Day riot of 1517 was focussed on those living within St. Martin le Grand.[104] Indeed, it was precisely the arrival of large numbers of Protestant refugees following the Reformation, who took up residence within the liberties and monasteries, that led Henry VIII to consider the first legislation to restrict and control activities within the precincts.[105]

Violations of sanctuary

In spite of the strength of church sanctuary as an institution throughout the mediaeval period, there were often violations. I have already mentioned one example that took place at St. Frideswide's in Oxford, but perhaps the most famous one is that of St. Thomas à Becket's murder in his own cathedral at Canterbury as he made his way to vespers. Although, of course, this was not a case of asylum, it was a blatant example of violation of church *fryth* by the sovereign. It was also suggested by the chronicler Henry Knighton that one of the causes of conflict between the archbishop and the king was Becket's resistance to Henry II's attempts to restrict the right of church sanctuary.[106] The widespread outrage at the 'threefold violation of sacred person, place, and time' led to both Becket's swift canonisation and King Henry II's public act of penance for his murder.[107] Becket's murder, so Isobel Thornley claims, hobbled Henry II's desire to end the practice of the liberties of the chartered sanctuaries, due to the public backlash it caused.[108] As Cox puts it, this is but one example where 'the whole course of events was completely changed, and dynasties shaken by violations of sanctuary'.[109]

Another archbishop, this time of York, was hunted down and removed from sanctuary by agents of Richard I (The Lionhearted) for his disobedience. This was in spite of the fact that this archbishop, Geoffrey, was the brother of the king. The Bishop of Ely, who was the king's chancellor and the chief violator of Geoffrey's sanctuary, was promptly forced to go into exile himself due to the outrage that followed.[110] During the twilight years of the twelfth century, an insurgent movement, led by William Fitz Osbert, known as 'Longbeard', rose up against a proposed poll-tax. Some 52,000 of London's poor were mobilised, threatening the men of property. Fitz Osbert was hunted down, and managed to take refuge in the church of St. Mary le Bow; the then Archbishop of Canterbury, Hubert Walter, who was also the Chief Justiciar of England, came down squarely on the side of the aldermen, demanding that he leave. Fitz Osbert refused, but the archbishop ordered his own church to be burned down for the purpose of 'smoking out' the

---

104   Ibid 491, 504.
105   Kershaw R and Pearsall M, *Immigrants and Aliens: A Guide to Sources on UK Immigration and Citizenship* (2nd edn, The National Archives, 2004), 89.
106   Cox (n 2), 35.
107   Hayes (n 18), 21.
108   Thornley ID, 'The destruction of sanctuary' in RW Seton-Watson (ed), *Tudor Studies* (Longmans, 1924), 184.
109   Cox (n 2), 34.
110   Ibid 38.

fugitive. It appears that, in defence of the established order, the senior clergy were even prepared to violate church sanctuary. As Mazzinghi argues, the 'gravity of the crisis' was such as to provoke the clergy to this extreme position – although the accusation that Fitz Osbert was a heretic might have also loaded the scales against him.[111] Fitz Osbert was captured and executed, but just 2 years later, Walter was forced to resign as justiciar, partly due to complaints made to the Pope about his blatant violation of sanctuary in that case.[112] However, over the next century, there were many instances where the king was forced to restore fugitives to sanctuaries from which they had been forcibly seized, sometimes by the king's own agents. On at least one occasion, in 1334, the Mayor of London and his officials were forced to pay penance for their removal of fugitives from sanctuary.[113]

One notable incident, in 1378, involved an escaped prisoner from the Tower of London who sought refuge in the chartered sanctuary at Westminster. The guards from the Tower pursued and then cut him down within the precincts of the sanctuary. Such was the outrage at such a violation that all religious rites at Westminster Abbey were cancelled for 4 months and 'sittings of Parliament were suspended lest they should be contaminated by assembling near the scene of the outrage'.[114] Ten years later, a clerk charged with treason took sanctuary in Westminster and, despite repeated demands from both Houses of Parliament, he was not given up to the secular authorities.[115] The absolute right of all, regardless of who they were or what their alleged crime, to take sanctuary at Westminster and the other chartered sanctuaries was reaffirmed in that same year (1388) by Richard II.[116] However, the fact that just 5 years later the chartered sanctuary at Culham had to present documentary proof to Parliament that it enjoyed the same rights as Westminster suggests that the extent of their privileges were constantly being challenged throughout this period. As late as the Wars of the Roses partisans of both sides at various times took sanctuary, and by and large this was respected by their enemies in victory.[117] Indeed, it was their continued presence

---

111   Mazzinghi (n 7), 77.
112   Cox (n 2), 40; Mazzinghi (n 7), 76–77.
113   Thornley (n 100), 297.
114   Cox (n 2), 52.
115   Ibid 54.
116   Ibid 56.
117   Many Lancastrians had taken sanctuary at Beaulieu. Mazzinghi (n 7), 51. These were what today we would call 'political refugees'. The boy-king Edward V was actually born in Westminster sanctuary where his mother had taken refuge after the fall of the House of York in 1470. Another sanctuary-seeker, John Morton, ended up as Henry VII's Archbishop of Canterbury. McSheffrey (n 20), 498. Henry Tudor, who would begin in earnest the first attacks on sanctuary as King Henry VII, took refuge in St. Malo in 1479. Timbal (n 1), 177. The two major sanctuaries in London – Westminster and St. Martin le Grand – were 'full of the adherents of Edward IV'. Thornley (n 100), 314. Some years later, Richard III had roads to Westminster as well as access to it from the Thames blocked so as to prevent supporters of Edward V from seeking sanctuary there, and thus easing his own path to the crown. See Cox (n 2), 59–60. Yet it is telling that here again the pursuers see themselves barred from violating the sanctuary, even in such volatile and chaotic times.

in sanctuaries, especially within the capital, which allowed each faction to regroup and effectively counter-attack. As Thornley notes, Wycliffe's warnings of a century earlier that the privileges of sanctuary, granted by the monarch, could be used to undermine his realm were coming true.[118] What all this suggests is that, whatever the reasons behind the original grant of chartered status, their continued existence signified a real weakness in the sovereign order.

One point on which violation of sanctuary was most definitely not an issue was in cases where the alleged crime was committed within the sanctuary precinct itself. For example, in a case dating from 1321, a woman killed the clerk of the church of All Saints by London Wall within the church precinct and then claimed sanctuary within the same. The Bishop of London declared this use of sanctuary invalid; she was removed and later hung without, it appears, much controversy.[119]

It was at the height of the civil wars of the late fifteenth century that Richard III's key advisor, the Duke of Buckingham, condemned the sanctuaries, but in doing so expressed accurately a crucial aspect of their existence:

> A Sanctuary serueth always to defend the body of that man that sandeth in danger abroad, not of great hurt onely, but also of lawfull hurt; for against unlawfull harmes neuer Pope nor King intended to Priuiledge any one place, for that Priuiledge hath euery place: knoweth any man any place, wherein it is lawfull for one man to doe another wrong? . . . *but where a man is by lawfull meaner in peril, there needeth he the tuition of some speciall priuiledge*, which is the onely ground & cause of all Sanctuaries.[120]

Buckingham hits the mark in identifying sanctuary as being about protection *from* the law, not a function of the law itself. But the modern claim of law, that it is synonymous with justice, finds its germ in Buckingham's speech. It is telling, therefore, that it dates from the eve of the Tudor period, one where the claim of sovereign power reinforced by a unified and decisive force of law would usher in law's modern imperium, and with it, the end of a 1000-year tradition of sanctuary.

It is common to date the end of sanctuary from around the sixteenth century, with the establishment of the supremacy of the secular sovereign under the Tudors. This is not wholly wrong, but it does ignore the long gestation of law that preceded these seminal events, and its role in undermining sanctuary and laying the basis for its destruction. Law did not, Athena-like, suddenly appear at a moment of genesis for modernity, whether that be the Papal Revolution, the Tudor period or the French Revolution. Instead, there was a long process from

---

118 Thornley (n 100), 315. However, on one occasion, Edward IV had twenty of his Lancastrian enemies dragged out of sanctuary and summarily beheaded. Mazzinghi (n 7), 82–83.
119 Cox (n 2), 230.
120 Quoted in Ibid 66–67 (emphasis added).

germination to complete hegemony. Indeed, as I will show in Part II, in relation to the refugee, this process was not complete until the 1951 Convention, and perhaps even later with its incorporation into various domestic legal regimes over recent decades. In addition, although there had long been hostility towards sanctuary from the crown, eliminating it was not merely a case of will. The late twelfth century witnessed a series of attacks upon sanctuary, some of which we have already mentioned: Henry II's attempt to restrict church sanctuary to 40 days in 1164; the murder in 1170 of Becket in Canterbury Cathedral; in 1191, the seizure of the Archbishop of York from sanctuary in Dover by agents of Richard I; and in 1196, the smoking-out of Fitz Osbert from St. Mary le Bow. And yet, sanctuary was to continue for several centuries more, with kings frequently forced to respect the practice. Thornley, a leading historian of medieval sanctuary, states that as late as the fifteenth century, the strength of sanctuary was such that efforts to restrict it were in vain.[121] In the West, law re-emerged from the late eleventh century onwards, but the time for its hegemony was not yet ripe. Its gestation period lasted centuries, and the rest of this chapter tells that story as it related to sanctuary. As we will see, it is precisely at that historical moment in England when the various elements of modernity begin to fall into place – i.e., with the Tudor period – that the death-knell for sanctuary is finally sounded.

The rise of canon law

One of the pre-eminent historians of the Western legal tradition, Harold J. Berman, has located the rebirth of law in the West during the late eleventh century and early twelfth century, a period known as the Papal Revolution.[122] This was a time in which the Papacy sought to establish a firm authority over the Church throughout Europe: a break from the much greater autonomy enjoyed by monasteries and clerics hitherto. It was during this time that the term 'canon law' (*jus canonicum*) was coined. In the early mediaeval period, church and secular authority were so intertwined and inseparable that one cannot speak of a separate thing as law, nor of legal professionals, nor courts, etc., until around the late eleventh century.[123] So, for example, King Ine's council, which promulgated some of the founding laws of sanctuary in England, had a majority composed of bishops. As Stephen Pope writes: '[the] ends of both ecclesiastical and secular governments were indistinct . . . the care of men's souls was clearly a governmental as well as an ecclesiastical concern'.[124] The legal paradigm, insofar as its presence was felt, had no life separate from faith, and indeed appears in respect of sanctuary to have been subordinate to theological considerations.

---

121 Thornley (100), 315.
122 Berman HJ, *Law and Revolution: The Formation of the Western Legal Tradition* (Harvard University, 1983).
123 Ibid 76; Ryan (n 24), 215.
124 Pope (n 25), 681.

The Papal Revolution represented an attempt by the Pope to establish complete hegemony over the various elements of the Church spread out across Europe. Part of this strategy was that the Papacy sought to create a clearer division between itself and the secular powers; by disentangling the clergy from their ties with kings and emperors, the Pope could bring them under more direct control from Rome. The development of civil and canon law became a means by which the relationship between these two increasingly autonomous sectors could be regulated. Gratian's *Concordance of Discordant Canons*, which Berman refers to as the first comprehensive legal treatise, appeared in the mid-twelfth century, and around the same time, we see the publication of a set of legal rules for magistrates in Provence.[125] Gratian's work would end up as the first volume of the *Corpus Juris Canonici* as codified in the sixteenth century. In 1234, the Church issued its first collection of canon law.[126] Fifty years later, a French crown official compiled customary law from around the kingdom into the *Coutumes de Beauvaisis*.[127] Even Roman law had never had quite the same character as this, 'as a coherent whole, an integrated system, a "body" '.[128] Justinian's *Corpus*, by contrast, had been a collection of commentaries and other sources dating back over centuries. In fact, the term *'corpus juris'* is absent from Justinian. It was, instead, the name given to the collection when it was rediscovered in the eleventh century.[129] Evidence, perhaps, of the growing influence of the law is that 'every notable pope from 1159 to 1303 was a lawyer'.[130]

In addition to claiming for itself a more comprehensive and integrated character, by regulating the relationship between the Church and the secular power, the law began to establish itself as something separate from and above both theology and politics; it became the thing that 'binds the state itself'.[131] Pashukanis makes a similar point, locating the rise of law's hegemony in its role as a third party standing above a set of conflicting interests. Pashukanis, however, sees this development in relation to the regulation of commercial activity in the emerging market towns.[132] It could be argued that the same phenomenon is being identified by both Berman and Pashukanis, except that the former sees it in its higher stage, while the latter recognises the phenomenon as it permeates into daily life. Certainly Berman is at one with Pashukanis and with the Marxist

---

125 Berman HJ, *Faith and Order: The Reconciliation of Law and Religion* (William B Eerdmans Publishing, 2000), 27; Tigar ME, *Law and the Rise of Capitalism* (Monthly Review Press, 2000), 39.
126 Berman (n 125), 44.
127 Tigar (n 125), 39.
128 Berman (n 125), 27.
129 Ibid 27.
130 Southern RW, *Western Society and the Church in the Middle Ages* (Penguin, 1970), 131.
131 Berman (n 125), 27.
132 Pashukanis EB, *Marxism and Law: A General Theory* (Barbara Einhorn tr, Pluto, 1989), 135–136.

legal historian, Michael E. Tigar, in seeing the rise of law as tied to the rise of commodity exchange during the eleventh and twelfth centuries.

It is around this time that we find many debates among canon lawyers about several practical issues, some of which were described above. For example, this was a period that saw an ideological battle between the Franciscans and the canon lawyers, with the lawyers deploying sophist arguments around questions over consumption of food and clothing to defeat the theological rejection of property by followers of St. Francis.[133] In relation to sanctuary, the canon lawyers argued over such questions as whether asylum should be denied to those who planned crimes from within the church, but gave orders for them to be carried out by associates on the outside, or whether someone who committed a crime in one church could then claim asylum in another.[134] As we have already seen in the chartered sanctuaries, within which fugitives could spend years, or even lifetimes, it was possible for them to continue to engage in criminal transactions with those outside. But whereas St. Martin le Grand had a bad reputation in this respect, this was not the general rule.[135] Thus, the canonists' concerns were only relevant to, at best, marginal cases of sanctuary. And even there, the complaints may have been inspired more by prejudice than facts. What appears to have been of greater concern was that law should be universal and possess supreme authority. It was these arguments that would later add grist to the mill for the secular authorities whose agenda became the complete destruction of sanctuary.

A theological dualistic conception of power, with the Church autonomous in the sacred sphere, and the monarch possessing absolute power in temporal matters developed and was codified by St. Thomas Aquinas in his *Scriptum super Sententiis*.[136] This strengthened the power of the church as a separate and legitimate body within a society that was fast developing a much more systematic and centralised form of sovereign power. But it also laid the foundations for an argument that would become increasingly prevalent over the next two centuries: sanctuary, by granting immunity – at least for a time – to those who had breached the king's peace, served to undermine and encroach upon secular law and order. This was the logic that led from mere separation of the two spheres of authority

---

133 Agamben G, *De la très haute pauvreté: Règles et forme de vie* (Joël Gayraud tr, Bibliotèque Rivages, 2011), Part III.
134 Helmholz (n 54), 55.
135 Indeed, St. Martin le Grand was full of artisans who carried out a legitimate trade in goods, often of high quality, from within the sanctuary. A number of sanctuary men there had premises which had a door or window that faced out of the precinct as shop fronts for them to sell their goods. McSheffrey (n 20), 489, and generally. In Beverley, where the sanctuary precinct covered the whole town, the sanctuary men and women were allowed to engage in whatever trade or profession they wished, including the right to join guilds. Cox (n 2), 144. They were also free to live anywhere they wished within the town. As such, they formed an integral and integrated part of the community.
136 Pope (n 25), 683.

to, in the Tudor period, the one destroying the other. However, between the twelfth and the fifteenth centuries, while the secular and ecclesiastical realms divided, there remained a great deal of intellectual solidarity between the civil and canon lawyers.[137]

The undermining of sanctuary by canon law

As we have seen, the principle of ecclesiastical immunity was one of the key elements that sustained the church as a place of sanctuary into the Middle Ages.[138] Rosenwein writes:

> In the late [Roman] Empire asylum and immunity were entirely separate concepts. Nevertheless, the law of asylum was an important precedent for later immunities because it prohibited state agents from entering church precincts to apprehend a refugee.[139]

It should be noted that church sanctuary was not rooted in a subjective right of asylum, but was a function of the rights and obligations of clergy to offer protection and intercession on behalf of the suppliant.[140] However, from the turn of the second millennium onwards, the inviolability of the church became a tricky problem, with the resurgence of the state and organised polities, and their separation from the Church. Specifically, the problem arose as to what extent the canon law of sanctuary could effectively negate the growing body of temporal law. Could not the right of asylum effectively give people immunity from temporal law *in toto*? Helmholz gives a fascinating account of the theological debates within the Church over this question. Some of the conclusions allowed for some accommodation with the temporal law on this point, and eventually opened the door for the effective emasculation of the right of asylum. The role of canon law was crucial, as in the medieval period Roman law on sanctuary played 'a secondary role' to it.[141] However, that is not to say that the Church did not appropriate aspects of Roman law when it suited it:

> [P]arts of the Roman law filled gaps in the canon law. No canon law excluded Jews from sanctuary, for example. However, Roman law did, and the canon law embraced it as a worthy addition to the *casus excepti*.[142]

---

137 For the continuous overlapping of understandings of sovereign authority between these two spheres, see Kantorowicz EH, *The King's Two Bodies: A Study in Mediaeval Political Theology* (Princeton University, 1957).
138 Helmholz (n 54).
139 Rosenwein (n 54), 37.
140 Timbal (n 1), 158, 161; Shoemaker (n 1), 22, 69; Helmholz (n 54), 28.
141 Helmholz (n 54), 37.
142 Ibid 38. The reference to Roman law can be found in Justinian Watson A (tr), *The Digest of Justinian* (University of Pennsylvania, 1985), 1.12(15).1.

Beginning in the twelfth century with Gratian's inauguration of a systematic canon law, the Church lawyers would ensure the 'intellectual groundwork' necessary for the eventual destruction of sanctuary.[143] Following agitation by the canon lawyer Hostiensis in 1281, Pope Martin IV declared Jews to be 'unworthy' of sanctuary – a ruling confirmed 30 years later by Pope John XXII.[144] Helmholz, along with others, rejects the argument put forward by historians of asylum throughout the last two centuries who pitched the Church as the absolute defenders of sanctuary against the secular abolitionists. Instead, the development of canon law was the medium through which church sanctuary could be restricted and then delegitimised.[145] In short, the two wings of medieval law, canon and secular, complemented each other in respect of sanctuary. 'The common law coincided with the canon law in its principles and in most of the ways it worked in practice'.[146] Indeed, Helmholz argues that, in fact, in contrast to canon law, it was the common law 'that encouraged the broader availability of sanctuary during the Middle Ages'.[147] As sanctuary headed for its denouement in the fifteenth and sixteenth centuries, it was the combined canon and Roman law of the *ius commune* which provided the source for 'some of the ideas expressed by common lawyers in describing their own law of sanctuary or arguing for its restriction'.[148]

Helmholz schematises the canon law on asylum into three separate categories: immunity of churches, treatment of refugees and the *casus excepti*.[149] The first of these, church immunity, was about ensuring the physical protection of the church and of creating a separation from the world around it. From the late eleventh century onwards, this principle would have suited the Church in its attempt to create a structural distance from secular power. If the principle of church immunity was relatively straightforward, the treatment of the refugees themselves was far more problematic. To harbour criminals would be a violation of canon law and the prohibition against the Church becoming a 'den of thieves'. The compromise was to ensure that those who had sought sanctuary in a church would not face execution or mutilation, but would nevertheless face some sort of punishment. In practice, this meant that the fugitive would have to make amends to his or her victim, usually in monetary terms.[150] The second category identified by Helmholz dealt with ensuring a basic humanitarian treatment of the refugees in sanctuary. The third category of canon law that dealt with sanctuary was, crucially, concerned with who should be prohibited from the protection of the Church. The *casus excepti* are a classic example of the legal paradigm: defining the subject of rights.

143 Shoemaker (n 1), 154.
144 Timbal (n 1), 19.
145 Helmholz (n 54), 74. Rosenwein (n 54) and Schoemaker (n 20) make the same argument.
146 Helmholz (n 54), 69.
147 Ibid 22.
148 Ibid 73.
149 Ibid 25–37.
150 Ibid 30–31.

They consisted of a series of categories of people deemed unworthy of sanctuary and thus prohibited from access. The *casus excepti* first appeared in the eleventh century; thus, they lay at the base of canon law, and continued to expand in scope all the way up to the nineteenth century, in principle as part of maintaining 'public order'.[151] They reflect backwards to the laws of the late Roman Empire that attempted to restrict access to sanctuary, and forwards to the modern law of asylum that sets objective criteria for the undeserving asylum-seeker.[152] It was the legal category of *casus excepti* that was central to the undermining of sanctuary.

The canon lawyers carried on an unending debate on the *casus excepti*. On the one hand, there were those who took the position that one had to first prove one's piety and loyalty to the Catholic Church in order to claim sanctuary. This logic would also place those who had been excommunicated – who, in principle, were not allowed to enter a church anyway – or those put under a secular ban within the category of those who could be forcibly and legitimately removed from sanctuary. Yet, on the other hand, as many theologians held, if one were to exclude suppliants who lacked piety, then that could easily exclude the majority of Christians whose main motive for seeking sanctuary was a self-interested desire to avoid secular punishment.[153] Helmholz asserts that canon law, 'like many ancient systems of asylum ... welcomed only entrants from its own circle of belief'.[154] However, the Israelites did not exclude non-Jews who lived among them from the Biblical sanctuary cities.[155] And Helmholz's assertion also ignores Augustine's plea that sanctuary be available to all, and the fact that, on many occasions, outsiders were indeed welcomed. Examples of this are the Jewish High Priest Onias who was welcomed at the Temple of Apollo, and the many pagans who were sheltered by the early Christians from the might of Rome. Moreover, as J.H. Baker argues, since in fact 'sanctuary was not a personal privilege, but a privilege attaching to a sanctified place, it was in theory available to Jews and infidels as well as Christians'.[156] However, in place of this non-sectarian theological tradition came a juridical process. And Timbal succinctly describes the effect of juridical rationality on the practice of asylum:

> While the classical law of the Church asserted the principle of asylum as open to all, with rare exceptions, the jurists took the opposite position. When an individual invokes the right of asylum . . .he must be asked if he is Catholic or not. If he is not, he is excluded. If he is, then one has to determine if his wrong was committed in the church – meaning he would not have the right of asylum – or outside of the church. If the latter, and if he is a serf then he

151 Timbal (n 1), 210.
152 E.g. Article 1F, Convention Relating to the Status of Refugees, 28 July 1951, United Nations, Treaty Series, vol 189.
153 Helmholz (n 54), 50.
154 Ibid.
155 Timbal (n 1), 11. The biblical references are Numbers 35:15; Joshua 20:9.
156 Baker (n 31), 8.

will not be admitted unless he can demonstrate [that he is fleeing the threat] of serious cruelty; otherwise he is to be returned to his master who must take an oath [not to harm his serf].[157]

Yet in spite of canon law restricting sanctuary to certain classes of people, there is actually little evidence that bishops, in practice, attempted to exclude those who fell within the *casus excepti*, suggesting a split between the lawyers and the theologians within the Church on the question of sanctuary. In fact, there were many instances where the clergy, together with many of the local population, fought pitched battles to defend refugees in sanctuary from being seized by royal agents.[158] During the thirteenth century, Hostiensis felt compelled to rebuke bishops for extending sanctuary to those who fell outside of the protection of canon law. And as late as the fifteenth century, the bishop of Noyon in France challenged the king's procurer, who had ordered that those subjected to a secular ban, or who were otherwise enemies of the state, were excluded from the right of asylum. The bishop based his opposition on the precedent of the Biblical sanctuary cities that made no such distinction.[159] No evidence has been found in bishops' registers for any kind of formal procedure to test whether or not sanctuary-seekers had a right to asylum before entering the church. In the great sanctuaries, however, there does seem to have been some kind of perfunctory ceremony, involving the suppliant taking some form of oath, although again this appears to have been more a formality than something substantively procedural. Helmholz writes: 'The English bishops appear, on balance, not to have wished to limit the claim of fugitives to ecclesiastical immunity, even though it would have been consistent with the canon law to have done so'.[160]

The clergy were faced with the dilemma that systematically excluding those who fell within the *casus excepti* conflicted with the principle of clerical tenderness (*lenitas*) towards suppliants. To get around this, some could simply take a *laisser faire* attitude while allowing the secular authorities to play the 'active role' in actually removing them from sanctuary.[161] At the same time, the secular agents were able to rely more and more on the canon law's ever-growing class of *casus excepti* as justification for violating church sanctuary and forcibly removing fugitives.[162]

Thus, it would not be correct to say that 'the Church' was in favour of restricting access to sanctuary only to pious Christians, but rather it was the Church lawyers who were anxious to limit and restrict the right of asylum, while clergy appeared to stick more closely to a more open approach. Helmholz argues that bishops felt able to violate the canon law on the *casus excepti* because the

---

157 Timbal (n 1), 266.
158 Ibid 396–397.
159 Ibid 357.
160 Helmholz (n 54), 63–64.
161 Timbal (n 1), 222.
162 Ibid 384.

common law, being more expansive in its approach, tended to ignore them.[163] Perhaps, but this begs the question as to why the common law would be so generous, and also why the bishops felt confident enough to defy the not inconsiderable power of the Church hierarchy. In my opinion, this could only have been a result of popular support and reverence for more open access to sanctuary, many examples of which I have already discussed. The numbers fleeing to sanctuary annually, and the ever-present possibility that anyone may need to take advantage of sanctuary themselves, probably helped ensure this popular endorsement of sanctuary, at least for a time.

The coming of the modern state and the destruction of sanctuary

Several centuries of canon law creating prohibition after prohibition on certain classes of people allowed to take sanctuary, and legitimising the removal by state agents of persons belonging to those groups, had taken its toll by the fifteenth century. Popular support for sanctuary appears not to have been as wide or, at least, as active as it once was. The secular authorities were also now emboldened to make more aggressive attacks on sanctuary, often using the principle of the *casus excepti* as a starting point. The time was also ripe, in that the Tudors, emerging victorious from the long civil war between the houses of Lancaster and York, sought to impose stability and authority with the creation of the modern state. Partly as a result of the trauma of this long war, the Tudors were anxious to close off spaces outside of the sovereign authority of the crown which might threaten the existing settlement.[164] With the coming of the modern state in England, a new way of 'conceptualizing, organizing and controlling space' was inaugurated.[165] As with the Romans, the Tudors were concerned to establish a centralised and uniform source of power. As a result, the right of sanctuary was greatly reduced. The general shift away from immunities was part of a process in which the king's agents were granted far greater leeway to enter private property. And indeed, over the next two centuries, 'the occasions for search and seizure "proliferated from three to fifteen categories" '.[166]

A turning point in English law was the case of *Rex v. Sir Humphrey Stafford* [1486].[167] Stafford was a Yorkist who, following defeat at Bosworth Field, attempted a rebellion against Henry VII. With the failure of this uprising, Stafford fled to the chartered sanctuary at Culham in Oxford, only to be dragged out and taken to the Tower of London to await execution. He pleaded that his right of sanctuary had been violated and that he should be returned whence he had been seized by the king's men. The court demanded from the Abbot of Culham

163 Helmholz (n 54), 70.
164 Cox (n 2), 319.
165 Rosenwein (n 54), 207.
166 Ibid, citing William J Cuddihy.
167 1 Henry 7 ff 22–24, pl 15 [1486].

proofs of the original grant of sanctuary. This he could not do, so Stafford lost his claim and was duly executed. There are clear echoes here of the Tiberian attack on *asylia* through the imposition of a requirement of legal proof of possession of immunity. The case of *Stafford* was undoubtedly a blow against the old chartered sanctuaries, as many of their privileges dated so far back that documentation would be hard to provide. From now on, the sovereign would apply the law as forcefully as possible to deny political enemies sanctuary, and increasingly the rights of sovereign command would edge out the immunities and other competing spaces of authority.[168]

From 1487 onwards, Henry VII was able to secure papal bulls authorising the removal from sanctuary of those who had left the place of sanctuary to commit further crimes, and of those who owed debts to the state. This followed an earlier ruling almost 40 years previously by Pope Pius II, granting the city of Antwerp the right to remove murderers from sanctuary.[169] The effect of these initial papal bulls was the gradual exclusion of public debtors until, by 1562, canon jurisprudence excluded all who owed such debts from asylum.[170] Further, these bulls allowed creditors to seize any property owned by sanctuary men, and bestowed the power on the king to provide his own guards to watch from within the sanctuary anyone accused of treason.[171] One man, William Oldhall, who took sanctuary at St. Martin le Grand, complained that this measure effectively turned the asylum into a prison. Indeed, this may have been a deliberate goal of early Tudor penology.[172]

A further key stage in the decline of sanctuary came in 1516 in the notorious case of *Rex v. Savage*,[173] involving the brutal murder of a justice of the peace, and the murderer's subsequent resort to sanctuary.[174] Just as with Stafford, the assailant, Savage, was then forcibly removed from the sanctuary and placed in the Tower of London to await trial for murder. Such was the scandal surrounding the violation of sanctuary in addition to the original crime that the case was heard in the presence of Henry VIII himself along with 'a swarm of bishops, canonists and other ecclesiastics, and all the judges'. The case report goes on to note that: 'Many mischiefs were rehearsed which had been done in time past and which increased from day to day because of the Sanctuaries of Westminster and St. John's, etc., and what remedy and redress could be provided was the

---

168 Ryan (n 24), 225; Thornley (n 108), 185.
169 Helmholz (n 54), 48.
170 Timbal (n 1), 369.
171 Mazzinghi (n 7), 15.
172 Kaufman (n 99), 474.
173 *Rex v. Savage*, 72 ER 365 [1516].
174 Baker (n 31), 12. See Ives EW, 'Crime, sanctuary, and royal authority under Henry VIII: the exemplary sufferings of the savage family' in Morris S Arnold and others (eds), *On the Laws and Customs of England* (University of North Carolina, 1981) for a fascinating in-depth discussion of the historical and political context of this case.

principle reason why the King was there in his royal person that day'.[175] The earlier case of *Stafford* was cited, but in this case, the chartered sanctuary in question, St. John's in Clerkenwell, was able to provide the necessary proofs of its privilege. Eventually, after the case had dragged on for several years, Savage withdrew his claim regarding the violation of sanctuary. One reason why his claim was withdrawn became evident when Chief Justice Fineux made his subsequent ruling, for Fineux made new law by stating that the original proofs were no longer sufficient. Instead, evidence of use as a sanctuary 'time out of mind', i.e. before 1189, also had to be established in order to show that sanctuary could be granted for more than the standard 40 days. He went on to state that indefinite sanctuary 'is a thing so derogatory to Justice and contrary to the common good of the Realm that it is not sufferable by the law'.[176] And in this case, it was denied. E.W. Ives suggests that the forcible removal of Savage from St. John's might have been part of a deliberate plan by the crown lawyers to use it as a test case for further restricting the right of sanctuary.[177] One outcome of this case, which presages the coming split with the Papacy, was that it was decided in the Star Chamber that a sanctuary could not be created by a pope. Instead, it could only be granted by the king, with the pope relegated to simply confirming the grant.[178] But most tellingly, it was the canon law that was also invoked – the fugitive was deemed to fall within the *casus excepti* – in order to exclude Savage from sanctuary.[179] Here is but one explicit example of the secular law relying on its canon equivalent as part of the campaign to dismantle sanctuary.

A period of sustained attacks upon sanctuary began in 1530 when Henry VIII passed an Act banning abjurers from leaving the realm,[180] although, prior to this, legislation had been passed decreeing that all who chose to abjure the realm were to have the thumb of their right hand branded with the letter 'A', 'to the intent that he might be better known among the King's subjects to have abjured'.[181] Under the new Act, those who wished to abjure the realm were instead to choose a sanctuary within England to which they would remain for the rest of their life. Following this, Henry banned anyone accused of high treason from sanctuary altogether.[182] And then, in a piece of legislation designed to humiliate and stigmatise those in sanctuary, a further Act was passed, making it compulsory for all sanctuary men to wear a 20-inch square badge identifying themselves as such.[183]

A petition was sent to Thomas Cromwell, Henry VIII's chief minister, in 1534 complaining that the chartered sanctuaries were undermining royal justice and

---

175 Cited in Ives (n 174), 300.
176 Ibid 298–299.
177 Ibid 300–301.
178 Baker (n 31), 12.
179 Helmholz (n 54), 77.
180 22 Henry 8, c 14.
181 21 Henry 8, c 2.
182 26 Henry 8, c 13 and 28 Henry 8, c 7.
183 27 Henry 8, c 19.

reducing revenues due the king.[184] Two years later, Cromwell, in surviving notes he made for his audiences with the king, wrote of the need to seek 'the utter destruction of sanctuaries'.[185] That same year, an uprising in the north of England, known as the Pilgrimage of Grace, directed itself against Henry's general policy towards the Church and, in particular, his changes to the laws of sanctuary.[186] Thornley argues that this rebellion was, in effect, an attempt by the North to recover its ancient liberties.[187] Following the accession of Edward VI, there was an attempt at Beverley to resurrect the right of sanctuary there.[188] This was swiftly suppressed, only for a further attempt to re-establish sanctuary after the accession of the Catholic Queen Mary in 1553, with the final abolition of the sanctuary following the end of her reign. This suggests a continuing belief and attachment to the principle of sanctuary some years after their effective suppression by Henry VIII, not to mention resistance to the attempt at the suppression itself.

In 1540, Henry VIII passed an Act that finally abolished all the chartered sanctuaries.[189] However, ordinary sanctuary was still permitted solely within the boundaries of churches and churchyards. But even there, all of those accused of the most serious crimes – homicide, rape, theft, treason, etc. – were excluded. It is estimated that following the Act of 1540 and the dissolution of the monasteries, the number of sanctuaries in England was reduced to around half their previous number.[190] At Beaulieu, the clergy pleaded with Thomas Cromwell for the right of those sanctuary men who were there at the time to be allowed to remain with their wives and children for the remainder of their lives, on condition that no others were henceforth admitted. This request was apparently acceded to.[191] To replace the chartered sanctuaries, the Act stipulated that eight towns were to serve as secular and crown-controlled replacements. These initially included Wells, Westminster, Northampton, Norwich, York, Derby, Launceston and Manchester.[192] It is possible, even likely, that this statute was influenced by the Biblical sanctuary cities by the Jordan.[193] The burden of state regulation and supervision of those seeking sanctuary in these towns, the fact that they could offer asylum for little other than private debt, plus the strict limitation of only twenty sanctuary men and women at any time, made these new sanctuaries a

---

184 Trenholme (n 4), 59.
185 Cox (n 2), 322.
186 Ibid 323–324.
187 Thornley (n 108), 203.
188 Cox (n 2), 147.
189 32 Henry 8, c 12.
190 Trenholme (n 4), 30–31.
191 Cox (n 2), 188.
192 Ibid 326.
193 Mazzinghi (n 7), 83–84. Other examples from this time of secular asylum cities/ towns can be found among the Flemish and Germans. Sanctuary towns also existed in the Netherlands until 1795, and in Denmark, one sanctuary town contained thousands of fugitives until as late as 1827. Logan WA, 'Criminal Law Sanctuaries' (2003), 38, *Harvard Civil Rights-Civil Liberties Law Review*, 321, 369.

mere shadow of their predecessors.[194] And indeed, all of them, with the exception of Westminster, fell quickly into complete desuetude, only to be unceremoniously abolished altogether just 60 years later.[195] With James I's Act of 1623 abolishing these sanctuary cities, the tradition of sanctuary in England, having survived for more than 1,000 years, came to an end.[196]

An addendum on the creation of these new sanctuary cities provides an interesting glimpse into ways of thinking that were perhaps new then, but which have today become ubiquitous in the discourse on asylum: security and economic burden. Manchester petitioned Henry VIII against its designation as a sanctuary city. The reasons given were that an influx of destitute sanctuary-seekers would depress the local economy of the cloth and cotton trade, and in addition Manchester had no city walls, nor a mayor, sheriff or bailiff to ensure public order. Henry acceded to the Mancunian request and moved the sanctuary to Chester, which had little or no trade but did have the necessary security apparatus, e.g. a gaol, mayor and bailiff – although, following protests from Chester, the sanctuary was eventually moved to Stafford.[197] With a modern attempt to impose universal law and sovereign power, came some peculiarly modern prejudices about asylum and asylum-seekers, namely that they represented an economic cost and/or a security risk.

If sanctuary has 'its root in a sentiment . . . that a peculiar sacredness attaches to particular places', then once such a sanctified approach was removed, sanctuaries were liable to exposure to the ruthless calculating approach of modern rationalism.[198] At no point during its long history would church sanctuary have been able to withstand determined physical attacks by secular authorities.[199] What preserved their immunity in practice was the reverence and respect in which they were held by the society around them from top to bottom. Baker states that by the early seventeenth century, public opinion had shifted so that it 'would not stand' for an institution such as sanctuary.[200] But as we saw earlier, the church itself began the process of undermining sanctuary via canon law several centuries previously. Once again, as in Greece and Rome previously, the rot set in once sanctuary/asylum was reconfigured within a legal paradigm.

The twilight of sanctuary

In 1563, the Council of Trent issued a call for a return to the 'due reverence' for ecclesiastical immunity. This was a last gasp of such a notion. Certainly in

---

194   Thornley (n 108), 204.
195   1 James I, c 25.
196   21 James I, c 28.
197   Trenholme (n 4), 88.
198   Mazzinghi (n 7), 1. See also Hayes (n 18); Rosenwein (n 54).
199   Baker (n 31), 8.
200   Ibid 13.

England, the legislation of Henry VIII and then James I abolished sanctuary as a plea in a court of law, but, as Ryan points out, it did not declare the institution itself as illegal: 'Thus, merely the procedural, rather than the substantive right, was abolished'.[201] This would explain how various sanctuaries, mostly for debt, were able to survive in places such as Holyrood, the Southwark Mint and Whitefriars until late into the eighteenth and nineteenth centuries, 'from which the instruments of public authority were excluded'.[202] The 'counties palatine' – those which possessed historical immunities from the king – such as Chester, Durham and Lancashire retained some of their immunities into the eighteenth century.[203] In Scotland, debtors could seek sanctuary right up until 1880 when imprisonment for debt was abolished, thus making the right of sanctuary super-fluous. This was probably the last example of the ancient right of sanctuary in the British Isles.[204]

The medieval European institution of sanctuary found its way as far afield as New Mexico in the seventeenth century, via the Spanish *conquistadors*.[205] It survived there until the late nineteenth century when it too was abolished.[206] Even in the wake of uprisings by Native Americans, those accused of sedition and rebellion who sought church sanctuary were left unmolested by the colonial authorities.[207] The historian of these sanctuaries, Elizabeth Howard West, reaches a conclusion on their decline that chimes with her European counterparts: 'Naturally as the civil courts became stronger, the practice lost in efficacy and was bound in the natural course of events to disappear'.[208]

As the modern state was forged throughout Europe and beyond, the last remnants of sanctuary were erased. In France, although a *droit d'asile* was severely limited in 1539, just a year before Henry VIII's seminal Act in England, it was only finally abolished during the French Revolution.[209] Sanctuary was severely truncated in Spain during the restoration of absolute monarchy from the early nineteenth century onwards.[210] It was abolished in Austria in 1776, Silesia in 1743, Tuscany in 1769, Prussia in 1794, Franconia in 1799, Baden in 1803, Wurtemberg in 1804, Rome in 1815, Saxe-Weimar in 1823 and Saxony in

---

201 Ryan (n 24), 229.
202 Rigsby KJ, *Asylia: Territorial Inviolability in the Hellenistic World* (University of California, 1996), 2; Haagen P, 'Imprisonment for Debt in England and Wales' (PhD Thesis, Princeton University, 1986), 270–311.
203 Ryan (n 24), 229; Thornley (n 108), 184.
204 Trenholme (n 4), 92–93.
205 West EH, 'The Right of Asylum in New Mexico in the Seventeenth and Eighteenth Centuries' (1928), 8, *Hispanic American Historical Review*, 357, 361.
206 Ibid 362.
207 See, e.g., the case of Juan de Tafoya in Ibid 369–371.
208 Ibid 391.
209 Coursier H, 'Restauration du droit d'asile' (1950), 32, *Revue Internationale de la Croix-Rouge et Bulletin international des Sociétés de la Croix-Rouge*, 909, 910; Trenholme (n 4), 97. See also Reyerson (n 64), 623–624.
210 West (n 205), 361.

1827.[211] Sanctuary cities survived in Holland until 1798 and in Denmark until 1827.[212] The Vatican signed concordats with Austria in 1855 and Ecuador in 1862, which stated that the right of asylum could be vitiated in the interests of 'justice' and 'public security'.[213] Such was the almost complete erasure of asylum by the turn of the twentieth century, that in a standard textbook on international law published in 1906, James Bassett Moore could spend over a hundred pages discussing the question of a possible right of asylum solely in terms of a right vested in states within their diplomatic missions abroad. Moore's conclusion was therefore that: 'The word asylum has in its legal relations become to a great extent metaphorical'.[214] Thirty years later, Timbal identifies the right of asylum persisting only in places 'at a certain level of civilisation', namely in parts of Asia and Africa.[215] There, as in Europe, the right was associated with temples, woods, shrines, etc. In Persia, it survived until the early twentieth century, but following the establishment of a constitutional government, asylum 'lost its importance' and was eventually abolished a few years later.[216] Typically perhaps, the Catholic Church only finally admitted the obvious long after the question had become moot, when in 1983 a revision of the canon law finally dropped any reference whatsoever to sanctuary.[217]

The historical judgement on sanctuary

Most historians writing over the last three centuries have concurred with the lawyers of the late Middle Ages, arguing that sanctuary had its place during 'barbarous times' and a 'low state of civilisation', as 'mitigating the cruelties of a cruel age', but was obsolete or even offensive under a modern rule of law.[218] In *Memorials of Westminster Abbey* (1865), the then dean of the Abbey and professor of ecclesiastical history at Oxford, Arthur Stanley, wrote a classic statement on how modernity perceived sanctuary:

> The (chartered) sanctuaries of mediaeval Christendom may have been necessary remedies for a barbarous state of society, but when the barbarism, of which they formed part, disappeared, they became almost unmixed evils.[219]

211 Timbal (n 1), 449; Moore JB, *A Digest of International Law: Volume II* (US Government Printing Office, 1906), 767.
212 Bianchi H, *Justice as Sanctuary: Toward a New System of Crime Control* (Indiana University, 1994), 144–145.
213 Timbal (n 1), 451.
214 Moore (n 211), 755.
215 Timbal (n 1), 455.
216 Ibid 457.
217 Carro (n 13), 767.
218 Mazzinghi (n 7), 101; Trenholme (n 4), 96; Timbal (n 1), 453; West (n 205), 359.
219 Stanley A, *Historical Memorials of Westminster Abbey* (John Murray, 1886), 414.

Cesare Beccaria captures the peculiarly modern concern that multiple sites of sovereign authority undermined a civilised way of being in his seminal work, *On Crimes and Punishments*, published in 1764:

> Within the borders of a country there should be no place independent of its laws [and] to multiply such places of asylum is to create so many small sovereignties . . . where laws have no say.[220]

Carro, marshalling his arguments against the US Sanctuary Movement's defiance of the law during the 1980s – as discussed in Part III – suggests that the abolition of sanctuary was a necessary pre-condition for modern individual rights and the extrication of sovereign authority from the grip of the Church. He then goes on to quote the Fifth Amendment to the US Constitution, a classic statement of absolute confidence in the efficacy of the liberal rule of law and property rights as the sole guarantors of justice.[221] This together with a more direct claim made by the French revolutionaries – 'The right of asylum is being abolished in France, for it's now the law being the asylum of all people'[222] – demonstrates law's claim to an all-encompassing *imperium*, a feature of the modern state, which cannot abide the principles on which sanctuary has historically stood: a space of otherness to the authority of law and sovereign power.

Thornley describes Henry VIII's destruction of the sanctuaries as one of 'level[ing] liberties to make a foundation for liberty'.[223] This is in spite of her showing the utter cynicism of Henry's attacks on sanctuary. But for her, the fate of sanctuaries was already sealed by the coming break with Rome, and its attendant anti-clericalism. In addition, these privileges were casualties of modernity's 'inevitable' process of sweeping away all jurisdictions which stood outside the sovereign authority.[224] Along similar lines, Pope argues that the key determining issue in the abolition of sanctuary was simply that the king could no longer tolerate a 'foreign authority' within his realm.[225] However, McSheffrey challenges these conclusions by pointing to contemporary evidence showing that almost up to their dissolution, the chartered sanctuaries operated on the basis of lively, functional and accepted practices, even if they were sometimes controversial.[226] Moreover, most people at the time would have seen no inherent problem with the Church giving sanctuary to criminals, as this fit with common notions of Christian mercy, charity and the possibility of redemption.[227]

---

220 Beccaria C, *On Crimes and Punishments and Other Writings* (Aaron Thomas ed, Aaron Thomas and Jeremy Parzen trs, University of Toronto, 2008), 92.
221 Carro (n 13), 767.
222 Quoted in Bianchi (n 212), 144.
223 Thornley (n 108), 185.
224 Ibid 200.
225 Pope (n 25), 697.
226 McSheffrey (n 20), 493 and generally.
227 Ibid 509.

Almost alone among historians of sanctuary, Mazzinghi admits the limitations of law and the crucial role that sanctuary did, and potentially could have, in mitigating its flaws. For him, the inherent 'generality' of law makes 'every system or code of laws' imperfect; 'Immunities suppose the law deficient, and the right to sanctuary was such [an] immunity'.[228] As such, a more well-rounded approach, more respectful of the specific circumstances in each case, was lost with the destruction of sanctuary under the Tudors,[229] although in a weak statement of qualification, Mazzinghi suggests that, over time, as law became a 'less imperfect' system, so the institution of sanctuary necessarily went into decline.[230] The question as to how this should be if 'every system or code of laws' is imperfect is, of course, not resolved. Writing just a few years ago, William Chester Jordan posits that sanctuary mainly served the purpose that plea-bargaining does today: as a means to temper the harshness of the law. As such, its popularity in its day and its continued resonance down to the present, including the US Sanctuary Movement of the 1980s, was largely due to its major effect: that 'it saved lives'.[231] Yet, plea-bargaining is an integral and well-accepted part of the legal system; sanctuary never has been. Karl Shoemaker rightly identifies most of these historians as displaying 'an acute feeling of their superiority over legal practices of the earlier age'.[232] However, as we survey the treatment of refugees by law under modernity – the subject of the next section of this book – as compared to earlier epochs, it should become clear that such a sense of superiority is misplaced.

228 Mazzinghi (n 7), 100.
229 Ibid 106.
230 Ibid 101.
231 Jordan (n 3), 31–32.
232 Shoemaker KB, 'Sanctuary Law: Changing Conceptions of Wrongdoing and Punishment in Medieval European Law' (PhD Thesis, University of California, Berkeley, 2001) (n 20), 17.

Conclusion to Part I

There are a few essential points that can be taken from this traversal of several thousand years of asylum/sanctuary. First, and most importantly for this book's thesis, asylum has repeatedly come into conflict with law. Whether it was Solon's attempts at a comprehensive legal code, the Tiberian 'reform' or the re-emergence of law in the later half of the Middle Ages, at each juncture, asylum found itself bound to such an extent that it either ceased to exist outright or was slowly marginalised out of existence. The one exception was the legalisation of church sanctuary in the closing decades of the Western Roman Empire. But here the failure of law to stamp out asylum was largely due to the collapse of the legal order that immediately followed. The reasons for this inverse relationship between asylum and law are tied to a second conclusion that we can draw from this history. Asylum consistently arose as a space that existed beyond that of law and the state.

Asylum, understood in its original meaning – *a* (not); *sylia* (subject to seizure) – has generally been interpreted as freedom from seizure from one's pursuers. Certainly this is one very important aspect, which survives into our contemporary law of asylum. But for the Greeks, the *asylia* had this characteristic *because* they possessed a more general concept of 'freedom from seizure': they were places beyond the control of any state or its law, whether of their fellow Greeks or the occupying Romans. In the case of the Romans, for whom a unitary political and legal authority was paramount, the *asylia* could not be allowed to survive. The Roman Empire can thus be bookended in its confrontation with asylum/sanctuary: at its height, the former extinguished the latter; at its nadir, Rome found itself unable to hold the line against the Church and those who sought succour within its walls. It is precisely during the epoch that followed, which saw the most profound retreat in the West of law and the state, that sanctuary was able to flourish to perhaps its fullest extent.

Atle Grahl-Madsen writes:

> Throughout history sovereigns have maintained the right to decide whether a refugee shall be given shelter, be ordered to leave the territory, or be handed over outright to the ruler whom he has tried to escape.[1]

---

1 Grahl-Madsen A, *The Status of Refugees in International Law: Volume One* (AW Sijthoff, 1966), 9.

And yet, as we have seen, it has not always been so straightforward. Sovereigns have frequently had to defer to religious or other authorities on such matters, even when the ruler from whom the refugee has fled has been that particular sovereign. In describing the genealogy of asylum, there is one aspect that appears strikingly different from the system of refugee law today. Almost without exception, what we have discovered have been spaces which in one way or another stood beyond the reach of the sovereign power. Today, in contrast, refugee law is about the movement from one sovereign order to another, but never about escaping it altogether. Indeed, one of the central hypotheses of this book is that it is the practice of recognising the refugee almost exclusively in terms of the law, which has landed the refugee in the degraded existence that she now experiences most of the time. This theme will become most evident in Part II on modern refugee law, and Part III on the US Sanctuary Movement and the Sans-Papiers. In a sense, the concept of sanctuary has been turned inside out; instead of a space within, yet without, we now have a space that is without (of the country of origin), yet inescapably within (the law). Instead of space, refugee law is centrally concerned with defining the contours of the refugee subject himself. This biopolitical concern with the measuring and controlling of the subject is evidently latent in law, for it appears in the first laws of asylum from the end of the Roman Empire that restricted sanctuary to certain classes of persons such as public debtors and 'bogus' converts to Christianity. A similar paradigm is at work in the canon law's *casus excepti*, which too concerns itself with the character of the refugee subject.

A final conclusion we can draw is that, while the integrity of asylum has never been absolute, the question of political, religious or social solidarity with its ideals has been indispensable to its functioning, much more so than law. Sanctuary in England was more or less abolished in 1623. Yet, just 60 years later, one of the largest ever movements of refugees into England took place with the arrival of the Huguenots. In relation to the current population of the United Kingdom, the equivalent proportion of refugee arrivals today would number more than 1.5 million people. Yet, the absence of law was no barrier to asylum. Grahl-Madsen argues that the sequence of events – the effective expulsion of the French Protestants and their reception in England, Germany, Holland, etc. – represents the origins of the 'modern European tradition of asylum'.[2] Insofar as it does, it can be understood not necessarily as founding a right of individuals to asylum, but rather of states to grant asylum, for the essential act here was the freedom of receiving states to welcome unwanted subjects of sending states without having to incur the hostility of the latter; the individual refugee was merely a beneficiary of this right.[3] Philip Marfleet reflects on the transformation from the ancient practice of sanctuary, abolished by James I in 1623, and its resurrection in a new guise some 60 years later:

2   Grahl-Madsen A, *The Status of Refugees in International Law: Volume Two* (AW Sijthoff, 1972), 8.
3   Ibid 7.

The idea of protection remained but the practice of providing security had changed profoundly. The territory of the national state now defined the boundaries of refuge: the state itself had in effect been sacralised and provided space within which fugitives might find protection. They must be aliens, however: subjects of another state authority and ready to submit themselves to English Law.[4]

The space of asylum in this modern conception was not outside sovereign control. Indeed, it was only at the invitation of the Crown, no doubt encouraged by popular feeling, that the Huguenots were admitted. However, this right of the state remained discretionary and thus open to political influence and pressure. Again, throughout most of the nineteenth century, Britain had no laws restricting entry to the country, and in fact became known as a haven for refugees. Indeed, one attempt by Palmerston's administration in 1858 to enact a very minor restriction on refugees led to mass popular resistance and the fall of the government.[5] And yet today, in spite of the panoply of international and domestic laws supposedly guaranteeing the right of asylum, lack of sympathy or support has rendered it increasingly meaningless. In other words, the more law has come to concern itself with asylum, the less space there has been for the political element. Popular support for asylum has arguably been compromised by an unending discourse over legitimacy and 'bogus' asylum-seekers, a discourse that is framed in legal terms.

As has been apparent over the preceding chapters, there have been many alterations and variations of asylum in the course of the last few thousand years. But a common thread throughout has been fidelity to a greater or lesser extent to the etymology of 'asylum' – freedom from seizure. Milligan makes the point that the history of legal sanctions in respect of sanctuary in the pre-modern world is overwhelmingly in respect of violations of sanctuary.[6] By contrast, today the reverse is true: the force of law is directed against those who would either seek or offer sanctuary outside of the sovereign order.

4   Marfleet P, 'Understanding "Sanctuary": Faith and Traditions of Asylum' (2011), 24, *Journal of Refugee Studies*, 440, 448.
5   Porter B, *The Refugee Question in Mid-Victorian Politics* (Cambridge University, 1979), 196–199.
6   Milligan CS, 'Ethical aspects of refugee issues and U.S. policy' in Ved P Nanda (ed), *Refugee Law and Policy: International and U.S. Responses* (Greenwood Press, 1989), 175.

Part II
The creation of the refugee subject

Introduction to Part II

> The 1951 Convention Relating to the Status of Refugees and the 1967 Protocol to the Convention are the modern legal embodiment of the ancient and universal tradition of providing sanctuary to those at risk and in danger.[1]

In the preceding chapters, we have explored the genealogy of asylum and found that, as a concept, it has been repeatedly in conflict with law. If Volker Türk and Frances Nicholson, writing under the auspices of the United Nations High Commissioner for Refugees (UNHCR) itself, are correct that the 1951 Convention is the embodiment of this tradition, then it would seem as if somehow modern refugee law has managed to square asylum into the legal circle. Yet, the fallaciousness of this argument can be demonstrated by examining the origins and development of this body of law. Whereas the roots of asylum lie in 'freedom from seizure' by sovereign power, and solidarity with the refugee, the impetus for the development of refugee law has instead been the preservation and strengthening of sovereign right. What should become clear, is the striking difference of this process, and the concerns that dominate it, from that which governed the evolution of asylum. In particular, it is noticeable the extent to which refugee law from the beginning has had a biopolitical focus on identifying, measuring and judging the refugee; its primary concern has been to control and manage movement.

Most writers on refugee law begin either with the post-World War II process that culminated in the 1951 Refugee Convention or with the earlier attempts to establish basic forms of legal protection in the aftermath of World War I.[2]

---

1 Türk V and Nicholson F, 'Refugee protection in international law: an overall perspective' in Erika Feller, Volker Türk and Frances Nicholson (eds), *Refugee Protection in International Law: UNHCR's Global Consultations on International Protection* (Cambridge University, 2003), 3.

2 Non-legal writers tend to avoid this myopia, e.g., Marfleet P, 'Understanding "Sanctuary": Faith and Traditions of Asylum' (2011), 24, *Journal of Refugee Studies*, 440; Malkki LH, 'Refugees and Exile: From "Refugee Studies" to the Natural Order of Things' (1995), 24, *Annual Review of Anthropology*, 495; Price ME, *Rethinking Asylum: History, Purpose, Limits* (Cambridge Univesity, 2010). Dallal Stevens is a notable exception of a legal writer who does explore the deeper history involved. Stevens D, *UK Asylum Law and Policy: Historical and Contemporary Perspectives* (Sweet and Maxwell, 2004).

These accounts therefore miss on two things: first, an explanation as to how refugee movements prior to the twentieth century were perceived and managed, and second, they lack an appreciation of the concerns and outlook that shaped the refugee subject as it would become defined in law. The insistence upon a fixed, universal refugee subject, one that is necessarily exclusionary and that must be managed, is very recent. Moreover, it is a function of a sovereign legal order in which the concept of asylum is completely reversed. No longer is it a space beyond the reach of the state; instead, asylum, such as it is, is reconfigured as being solely in the gift of this or that state. In short, in the modern age, the space of asylum has been subsumed within law and the state. Thus, the focus has shifted from demarcating and protecting the space of asylum, to delineating the subject of asylum, i.e. the refugee.

At the outset, it is worth pointing out how malleable the concept of the refugee has been historically. The use of the term 'refugee' is relatively recent, certainly as currently understood. Until the mid-nineteenth century, it was commonly used only in relation to the specific instance of the French Huguenots of the sixteenth and seventeenth centuries. French and English dictionaries continued to define 'refugees' in such a way, and German dictionaries only contained the French word *réfugié*, again referring only to the Huguenots; it was only after World War I, around the time of the first instruments of international refugee law, that *flüchtling* came into use designating refugees in general.[3] The word itself is derived from the French verb *se réfugier*, which means simply to seek shelter from danger or even just something unpleasant.[4] Even today, other languages use terms that suggest a similarly broad understanding of the concept of a refugee. For example, the literal meaning of *flüchtling* is a person in flight, whereas in Japanese, *nanmin* translates as a person in difficulty. Beyond the specific use of the word 'refugee', as we saw in Part I, a very wide variety of circumstances have given rise to the need for asylum. It is only when law becomes concered with the question that the concept becomes fixed within certain boundaries.

Nergis Canefe argues that international refugee law has essentially comprised two different stages.[5] The first was inaugurated by the Treaty of Westphalia and ended around the time of World War I. There then followed an interregnum where the international regime was in crisis and flux. The second regime of international refugee law dates from 1951, with the Convention and its 1967 Protocol at its heart. The Westphalian regime was characterized by the principle

---

3   Marrus MR, *The Unwanted: European Refugees from the First World War Through the Cold War* (Temple University, 2002), 9.
4   Larousse defines the verb as: 'Se retirer en un lieu ou auprès de quelqu'un pour échapper à un danger ou à une chose désagréable'.
5   Canefe N, 'The fragemented nature of the international refugee regime and its consequences: a comparative analysis of the applications of the 1951 Convention' in James C Simeon (ed), *Critical Issues in International Refugee Law: Strategies Towards Interpretative Harmony* (CUP, 2010), 182.

that state sovereignty entailed the right of states to grant asylum to nationals of other states without fear of reprisals from the state of origin. Canefe argues that this regime was largely defined by a *laissez-faire* attitude, i.e. there was very little in the way of positive norms in international law regarding the rights of refugees and the practice of asylum, except for the negative obligation not to interfere in the rights of states to grant asylum to whomever they so wished. The second regime, the one that now polices a division between the 'genuine' refugee and others, has been far more comprehensive, revolving around a detailed set of definitions and rights.

James C. Hathaway opens his discussion of the origins of international refugee law by laying out the common sense definition of a refugee: 'a person compelled to flee his State of origin or residence due to political troubles, persecution, famine or natural disaster'.[6] Certainly this is far broader than any legal definition that we have had, for it includes economic refugees (victims of famine) as well as victims of natural disasters. However, it remains restricted to those fleeing across borders. The refugee of modernity is indeed inextricably tied to the question of the state. This is another clear divide from the tradition of asylum, which made no distinction on this question. In fact, most asylees of the past were from the local area or from within the state in which asylum was sought. The Ancient Greek *asylia* or church sanctuary would therefore not have fitted within the contemporary notion of asylum. Neither would the Cathar refugees from the Church's inquisition, who moved with ease across the Pyrenees and back again, often as part of the annual transhumance, as well as further afield to Valencia, Majorca, Lombardy and Sicily.[7] As both Patricia Tuitt and Caren Kaplan have discussed, the question of movement as determinative of the refugee is highly contingent, particularly in the modern context.[8] And of course, the tens of millions of Internally Displaced Persons (IDPs) today are testament to the restrictiveness of that particular aspect of the refugee definition. The growing phenomenon of 'climate refugees' also demonstrates how exclusionary notions, not just of cross-border movement but also of persecution, deny protection to a great many who need it.[9] But for roughly the first four centuries of the modern nation-state until 1920, 'there was little concern to delimit the scope of the refugee definition'.[10] As Terje Einarsen points out, 'persecuted people before the

---

6 Hathaway JC, 'The Evolution of Refugee Status in International Law: 1920–1950' (1984), 33, *International and Comparative Law Quarterly*, 348, 348.

7 Ladurie ELE, *Montaillou: Cathars and Catholics in a French Village 1294–1324* (Barbara Bray tr, Penguin, 1980), 187, 195, 238, 246, 286.

8 Tuitt P, 'Rethinking the refugee concept' in Frances Nicholson and Patrick Twomey (eds), *Refugee Rights and Realities: Evolving International Concepts and Regimes* (Cambridge University, 1999); Kaplan C, *Questions of Travel: Postmodern Discourses of Displacement* (Duke University, 1996).

9 For a detailed discussion and defence of the term 'climate refugees', see Kent A and Behrman S, *Facilitating the Resettlement and Rights of Climate Refugees: An Argument for Developing Existing Principles and Practices* (Taylor and Francis, 2018), chapter 2.

10 Hathaway (n 7), 348.

20th century often simply moved to new countries or even new continents without many immigration restrictions'.[11] Erskine May, in his *Constitutional History of England*, writes:

> The Crown indeed had claimed the right of ordering aliens to withdraw from the realm: but this prerogative had not been exercised since the reign of Elizabeth (viz. in 1571, 1574 and 1575). From that period, through civil wars and revolutions, a disputed succession, and treasonable plots against the state, no foreigners had been disturbed.[12]

However, as the system of nation-states developed and spread from the seventeenth century onwards, and along with it a theory and practice of international law as the law of states, so the concept of asylum was turned inside out. Instead of being a space beyond the law, it became a right of states *vis-à-vis* one another, with the refugee reduced merely to a 'unit of displacement' between them.[13]

11 Einarsen T, 'Drafting history of the 1951 Convention and the 1967 Protocol' in Andreas Zimmermann (ed), *The 1951 Convention Relating to the Status of Refugees and its 1967 Protocol: A Commentary* (OUP, 2011), 43.

12 Quoted in Greig DW, 'The Protection of Refugees and Customary International Law' (1978), 8, *Australian Year Book of International Law*, 108, 120.

13 The phrase is taken from, Goodwin-Gill G, 'Refugee identity and protection's fading prospect' in Frances Nicholson and Patrick Twomey (eds), *Refugee Rights and Realities: Evolving International Concepts and Regimes* (Cambridge University, 1999), 246.

3 The nation-state origins of refugee law

The modern law of asylum as the right of states

The founding theorists of international law laid out certain key principles in relation to asylum, which have remained at the heart of refugee law today. Hugo Grotius sought asylum in France and was one of the first modern jurists to call for a right of asylum to be recognised in international law.[1] Yet, he qualified this by denying such a right to the undeserving, namely those guilty of having done something 'injurious to human society or to other men'.[2] Christian Wolff sets out a natural law by which 'in primitive society any man is allowed to dwell anywhere in the world', while on the other hand considering the right of the sovereign to decide 'whether or not he desires to receive an outsider into his state'.[3] On balance, the right of the state in civilised society must be preferred: 'if admittance is refused, that must be endured'.[4] Samuel von Pufendorf believed that it was a matter exclusively for the state to decide whether or not it was in its own interests to allow entry for the refugee in question.[5] And Emmerich de Vattel perhaps expressed the problem from the point of states most clearly when he wrote:

> [I]f in the abstract this right is a necessary and perfect one . . . it is only an imperfect one relative to each individual country; for . . . every Nation has the right to refuse to admit an alien into its territory when to do so would expose it to evident danger or cause it serious trouble . . . By reason of its natural liberty it is for each Nation to decide whether it is or is not in a

---

1   Grotius H, *The Law of War and Peace* (Francis W Kelsey tr, Bobbs-Merrill, 1962), ii.2.XVI.
2   Ibid ii.21.V.
3   Wolff C, *Jus Gentium Methodo Scientifica Petractatum: Volume Two* (Joseph Horace Drake [trans], Clarendon Press, 1934), s 147, 148.
4   Ibid 148.
5   Quoted in Einarsen T, 'Drafting history of the 1951 Convention and the 1967 Protocol' in Andreas Zimmermann (ed), *The 1951 Convention Relating to the Status of Refugees and its 1967 Protocol: A Commentary* (OUP, 2011), 42.

position to receive an alien. Hence an exile has no absolute right to choose a country at will and settle himself there as he pleases.[6]

Grahl-Madsen writes that both Grotius and Vattel, although arguing from quite different standpoints, recognised a ' "right of asylum" for the individual, but it was undoubtedly what Vattel called an "imperfect right", meaning that the corresponding obligation depends upon the judgement of him who owes it'.[7] This may be so, but if the individual right of asylum is imperfect, then the classic authors on international law are much clearer in asserting a far more 'perfect' and secure right of asylum when understood as that which belongs to the state. Grahl-Madsen recognises this when citing Vattel: a state is 'free to act as it pleases, so far as its acts do not affect the perfect rights of another Nation'.[8] Léopold Bolesta-Koziebrodzki has pointed out that the right of asylum is founded upon the inherent right of the state to territorial integrity and the right to admit into its domain whomever it so wishes,[9] whereas in *Réfugiés et Sans-Papiers: La République face au droit d'asile*, Gérard Noiriel identifies the modern principle of state sovereignty as the link between the destruction of the ancient sanctuaries and the modern law of asylum:

> From the beginning of the 16th century, the right of asylum became the prerogative of royal power. It presupposed the sovereignty of the refugee's state of origin (the principle of territorial plenitude excluding the possibility of the domestic spaces which had constituted the religious refuges of earlier centuries) and the sovereignty of the state of reception (which alone decided whether or not to receive the exile). The right of asylum was therefore a consequence and not a limitation of the principle of sovereignty.[10]

Henri Coursier describes very well the transformation following the French Revolution:

> With the new regime, the right of asylum ceases to be a right which the person can claim, relying on the principles of humanity as being above the law of the State, to become instead a right which, while it operates in the interests of the individual on the basis of humanitarian norms, is one that the state asserts for itself.[11]

6 Quoted in Grahl-Madsen A, *The Status of Refugees in International Law: Volume Two* (AW Sijthoff, 1972), 14.
7 Ibid 16.
8 Ibid.
9 Bolesta-Koziebrodzki L, *Le Droit d'asile* (AW Sythoff, 1962), 79.
10 Noiriel G, *Réfugiés et sans-papiers: La République face au droit d'asile XIXe–XXe siècles* (Hachette, 1998), 20, footnote 1.
11 Coursier H, 'Restauration du droit d'asile' (1950), 32, *Revue Internationale de la Croix-Rouge et Bulletin international des Sociétés de la Croix-Rouge*, 909, 911.

Put another way, Richard J. Fruchterman has written that the birth of the modern age brought with it 'a shift away from the idea that the individual had a right to territorial asylum and toward the concept that it was solely the right of the State to grant or deny territorial asylum'.[12] In the original draft of the 1951 Convention, what is now paragraph 4 of the Preamble referred to the 'right of asylum' and the consequent burden it placed on states of refuge. During the *travaux préparatoires*, concern was expressed by a number of delegates at this wording. But the President of the conference reassured them that the right being described was that of the state to grant asylum, not of the individual who benefits from it.[13] María-Teresa Gil-Bazo has presented a revealing study on how asylum has become written into a number of constitutions around the world today, and argues that asylum now has the status of a general principle in international law.[14] Yet, insofar as this may be true, it still represents a break from pre-modern asylum, as its modern guise is in the sole gift of the state, not a space outside of it.

Noiriel sheds light on a crucial difference between the reception of refugees under the *ancien regime* and that which emerged following the French Revolution. During the earlier period, the reception of refugees was not an area in which the state had a particularly strong role. Instead, the reception and support of refugees was decided within local communities, guilds and the like, with the active participation of the refugees themselves in reconstituting their social lives within the host community. As such, asylum still retained a distance from the sovereign legal order. By contrast, following the Revolution, the state began to assume the sole role in managing and regulating the reception of refugees. This was the inevitable result of the modern ideology of power organised vertically and centralised in the state.[15]

Granting asylum had been a common practice under the monarchy through-out the eighteenth century, particularly for Catholics fleeing repression in the Protestant countries. However, the role of royal power was not to determine who should or should not be granted asylum, but rather was to decide on the distribution of public monies to support the asylees. It was only with the advent of the republican idea of the indissolubility between state and people that it became the business of the state to cast its eyes upon the person of the refugee.[16] Yet, for much of the nineteenth century, just as in broader terms France continued to wrestle with a forward-looking republicanism constrained by repeated

---

12 Fruchterman RL, 'Asylum: Theory and Practice' (1972), 26, *Judge Advocate General Journal*, 169, 171.

13 Weis P, *The Refugee Convention, 1951: The Travaux Préparatoires Analysed with a Commentary by Dr Paul Weiss* (Cambridge University, 1995), 30. The final draft, to clarify the point, refers to the 'grant of asylum'.

14 Gil-Bazo M-T, 'Asylum as a General Principle of International Law' (2015), 27, *International Journal of Refugee Law*, 3.

15 Noiriel (n 10), 45.

16 Ibid 35.

throwbacks to the old society, so too an encroaching biopolitical paradigm only gradually edged out the more open practice of asylum that had hitherto existed.

In France and elsewhere, the advent of the modern nation-state reframed asylum as a species of immigration policy, with a focus on the need to account for and manage population flows. This was not a sudden development, but one that gestated over the course of the nineteenth century and into the early twentieth century, culminating in the rapid spread of border controls, and the equally rapid spread of refugee law that resulted from those controls in the years surrounding World War I. The concerns that drove this process were dominated by two elements of the biopolitical paradigm: the effective management of population as a source of wealth and the use of a security discourse to control and monitor population flows. Furthermore, a managerial rather than a political framework increasingly came to dominate asylum policy. What should become clear in this and the following chapter is that far from international refugee law acting as a break on this phenomenon, as is commonly supposed, it regularised and normalised it.

It was the Montagnard Constitution of 24 June 1793 that proclaimed for the first time in modern law the right of asylum. Article 120 declared that the French Nation 'serves as a place of refuge for all who, on account of liberty, are banished from their native country. These it refuses to deliver up to tyrants'. Yet, already the legal right is circumscribed: flight on grounds of political or religious persecution alone defines those as worthy of asylum. Moreover, we find here too a distinction drawn between those who are fleeing due to their adherence to liberal democratic principles and others less deserving. Thus, some of the key frameworks of the modern legal definition of the refugee are present at its inception. It is sometimes claimed that the 1793 legislation was merely a secular updating of the ancient custom of sanctuary.[17] But, as we have already seen, that tradition had a quite different character, based on different criteria and conceived of as spaces beyond the realm of sovereign power and law. Moreover, as generous as it was, this Constitution, although endorsed overwhelmingly by a referendum based on universal male suffrage, was suspended by the Convention on the grounds that the emergency war situation made its implementation impossible for the time being. In fact, following the Thermidorian Reaction of the following year, it was effectively abolished. This early attempt at a relatively generous refugee law thus fell victim to the emerging security paradigm. So this often quoted instrument of refugee law was never actually in force. Nonetheless, Article 120 does reflect the earlier tradition in being more openly political, an aspect that would be denied or covered over by later refugee law, concerned as it is with a supposedly universal concept.

---

17 Ponty J, *L'immigration dans les textes: France, 1789–2002* (Belin, 2003), 13; Noiriel (n 10), 307.

The United Kingdom effectively had no border controls right up until the seminal 1905 *Aliens Act*.[18] Bernard Porter has described the period prior to that as being one where 'asylum was maintained not by law, but by the absence of laws'.[19] Indeed, prior to the eighteenth century, there was very little legislation regulating entry, settlement or even the grant of citizenship.[20] Dallal Stevens summarises asylum policy at this time as having been based on the recognition of 'genuine suffering, religious affinity and politics'.[21] In 1708, the Act for Naturalisation of Foreign Protestants, introduced as a response to the huge numbers of Huguenot arrivals in the previous decades, actually relaxed what controls existed. The provisions of the Act required the refugee only to offer proof that they had taken the sacrament in a Protestant or Reformed church in the preceding 3 months.[22] However, Parliament was clear in laying out its motives for such openness, which expresses clearly one of the key aspects of Foucault's biopolitical paradigm: 'the increase of people is a means of advancing the wealth and strength of a nation'.[23] This Act was repealed just 3 years later, with Parliament declaring that it had since become apparent that the new arrivals had contributed to 'the discouragement of natural-born subjects and to the detriment of the trade and wealth thereof'.[24] The issue of asylum would return to the United Kingdom in the context of a percieved national security threat in the years following the French Revolution.

For the remainder of this chapter, we will explore how the refugee subject emerged through the prism of developments in three countries: France, United Kingdom and United States. They provide useful case studies for three reasons. First, they are all historic countries of asylum. Second, they all played a central role in the development of international refugee law in the twentieth century, as discussed in the next chapter. Third, two of them – United States and France – have become the sites of significant resistance movements against the legal framing of asylum, as discussed in Part III.

The emerging security paradigm – stage one: fallout from the French Revolution

The political instability unleashed by the events of 1789 and the Napoleonic Wars led to some legislative controls in the 1790s. The security paradigm emerged

---

18 Aliens Act 1905, 5 Edw. VII, c 12.
19 Porter B, *The Refugee Question in Mid-Victorian Politics* (Cambridge University, 1979), 3; See also Noiriel (n 10), 307, footnote 1.
20 Kershaw R and Pearsall M, *Immigrants and Aliens: A Guide to Sources on UK Immigration and Citizenship* (2nd edn, National Archives, 2004), 8.
21 Stevens D, *UK Asylum Law and Policy: Historical and Contemporary Perspectives* (Sweet and Maxwell, 2004), 7.
22 Kershaw and Pearsall (n 23), 9.
23 7 Ann, c 5.
24 10 Ann, c 5.

on both sides of the conflict. Already in 1797, for example, in France, at the height of the Thermidorian reaction, a law was passed allowing for the expulsion of aliens whose continued presence was considered likely to upset '*l'ordre et la tranquilité publique*'.[25] However, most of the running in the development of law in this respect took place in the United Kingdom. The Aliens Acts of 1793 and 1798 made it mandatory for all immigrants to register on arrival at ports of entry.[26] These registration documents contained their names, occupations, ranks and addresses, and had to be lodged with the local authorities, usually in the form of the local justices of the peace. This system, in turn, made possible for the first time a systematic collection of data by the government. For example, in 1797, the government issued a directive to local authorities calling for the reporting of all aliens who had arrived in the previous 5 years. The reporting of aliens was also extended under the legislation to householders who gave lodgings to these foreigners. Moreover, all aliens had to apply for passports should they wish to leave London, and faced restrictions as to where they could live outside the capital. In order to facilitate the huge growth in the control and management of immigrants, a whole new government department was set up: the Aliens Office. One of its primary goals was to ascertain from local authorities the character of any and all aliens.[27] In a precursor of things to come, these pieces of legislation, enacted as an emergency response to war conditions in the wake of the French Revolution, ended up having a far longer life beyond the emergency situation. So, for example, Vaughan Bevan writes of the 1793 Act:

> The Act's real importance lay in the fact that so many of the features of modern control appeared within it e.g. entry via designated ports, licences to enter, a central system of record keeping including reports of hoteliers, control on internal movement by passports and an unfettered and expeditious power of removal.[28]

In addition, the overall picture is one that sees the yoking together of national security fears with the arrival of refugees, another leading trope of modernity that continues to dominate the issue of asylum today. This aspect becomes most evident in the 1798 Act, which sought to toughen the restrictions imposed by the Act of 1793, specifically targeting asylum-seekers: 'Refuge and Asylum which . . . have been granted to persons flying from the oppression and tyranny exercised in France . . . may . . . be abused by persons coming to this Kingdom for purposes dangerous to the interests and safety thereof'.[29] Among other things, this Act also made it compulsory for aliens to produce their licence of residence to the

---

25   *Loi relative aux passports*, No. 1502, 28 Vendémiaire An VI (19 October 1797), Article 7.
26   Aliens Act 1793, 33 Geo. III c 21; Aliens Act 1798, 38 Geo. III, c 50.
27   Kershaw and Pearsall (n 23), 45.
28   Bevan V, *The Development of British Immigration Law* (Croon Helm, 1986), 60.
29   Aliens Act 1798, 38 Geo. III c 50.

local magistrates on demand,[30] and allowed indefinite detention of any alien deemed to be a 'dangerous person'.[31] These measures, so familiar to us in the present scene of refugee law, are creatures of early modernity, and not such recent developments as is commonly supposed.

These provisions were repealed following Napoleon's defeat in 1814, only to be reintroduced a year later. Then in 1816, a further Act was passed.[32] This contained many of the original provisions of the earlier acts, only this time the register of aliens was to be compiled and kept by central government rather than by local authorities. This legislation only applied to new arrivals and not to those already in the United Kingdom. However, in 1826, the Aliens Registration Act extended such controls over already settled immigrants.[33] It required all aliens to register with the government giving their personal details within 14 days of the passing of the Act. Following this, they were then required to report their address to the Aliens Office every 6 months. This Act was later repealed and replaced by a new Act in 1836, which abolished many of the more onerous requirements such as registration with the Aliens Office.[34] Indeed, the main provision that remained, for an initial declaration on arrival in port, was hardly enforced. In 1842, for example, some 11,600 aliens arrived in the United Kingdom, with only 6,000 registering. In some areas, the proportions were even lower; in Hull, 794 arrived and just 1 registered, while in Liverpool, no lists were kept at all.[35] A Select Committee report in 1843 noted that: 'it is very generally disregarded by Foreigners and it is never enforced by the authorities'.[36] There are a few possible reasons why the draconian approach to asylum and immigration should have apparently abated by the 1830s. The war fever and concomitant fears for national security of the preceding decades had receded. Bevan argues that the marked liberalisation of immigration controls in mid-nineteenth-century Britain was largely down to Victorian self-confidence, and a recognition that immigrants provided 'vitality . . . to an already energetic population'.[37] Equally, it has been argued that the prevailing sentiment of *laissez-faire* made the idea of state controls *per se* unpalatable.[38] In essence, while immigration policy was fairly liberal in the United Kingdom, it was a function of the priorities and ideology of the state at the time.

With a mass immigration of Poles in 1830, France began to number its asylees in the thousands rather than the hundreds, and within a decade, there were some

30 Ibid s 15.
31 Ibid s 16.
32 Regulations of Aliens Act 1816, 56 Geo. III c 86.
33 Regulations of Aliens Act 1826, 7 Geo. IV c 46.
34 Aliens Act 1836, 6 & 7 Will. IV c 11.
35 Kershaw and Pearsall (n 23), 49.
36 Cited in Bevan (n 31), 64.
37 Ibid 64.
38 Ibid 65; Foot P, *Immigration and Race in British Politics* (Penguin, 1965), 83; Porter (n 22), 93–94.

30,000 refugees residing in France.[39] There was widespread political solidarity, with the Polish exiles among the population. As a result, a great many committees and support groups sprang up to welcome and support their integration into local communities.[40] By this time, the Republic had been replaced by the restoration of the Bourbon monarchy, and the arguments for granting asylum rested on the tradition of hospitality under the *ancien regime*. But the logic of biopolitical law remained a consistent thread. On the basis of preserving public order, laws were passed in 1832 and 1834, giving the state the power to assign places of residence to the exiles on pain of arrest and deportation.[41] Janine Ponty suggests that these laws were partly in response to demands from other governments to move various of the refugees in France farther from the border, and to more isolated places, in order to prevent them from being able to remain in regular contact with subversives who had remained in their countries. One such request, for example, involved a demand by Metternich regarding the Italian radical republican Giuseppe Mazzini.[42] Grahl-Madsen points out that the 1832 law was the first to 'institute "internal measures" in lieu of expulsion'.[43] In other words, it created the legal framework under which the sovereign order extended its grip over the refugee rather than merely abandoning them. The discussions in the National Assembly at this time again reflected, only in stronger terms, the concerns of the rights of the nation-state in relation to the granting of asylum. The law of 1832 gave the government the right to expel refugees 'if it judged their presence as likely to disturb law and order'.[44] Nonetheless, the Minister still claimed that the offering of asylum was based on 'conscience' and not a 'system'.[45] So at this stage, the logic of asylum was facing both ways: forwards to the modern rights of the nation-state and backwards to the arbitrary and sentimental norms of the *ancien regime*.

Along with the growing claim of the state to the regulation of asylum and a concern with the burden of financing support for asylees, so also began a concern with determining the 'genuineness' of the refugees. In 1832, Francois Guizot, a leading statesman of the period, called on the government to give assurances that refugees being granted public assistance had been 'really compelled to leave their countries as a result of political events' and were not 'vagabonds', criminals or merely 'unfortunates'.[46] Indeed, the question of who was legitimately a refugee dominated discussions in the National Assembly on the 1832 legislation.[47]

---

39 Noiriel (n 10), 37; Ponty (n 20), 27.
40 Noiriel (n 10), 63–64.
41 *Loi relative aux Etrangers réfugiés qui résideront en France*, 21 avril 1832, Article 1; Circulaire du ministre de l'Intérieur adressée aux préfets, 5 septembre 1834.
42 Ponty (n 20), 28.
43 Grahl-Madsen (n 6), 21.
44 *Loi relative aux Etrangers réfugiés qui résideront en France*, 21 avril 1832, Article 2.
45 Noiriel (n 10), 40.
46 Ibid 42.
47 Ponty (n 20), 26.

Yet it remained the case for some time that the law was imposed only very rarely.[48] In the 5 years after the law of 1832, just 4 refugees out of a total of 13,000 were actually expelled.[49] In general, as Catherine Wihtol de Wenden has pointed out, state controls on immigration were so lax that it was not clear to anyone, even to the authorities, until the middle of the nineteenth century just how many non-nationals resided in France.[50] For example, it was only in 1851 that nationality of residents became a measurement in the census. Nonetheless, Noiriel argues that this period marks the beginning of a paradigm, whereby the 'French state imposes its law from the outset on those [refugees] whom it receives (*qu'il accueille*)'.[51]

A major shift in French immigration policy came with the move away from the Napoleonic focus on the *jus sanguinis* towards a policy of *jus soli* after 1851. Although this opened up the possibility of citizenship to a wider class of persons, this shift in policy also represented a 'nationalisation' and juridification of the issue, for it made the border the determining aspect in the granting of citizenship. The impetus for this was grounded in the realities of France's transformation into an industrialised country in need of an influx of labour rather 'than for any idealistic concerns about liberty, equality and commitment to the land of asylum'.[52] A particularly draconian piece of legislation of this period is the law of 3 December 1849, enacted in the wake of Louis Bonaparte's counter-revolution. This gave the Minister of the Interior the right to order the deportation of any alien.[53]

Yet the determination of immigration status and support remained somewhat open. Noiriel has analysed in detail the archives of communications between refugees and local and national administration during the middle of the nineteenth century. What is most notable, compared to today, is the directness of appeal couched as it was in terms of claims to Christian charity and sympathy. This was largely due to the wide measure of discretion in the process of granting relief, and the absence of abstract criteria.[54] As such, claims for assistance were always contestable. It was also testimony to the holdover from an earlier age in which Christian mercy and charity held sway. The result was that the coldness of a more formal bureaucratic and legal process was much less than it would later be. Moreover, there was less mediation between the experiences and needs of the refugee and the authorities granting assistance.

48 Marrus M, *The Unwanted: European Refugees in the 20th Century* (Temple University, 2002), 16.

49 Noiriel (n 10), 62.

50 de Wenden CW, *Les immigrés et la politique: cent cinquante ans d'évolution* (Sciences Po, 1988), 18.

51 Noiriel G, *Le Creuset français. Histoire de l'immigration XIXe – XXe siècle* (Seuil, 1988), 335.

52 Silverman M, *Deconstructing the Nation: Immigration, Racism, and Citizenship in Modern France* (Routledge, 1992), 146–147.

53 *Loi du 3 décembre 1849 sur la naturalisation et le séjour des étrangers en France*, Article 7.

54 Noiriel (n 10), 60–61.

The US experience

Many of the same issues that drove the development of asylum and immigration policy in Europe have their echoes in the United States during the same period. Erika Lee summarises her historical study of US immigration policy by noting how across the developed world the legal framework for refugee admissions has been deployed as a key plank in the control of immigration.[55] The Unites States is, of course, known as a nation of immigrants, in particular of refugees. The pilgrims fleeing religious intolerance in the seventeenth and eighteenth centuries have achieved immortality as founders of what was later to become the first modern liberal republic. And yet, within the first decade of the republic's founding, anti-alien sentiment was rife and Congress enacted its first immigration controls. This had already been presaged in Article 1, Section 8 of the US Constitution (1787), which among other things granted the federal government the power to 'establish a uniform Rule of Naturalization'. First came the 1790 Naturalization Act, which on the one hand granted citizenship to all 'free white persons' who had resided in the Unites States for a minimum of 2 years, while at the same time explicitly excluding people of colour, whether African-Americans or Native Americans.[56] Although this Act dealt only with the grant of citizenship and not entry into the country *per se*, Lee argues that this effectively marked the beginning of the US government's 'gatekeeping function', decades before the first systematic immigration controls some 80 years later.[57] The Alien Act 1798 gave the President the power to deport any non-citizens 'as he shall judge dangerous to the peace and safety of the United States'.[58] Already in 1801, in his presidential inauguration address, Thomas Jefferson lamented these early immigration controls with special reference to the plight of refugees:

> And shall we refuse to the unhappy fugitives from distress that hospitality which savages of the wilderness extended to our fathers arriving in this land? Shall oppressed humanity find no asylum in this globe?[59]

The 1798 Act was to be the last set of federal immigration controls until 1875. However, in the 1830s, the United States had it first real test in receiving large numbers of refugees. In common with France, the United States became one of the main destinations for Poles fleeing Russian repression. They were welcomed

---

55 Lee E, 'A nation of immigrants and a gatekeeping nation: American immigration law and policy, 1875-Present' in Reed Ueda (ed), *A Companion to American Immigration* (Blackwell Publishing, 2006), 29.

56 An Act to Establish an Uniform Rule of Naturalization, 26 March 1790 [First Congress, Session II, chapter 3. 1790].

57 Lee (n 58), 9.

58 Section 1, An Act Concerning Aliens, 25 June 1798 [Fifth Congress, Session 2, chapter 54, 1798].

59 Cited in Hutchinson EP, *Legislative History of American Immigration Policy 1798–1965* (University of Pennsylvania, 1981), 17

as ambassadors of the republican ideal escaping Old World absolutism. In common with the political dynamics of Victorian Britain and the Cold War a century later, great ideological battles opened up the space of asylum. An act was passed in May 1834, granting 500 acres of land to each Polish refugee at the minimum price of $1.25 per acre, specifying that the land in question would be in Illinois and Michigan.[60] Political solidarity was thus married to a desire to see an influx of White Europeans who could cultivate the large expanse of land in the Mid-West. States in that part of the country positively encouraged immigration so as to spur population growth.[61] Indeed, economic concerns were at the forefront when in the following year there were attempts to force the exiles to both live on and cultivate these gifts of land. The biopolitical concern with managing population as a source of wealth is particularly evident here. Nevertheless, there were no controls on the actual entry into the country of refugees, either for the Poles or the many German liberals who arrived following the defeat of the 1848 revolutions.[62] The federal government, in fact, played little role in processing immigrants at all; this was left primarily to the states. E.P. Hutchinson points out that immigration controls were so negligible throughout much of the nineteenth century that 'the question of differential treatment for refugees did not really arise except when public opinion and sympathy were aroused as in the case of the Polish exiles'.[63] And in that case, the effect of public opinion was to give *added* assistance to the refugees. One reason for the United State's generosity during this period, which has echoes in Victorian Britain's motives for its hospitality, might have been because the arrival of refugees from the Old World 'reinforced the American sense of the superiority of their own government and political institutions', which would have had significant purchase at a time when the country was still a relatively weak and fledgling state.[64]

The point at which immigration controls began to really tighten came with the arrivals of large numbers of Chinese immigrant workers in the 1860s and 1870s. A series of restrictions on their entry culminated in the notorious Chinese Exclusion Act 1882, at first a temporary piece of legislation, but eventually made permanent and not repealed until 1943.[65] Of course, one of the key motivations behind these measures was a barely concealed racism. However, these new laws had a far wider resonance. As Lee writes, they:

> set in motion new bureaucracies, modes, and technologies of immigration regulation, such as federal immigration officials who inspected and processed newly arriving foreigners, government-issued identity and residence

---

60 Ibid 24.
61 Lee (n 58), 9.
62 Hutchinson (n 62), 522.
63 Ibid 523.
64 Ibid.
65 Chinese Exclusion Act of 1882, 126 (22 Stat. 58).

documents, such as U.S. passports and "green cards", and further regulations such as illegal immigration and deportation policies.[66]

Previously, when the United States had needed immigrant labour, in particular relying on Chinese labour to build the Transcontinental Railway, immigration had been encouraged.[67] But with the completion of work on the railway and with economic depression, there was a complete reversal of policy, both in terms of the Chinese Exclusion Act and the Immigration Act introduced later the same year.[68] Other factors were also at work too. Between 1880 and 1920, 23.5 million immigrants, many of them refugees, arrived in the United States. This huge number of new arrivals, and their multi-ethnic makeup, led to an 'explosive xenophobic reaction based on racial and religious prejudice, fears of radicalism, and class conflict'.[69] This came at the same time as a new national identity was being forged which tied the question of immigration to sovereignty; the authority of the state was becoming in the United States, as well as elsewhere, measured by the extent of border control. Moreover, post-Civil War, the federal government was immensely strengthened and was thus able to deploy its much greater administrative muscle to manage and control immigration into the vast continental United States.[70]

One Chinese worker, Chae Chan Ping, challenged his exclusion under the 1882 Act, having lived and worked in the country for 12 years. The Supreme Court in its ruling on his case declared:

> That the Government of the United States, through the action of the legislative department can exclude aliens from its territory is a proposition which we do not think open to controversy. Jurisdiction over its own territory to that extent is an incident of every independent nation. It is a part of its independence. If it could not exclude aliens it would be to that extent subject to the control of another power.[71]

Until then, the question of admission had mainly been one for the individual states depending on the port of entry.[72] It is only during this period, as with the United Kingdom and France, that the national state begins to centralise and formalise immigration controls. For certain refugees, however, there remained some level of protection. For example, in an echo of the common exception to

---

66 Lee (n 58), 11.
67 Koulish R, *Immigration and American Democracy: Subverting the Rule of Law* (Routledge, 2010), 31–32.
68 Chinese Exclusion Act of 1882, 126 (22 Stat. 58); Immigration Act of 1882, 376 (22 Stat. 214).
69 Lee (n 58), 10.
70 Ibid.
71 *Chae Chan Ping v. United States* [1889] 130 U.S. 581, per Justice Field.
72 Koulish (n 70), 128.

extradition agreements, the compulsory deportation of foreign criminals man-dated under the Immigration Act 1882 exempted those convicted of a political offence.[73] This exemption was strengthened by the 1891 Immigration Act, which made it clear that political offences might be so, even if the state from which the refugee had fled claimed the offence committed to have been simply a common crime.[74] While of course this was, in principle, of benefit to many refugees, it did also mark a distinction between deserving and undeserving migrants/refugees in law. The subsequent history of the political offence exception bears out how once such a separate category was created, it became easy for the law to gradually wittle it down.[75]

The 1891 Act, through the creation of the Bureau of Immigration, also vested sole control of immigration matters in the federal government, thus marking yet another stage in the centralisation of border controls, and the effective tying together of state sovereignty with immigration policy.[76] Writing in 1939, Louis Adamic observed that US immigration policy could be divided into four periods: 1) the period of colonisation prior to 1783; 2) more or less 'free immigration' from 1783 to 1830; 3) controls over immigration operating at the level of the states; and finally, 4) the period of federal controls over immigration beginning in 1882.[77] Adamic comments that the latter period is 'likely to continue indefinitely'; almost 80 years later, his prediction appears to have been confirmed.

Implanting regimes of control

Victorian Britain was not as liberal on immigration and asylum as is commonly assumed. Yes, it is true that legislation remained largely weak on the question, and it is a frequently remarked upon fact that not a single foreigner was deported by the authorities throughout the period. But it is also true that the state regularly sought to impose greater restrictions. What held it back most of the time was popular opposition to increased controls, born partly as a result of sympathy for the wave of political refugees from Poland, Hungary, France and Italy, and a proud self-image of the United Kingdom as a bulwark of liberalism against the

---

73 Section 4, Immigration Act of 1882, 376 (22 Stat. 214).
74 Section 1, Immigration Act of 1891, 551 (26 Stat. 1084).
75 The cases of Re: Castioni [1891] 1 Q.B. 149; Re:Meunier [1894] 2 Q.B. 415 are discussed subsequently in the UK context. In addition, further restrictions have been placed in the Swiss case *Ktir v. Ministere Public Federal* [1961] 34 ILR, and in the US case *Eain v. Wilkes* [1981] F.2d 504. Moreover, Article 1 of the 1977 European Convention on the Suppression of Terrorism excludes most acts associated with violent political resistance from the political offence exception, and the EU's Council Framework Decision of 13 June 2002 on the European arrest warrant and the surrender procedures between Member States 2002/584/JHA does not recognise the political offence exception at all.
76 Section 7, Immigration Act of 1891, 551 (26 Stat. 1084).
77 Adamic L, *America and the Refugee* (Public Affairs Committee, 1939), 6.

backward semi-feudal regimes of the continent.[78] However, in response to the outbreak of revolution across Europe in 1848, the government, citing claims of possible domestic insurrectionary activities, introduced a Bill that allowed for the removal of aliens in the interests of the 'preservation of the peace and tranquillity of the realm'.[79] Political instability at home as well as abroad gave an impetus (or possibly an excuse) for a renewed attempt at controls. It is significant that this Bill was announced just the day after one of the largest Chartist demonstrations.[80] The Bill became law, but the provisions for deportation were never acted upon and the Act lapsed after 2 years. Palmerston's government then introduced a *Conspiracy to Murder Bill* in 1858 seeking *inter alia* to increase the penalty for this offence from 2 years to life imprisonment and, of particular relevance for refugees, to extend the scope of the offence to cover conspiracies to commit murder abroad.[81] This last point was in direct response to the 'Orsini Plot' that had been revealed just a few weeks before the Bill was introduced in Parliament. The Italian nationalist Felice Orsini, who had taken asylum in the United Kingdom, had assembled bombs there that were later used in an assassination attempt upon Louis Napoleon. The perceived attack on political refugees contained in this Bill provoked rapid and widespread resistance, including petitions to Parliament and mass demonstrations. In quick succession, the Bill was abandoned and Palmerston's government collapsed. Then in 1870 came the *Extradition Act*, Section 3 of which effectively defined a *bona fide* refugee solely on the grounds of political persecution.[82] Even the scope of this 'political offence exception' in extradition proceedings was severely circumscribed in the cases of *Re: Castioni* [1891] and *Re: Meunier* [1894], which, respectively, excluded from this exception people who had instigated violent political acts outside of an already existing conflict and anarchists.[83]

So, in truth, in almost every decade from the 1830s through to the 1890s, the British state sought greater controls over immigration, largely in response to the claimed threat posed by political events abroad. It was instead popular opinion and agitation, coupled with an overarching ideology that posited the United Kingdom as the home of liberty amidst a Europe dominated by backward authoritarian regimes that kept the doors open. However, with the gradual spread of the modern liberal state in Italy, Germany and France and beyond, so this latter element held diminished value in political discourse. Cedric Thornberry identified a key element in the transformation of official attitudes post-1870:

> The succession to power of the bourgeois liberal refugee marked the demise of the romantic image of the alien as a popular British hero. In his stead

---

78 Porter (n 22), 124.
79 Aliens Act 1848, 11 Vic., c 20.
80 Bevan (n 31), 65, footnote 95.
81 Porter (n 22), 176.
82 Extradition Act 1870, 33 & 34 Vic., c 52.
83 *Re: Castioni* [1891] 1 Q.B. 149; *Re: Meunier* [1894] 2 Q.B. 415.

appeared a more sinister alien figure – saturnine and be-bombed – socialist, communist or anarchist. This was the new political deviant, and, an internationalist rather than a nationalist, he was stigmatised as the "enemy of all government". When Balfour in 1905 irreligiously said that the only right of asylum Britain had traditionally recognised was to let in people with whom we agreed he may have overstated his case – but there was a substantial grain of truth in what he said.[84]

Paul Foot makes a similar point, describing the openness of the United Kingdom to refugees such as Mazzini and Garibaldi who were seen by the British ruling class as 'fighting the same struggle . . . against feudalism and reaction', and in defence of liberal values.[85] But when in the later half of the century refugees bore the new revolutionary politics of socialism and anarchism, which were not in support of free trade and capitalism, but against it, then the refugee-as-hero was transformed into the refugee-as-threat.[86] Foot comments that the Liberals in Parliament 'favoured all political offenders with whose politics they agreed', and paints this as 'cynicism'.[87] But it could be looked at another way, as simply yet further testimony to the fact that, by definition, a judgement on giving asylum to political offenders involves, to some degree at least, viewing their political motives and practice as legitimate, and that as such asylum is contingent upon a subjective view of the refugee's motives. Certainly this was the basis on which the Huguenots had been received; and going much further back was also reflected in the sanctuary given by the Church to those resisting the Romans during the twilight of the Empire, and even further back to the granting of asylum to various leading political and military figures in Ancient Greece.

By the 1890s, the United States, like European states, saw anarchism as the big political threat. An attempt was made in 1894 to pass a Bill through Congress that sought *inter alia* to exclude anarchists from being granted asylum as political refugees. In addition, if anarchist aliens were convicted of a common crime in the United States, they could be deported.[88] The Bill failed, but it was a harbinger of things to come. By the turn of the century, the panic over anarchism, closely tied to whipped up concerns over immigration, came to a head following the assassination of President William McKinley by the anarchist Leon Czolgosz. Although Czolgosz was born in the United States, he was the child of Polish immigrants. On taking up office following the assassination, President Theodore Roosevelt made it clear that new controls targeting anarchist aliens would be pursued, as part of a package of comprehensive immigration controls:

84 Thornberry C, *The Stranger at the Gate: A Study of the Law on Aliens and Commonwealth Citizens* (The Fabian Society, 1964), 3.
85 Foot (n 41), 84–85.
86 Ibid 84.
87 Ibid 85.
88 Hutchinson (n 62), 112–113.

> I earnestly recommend to the Congress that in the exercise of its wise
> discretion it should take into consideration the coming to this country of
> anarchists or persons professing principles hostile to all government ...
> They and those like them should be kept out of this country; and if
> found here they should be promptly deported to the country whence they
> came.[89]

In the United Kingdom, the case of *Re: Meunier* [1894] targeted anarchists, and
from then on, a growing legal distinction was drawn between desirable and
undesirable categories of refugees.[90] Yet the development of immigration controls
was initially a slow process that progressed in fits and starts. In 1889, a House
of Commons Select Committee reported that controls were not necessary as the
numbers of aliens in Britain was 'not large enough to cause alarm'. However,
the Committee also 'contemplated the possibility of such legislation becoming
necessary in the future'.[91] From around this time, an anti-immigrant faction
began to cohere within Parliament, driven by fear of anarchism, and a large dose
of anti-Semitism. In 1894 and 1898, there were attempts to introduce legislation
to control the influx of mainly Jewish refugees from Eastern Europe, although
neither made it to the statute book.[92] Pressure from the reactionaries eventually
led the government to set up a Royal Commission on the Aliens Question. The
key recommendation of the Commission was that a distinction should be made
between 'desirable' and 'undesirable' immigrants. In this, the Commission was
heavily influenced by the recent advent of controls on a similar basis in Canada,
South Africa and the United States.[93] Moreover, the Commission argued that
the power to decide on this question should reside with immigration officers at
the ports of entry.[94] In other words, the decision on whom to admit should be
moved to the administrative sphere and depoliticised.

The Report was delivered in the middle of 1903. By the following year, the
Conservative government had a Bill described in the King's Speech as intended
to deal with 'the evils consequent on the entry of destitute aliens'.[95] At the same
time, the right-wing periodical, *National Review*, claimed that 'the so-called right
of asylum' had made the country 'the happy hunting-ground of foreign anarchists and assassins'.[96] The Liberal opposition submitted an amendment that,
while accepting the case for controls to limit poor people entering the country
unchecked, would ensure 'the retention of the principle of asylum for the victims

---

89 Cited in Ibid 127.
90 *Re: Meunier* [1894] 2 Q.B. 415
91 Quoted in Foot (n 41), 86.
92 Bevan (n 31), 67.
93 Ibid 69–70.
94 Foot (n 41), 91.
95 Quoted in Ibid 93.
96 Quoted in Glover D, *Literature, Immigration, and Diaspora in Fin-de-Siècle England:
   A Cultural History of the 1905 Aliens Act* (Cambridge University, 2012), 169.

of persecution'.[97] We find here already the circumscribing of asylum solely on grounds of persecution. But also the fundamental distinction between the deserving and the undeserving immigrant is accepted, even by those wary of immigration controls. In the face of attacks on asylum and what had hitherto been effective open borders, defenders of refugees crossed the Rubicon by making a claim for 'good' or 'genuine' refugees, distinguishing them from subversive or burdensome arrivals.

Due to concerted opposition to the Bill, it eventually fell. But the government brought forward a new Bill, which ended up on the statute books as the *Aliens Act* 1905, the first comprehensive legislation in the United Kingdom on immigration controls.[98] Although it was not as severe as the failed Bill of the previous year, it enshrined the principle in law of restricting the flow of undesirable immigrants. For example, entry for those who arrived by ship containing more than twenty third-class passengers was subject to contols. Moreover, inspection was only required for those in steerage, i.e. all those not travelling first class.[99] It thus demarcated the line between a poor immigrant mass on the one hand and well-heeled émigrés and travellers on the other. It further created a distinction between immigration and asylum, by stating that the latter was an ancient right to be preserved. Although the principle of asylum continued in theory to be respected, refugees would now find themselves having to be sieved through ever more extensive border controls. As such, they would have to justify themselves as genuine refugees, and over time, the principle of control would apply equally to them. This was evident at the outset. According to section 8(4) of the Act, the Home Secretary had absolute discretion in determining whether or not, for the purposes of extradition, the refugee was covered by the political exception. Crucially, refugees had, for the first time, to prove to the Immigration Board that they were genuine refugees.[100] A year after the passage of the Act, the Home Secretary of the new more sympathetic Liberal government felt compelled to issue a circular to the Immigration Board, 'expressing concern at the rigid application of the Act and hoping that the benefit of the doubt would be given to those alleging persecution and who were thus seeking refugee status'.[101] However, this entreaty appears to have had little or no effect. From 505 people admitted as refugees in 1906, the figure fell to 43 in 1907, and just 5 by 1910.[102]

Dallal Stevens writes that in relation to asylum, the impact of the 1905 Act was that it 'established an administrative and legal framework for deciding refugee cases'.[103] For Knox and Kushner, the 1905 Act 'undermined' the notion of 'free

---

97 Quoted in Foot (n 41), 94.
98 Aliens Act 1905, 5 Edw. VII, c 12.
99 Goodwin-Gill G, *International Law and the Movement of Persons between States* (OUP) 1978, 98.
100 Glover (n 99), 5; Marrus (n 51), 37.
101 Bevan (n 31), 72.
102 Glover (n 99), 165.
103 Stevens (n 24), 42.

entry for refugees'.[104] In the Privy Council case of *A.G. for Canada v. Cain*, heard just 1 year after the passing of the 1905 Act, Lord Atkinson clearly expressed the new legal paradigm attached to immigration, one which clearly echoed the reasoning in the *Chae Chan Ping* case in the United States two decades earlier:

> One of the rights possessed by the supreme power in every State is the right to refuse to permit an alien to enter that State, to annex what conditions it pleases to the permission to enter it, and to expel or deport from the State, at pleasure, even a friendly alien, especially if it considers his presence in the State opposed to its peace, order, and good government, or to its social or material interests.[105]

Insofar as the principle of asylum was upheld, debates and discussion around the Act had implanted the notion that asylum was a privilege granted by the state, rather than a right belonging to the refugee. For example, during the debate on the second reading of the Bill, the prime minister, Arthur Balfour, attempted to resist the claim of an inaliable right of asylum by arguing that, 'who is to be added to its community from outside, and under what conditions . . . is a final and indestructible right of every free community'.[106] Balfour repeated the sentiment in his winding-up speech on the third reading, arguing that the principle of 'hospitality' that underlie asylum was a mere 'virtue' that was otherwise not 'obligatory upon individuals or upon nations'.[107]

The emerging security paradigm – stage two: World War I

With the outbreak of World War I, whipped up fears about the 'enemy within' formed a background for furthe controls over the movements of migrants and refugees. As soon as war was declared, a decree was issued in France demanding that all resident aliens report to the local police with immediate effect.[108] In 1917, identity cards for foreign residents were inaugurated.[109] Up until 1917, immigrants in France only had to make a formal declaration at the local Mairie (council office) in order to legitimately live and work. However, a government decree published in that year introduced for the first time a residency permit for those foreigners who had been resident in France for at least 15 years. Smaïn Laacher describes this measure as an attempt by the government to monitor and control the movements of the immigrant population.[110] As we will see in the case of the United Kingdom and United States too, World War I and its aftermath gave an

---

104   Kushner T and Knox K, *Refugees in the Age of Genocide* (Frank Cass, 1999), 29.
105   *A.G. for Canada v. Cain* [1906] AC 542, at 546 per Lord Atkinson.
106   Glover (n 99), 143.
107   Ibid.
108   Wihtol de Wenden (n 53), 29.
109   *Décret du 2 avril 1917 portant création d'une carte d'identité à l'usage des étrangers.*
110   Laacher S, *Mythologie du Sans-papiers* (Le Cavalier bleu editions, 2009), 11.

impetus to a significant securitisation of asylum and immigration policy. Indeed, this period arguably marks a key stage in the evolution of the paradigm of the state of exception as the norm in general, and as regards immigration policy.

The outbreak of war in 1914 led to another qualitative shift in UK immigration law, following on from the 1905 Act. On August 5, the Aliens Restrictions Bill was introduced by the government. Its stated aim was 'in time of war or imminent national danger or great emergency to impose restrictions on aliens'.[111] Further, it would grant powers to the Home Secretary to prohibit aliens to enter or to deport them, and it required that all aliens in the country had to register with the police.[112] The Bill was passed through all its parliamentary stages within a single day. During the truncated 'debate', just one voice, that of the Labour MP Sir William Byles, was raised questioning the time limit of these 'dangerous powers'. He was shouted down from all sides of the House, and the Home Secretary assured him that the measures would end with the conclusion of the war.[113] The wide scope allowed under the rubric of 'national danger' and 'great emergency' meant that, in fact, this legislation remained in force for almost 60 years until the *Immigration Act* 1971 replaced it.[114] The state of exception as the norm was now in place in relation to all aliens including refugees, as the reserved provision for refugees contained in the 1905 Act was erased under the new Act. Over half a century later, in the *Soblen* case, the Court of Appeal held that the powers of the 1914 Act, as amended by the 1919 Act, to refuse admission to asylum-seekers, were indeed applicable even in peacetime.[115] Writing in 1963, Thornberry accurately states: 'The "emergency" of 1914 has never fully receded'.[116] And as Stevens notes, as a result of this wartime legislation, 'refugees and asylum seekers reverted to the status of "alien" and were no longer viewed as warranting exceptional treatment'.[117] The point is that once the law had assumed the right to decide on categories of 'refugee', 'immigrant', 'illegal alien', etc., it retained the prerogative to alter or subsume these categories into one another. The outbreak of war simply presented itself as an opportune time to exercise this prerogative.

The Belgian refugees, some 260,000 of them, who arrived in the United Kingdom in the early months of the war, were perhaps the first to feel the effects of this new legislative paradigm. They were generally welcomed, and it appears that little was done to ascertain whether they were 'genuine' refugees fleeing persecution.[118] However, one of the reasons we can be fairly precise on their

---

111 Aliens Restriction Act 1914, 4 & 5 Geo. 5, c 12.
112 Foot (n 41), 101.
113 Ibid.
114 Immigration Act 1971, c 77. The provisions of the 1914 Act were made permanent by the Aliens Restriction (Ammendment) Act 1919, 9 & 10 Geo. 5, c 92.
115 *R. v. Governor of Brixton Prison Ex p. Soblen* (No. 2) [1963] 2 Q.B. 243.
116 Thornberry (n 87), 415.
117 Stevens (n 24), 54.
118 Ibid 44.

numbers was that for the first time a central government register was compiled of all of their details. Many of them were kept in camps, although at this stage, the camps were self-administered by the refugees themselves.[119] With the end of the war, however, the government was anxious to assure Parliament that 'pure Belgian refugees . . . are as rapidly as possible being returned to their own country'.[120] Then in 1920 came the Aliens Order, which effectively reintroduced many of the controls on immigrants already in the country that had been present in the legislation of the Napoleonic period, e.g. presentation of immigration papers to the police on demand, registration by hoteliers of alien guests.[121] According to one commentator, by the time of the arrival of large numbers of Jewish refugees in the 1930s, the 'principle and tradition of asylum were not so sacrosanct but had to be measured against the economic and social effects of large-scale immigration'.[122]

In the United States, the *Naturalization Act of 1906* was passed, which among other things excluded arrivals reliant on public welfare.[123] There was a provision that exempted from this prohibition those 'seeking admission to this country solely to avoid prosecution or punishment on religious or political grounds'. An amendment had inserted the word 'solely', thus making it clear that a high bar had to be reached for the test of deserving refugees.[124] The *Immigration Act of 1917* created a legal bar on a broad range of perceived subversives entering the country.[125] It also introduced a literacy test for the first time.[126] In 1921, the United States introduced the quota system for immigration. The *Emergency Quota Act* defied its nomenclature, with the quota system remaining the key plank of immigration policy to this day.[127] There was an attempt to include within the class of exceptions refugees fleeing religious persecution, but this

119 Kershaw and Pearsall (n 23), 27.
120 Home Secretary speaking in the debate on the 1919 Aliens Bill, quoted in Stevens (n 24), 53.
121 Bevan (n 31), 73.
122 Ibid 74.
123 Naturalization Act of 1906 (34 Stat. 596).
124 Hutchinson (n 62), 141.
125 'The following classes of aliens shall be excluded from admission into the United States . . . anarchists, or persons who believe in or advocate the overthrow by force or violence of the Government of the United States, or all forms of law, or who disbelieve in or are opposed to organized government, or who advocate the assassination of public officials, or who advocate or teach the unlawful destruction of property; persons who are affiliated with any organization entertaining and teaching disbelief in or opposition to organized government, or who advocate or teach the duty, necessity, or propriety of the unlawful assaulting or killing of any officer or officers, either of specific individuals or of officers generally, of the Government of the United States or of any other organized government, because of his or their official character, or who advocate or teach the unlawful destruction of property'. S.3, Immigration Act of 1917 301 (39 Stat. 874).
126 Ibid.
127 Emergency Quota Act of 1921 67–5 (42 Stat. 5).

amendment failed.[128] As such, refugees were included within the quota of admissions, so once that had been filled, no one, not even refugees from that country, could gain admittance.[129] Two years later, Congress was faced with the plight of the Armenian refugees, far exceeding the quota restrictions. A Bill was proposed specifically to aid them, entitled *The Near East Refugee Act*, yet this failed to pass.[130] The overall effect of this plethora of border controls was that the number of immigrants to the United States fell from 23.5 million in the period 1880–1920 to less than 6 million in the years 1920–1965.[131]

From national to international refugee law

Given the development of laws concerning refugees within the national context, it should not be surprising that international refugee law, instead of being the institutional expression of humanitarian concern for the refugee, has revealed itself to be 'a basis for rationalizing the decisions of states to refuse protection'.[132] In answer to those who would maintain that international law represents some kind of higher authority descending from the heavens to mitigate the power of the nation-state, Hathaway puts his finger on the critical point when he writes that international law 'must be agreed to by, rather than imposed upon, states'.[133] More specifically, Fruchterman is correct to point out that:

> The . . . [1951] Convention is not in derogation of the State-supremacy doctrine, but is rather a voluntary undertaking by the signatories to provide assistance to refugees. The States still retain full authority to grant or deny asylum to persons who do not qualify as refugees as that word is used in the Convention.[134]

The current system of international refugee law as one whose origins are rooted in the perceived need to 'govern disruptions of regulated international migration in accordance with the interests of states' is a prime example of this truism.[135]

And yet in Europe and North America, for a long time, there was no clear categorisation in law between different classes of immigrants, including refugees. One was either admitted or not, and if one was, then usually it was a relatively

---

128 Hutchinson (n 62), 178.
129 Simpson JH, *Refugees: Preliminary Report of a Survey* (Royal Institute of International Affairs, 1938), 164.
130 Hutchinson (n 62), 184.
131 Lee (n 58), 12.
132 Hathaway JC, 'A Reconsideration of the Underlying Premise of Refugee Law' (1990), 31, *Harvard International Law Journal*, 129, 130.
133 Ibid 134.
134 Fruchterman (n 12), 177.
135 Hathaway (n 136), 133.

simple matter to establish permanent residence or to get citizenship in the country of choice. In an illuminating study, Reiko Karatani has shown how, at the level of international legal regimes, there was little or no distinction made between refugees and migrants generally, until the immediate post-World War II period.[136] Refugee law only later grew out of a general concern among states to control borders and re-assert their rights to decide on who could enter their territories. Immigration control and asylum are inextricably bound together in the modern period. Indeed, the concerns and paradigms used for refugees were essentially the same as those for overall immigration control. As Guy Goodwin-Gill writes:

> Refugee law ... developed alongside immigration control and the rise, or entrenchment of the nation-state. Coerced and other uncontrolled population movements challenge that aspect of sovereignty subsumed within the principle of community and self-determination. Refugee law – the identification and selection of a limited class of persons in need who are to be considered worthy of protection and assistance – meets halfway or less the challenge of the inevitable.[137]

John Hope Simpson makes the point that mass forced migration is not a modern phenomenon. However, the modern refugee phenomenon *is* indelibly bound up with the conditions of a world of border controls, for refugees 'have found themselves in a world in which free migration has ceased, and the pandemic condition of national exclusiveness, which has caused their departure from their own country, militates their absorption in any other'.[138] It is the period since World War I, with its rapid development of border controls, which has marked a sea-change in the condition of the modern refugee. I would agree with that view, except that it is important to add that the seeds of that shift were planted decades earlier. As we have seen, a security paradigm has been evident since at least the end of the eighteenth century, and many of the concerns and prejudices about deserving and undeserving refugees were already present during the nineteenth century. I have focussed on the United Kingdom, France and the United States, but similar processes were at work in Holland and Switzerland and elsewhere.[139] Noiriel argues that by the end of the nineteenth century, the hegemony of the nation-state had 'rendered impossible' any notion of social life 'not founded upon the principle of nationality'.[140] As such, it increasingly became necessary to determine, in law, the status of those outside their country of nationality, and to establish a set of further sub-categories such as immigrants

---

136   Karatani R, 'How History Separated Refugee and Migrant Regimes: In Search of Their Institutional Origins' (2005), 17, *International Journal of Refugee Law*, 517.
137   Guy Goodwin-Gill cited in Hathaway (n 134), 133, footnote 20.
138   Simpson (n 133), 2.
139   Noiriel (n 10), 93.
140   Ibid 22–23.

and refugees. The institution of a permanent and widespread regime of passports and immigration controls following the 'emergency' measures of World War I contributed to the situation described by Egidio Reale, where refugees had become the 'excommunicated of the world; they live *extra legem*'.[141] What follows is an attempt to sketch out how the regime of international refugee law has been framed within the biopolitical framework of management and security through a developing legal categorisation of the refugee. I make no claim to a comprehensive treatment of the subject – such a thing would require a whole book in itself. My aim is simply to challenge the dominant narrative which presents international refugee law as primarily a species of human rights law, and instead to present it as mainly an apparatus of control, which follows along many of the lines laid out by states over the century or more preceding it.

141 Quoted in Ibid 101.

4 The evolution and impact of international refugee law

Introduction

According to Noiriel, across the Western world from World War I onwards, a new paradigm emerged in the control of immigration. Everyone becomes a '*demandeur*', one who seeks something such as a job or the right of residence within the country.[1] In order to have such a request processed and decided upon, the individual must offer proof to the authorities of their identity and their rights. But it is the state that determines the criteria and the standard of such proofs. This paradigm, inaugurated along with the introduction of ID cards and the standard use of passports, became the form applied to the control of refugee admissions during the inter-war period.[2] Simpson, writing in 1938, stated that:

> Any alien finds himself in a network of legal and administrative restrictions almost all of which are [First World] War, or post-War creations . . . It is scarcely an exaggeration to say that the alien in a legal sense is a creature of the post-War world, and to meet some of his more urgent needs a complex scheme of arrangements has been elaborated.[3]

Indeed, elsewhere Simpson reflects on how, prior to World War I, he had travelled extensively without ever needing to possess a passport.[4] By contrast, Leon Trotsky could lament his situation 12 years after the war, as an exile on a 'planet without a visa'.[5] Beyond these individuals, refugees on a mass scale were

---

1 Noiriel G, *Réfugiés et sans-papiers: La République face au droit d'asile XIXe–XXe siècles* (Hachette, 1998), 192.
2 Ibid.
3 Simpson JH, *Refugees: Preliminary Report of a Survey* (Royal Institute of International Affairs, 1938), 99.
4 Simpson JH, 'The Refugee Problem' (1938), 17, *International Affairs*, 607. The writer Norman Angell described similar experiences as a traveller in the 1890s, cited in Marrus MR, *The Unwanted: European Refugees from the First World War through the Cold War* (Temple University, 2002), 92.
5 Trotsky L, *My Life: An Attempt at an Autobiography* (Penguin, 1975). The quote is taken from the title of chapter 45.

facing similar crises as they were shunted from border to border. And it was during this period that certain terms such as 'undesirables' and 'false refugees' became widespread.[6] It was also during this period that control of population movement was reframed, at least partly, through the development of international legal definitions of those moving across borders. In the 1920s, refugees were 'for the first time ever, defined in legal terms'.[7] In addition to the evolving definition of a refugee, in 1924, the Rome International Convention 'proposed the first precise definition of an "emigrant" and an "immigrant"'.[8]

The paradigm that Noriel describes applies to the structure of international refugee law, particularly as it has developed since the 1951 Convention; namely, the basis for the justification of all liberal democracies in rejecting asylum-seekers: if one cannot furnish sufficient proof, then asylum is denied.[9] The power relationship is that of a suppliant before the state which alone decides on the criteria for admission and protection. The key point, however, is that the development of international refugee law places the refugee as the object of the relation rather a subject involved in making it. This in turn has transformed the discourse on the refugee from a 'person with problems' into being the 'problem' itself.[10]

Re-establishing order

International refugee law has its origins in the chaotic conditions following World War I. In particular, the huge numbers of people forced to flee as a result of the Russian Revolution and the breakup of the Ottoman Empire demanded some kind of response. By 1926, the number of refugees in Europe was estimated to be around 9.5 million.[11] The first initiative was the creation by the League of Nations of the office of High Commissioner for Refugees, with the Norwegian Fridtjof Nansen appointed to the role. He in turn created the Nansen Passport system, based on a temporary document issued to refugees in order to allow them at least some limited travel in exile. However, one had to be either Armenian or Russian to qualify as a recipient of this document. For the Armenians, and other minorities of the former Ottoman Empire, they had possessed citizenship of a state that no longer existed. In the case of the White Russians, they had been

---

6 Noiriel (n 1), 226.
7 Zimmermann A and Mahler C, 'Article 1 A, para. 2 1951 Convention' in Andreas Zimmermann (ed), *The 1951 Convention Relating to the Status of Refugees and its 1967 Protocol: A Commentary* (OUP, 2011), 302.
8 Noiriel G, *Le creuset française: Histoire de l'immigration XIXe-XXe siècles* (Seuil, 1988), 115. 'An emigrant is considered to be one who leaves their country with the aim of seeking work . . . An immigrant is considered to be a foreigner who arrives in a country in search of work there and who has the express or presumed intention to settle in a permanent manner there'.
9 Noiriel (n 1), 313.
10 Harrell-Bond B, 'Camps: Literature Review' (1998), 2, *Forced Migration Review*, 22.
11 Marrus (n 4), 51.

stripped of their Russian nationality by the Bolshevik government in 1921. The Russian refugees had an ambiguous legal status for a few years, as most other states did not recognise the Soviet government. But by the end of the 1920s, this was no longer the case. In contrast to the Russians, the Italian government of Mussolini decided against revoking the nationality of the large number of its political exiles, partly, at least, because the renewal of passports to the exiles helped facilitate continued surveillance over their movements.[12] Because these Italian refugees therefore did not formerly fall outside of a state/individual relationship, they were not covered under the Nansen system. Hathaway describes this period as one in which 'refugees were defined in largely *juridical* terms', so as to remedy the fact that a mass of stateless persons in Europe was creating 'a malfunction in the international legal system',[13] while Claudena Skran suggests that, as well as assisting some refugees to travel, the Nansen Passport 'would help governments to count and monitor their refugee populations'.[14] Noiriel argues that the relative ease with which the Nansen Passport was instituted in the years after World War I was possible only because European states believed that it would facilitate the mass repatriation of refugees caused by the war and the revolutionary upheavals in Russia.[15] In short, the Nansen Passport system was primarily about stabilising, monitoring and controlling the movement of refugees. Insofar as it had a humanitarian effect in facilitating greater ease of movement to refugees who would otherwise have been without travel documents, this was a secondary aim. Moreover, such a scheme was only necessary because of the plethora of border controls that had become the norm across Europe over the preceding decades.

The first explicit definition of a refugee in international law occurs in the 1926 Arrangement agreed by thirty-nine states. This treaty was intended to formalise the status of the Russians and Armenians, who, it was now clear, would not be able to return to their homelands anytime soon. In the Arrangement, refugees were defined as:

> Russian: Any person of Russian origin who does not enjoy or who no longer enjoys the protection of the Government of the Union of Socialist Soviet Republics and who has not acquired another nationality.

> Armenian: Any person of Armenian origin formerly a subject of the Ottoman Empire who does not enjoy or who no longer enjoys the protection of the

12 Simpson (n 3), 56.
13 Hathaway JC, 'The Evolution of Refugee Status in International Law: 1920–1950' (1984), 33, *International and Comparative Law Quarterly*, 348, 349, 358.
14 Skran, 'Historical Development of International Refugee Law' in Andreas Zimmermann (ed), *The 1951 Convention Relating to the Status of Refugees and its 1967 Protocol: A Commentary* (OUP, 2011), 7.
15 Noiriel (n 1), 106.

Government of the Turkish Republic and who has not acquired another nationality.[16]

Skran points out that this definition rested on the assumption that the refugee problem was tied to the lack of a link between themselves and a nation-state. This legal 'black hole' led the League of Nations to take a 'juridical approach' to the refugee question.[17] Two years later, the 1928 Arrangement on Russian and Armenian Refugees, drawn up by Nansen, gave the High Commissioner powers, in tandem with national governments, to regulate and adjudicate on the quality of claimants for refugee status. These included the following:

(a) certifying the identity and the position of the refugees;
(b) certifying their family position and civil statue, in so far as these are based on documents issued or action taken in the refugees' country of origin;
(c) testifying to the regularity, validity and conformity with the previous law of their country of origin, of documents issued in such country;
(d) certifying the signature of refugees and copies and translations of documents drawn up in their own language;
(e) testifying before the authorities of the country to the good character and conduct of the individual refugee, to his previous record, to his professional qualifications and to his university or academic standing;
(f) recommending the individual refugee to the competent authority, particularly with a view to his obtaining visas, permits to reside in the country, admission to schools, libraries, etc.[18]

At first glance, we might recognise a humanitarian impulse; essentially the High Commissioner would act as an advocate for the refugees *vis-à-vis* national governments. However, if we think more carefully about the implications of these provisions, then two much less positive aspects also present themselves. First, in order to have the High Commissioner act on their behalf, the refugees would have to provide to him all the necessary proofs of their *bona fides*. Second, it places the refugees in a passive, almost infantile, position in which they need to be spoken for, and to have someone act as a guarantor as to their identity. This passive role allocated to the refugee was something new then, yet has now become ubiquitous. Indeed, it has become a key bone of contention among refugees in contemporary movements of resistance, as we will see in Part III.

---

16 League of Nations, Arrangement Relating to the Issue of Identify Certificates to Russian and Armenian Refugees, 12 May 1926, League of Nations, Treaty Series Vol. LXXXIX, No. 2004, point 2.
17 Skran (n 14), 9.
18 League of Nations, Arrangement Relating to the Legal Status of Russian and Armenian Refugees, 30 June 1928, League of Nations Treaty Series, Vol. LXXXIX, No. 2005, resolution 2.

First attempts at establishing a system of international refugee law

These *ad hoc* and 'rudimentary'[19] arrangements of the 1920s were followed by more formal and far-reaching attempts to create a system of international refugee law with the 1933 Convention, and a further international agreement at Evian in 1938.[20] But the process of developing these various instruments was governed not by universal principles or a guiding concept of who a refugee was but rather again on an *ad hoc* basis as the need arose. Indeed, it is arguable that, until the 1967 Protocol removed the temporal and geographical limitations in the 1951 Convention, refugee definitions were to a greater or lesser extent related to specific circumstances or groups of refugees.

The 1933 Convention was the first legally binding international treaty on asylum, and would form the basis for the 1951 Convention.[21] A major impetus for the creation of the 1933 Convention was to put in place a framework of international law that could deal with refugees beyond the anticipated lifetime of the Nansen Office.[22] But, again, in the definition it gave of a refugee it remained highly specific. Only Russians, Armenians and a few other small groups such as Christian minorities from the former Ottoman Empire were included. The plight of those forced to flee the new Nazi government in Germany was completely ignored, in spite of some 50,000 refugees fleeing the country in the early part of that year.[23] The 1933 Convention also allowed signatories to derogate from all aspects, except for one: chapter XI, General Provisions. By the outbreak of World War II, however, only eight countries had formally adopted the Convention, and many of them had derogated from some of the most important provisions such as Article 3 on *non-refoulement*.[24] This was the first enunciation of this principle, which has since become a critical aspect of international refugee law. However, states could still expel refugees for 'reasons of national security or public order'.[25] For example, the United Kingdom made a reservation to Article 3 stating that 'public order' could include criminal or 'moral' issues.[26]

---

19 Weis P, 'The International Protection of Refugees' (1954), 48, *The American Journal of International Law*, 193, 194.
20 League of Nations, Convention Relating to the International Status of Refugees, 28 October 1933, League of Nations Treaty Series, Vol. CLIX No. 3663; League of Nations, Convention Concerning the Status of Refugees Coming From Germany, 10 February 1938, League of Nations Treaty Series, Vol. CXCII, No. 4461.
21 Skran (n 14), 14.
22 Simpson (n 3), 86. In 1931, The League of Nations had stipulated 31 December 1938 as the date by which the Nansen Office's work would cease.
23 Simpson (n 3), 59; Skran (n 14), 18.
24 Skran (n 14), 24–25.
25 1933 Convention (n 20), Article 3.
26 Jennings RY, 'Some International Law Aspects of the Refugee Question' (1939), 20, *British Year Book of International Law*, 98, 105, footnote 3.

Similar exclusion clauses were later included in the 1936 Arrangement and in Article 5 of the 1938 Evian Convention.[27]

More than 400,000 refugees fled the Nazis from 1933 until the outbreak of war. Because governments were very wary of giving them asylum, the Nansen system was not extended to them, but rather a separate legal structure was created to deal with these refugees.[28] Also, initially member states of the League of Nations were concerned should any of its activities be seen to infringe on the internal affairs of Germany.[29] As a result, when a High Commissioner was appointed specifically to deal with the plight of refugees coming from Germany, the office was deliberately kept at organisational arm's length from the League, and all funds for it had to come from private sources.[30] In frustration at the resistance among states to respond adequately to the refugee crisis instigated by the Nazi regime, the first High Commissioner, James G. McDonald, felt himself compelled to resign in December 1935. In his resignation letter, he made it clear the question of the refugees was of a political rather than a merely legal or humanitarian nature. He wrote:

> [I]t will not be enough to continue the activities on behalf of those who flee from the Reich. Efforts must be made to remove or mitigate the *causes* which create German refugees.[31]

In the same year, Norway had put a resolution forward to the League that a permanent organisation of the League should be established to assist all refugees, but this was rejected.[32]

In 1936, another *ad hoc* agreement, the Provisional Arrangement Concerning the Status of Refugees Coming from Germany, was drafted. Article 1 of that agreement established that,

> the term 'refugee coming from Germany' shall be deemed to apply to any person who was settled in that country, who does not possess any nationality other than German nationality, and in respect of whom it is established in law or in fact he or she does not enjoy the protection of the Government of the Reich.[33]

---

27 Simpson (n 3), 106.
28 Skran (n 14), 26.
29 Simpson (n 3), 87.
30 Ibid.
31 Quoted in Jennings (n 26), 110 (emphasis added).
32 Simpson (n 3), 89.
33 League of Nations, Provisional Arrangement Concerning the Status of Refugees Coming From Germany, 4 July 1936, League of Nations Treaty Series, Vol. CLXXI, No. 3952, Article 1.

As Skran points out, this definition shares with earlier ones a concern with those whose relations with their state of nationality has broken down.[34] It is also, again, highly specific in relation to the group of refugees concerned. By 1938, it was clear that there needed to be a more significant response to the exodus of Jews fleeing Nazi Germany. The matter became even more urgent following the annexation of Austria in March of that year. So, at the instigation of the US government, a meeting was convened at Evian in July. Although the Evian conference has gone down in history as one of the more shameful episodes in the closing of doors by Western countries to the Jewish refugees, it did result in a new convention specifically to deal with assisting them.[35] Article 1 built on the definition contained in the earlier Article 1 of the 1936 Provisional Agreement by defining 'refugees coming from Germany' as:

1. (a) persons possessing or having possessed German nationality and not possessing any other nationality who are *proved* not to enjoy, in law or in fact, the protection of the German Government;
    (b) stateless persons not covered by previous Conventions or Agreements who have left German territory after being established therein and who are *proved* not to enjoy, in law or in fact, the protection of the German Government.
2 Persons who leave Germany *for reasons of purely personal convenience* are not included in this definition.[36]

Two things are most striking about this definition. First, it is the first time that an international agreement insists on proof that the person being helped is a refugee as so defined. We have here the inauguration of a key aspect of contemporary refugee law, namely that assistance is conditional upon the offering of proof by the refugee that they fit the juridical definition of a refugee. In addition, the second clause, excluding those who have left Germany 'for reasons of purely personal convenience' also represents the first time in international law that a group is specifically excluded from protection. Skran writes: 'This clause makes a distinction inherent in refugee law as a whole – that refugees were a separate, special, and deserving category of international law'.[37] I would add to that, that it also assumes such a distinction is clear and can be expressed in law without in fact denying protection to those who need it. One can easily imagine Germans, Jewish or otherwise, who having felt merely harassed or uncomfortable living under the Nazi regime, had chosen for reasons of 'personal convenience' to move elsewhere. The concept of 'personal convenience' is certainly not an

---

34 Skran (n 14), 27.
35 The extent of the shabby attitude of state delegations' towards refugees and indeed the whole purported task of the conference is well described in Marrus (n 4), 171.
36 1938 Convention (n 20), Article 1 (emphasis added).
37 Skran (n 14), 31.

objective one. But what such a clause does is not simply to make a distinction between two objectively pre-determined groups, it also necessarily involves a level of suspicion or scepticism about all claims for protection, for it becomes necessary to judge all as to whether or not they are 'genuine' refugees or merely migrants for personal convenience. It is therefore easy to accept Loescher's claim that 'the term *economic refugees* was first used to describe Jews leaving Germany in the 1930s; they were referred to as the *Wirtschaftsemigranten*'.[38]

Neither the 1933 Convention nor the 1938 Convention guaranteed any right of asylum.[39] The earlier arrangements of the 1920s dealt with people who had already found asylum, but who required travel documents and some guarantees of their personal status in their countries of refuge. But the problem faced by the Jews fleeing Nazi Germany was their inability to secure entry to countries of refuge in the first place. Prior to the Holocaust, this was never resolved at the level of law. Many Jewish and other refugees from Nazi Germany did in fact find sanctuary, but this was facilitated through political means, either by governments taking a policy decision or through pressure exerted by groups agitating in their support.[40] One practical outcome of the Evian Conference was the setting up of the Inter-Governmental Committee on Refugees. This body issued its own definition of refugees coming from Germany as those who had fled their country of origin on account 'of their political opinions, religious beliefs and racial origin'.[41] This definition of a refugee was 'innovative' as it 'focused on personalised criteria' of belief, opinion or origins to 'evaluate the merits of claims to refugee status', and 'further signalled a new, more individualistic approach to defining refugeehood'.[42]

It can therefore be said that 'the interwar years . . . helped to establish refugees as a special category of migrant'.[43] For most commentators at the time and since, this was a sign of progress as it appeared to create special privileges for refugees in the context of closing borders and more stringent measures on entry. Certainly in the context of the specific needs of the refugees fleeing Nazi Germany, and with hindsight refracted back through the Holocaust, such a view is understandable. However, in the light of more than 60 years of experience of solid legal regimes at both international and domestic levels that specifically categorise the refugee as distinct from other types of migrant, such a positive spin on these inter-war developments is at least questionable. Moreover, much of the detail of the legal provisions discussed so far in this chapter suggests a far greater concern even at the time with control of the refugee rather than assistance or protection.

---

38 Loescher G, *Beyond Charity: International Cooperation and the Global Refugee Crisis* (OUP, 1993), 17.
39 Skran (n 14), 34.
40 Behrman S, 'Legal Subjectivity and the Refugee' (2013), 26, *International Journal of Refugee Law*, 1, 5.
41 Skran (n 14), 34.
42 Hathaway (n 13), 371; Skran (n 14), 34.
43 Skran (n 14), 36.

Writing in 1938, Louise W. Holborn, later to be the official historian of UNHCR, accurately identified the key problem from the point of view of nation-states:

> Disorganized groups of refugees are more difficult . . . to deal with than are organized groups, even if the latter are larger in number. A clearly defined status for refugees would aid efforts to make refugee status transitory in character and would facilitate settlement. If coupled with adequate technical organization, refugees would be under more direct control than at present, and the possibility of subversive political activity against governments respons-ible for their exile would be greatly lessened. The political complications often connected with aiding refugees would be practically eliminated also, particularly if the local offices concerned with refugees were qualified to decide which people fell within the accepted definition of 'refugee'.[44]

Here, in essence, is revealed the cynical approach that was evidently current in the pre-war period: the focus of refugee law was to be on managing refugees, rather than assisting them. At around the same time, another commentator, R. Yewdall Jennings, made a similar point: that for there to be an effective legal system governing refugees, the 'first step' would have to be 'a definition of the term "refugee"'. The definition he offers is one who has lost the protection of their state, and for whom therefore, 'the link between him and international law' has broken down.[45] Also writing in 1938, although from perhaps a less cynical perspective, Simpson, as part of his survey into the refugee crisis in Europe, argued that refugee assistance had been hobbled by political partisanship.[46] Specifically, he criticises as 'political sectionalism' attempts made by refugees themselves to add to the refugee program of the League an anti-fascist aim in order to address the root cause of refugee problems. Instead, Simpson pro-poses that refugee assistance be made, as far as possible, a technical procedure. Repeatedly then, the concerns on the refugee question expressed by leading commentators – ones, moreover, who tended to be sympathetic to the plight of the refugees – at the close of this first period of the development of international refugee law, are all to do with controlling, managing and depoliticising asylum, their solution being to make it more a juridical and administrative affair.

Post-1945

During World War II, the first step towards the creation of a global refugee relief organisation was taken and voluntarily placed itself, curiously enough, under the

---

44 Holborn LW, 'The Legal Status of Political Refugees 1920–1938' (1938), 32, *American Journal of International Law*, 680, 703.
45 Jennings (n 26), 99.
46 Simpson (n 3), 97.

direct control of the military Supreme Commander of Allied Forces.[47] And they appeared most concerned not for the welfare of the refugees but rather for the disruption that might be caused by 'uncontrolled self-repatriation of displaced persons who might form themselves into roving bands of vengeful pillaging looters on trek to their homes'.[48] Following the end of the war, many former Nazi concentration camps were turned into 'Assembly Centres' for refugees. Liisa H. Malkki argues that it was in these centres that the bureaucratic monitoring and documenting of refugees was first initiated, out of which the 'postwar figure of the modern refugee largely took shape'.[49] As we saw in the previous chapter, this practice was already being developed in the nineteenth century in various domestic regimes, although certainly this period marks a key stage in relation to international law and the refugee. Malkki continues:

> The legal apparatus that has developed [since 1945] has been of forma-tive importance in the orders of knowledge in which 'the refugee' makes its appearance, and in practice, this legal apparatus tends to take the contem-porary order of sovereign nation-states as given.[50]

A result of this system of refugee law that has developed since 1945 has been the 'leaching-out' of the politics that lays behind refugee movements; this depoliticisation has in turn become pervasive among the various humanitarian and policy organisations concerned with refugees today.[51] In addition, the initial placing of the military in control suggested that with an emerging Cold War, European security and reconstruction became of vital importance. Therefore, 'addressing the refugee crisis became a geopolitical imperative', whereas in the specific US context, 'foreign policy interests dictated that the United States take some responsibility for resettling war refugees'.[52] However, as Mae M. Ngai notes, no consideration was given to the many Asian refugees created as a result of the war in the Pacific; at this time, before the Chinese Revolution and the Korean War, this region was not considered to be a significant arena of conflict between the United States and the USSR.

In the initial post-World War II period, the distinction between refugees and what were known as 'surplus workers' was unclear, with many of the former

47 Noiriel (n 1), 120; Marrus (n 4), 319.
48 Supreme Headquarters Allied Expeditionary Force (SHAEF) Plan, quoted in Malkki LH, 'Refugees and Exile: From "Refugee Studies" to the Natural Order of Things' (1995), 24, *Annual Review of Anthropology*, 495, 499. Similar sentiments were expressed by General Patton in language that was only slightly more offensive, describing DPs as 'locusts' who needed to be kept behind barbed wire. Marrus (n 4), 322.
49 Malkki (n 48), 500.
50 Ibid 502.
51 Ibid 505. Agier M, *On the Margins of the World: The Refugee Experience Today* (David Fernbach, tr, Polity, 2008).
52 Ngai MM, *Impossible Subjects: Illegal Aliens and the Making of Modern America* (Princeton University, 2004), 235–236.

being lumped in with the latter. Rieko Karatani argues that the emerging refugee regime essentially reflected the concerns of states that this 'surplus population' not endanger post-war political stability and economic recovery.[53] The inter-war conventions on refugees suffered from the general weakness of international law during that period. But after World War II and the strengthening of international legal institutions, states became even more concerned to restrict as much as possible the admission of refugees. Thus, much of the discussions on the various instruments of international law, culminating in the 1951 Convention, were dominated by state representatives emphasising defence of national interests and the need for a strict codification in law of the category of refugee.[54] In June 1946, for example, the French delegate to the UN remarked that the question of the refugee definition was far from being a merely academic one. A broad definition, he argued, such as the one proposed initially by the United Kingdom, would lead to a potential difference in the number of refugees entitled to protection ranging from 200,000 to 1 million.[55] In the following month, the United Nations Relief and Rehabilitation Administration (UNRRA), which had been set up in 1943 to manage aid and resettlement for refugees, compelled those seeking refugee status to provide 'concrete evidence' of persecution.[56] Thus, states and international bodies were quickly fastening on to the notion that a formal legal definition of the refugee would assist in controlling population movements.

The International Refugee Organisation (IRO) was set up in 1946 as a successor to UNRRA. The replacement of UNRRA with the IRO was driven in large part by Cold War politics. The United States, along with its allies, considered the former to have pro-Soviet sympathies, and therefore led efforts in the UN to replace it with a more Western-controlled body. Loescher and Scanlan write: 'By taking these steps, the Truman administration converted the refugee issue into an aspect of the emerging Cold War, and thus provided a new basis for [domestic] conservative support which was only marginally related to traditional [refugee supporting] interest group politics'.[57] Ostensibly, the creation of the IRO was mainly concerned with encouraging and facilitating resettlement of those who felt unable to return to their countries of origin. This was a reaction to Soviet attempts to have their citizens forcibly returned, many of whom had been displaced and interned by the Germans during the war.

The IRO also introduced or reinforced prior concepts that would become key elements of the definition of the refugee in the post-war period. The Preamble of the IRO's Constitution makes repeated reference to '*genuine* refugees and

53 Karatani R, 'How History Separated Refugee and Migrant Regimes: In Search of Their Institutional Origins' (2005), 17, *International Journal of Refugee Law*, 517, 519.
54 Noiriel (n 1), 121.
55 Ibid 123.
56 Hathaway (n 13), 373.
57 Loescher G and Scanlan JA, *Calculated Kindness: Refugees and America's Half-Open Door, 1945 to the Present* (The Free Press, 1986), 14–15.

displaced persons'.[58] Annex 1 then lists those worthy (or not) of being refugees, creating categories of those considered to be 'unworthy of international protection and assistance'.[59] In the main, this referred to former Nazis or their collaborators.[60] Also specifically excluded are economic migrants.[61] The IRO Constitution further excluded from the remit of protection those who:

(a) have participated in any organization having as one of its purposes the overthrow by armed force of the Government of their country of origin, being a Member of the United Nations; or the overthrow by armed force of the Government of any other Member of the United Nations, or have participated in any terrorist organization;

(b) have become leaders of movements hostile to the Government of their country of origin being a Member of the United Nations or sponsors of movements encouraging refugees not to return to their country of origin.[62]

At a time when national liberation movements were beginning to flare up with intensity in India, Algeria, Indochina and elsewhere, this must be understood as a means to shore up the integrity of the imperial states of Europe. Thus, the refugee policy not just of the United States, but of the UN, became even more a tool reinforcing the sovereign rights of states and for mediating the geo-political rivalries between them, rather than a humanitarian goal of protection.

Critical to the undermining of the refugee and the shoring up of states' rights was the combination of an international system of refugee law, a set of norms, together with the retention by states of refugee status determination procedures. Thus, states were able to apply an international set of norms, with all the authority that it carried, via a screening procedure over which they would have control.[63] Hathaway identifies three different approaches to the refugee problem between the wars: juridical, social and individual. Yet, in spite of the varying approaches, he concludes that each turn was determined by the perceived needs of states.[64] From 1938 onwards, a key element appears which would form the basis of refugee law in the second half of the twentieth century and beyond: the emphasis on the refugee establishing proof of their persecution; both UNRRA and its successor organisation, the IRO, 'insisted on concrete evidence' from the refugee

---

58 United Nations, Constitution of the International Refugee Organisation (IRO) A/RES/62 (1), 15 December 1946, Preamble (emphasis added).
59 Hathaway (n 13), 376.
60 IRO (n 58) Annex 1, Article 1(c).
61 Ibid Article 1(e).
62 Ibid Section D, II (6).
63 Hathaway JC, 'A Reconsideration of the Underlying Premise of Refugee Law' (1990), 31, *Harvard International Law Journal*, 129, 144.
64 Hathaway (n 13), 380.

that would back up their claim for refugee status.[65] Along with an individualist approach to determining who was deserving of assistance came a set of objective criteria for judging the 'genuine' refugee.

The 1951 Convention

> In the genealogy of 'the refugee' one such moment [in its development] can be located in post-World War II Europe ... 'the refugee' as a specific social category and legal problem of global dimensions did not exist in its full modern form before this period ... The standardizing, globalizing processes of the immediate postwar years occurred, importantly, in the institutional domain of refugee settlement and refugee camp administration, and in the emerging legal domain of refugee law ... Through these processes, the modern, postwar refugee emerged as a knowable, nameable figure and as an object of social-scientific knowledge.[66]

> Asked 'What is a refugee?' an eminent international lawyer once answered: 'It is a person who satisfies the criteria laid down in Article 1 of the Refugee Convention'.[67]

As the central instrument of international refugee law, the 1951 Convention is the subject of much discussion in the general literature. What follows is focussed on completing the narrative of international refugee law's birth, by discussing the preoccupations that were instrumental in its drafting. Once again, the story we are told, of the 1951 Convention as fundamentally a humanitarian document, is betrayed by the evidence. Instead, the biopolitical framework identified by Malkki in the above quote was finally fully realised. To argue, as some continue to do, that the 1951 Convention can best be understood as a species of human rights law is therefore mistaken.[68] The 1951 Convention represents the final conquest of asylum by law, in which the former is all by erased by the latter. That is, it is the moment when the international legal order, i.e. the collective of states, stakes a global claim to the delineation of the refugee subject and the space of asylum.

Frank Krenz, a former member of the Legal Division of the UNHCR, makes the claim that the ancient institution of asylum had always been a function of territorial sovereignty, when in fact, as we have seen, for much of

---

65 Hathaway (n 63), 139. OFPRA refers to this period as inaugurating 'individual eligibility' as the basis for granting refugee status, as if this was a good thing. OFPRA, De la Grande guerre aux guerres sans nom: une histoire de l'OFPRA (OFPRA, nd), 10.
66 Malkki (n 48), 497–498.
67 Grahl-Madsen A, 'The European Tradition of Asylum and the Development of Refugee Law' (1966), 3, *Journal of Peace Research*, 278.
68 For example, Alleweldt R, 'Preamble to the 1951 Convention' in Andreas Zimmermann (ed), *The 1951 Convention Relating to the Status of Refugees and its 1967 Protocol: A Commentary* (OUP, 2011), 233.

its history, asylum/sanctuary had actually concerned spaces beyond sovereign-state territory.[69] Krenz then goes on to offer us a heroic description of the post-war evolution of refugee law:

> From [the end of the Second World War] onward the concept of 'Freedom of Movement' gained impetus, and rebellion took place against the supremacy of State sovereignty in matters relating to the release of subjects or the admission of aliens.[70]

Sadly, this rather overblown description does not fit the reality of what happened then. The state-centred concept of asylum that arose in the seventeenth century remained. A leading textbook on international law, in an edition published in 1948, stated:

> the so-called right of asylum is certainly not a right possessed by the alien to demand that the State into whose territory he has entered with the intention of escaping persecution in some other State should grant these things.[71]

In more positive terms, the prevailing view at the time on the law of asylum is best summed up in the description offered by the Institute of International Law in 1950: 'Asylum is the protection which a State grants on its territory or in some other place under the control of certain of its organs, to a person who comes to seek it'.[72] It further declared that the state has the right to expel the asylee, that such an expulsion might be impossible if other states refused to accept them, and that in situations involving mass refugee flows, it was up to states to best manage these on the basis of 'the most equitable way of sharing between their respective territories'.[73] Nowhere does this declaration on international law, by one of the leading authorities in the field, refer to the rights of the refugee. In other words, in the year before the adoption of the 1951 Convention, a leading body of international jurists identified the right of asylum as fundamentally vested in the putative host state, not the refugee herself. Grahl-Madsen adds that asylum can be understood within the framework of the 'territorial supremacy and integrity of States ... in the sense that [the refugee] is no longer subject to (lawful) seizure by the authorities of the country from

---

69 Krenz FE, 'The Refugee as a Subject of International Law' (1966), 15, *International and Comparative Law Quarterly*, 90, 91.
70 Ibid 90.
71 Oppenheim's International Law (7th edn), cited in Bevan V, *The Development of British Immigration Law* (Croom Helm, 1986), 214.
72 Institut De Droit International, *L'asile en droit international public* (Bath, 1950), Article 1.
73 Ibid Article 2.

which he has fled',[74] i.e. the territorial integrity of the country of asylum must be respected *vis-à-vis* the state seeking custody of the asylee. Felice Morgenstern writing on the eve of the 1951 Convention concurs:

> There is an undisputed rule of international law to the effect that every state has exclusive control over the individuals on its territory . . . A competence to grant asylum thus derives directly from the territorial sovereignty of states.[75]

This was also the view of the higher courts in Germany, Switzerland and the United States in rulings dating from 1900, 1921 and 1940, respectively.[76] And insofar as the rights of states are limited in their right to grant asylum, it is in relation to the rights of other states, e.g. in cases where extradition is being sought for non-political crimes.[77] Although writing before the final draft of the 1951 Convention, Morgenstern was in a position to reflect on the discussions that led to Article 14 of the Universal Declaration on Human Rights. The original draft read: 'Everyone has the right to seek and *to be granted*, in other countries, asylum from persecution' (emphasis added). This draft was vehemently opposed by a number of states on the grounds that it infringed upon the sovereign right of states to control entrance to their territory.[78] Australia, for example, insisted that the Declaration could not refer to any duties on states in respect of asylum. So the final draft replaced the phrase 'to be granted' with the rather more ambiguous 'to enjoy'. Morgenstern described, aptly perhaps, this final version of Article 14 as 'flippant'.[79] Further, Noiriel argues that the 1951 Convention was only acceded to by so many states, and has therefore succeeded over the past 60 years in becoming an established part of international law, precisely because it preserves the prerogatives of the nation-state to be the final arbiter of who can or cannot enter its territory.[80] Indeed, the mechanism of individualisation and control, and the techniques involved in determining eligibility and the veracity of the claim for asylum form the foundation without which a law of asylum could not exist within the context of a world hegemonised by the nation-state.[81] The point to emphasise, however, is that while one part of the context of the drafting of the 1951 Convention was the evolving human rights discourse of the post-war period, equally there was a widespread consensus

---

74 Grahl-Madsen A, *The Status of Refugees in International Law: Volume Two* (AW Sijthoff, 1972), 4.
75 Morgenstern F, 'The Right of Asylum' (1949), 26, *British Yearbook of International Law*, 327.
76 Ibid 335.
77 Ibid 330.
78 UN Doc A/C 3/285, Rev 1.
79 Morgenstern (n 75), 337.
80 Gérard Noiriel (n 1), 151.
81 Ibid 152.

among international lawyers and states that asylum was solely in the gift of states or it was nothing.

The drafting of the 1951 Convention

Drafting of the 1951 Convention began in early 1946. Loescher argues that for Western governments, the negotiations were mainly about 'limiting their legal obligations to refugees'.[82] Discussions on the refugee definition were perhaps the most extensive of the entire process, with more than 500 pages of official documents devoted to it alone.[83] There were many drafts of the refugee definition, and arguments over the exact wording lasted right up until the end of the drafting process 5 years later. The definition eventually agreed entailed 'substantial limitations' on who would be included, leaving out internally displaced persons, economic refugees, people made stateless for reasons not related to persecution, those fleeing general situations of violence or war and those fleeing natural or ecological disasters.[84] An innovation of the 1951 Convention definition was the insistence on 'persecution' as cause of the refugee's flight, although the term had been 'in the air', having previously been used by both UNRRA and the Allied military in reference to refugees at the end of the war.[85] The term is also present in Article 14 of the UN Declaration on Human Rights. It has sometimes been suggested that 'persecution' was also intended to be directed specifically towards people fleeing communist states, and thus was adopted for opportunist reasons at the height of the Cold War.[86]

Stephanie Schmahl, citing the French and Italian delegates to the Conference of Plenipotentiaries that drafted the 1951 Convention, describes the concern of European states as being to create a legal regime 'primarily designed to create secure conditions such as would facilitate the sharing of the refugee burden'.[87] There appears to have been a trade-off in the negotiations over Article 1, the 'key' to the system of rights for refugees under international law.[88] In return for a settled universal definition of a refugee, the temporal and geographical limitations (relating to events in Europe prior to 1951) had to be put in place.[89] The French delegation, following concerns expressed within

---

82 Loescher (n 38), 57.
83 Einarsen T, 'Drafting history of the 1951 Convention and the 1967 Protocol' in Andreas Zimmermann (ed), *The 1951 Convention Relating to the Status of Refugees and its 1967 Protocol: A Commentary* (OUP, 2011), 49.
84 Ibid 52.
85 Grahl-Madsen A, *The Status of Refugees in International Law: Volume One* (AW Sijthoff, 1966), 189.
86 Loescher (n 38), 57.
87 Schmahl S, 'Article 1B 1951 Convention' in Andreas Zimmermann (ed), *The 1951 Convention Relating to the Status of Refugees and its 1967 Protocol: A Commentary* (OUP, 2011), 469.
88 Einarsen (n 83), 40.
89 Ibid 55.

the French government that they would have to receive too many refugees, successfully insisted on these restrictions being included in the final draft.[90] The US delegation, among others, objected to a universal definition as it would force states to sign a 'blank check'. The US delegate, Henkin, pointed to the numbers of Palestinian refugees and of those who had fled as a result of Indian Partition as examples of why a more specific definition was necessary. The Italian delegate, Del Drago, expressed horror at the idea that European nations would have to accept refugees as a result of national movements in the East.[91] The Israeli delegate, Robinson, made the curious argument that people fleeing natural disasters could not be included because 'fires, floods, earthquakes or volcanic eruptions' did not differentiate 'between their victims on the grounds of race, religion or political opinion'. Robinson also made it explicit that 'persecution' meant that anyone merely fleeing a war situation would also be excluded.[92] It was left to the Pakistani delegate, Brohi, to express his government's opposition to a refugee convention that excluded all non-European from protection, such as the millions who suffered as a result of Partition.[93] It is therefore clear that the Convention refugee has its origins not in concern for refugees *per se* but rather as part of a compromise intended to assuage the concerns of states that they would be inundated with masses of unwanted asylum-seekers. In particular, the Western bias of the Convention is obvious in statements such as the following made in 1966 by UNHCR:

> The limitation did not give rise to any particular problem when the 1951 Convention was first adopted, since at that time the 1951 Convention extended in practice to all known groups of refugees.[94]

This claim is highly disingenuous, as the Convention excluded non-European refugee situations, thus ignoring at least three other major refugee crises of the time: the largest forced migration in world history involving some 14.5 million people who crossed the borders following the partition of India and Pakistan in 1947; the 800,000 Palestinians forced from their homes by the Zionists in the following year; and the refugees created by the outbreak of war on the Korean peninsula in 1950.[95] For geopolitical reasons to do with the Cold War, the UN, at the behest of Western states, was prepared to set up specific agencies to assist the Palestinians and Koreans, but those in the Indian subcontinent were denied aid, in spite of repeated requests from India and Pakistan.[96] Moreover, even the

---

90 Noiriel (n 1), 144.
91 Einarsen (n 83), 60.
92 Ibid 61–62.
93 Ibid 57.
94 UNHCR, UN Doc A/AC.96/346 (1966), paragraph 2.
95 The Convention allowed states voluntarily to accept non-European refugees, but this was not a binding commitment as it was with European refugees.
96 Loescher (n 38), 62.

'universality' of the definition, absent the temporal and geographical limitations, was clearly intended to exclude whole swathes of refugees, namely those fleeing general violence or natural disasters.

Writing in 1954, Paul Weis observed that both the discussions that led to the setting up of the IRO and then later the UNHCR demonstrated a 'keenness' among states to delimit the scope of people who would be assisted and given asylum.[97] In addition to the exclusive nature of the definition, the 1951 Convention ended up with a cessation clause – Article 1C – a novelty in international refugee law, thus creating a situation of permanent precarity even for those granted refugee status. Further, during the negotiations, states insisted on retaining the right to exclude refugees on the basis of national security and public safety whom they considered 'unworthy or undesirable',[98] something which found expression in Article 1F and Article 33(2). In discussions on Article 31 of the Convention, which ostensibly grants some leniency to refugees who illegally enter the putative host state, the Secretariat, in proposing the draft, began their commentary by stating categorically: 'The sovereign right of a State to remove or keep from its territory foreigners regarded as undesirable cannot be challenged'. The Secretariat did raise the issue of the refugee 'caught between two sovereign orders', but in the context not of the suffering of the refugee but rather that they might end up leading 'the life of an outlaw and may in the end become a public danger'.[99]

Until the 1946 IRO Constitution and the 1951 Convention, refugee definitions in the various international agreements had always been based on the group approach. However, from 1946 onwards, the individualized approach became institutionalized.[100] Schmahl suggests that one of the reasons for this shift was that, prior to the war, international law did not recognise individuals as subjects.[101] During that period, the key question was of the 'breakdown in the international legal order' due to the large numbers of people whose relationship to their home state, or indeed any state, had been dissolved.[102] Schmahl further argues that until 1935, this juridical approach held sway, but from then until the outbreak of war, there was a shift towards a more 'social' approach that saw refugees as 'helpless casualties of broadly-based social or political occurrences'.[103] But Schmahl, along with others, also sees in this latter stage the beginnings of a new stage in international refugee law in which there was increasing focus upon the individual refugee and the questions of establishing the veracity of their claim for assistance, and whether their character and circumstances made them deserving

---

97   Weis (n 19), 208.
98   Hathaway (n 63), 172.
99   Weis P, *The Refugee Convention, 1951: The Travaux Préparatoires Analysed with a Commentary by Dr Paul Weis* (Cambridge University, 1995), 202.
100 Zimmermann and Mahler (n 7), 299; Schmahl (n 87), 253.
101 Schmahl (n 87), 253.
102 Ibid 254.
103 Ibid.

of asylum.[104] This is certainly evident in the novel emphases on proof and exclusions in the 1936 Agreement and the 1938 Convention, as discussed above. The import of the phrase, 'Has been considered a refugee' contained in Article 1A, para. 1 of the 1951 Convention, is that the claimant 'must have been recognized by a competent municipal or international authority as a refugee in accordance with [the pre-war instruments]'.[105] According to both UNHCR and the higher courts in Germany, this meant that even had someone, e.g. an Armenian or a Russian, qualified for assistance under those arrangements or Conventions, if they had not by that point, or subsequently been actually determined by any authority to be a 'refugee', then they would not be covered by the 1951 Convention.[106] This, more than almost anything else, sums up the narrowness of the Convention's scope in relation to whom it would assist, compared to what had existed prior to this period in the development of international refugee law. It also illuminates the increased juridical nature of the refugee definition, and the manner in which refugees would now be forced to 'labour towards the law'.[107]

The negotiations that led to the 1951 Convention are probably best summed up by an NGO observer of them. He ironically noted that the discussions:

> had at times given the impression that it was a conference for the protection of helpless sovereign states against the wicked refugee. The draft Convention had at times been in danger of appearing to the refugee like a menu at an expensive restaurant, with every course crossed out except, perhaps, the soup, and a footnote to the effect that even the soup might not be served in certain circumstances.[108]

Defining and controlling the refugee subject

Unlike many other signatories of the 1951 Convention, France moved swiftly to implement it into domestic law. One might assume, therefore, that France led the way in refugee protection. Insofar as this might partly be true, it is also clear that the Convention also facilitated more sinister methods of controlling refugees that have sadly become ubiquitous today. Within months, the law of 27 July 1952 incorporated into the domestic legal regime the definition of a refugee contained in Article 1A of the 1951 Convention.[109] This law also created the *Office Français de Protection des Réfugiés et Apatrides* (OFPRA) in order to manage the implementation of refugee admissions and to ascertain refugee status on the terms of the Convention. This legislation therefore led to the principle of the

---

104   Ibid 255.
105   Ibid 260–261.
106   Ibid.
107   The concept of the dispossessed being forced to 'labour towards the law' is taken from Tuitt P, Race, Law, Resistance (Glasshouse 2004), Chapter One.
108   Quoted in Hathaway (n 63), 145.
109   Article 2, *Loi no 52–893 du 25 juillet 1952 relative au droit d'asile*.

right of asylum in France being definitively 'subordinated to establishing proof of persecution'.[110] The emphasis on establishing proof of identity led quickly to OFPRA relying heavily on the police and police methods. For example, the authorities began to screen Spaniards arriving over the Pyrenees, distinguishing between Convention refugees and economic migrants, and issuing 'eligibility certificates' to those deemed to be genuine refugees according to the definition in Article 1A.[111] Similar documents were also used by Italy and West Germany for their own refugee arrivals. Without these certificates, refugees were unable to get work or access other forms of assistance. As a result, a lack of documents, i.e. being denied refugee status, could easily lead to refugees facing highly exploitative conditions in the black economy, a situation that led directly to the Sans-Papiers movement discussed in Chapter 6

In its account of its own history, OFPRA states that the focus on judging the eligibility of the applicant is crucial, for 'the credibility of the narrative, its coherence and its accuracy, comes down to the question of proof'.[112] The refugee from then onwards carried the burden of establishing their right to asylum. In addition, the semi-autonomous refugee groups to aid Armenians, Russians and Spaniards, which had hitherto played the leading role in settling refugees, were effectively subsumed into this new administrative apparatus.[113] Similar practices resulted from the introduction of the 1951 Convention elsewhere. Almost immediately after it came into force, states began to use the Convention as a means to restrict the entry of those seeking asylum. West Germany, for example, set up a 'recognition procedure' based in Nuremburg, which assessed the 'refugee quality' of applicants against the definition in Article 1A. In Italy, those entering the country illegally were held in 'collecting centres' where they would also be assessed as to 'refugee quality' before being released.[114] The logic of control that guided the process leading up to the 1951 Convention naturally fed into the manner in which it was implemented. The burdensome apparatus of screening procedures, surveillance and detention that is so ubiquitous today is not a betrayal of the spirit of the 1951 Convention, but rather is an expression of it.

The 1980 Refugee Act

It is worth exploring the passage of the 1980 Refugee Act in the United States in a little detail, because it is instructive in how the humanitarian narrative attached to refugee law is so ingrained that it obscures some of the themes I have been highlighting so far: the focus on control and management and setting up

110   Noiriel (n 1), 200.
111   Weis (n 19), 196.
112   OFPRA, *De la Grande guerre aux guerres sans nom: une histoire de l'OFPRA* (OFPRA, nd), 17.
113   In 1945, an office, similar to those that had been set up in the 1920s to aid Armenian and Russian refugees, had been created for the Spanish exiles. Ibid 9.
114   Weis (n 19), 216.

barriers to asylum, rather than facilitating it. It also provides some useful background for the rise of the Sanctuary Movement, discussed in Chapter 5, which was formed in the immediate aftermath of passage of the Act. Just as with the 1951 Convention, it is frequently argued that the purpose of the 1980 Refugee Act, which formally abolished preferential treatment for refugees from countries in the Communist sphere and for the first time incorporated the Convention into domestic law, was to facilitate a more humanitarian and less political procedure for granting asylum.[115] As we shall see, this was certainly the line of sections of the Sanctuary Movement, and ended up severely compromising the movement's commitment to asylum. However, a humanitarian focus was clearly not the Act's effect, and arguably was not what lay behind its formation.

The large number of refugee arrivals in the late 1970s provoked much debate in Congress about how to restrict the numbers of refugees entering the country.[116] And throughout the 1970s, there had been various attempts to pass legislation to create a more statutory framework for adjudicating asylum claims and controlling refugee arrivals.[117] While the 1980 Act eliminated the 'seventh preference', which had privileged refugees coming from Communist countries, by adopting the 1951 Convention's definition of a refugee, it also 'destroyed the former presumption that all those fleeing Communist lands were in fact refugees'.[118] Thus, this group of refugees would now also be forced to prove themselves worthy of asylum, along with all other claimants. The Act also instituted the first delineation in law of a refugee, taken of course from Article 1A of the Convention. Indeed, rival bills had actually offered a wider definition including those fleeing natural disasters and armed conflict, yet these were all rejected.[119] In addition, many in Congress had decried the extensive use of the parole power exercised by the Executive to allow whole groups of refugees in at various times. This was a discretionary power that had been used repeatedly since the Eisenhower administration to allow in hundreds of thousands of Hungarians, Soviet Jews, Vietnamese, Cambodians and Laotians over and above the statutory quota restrictions.[120] The 1980 Act finally closed this mode of access to protection too.

It is perhaps in this context that the process that led to the 1980 Act can best be understood, not primarily as a humanitarian gesture but rather as a mechanism for a more controlled and less 'politicised' refugee admissions procedure. The

---

115   For example, Anker DE and Posner MH, 'The Forty Year Crisis: A Legislative History of the Refugee Act of 1980' (1981), 19, *San Diego Law Review*, 9.

116   Lee E, 'A nation of immigrants and a gatekeeping nation: American immigration law and policy' in Reed Ueda (ed), *A Companion to American Immigration* (Blackwell Publishing, 2006), 22.

117   Anker and Posner (n 115), 20.

118   Loescher and Scanlan (n 57), 155.

119   Anker and Posner (n 115), 22.

120   Lee (n 116), 22; Kurzban IJ, 'A Critical Analysis of Refugee Law' (1982), 36, *University of Miami Law Review*, 865, 872.

combination of an overtly political asylum paradigm, grounded in the ideology of the United States as the home of freedom and human rights, together with wide executive discretion in granting admission, meant that every refugee crisis led to political agitation in favour of their admission, whether it was Hungarians, Cubans, Haitians, Chileans or Vietnamese – although, of course, the executive operated a far more restrictive policy of paroling refugees from regimes friendly to the United States, such as Chile and Haiti, than from Communist countries.[121] Bill Ong Hing has noted that 'a major catalyst for the new refugee law was a disturbing anxiety felt by some members of Congress that thousands of Southeast Asians would destabilize many communities'.[122] Although the 1980 Act is usually associated with the haloed name of the liberal Senator Edward Kennedy, it was co-sponsored by one of the most reactionary senators of the time, Strom Thurmond, known mainly for his racism and hostility to Civil Rights. Ong Hing goes on to argue that the 'emphasis on "humanitarianism" . . . clouds other political motivations such as the desire to limit refugee admissions'.[123] Peter H. Schuck explains further the motivations that lay behind the Act:

> By the end of the [1970s], the [Congressional] committees' leaders could mobilize support for a new refugee admissions system. They envisioned a process that would be more predictable, manageable, and consultative, that would enhance Congress's policy influence, and that would limit the administration's parole power. The Refugee Act . . . was the result of this vision.[124]

Many of those in Congress who were especially hostile to the arrival of large numbers of Vietnamese refugees linked the issue with the problem of the parole power, already mentioned above. One such congressman, Representative Joshua Eilberg, specifically argued that parole was being used to flout the restrictions imposed under existing legislation.[125] In total, between 1975 and 1979, some 300,000 refugees were allowed into the United States under parole powers.[126] One of the key provisions of the 1980 Act was that it ended the wide discretionary powers of the executive to parole unlimited numbers of refugees into the country. So Section 212 of the Act severely restricts the parole power:

> The Attorney General may not parole into the United States an alien who is a refugee unless the Attorney General determines that compelling reasons

---

121 Kurzban (n 120), 872.
122 Ong Hing B, *Making and Remaking Asian America Through Immigration Policy 1850–1990* (Stanford University, 1993), 127.
123 Lee (n 116), 23.
124 Schuck PH, *Citizens, Strangers, and In-Betweens: Essays on Immigration and Citizenship* (Westview Press, 1998), 101.
125 Loescher and Scanlan (n 57), 153.
126 Ibid.

in the public interest *with respect to that particular alien* require that the alien be paroled into the United States rather than be admitted as a refugee . . . [emphasis added]

Note the emphasis on an individualistic determination and the 'public interest' as a key criterion. In addition, the Act reaffirmed that the burden of proof rested with the claimant for asylum.[127]

The numbers of refugees admitted into the United States fell from an average of 100,000 per year between 1975 and 1980 to around 50,000 in the years following the passage of the Refugee Act.[128] The potential for the 1951 Convention, as passed into law by the 1980 Act, to be an effective means for a cool and legalistic blanket refusal of claims can be seen in the following statement by Stephen E. Palmer, President Carter's deputy assistant secretary for Human Rights and Humanitarian Affairs, defending the large-scale refusal of asylum to Haitians:

> Determination of a particular asylum claim . . . is not a general referendum on human rights in the home country . . . Instead, we must apply a narrow and clearly focused standard established by treaty and by U.S. statutes. The question in passing on an asylum application is this: Does this particular individual have a 'well-founded fear of persecution' based on race, religion, nationality, membership in a particular social group or political opinion if he or she were to return to the home country?[129]

In the months following the passing of the Act, one of the largest arrivals of refugees into the United States took place with the Mariel boatlift of more than 100,000 Cubans to Florida. In order to assuage concerns, the Carter administration declared that all arrivals would be screened for their correspondence to the 1951 Convention standard of a refugee. However, the large and concentrated numbers made this impractical. In addition, the government refused to classify them as refugees, because to do so would 'reward illegal entry' and would thus set a 'dangerous precedent' for the future control of refugee arrivals.[130]

As we shall see, the attempt to depoliticise asylum was at one level unsuccessful. The Sanctuary Movement that almost immediately followed passage of the Act was perhaps the largest and most politicised pro-refugee movement in US history. Yet at another deeper level, the Act achieved its purpose in two ways. First, in confronting the Sanctuary Movement, the government was able to shield itself with the claim, on very similar terms to that of the Carter administration official quoted above, that the practice of refugee admissions was purely a legal and bureaucratic one. Indeed, it is striking how the arguments put forward by the

---

127   Kurzban (n 120), 874, 876, footnote 67.
128   Lee (n 116), 23.
129   Quoted on Loescher and Scanlan (n 57), 179.
130   Ibid 185.

liberal Carter administration and the hard-right Reagan administration are almost the same, both deploying the mantra of the 1951 Convention as reflected in the 1980 Act. Second, and more insidiously, the humanitarian claims of the Act led many in the Sanctuary Movement to have illusions that the problem was not the Act, but the failure of the government to abide by it. This, in turn, led the movement into practices that owed more to the paradigm of border control than to political liberation, as will become evident in Chapter 5.

Some argue that the Reagan administration's continued preference for refugees from Communist countries was a betrayal of the 1980 Act.[131] This was also the view of many in the Sanctuary Movement. However, one could equally argue that the Reagan administration was simply better able to obscure its political preferences behind the mask of a more 'objective' legal standard.[132] Moreover, it could also be argued that many, perhaps most, of those who crossed from Central America into the United States did not *sensu stricto* fit the definition of refugee contained in the 1951 Convention and the 1980 Act. This, too, would lead some in the Sanctuary Movement to make dubious distinctions and engage in some offensive practices, which will be discussed in detail. In the decades since, it is clear that the dominant discourse involving refugees has indeed become more legalistic and set in terms of border control and the 'problem' of undocumented migrants. Writing in 1996, Norman and Naomi Zucker described refugee policy as having become 'an exercise in alchemy: how to transform refugees into immigrants, immigrants who can be controlled, regulated, and above all, chosen'.[133] Subsuming the question of asylum into a legal framework has been key to achieving this policy objective, as can be seen from the following statistics. In the period 1980–1983, between 1 million and 1.5 million people were forced to flee the spiralling violence in Guatemala and Nicaragua as well as El Salvador. Of these, roughly 500,000 came to the United States.[134] This figure represented a number roughly equal to that of the Vietnamese refugees who came to the United States in the late 1970s; but whereas the latter had been received with relative openness as fugitives from a Communist regime recently at war with the US, as far as the Central Americans were concerned, the gates would be closed. Between June 1981 and March 1991, 2.8% of Salvadoran applicants were granted asylum, whereas the equivalent numbers were 74.5% for Soviets, 69% Chinese and 61% Iranians, all of them of course states hostile to the United States.[135] Zucker and Zucker put their finger on the key point when they

---

131   Ibid.
132   This is the argument put forward by Ann Crittenden and Ira J. Kurzban, although Kurzban attributes this to the residual executive power in the 1980 Act to designate refugee quotas. Crittenden A, *Sanctuary: A Story of American Conscience and the Law in Collision* (Weidenfeld & Nicolson, 1988), 22; Kurzban (n 120), 881.
133   Zucker NL and Zucker NF, *Desperate Crossings: Seeking Refuge in America* (ME Sharpe, 1996), 6–7.
134   Crittenden (n 132), xvi.
135   Zucker and Zucker (n 133), 85.

write: 'Salvadorans confronted a wall far more impenetrable than an inept bureaucracy and doctrinaire policy makers. That wall was the refugee law itself and the definition on which it is based'.[136]

The 1967 Protocol and regional instruments

Although the 1967 Protocol removed the temporal and geographic limitations of the 1951 Convention, the restrictive definition of a refugee as one fleeing their home state for reasons of persecution on grounds of the denial of social or political rights remained. Indeed, it was strengthened due to the fact that this definition now assumed a global and indefinite character: i.e. it completed the gesture towards universality. As a result, the overwhelming majority of contemporary forced migrants from the Global South, fleeing conditions of civil war, natural disasters and economic hardship, were placed outside this 'universal' refugee construct.[137]

The story, as often told, is that 1967 represents the fulfilment of the aspirations of 1951; it is a narrative of onward progress and the spread of refugee protection. Yet, other factors were at play too. As the concentration of refugee movements shifted away from Europe towards Africa the 1951 Convention was threatened with becoming, like its pre-war ancestors, obsolete. Recognising this, newly independent states in Africa were busy drafting their own treaty, eventually to become the 1969 Organisation of African Unity (OAU) Convention. The UNHCR, along with many state parties, were anxious lest the putative OAU Convention should threaten the hegemony of UNHCR and that of the 1951 Convention. It was only when the first drafts of the OAU Convention were being drafted in 1964–1965 that the UNHCR sprang into action with a proposal to remove the temporal and geographical limitations of the 1951 Convention.[138] The speed and alacrity with which state parties and the UNHCR thus agreed to the 1967 Protocol was arguably as much about preserving the integrity of refugee law itself as it was about extending protection to new groups of refugees. As Prakash Shah has written: 'the main intention behind the Protocol was to facilitate the retention of post-colonial influence in Africa through the agency of the UNHCR'.[139] Thus, while the narrative of the 1967 Protocol fulfilling the aspirations of the 1951 Convention is largely correct, it is not for the reasons that most people assume. What was achieved was not so much a universal humanitarian approach *towards* the refugee, but rather a universal claim of the refugee law regime *over* the refugee. However, in at least one crucial aspect, the newly independent African states were following the footsteps of the Europeans. A major concern among the drafters of the OAU Convention was that a legal

---

136   Ibid 89.
137   Hathaway (n 63), 162.
138   Holborn LW, *Refugees: A Problem of Our Time* (Scarecrow Press, 1975), 185.
139   Shah P, *Refugees, Race and the Legal Concept of Asylum in Britain* (Cavendish, 2000), 103.

framework for refugees *between states* was necessary in order to prevent asylees from committing subversive acts against their countries of origin.[140] Thus, the story of the spread of international refugee law to Africa is again one of extending control over the refugee and her movements.

The process used for getting the 1967 Protocol through the UN was designed precisely to prevent any wider political discussion on the question of the scope of protection and the question of the refugee definition; it is why the Protocol was drafted in a plain technical way, and why it makes no explicit reference to the 1951 Convention.[141] As Hathaway writes:

> The refugee definition established by the Protocol has enabled authorities in developed states to avoid the provision of adequate protection to Third World asylum claimants while escaping the political embarrassment entailed by use of an overtly Eurocentric refugee policy.[142]

Frédéric Tiberghien points out that the very fact of creating a definition of a refugee in law in turn creates the distinction between 'true' and 'false' refugees. The refugee determination procedure, ostensibly necessary to police this distinction, can also end up as a mechanism for making subjective judgements on whether or not the refugee is worthy of being granted asylum.[143] B.S. Chimni critiques the 1951 Convention when he writes that its 'objectivism tends . . . to substitute the subjective perceptions of the State authorities for the experiences of the refugee'.[144] In summary, all those aspects of international refugee law, as expressed primarily by the 1951 Convention, that are claimed to be positives – objectivism, universality and, most of all, legality – turn out on closer inspection to be key ingredients in the diminution of the refugee subject, and the placing of her under even greater control and management by states and the international legal order. We are a long way indeed from asylum as a space in which the refugee can enjoy freedom from seizure.

There have of course been many developments at the international level since the 1951 Covention and the 1967 Protocol, most notably the OAU Convention,[145] the Cartagena Declaration,[146] the Common European Asylum

---

140   Jahn E, 'Developments in refugee law in the framework of regional organisations outside Europe' (1966), 13, *Association for the Study of the World Refugee Problem Bulletin*, 75, 81.

141   Hathaway (n 63), 163–164.

142   Ibid 164.

143   Tiberghien F, *La protection des réfugiés en France* (2nd edn, Économica, 1988), 57.

144   Chimni BS, 'From Resettlement to Involuntary Repatriation: Towards a Critical History of Durable Solutions to Refugee Problems' (2004), 23, *Refugee Survey Quarterly*, 55, 62.

145   Organization of African Unity Convention Governing the Specific Aspects of Refugee Problems in Africa 1969, 1001 UNTS 45.

146   Cartagena Declaration on Refugees, Colloquium on the International Protection of Refugees in Central America, Mexico and Panama, 22 November 1984.

Policy,[147] the massive expansion of UNHCR's activities, and the proliferation of NGOs in everything, from running camps to providing assistance in host communities and giving legal advice to asylum-seekers. Many of these developments have acknowledged some of the limitations of the existing legal framework and have sought to fill gaps, e.g. the absence of a requirement for persecution in the OAU and Cartagena documents, and provision of miminum standards of life through the EU Qualification Directive[148] and the activities of NGOs. Some scholars, notably Barbara Harrell-Bond, have described how UNHCR and other NGOs organisations have in fact facilitated the process of maintaining refugees as passive recipients of aid and subjects of control.[149] And indeed, the humanitarian bent of these activities, with its concommitent papering over of the political, further reinforces the narrowness and passivity of the refugee subject as delineated by law. So, while refugee law has developed in certain respects since the 1951 Convention, the framework of asylum remains bound within the belief in an objective test for who is and is not deserving of being granted access to it, along with a depoliticised refugee subject as delineated by law. In Part III, we will see the extent to which this remains the case in relation to the US Sanctuary Movement and the Sans-Papiers.

---

147 European Union: Council of the European Union, Directive 2013/32/EU of the European Parliament and of the Council of 26 June 2013 on common procedures for granting and withdrawing international protection (recast).

148 European Union: Council of the European Union, Directive 2011/95/EU of the European Parliament and of the Council of 13 December 2011 on standards for the qualification of third-country nationals or stateless persons as beneficiaries of international protection, for a uniform status for refugees or for persons eligible for subsidiary protection, and for the content of the protection granted (recast).

149 Harrell-Bond B, *Imposing Aid: Emergency Assistance to Refugees* (OUP, 1986); Verdirame G and Harrell-Bond B, *Rights in Exile: Janus-Faced Humanitarianism* (Berghan, 2005); Stevens J, 'Prisons of the Stateless' (2006), 42, *New Left Review*, 53.

Conclusion to Part II

If the contemporary 'right of asylum' is fundamentally the right of the state to give shelter to fugitives on its territory, then it is at least doubtful that asylum as understood in the classical sense – as freedom from seizure by sovereign power – exists today. The right of asylum today, therefore, does not necessarily possess any objective free-standing characteristics, such as those based on faith and political solidarity, as it is a function of sovereignty itself. Contemporary asylum is therefore a legal fiction: the refugee has no protection from seizure by the host state, either literally, as is brutally self-evident in the global archipelago of detention centres and the like, or figuratively, in the sense of being forced into forms of subjectivisation and control via the process of refugee status determination and legal categorisation. Instead, freedom from seizure by the refugee's pursuers in the sending state is merely a consequence of the sovereign rights of the host states, not any rights borne by the refugee. Writing in 1938, Simpson was able to get to the heart of the matter on the question of a 'right of asylum':

> [A refugee] has no 'rights', both because as an alien he can have no complete rights against a sovereign state, and because legal rights originate from a sovereignty and as refugee he has no sovereign to endow him with or enforce his rights. He has no 'right' of asylum; it is a contradiction in terms. Asylum is a privilege conferred by a state, not a condition inherent in the individual. So far as it has a technical meaning in international practice the 'right of asylum' refers to the custom of not allowing the extradition of a person for a purely political offence. In a non-technical sense it is merely an impressive way of describing the wrong of exclusion.[1]

However, even the political offence exception to which Simpson refers is today being gradually eroded almost to extinction.[2] But even there, extradition is based

1 Simpson JH, *Refugees: Preliminary Report of a Survey* (Royal Institute of International Affairs, 1938), 100.
2 Behrman S, 'Accidents, Agency and Asylum: Constructing the Refugee Subject' (2014), 25, *Law and Critique*, 249, 254–255.

on the legal relations between states, of their rights and duties, rather than those of the refugee. Then there is the principle of *non-refoulement*, which some claim has become the kernel of a right of asylum. Although this principle prevents a state from deporting a refugee back to where they would face persecution, it does not prevent that state from deporting them elsewhere or placing severe restrictions on their freedom where no other state wishes to receive them.[3] Again, if we understand asylum in the classic sense of freedom of seizure, or sanctuary as a place of safety and security in which one can continue to live as normal a life as possible, then the systematic detention across the world of unwanted refugees who cannot be extradited for whatever reason negates the essence of asylum/ sanctuary. And yet, Simpson's diagnosis of the problem remains. So long as there are nation-states and legal sovereigns over territory then there will be refugees, and there cannot be any meaningful 'right of asylum'. So, then, what is the nature of contemporary refugee law if not to provide a framework of asylum in the proper sense? It is, as I have tried to show in the preceding chapters, the legal framework for the control of movements of forced migrants, the re-imposition of order upon a world disordered by wars and revolution, and a mechanism for managing the refugee 'burden' between nation-states. Or as Hathaway writes: 'Refugee law has historically been valued by states because it is a politically and socially acceptable way to maximise border control in the face of recurrent involuntary migration'.[4]

Writing in 1972, Grahl-Madsen notes that much consideration was then being given among scholars as to the development of a 'binding international instrument guaranteeing the individual a right to be granted asylum, should he be in need of it'.[5] A conference convened by the UN in 1977 to draft such a convention collapsed as states made it clear that in order to grant such a right, the legal definition would have to be made far more restrictive than even that contained in the 1951 Convention.[6] Forty years later, we are no closer to such an instrument,

---

3   Grahl-Madsen A, *The Status of Refugees in International Law: Volume Two* (AW Sijthoff, 1972), 94. The recent history in the United Kingdom, Australia and elsewhere of detention centres and control orders for such individuals demonstrates the paucity of the principle of non-refoulement when stripped to its essentials. In addition, in the landmark case of *Othman (Abu Qatada) v. United Kingdom* [2012] Application 8139/09, the European Court of Human Rights held that returning someone to a state with a history of torture would not necessarily violate the principle of non-refoulement where a so-called Memorandum of Understanding (MOU) was in place between the asylum state and the state of origin. These MOUs are supposed to guarantee humane treatment of the deportee, although they are highly controversial, with questions often raised as to how effective they are in preventing torture and other forms of serious maltreatment.

4   Hathaway JC, 'Why Refugee Law Still Matters' (2007), 8, *Melbourne Journal of International Law*, 89, 99–100.

5   Grahl-Madsen (n 3), 22.

6   Loescher G, *Beyond Charity: International Cooperation and the Global Refugee Crisis* (OUP, 1993), 140; Chamberlain MD, 'The Mass Migration of Refugees and International Law' (1983), 7, *The Fletcher Forum of World Affairs*, 93, 100.

and arguably much farther away. Indeed, such a prospect may be akin to the proverbial pot of gold at the end of the rainbow, at least in a world dominated by the nation-state and law. Grahl-Madsen perhaps hits the nail on the head when, in reference to the possibility of the existence of a right of asylum of the individual, he writes:

> If a State owes such a duty on the international plane, the subject of the corresponding right need not be the individual concerned. Actually . . . it is more likely that it would be one or more other States . . . to whom the duty is owed. A 'right of asylum' for the individual would then in strict terms mean the possibility for an individual to claim the benefit of a rule of inter-national law in force between two or more proper subjects of international law, to the effect that in given circumstances asylum shall be granted.[7]

In other words, insofar as forced migrants receive some benefit from refugee law, they are residual ones stemming from legal relations between states. As Grahl-Madsen writes elsewhere, the 'right of a State to grant asylum flows from its territorial integrity, which is a pillar of international law'.[8]

The flip side of refugee law operating as a function of the administrative management of refugee movements between states has been the draining away of the political subjectivity of the refugee herself. A central thesis in Noiriel's history of refugee law in France is that the organic social relationships within communities, which had hitherto been the basis on which refugees had been received and assisted, were undermined and dissolved over the course of the century after 1789. In their place came the system of abstract legal categories and relationships imposed from above. This development was critical in the historic downfall of the refugee and the concept of asylum.[9] Throughout most of the nineteenth century, the question of the refugee was still mainly a polit-ical one. From around 1880 until World War I, the question became increasingly one that surrounded the rights and duties of states in relation to extradition requests. But it was the 'emergency' measures taken during World War I – closure of borders, imposition of compulsory ID cards and passports, etc. – that reframed the whole question of asylum.[10] A key difference between the nine-teenth- and twentieth-century paradigms of asylum was that earlier asylum had not been a right granted by the state. Thus, the question of receiving the refugee was always contingent, and therefore always open and subject to open argument and pleas, including from the refugees themselves. Evidence gleaned from a comparison between correspondence between refugees and the French authorities in the nineteenth and twentieth centuries suggests that, whereas previously

7 Grahl-Madsen (n 3), 80.
8 Grahl-Madsen A, *Territorial Asylum* (Almqvist & Wiksell, 1980), 23.
9 Noiriel G, *Réfugiés et sans-papiers: La République face au droit d'asile XIXe–XXe siècles* (Hachette, 1998).
10 Ibid 180.

refugees pled on the basis of their political beliefs and activities, today they plead on the basis of persecution: from agent to victim. In the earlier period, refugees appealed to sentiment and solidarity, whereas today, they appeal to the reason of the judge or bureaucrat.[11] The refugee has thus become depoliticised and de-subjectivised as an active subject in the circumstances that have made them refugees. The appeal to reason is fraught with the problem that it is a concept that claims for itself objective truth, but which in reality is decided upon certain prejudices and beliefs. Solidarity and sentiment make no pretence to being objective or universal concepts. Reason is law; solidarity and sentiment are the stuff of politics and the contestable.

Aside from the occasional comment, such as that from Türk and Nicholson which appears at the beginning of this part of the book, and in spite of the common sense idea that the law of asylum that exists today is somehow the continuation of the ancient practice described in Part I, it is striking that almost no writers that I am aware of attempt to argue in detail for such a link. The only commentator who does so is Grahl-Madsen in his ground-breaking *The Status of Refugees in International Law*, published in the late 1960s and early 1970s. But even here, the attempt to make such a link is tenuous at best, and given in only the broadest of brushstrokes. In any case, Grahl-Madsen puts far greater stress and detail on the origins of refugee law within the framework of the classic model, from Grotius and Vattel onwards, of public international law as the law of states.[12] Alternatively, writers on the historical tradition of asylum approach the subject as of antiquarian interest. This is partly because many of them, although not all, are classical scholars. The point is that they are describing an institution or practice that has little or no visible existence in the modern world. This, I have been arguing throughout this book, is not in spite of the existence of a law of asylum but is because of it. Much more recently, Marfleet has written on the contemporary relevance of the ancient tradition of asylum.[13] For him, its resonance is found not in law but in resistance movements against the law, notably the US Sanctuary Movement.

In the next and final part of this book, I develop this point in greater detail and also draw out the lessons of the US Sanctuary Movement and the French Sans-Papiers in terms of the confrontation between the legal paradigm of asylum (what by now should be clearly a contradiction in terms) and the historical practice informed by theological and political considerations, which resists the methods of categorisation and control imposed by law.

11 Ibid 274–290.
12 Grahl-Madsen, *Status of Refugees* (n 3), 3–15.
13 Marfleet P, 'Understanding "Sanctuary": Faith and Traditions of Asylum' (2011), 24, *Journal of Refugee Studies*, 440.

Part III
Resistance
Grassroots asylum

Introduction to Part III

> Born in superstition, bred by religious dogma, and nurtured by the vanity of fifteenth- and sixteenth-century diplomats, asylum, the illegitimate child of law, refuses either to die or fade away.[1]

In exploring the development of both asylum and refugee law, it has been evident that they each spring from very different sources and are governed by different sets of norms. Asylum is grounded in religious and political notions of justice and redemption. In the case of refugee law, its more recent appearance on the scene has mainly been the result of concerns with the rights of states to control movement across borders and the biopolitical management of population within the sovereign terrain. Some key themes that have emerged have been the following. First, that law and asylum have been uneasy in each other's company; indeed, there have been repeated conflicts between the two. What appears to be a fundamental incompatibility has shown itself in the fact that asylum has tended to flourish in periods when legal structures have been relatively weak (post-Classical Greece, late Imperial Rome and Medieval Europe) and has been eclipsed during periods of resurgent sovereign power and the re-establishment of law (early Imperial Rome, early Modern Europe). Another major theme that has emerged has been the way in which certain contestable notions of justice that have surrounded asylum have been superseded by the claimed objectivity of refugee law, the latter precluding contestation at any substantive level. Linked to this development has been the question of judgement over the person seeking sanctuary/asylum. Prior to the modern age, the weight of regulation, such as it was, fell on determining the space of sanctuary, whereas today, the eye of the law falls overwhelmingly upon the person of the refugee.

At this point, a number of questions flow from this investigation: is asylum, as historically understood, any longer possible? What advantages, if any, would asylum today offer to the refugee in contrast to refugee law? What are the implications for law if such a resurgence of asylum were to occur? Some of

---

1 Fruchterman RL, 'Asylum: Theory and Practice' (1972), 26, *Judge Advocate General Journal*, 169.

the answers to these questions are revealed in this part of the book: an exploration of the US Sanctuary Movement and the Sans-Papiers and their relationship to law. Here, we find attempted resurrections of the ancient practice of sanctuary, perhaps in their most sustained form in the Western world since the decline of Church sanctuary in the sixteenth and seventeenth centuries. It is also the first time since then that we find sanctuary being used as a direct form of resistance against sovereign power. Perhaps most interestingly, they have transcended certain key distinctions between the asylum of old and its contemporary more secular setting. So, on the one hand, they have adopted the ancient practice of using church space as a sanctuary beyond the writ of law, and on the other hand, they also spread beyond this to the use of private homes, community centres, theatres, university campuses, trade union offices, workplaces and even to embrace the notion of sanctuary cities. Thus, sanctuary burst the bounds of the sacred and spread throughout society.[2] Also, whereas much of the earlier tradition of asylum was concerned only with the domestic – asylees fleeing within the realm to a church or shrine – the Sanctuary Movement facilitated the crossing of borders, and the Sans-Papiers have demanded a right of access to the community that is not beholden to the state. Together they have ruptured the paradigm of a state-centric view of asylum that has come to dominate in the modern age, from the writings of Grotius and Pufendorf to the 1951 Convention. In short, these movements have re-asserted the notion of asylum as 'freedom from seizure' from the clutches of both the state of origin and the state of asylum.

A further important aspect of the Sanctuary Movement and the Sans-Papiers that distinguishes them from earlier forms of asylum is that in these instances, sanctuary confronts not simply law but more specifically a developed system of refugee law, which claims to be based on protection of the refugee. As will become apparent, this fact led to much confusion and disorientation among Sanctuary Movement activists. Churches once again became spaces of protection from the forces of secular law. And yet, equally, aspects of juridical thinking, of legal processes, indeed of refugee law itself, found their way into the practice of sanctuary. This forces us to deal with the question of whether the power of legal ideology has infected and sullied the practice of asylum, even where it arises outside of the law, turning it into a pale shadow of its former self. Perhaps we are faced with the prospect of there being no space for a sustained alternative to law in dealing with the refugee question today? The hegemony of law eventually brought within its orbit many of the activists in this movement. In doing so, it not only corrupted much of the sanctuary tradition but it turned 'sanctuary' in many instances into an adjunct of the law rather than a challenge to it.

---

2   It is worth noting here that sacralisation functions to cleave aspects of life away from the everyday, 'removed from the free use . . . of men'. Thus, to break the bounds of the sacred through profanation is a form of resistance to such reification of objects, practices, spaces, etc. Agamben G, 'In praise of profanation' in *Profanations* (Jeff Fort tr, Zone Books, 2007), 73, and generally.

In the case of the Sans-Papiers, they were less beholden to legal categories. Indeed, one point of disctinction between them and the US Sanctuary Movement has been that their struggle comprised refugees whose asylum claims have been rejected in addition to other types of migrants. While, in fact, the lines were blurred between 'refugees' and 'economic migrants' in the case of the Sanctuary Movement, many activists seemed more concered with policing that distinction rather than overcoming it. This was far less in evidence with the Sans-Papiers. The reason for this is two-fold. First, there was the basis on which the claims were made in the first place. In the case of the Sanctuary Movement, the claim being asserted was on the basis of being a 'refugee'; for the Sans-Papiers, their claim has rested on broader notions of freedom of movement, and the duties owed by France to all refugees and migrants in the country, in particular those from the Global South, and especially those from former French colonies. Second, the movement of the Sans-Papiers has been initiated and led by refugees/migrants themselves, in contrast to the Sanctuary Movement which was mainly led by US-born activists. In both cases, the non-migrant activists were pulled towards the law and its categories, but with the Sans-Papiers, the migrants/refugees were better able to resist this, and they did so.

However, the Sanctuary Movement challenged the border in ways that the Sans-Papiers never did. The very fact of actually helping people to enter the country by evading border controls was one of the most scandalous aspects of the Sanctuary Movement. Whereas in the case of the Sans-Papiers, they did not do this, and were frequently concered to emphasise that they had entered France legally, thus perhaps reinforcing the legitimacy of the border itself. Again, the distinction was largely bred by the different circumstances. In the United States, the crisis was one of people being denied entry and protection at the Mexico-US border; in France, the issue mainly concerned people who had already spent many years in the country.

Taken together, though, these two movements represent what I call 'grassroots asylum'. That is, they have taken some of the essential principles of the historical tradition of asylum/sanctuary, of spaces of protection that are not beholden to sovereign law and legal subject categories, and given them new life as part of resistance movements from below that challenge the monopoly of the state in deciding who does and does not have the right to be part of the community. In this, they have followed in a tradition that has persisted even after the destruction of the old sanctuary tradition. There was the case of two of the signatories of the death warrant for Charles I who fled to New Haven following the Restoration, and were given asylum in the church there.[3] Another story is told of a homicide taking sanctuary in a church in Malta in about 1807. While the outcome of this incident is not known, Malta at that time still possessed a legal right of church sanctuary, which had survived the British occupation of the

---

3   Osterweis RG, *Three Centuries of New Haven* (Yale University, 1964), 55–64.

island.[4] In the mid-nineteenth century, the Underground Railroad spirited escaped slaves to freedom in the North using many churches and private residences as stops along the way.[5] Much more recently, in Europe during World War II, many churches and the communities around them gave sanctuary to those fleeing occupying forces. The most famous of these was in Le Chambon in France.[6] A couple of decades later, draft-resisters fleeing from federal authorities in the United States during the Vietnam War were given asylum in churches as well as in university campuses.[7] Indeed, some of the leading figures in sanctuary for Vietnam War draft-resisters such as The Revd William Sloane Coffin and The Revd Gustav Schultz would later play key roles in the Sanctuary Movement a decade later.[8] In the late 1970s, a movement arose in Holland in which churches gave sanctuary to immigrants and refugees threatened with deportation as a result of increasingly harsh immigration measures from the

---

4 de' Mazzinghi TJ, *Sanctuaries* (Halden & Son, 1887), 4.
5 The work of Wilbur Siebert is very revealing on the subject and benefits from being based on first-hand accounts of the movement given to him in the late nineteenth century. See Siebert WH, 'A Quaker Section of the Underground Railroad in Northern Ohio' (1930), 39, *Ohio Archaeological and Historical Quarterly*, 53; Siebert WH, *The Mysteries of Ohio's Underground Railroads* (Long's College Book Company, 1951); Siebert WH, *The Underground Railroad: From Slavery to Freedom: A Comprehensive History* (Dover Publications, 2006).
6 See Hallie PP, *Lest Innocent Blood Be Shed: The Story of the Village of Le Chambon, and How Goodness Happened There* (Harper and Row, 1979), for an absorbing account of this inspiring story. Robert McAfee Brown references Le Chambon at a rally for the Sanctuary Movement. Transcript of speech given on 23 March 1986 (GSSC).
7 Willigan JD, 'Sanctuary: A Communitarian Form of Counter-Culture' (1970), 25, *Union Seminary Quarterly Review*, 517; Foley MS, 'Sanctuary! A bridge between civilian and GI protest against the Vietnam War' in Marilyn B Young and Robert Buzzanco (eds), *A Companion to the Vietnam War* (Blackwell Publishers, 2002); Goldsmith-Kasinsky R, *Refugees from Militarism: Draft-Age Americans in Canada* (Transaction Books, 1976) provides an interesting contemporary account of those who crossed into Canada to avoid the draft or, in the case of deserters, to evade the Military Police. Although they were in effect seeking and were granted asylum, refugee law appears to have played little or no part. Instead, their reception remained primarily a question of politics, even though the numbers involved were substantial. Goldsmith-Kasinsky estimates that around 30,000 to 40,000 Americans took sanctuary in Canada at this time (5). At least some of those who had previously taken sanctuary in churches in the United States to resist the draft later fled across the Canadian border to seek sanctuary there too (45–46).
8 The link made by some of those who had been involved in both movements was that both cases involved people having to leave their homes against their will due to war, whether to resist fighting in one or to escape one, e.g. 'Sanctuary for Salvadorans', draft typed mimeographed document, 1 October 1982, 6 (GSSC). At the outset of the Sanctuary Movement, activists explicitly identified themselves within this tradition, stretching from the late Roman era through medieval church sanctuary, the Underground Railroad and the anti-Vietnam War movement, e.g. 'Historical and Theological Basis for Sanctuary', undated [early 1982?], unsigned typed mimeographed document (CRTFCAR).

government.[9] When a Turkish refugee, Kemal Altun, committed suicide by leaping out of the window in a courtroom in Berlin in 1983, a sanctuary movement developed in that city too.[10]

It is perhaps worth noting here that the sanctuary movement during the Vietnam War saw itself as quite clearly in opposition to the law and sovereign order. Coffin, for example, said:

> The underlying rationale for church sanctuary was theological and political rather than legal . . . there was no claim to any legal recognition of the privilege. Indeed, it was precisely the illegality of the act – an act of civil disobedience – that gave the concept of sanctuary its symbolic power as a confrontation with an unjust and illogical war.[11]

Another activist at the time identified the kernel of what sanctuary had always been, and the role it played for the movement then: ' "Sanctuary" has always meant a "holy place", a place in some way independent of the state's sovereignty'.[12] Perhaps this is indicative of a time when social orders were being challenged across the globe, and in which therefore the concept of asylum as freedom from seizure by law and the state held great purchase. The dichotomy between law and sanctuary would be much less clear in the Sanctuary Movement a decade later, when the sovereign order, particularly in the West, had re-established its poise and authority.

Nevertheless, all these represent important examples of 'grassroots asylum'. But the two that I focus on in the following chapters present the most sustained challenges to the legal framework of asylum as it exists today, and offer us the clearest picture of how asylum could be reconceived in the modern world.

While many criticisms can be made of the Sanctuary Movement and the Sans-Papiers in their limitations, and indeed I explicitly make many of these in the pages that follow, they demonstrate the potential to reconfigure asylum away from the degraded experiences imposed on refugees/migrants by the current system of refugee law, and of the legal paradigm in general. For they show us a potential way out of the demoralising binary of strict border controls versus reliance on international refugee law. Indeed, as I have tried to argue in

9   Sanctuary – The Congregation as a Refuge: Report of the international workshop, held under the auspices of the Council of Churches in the Netherlands and the Human Rights Desk of the National Council of Christian Churches in the United States of America – 26–30 August 1986 (Kerk en Wereld, 1986).

10 Cohen S, *From the Jews to the Tamils: Britain's Mistreatment of Refugees* (South Manchester Law Centre, 1988), 44–45.

11 Quoted in Francis ST, *Smuggling Revolution: The Sanctuary Movement in America* (Capital Research Center, 1986), 42. The same point is made by Walsh JH and O'Neill ME, 'Sanctuary: A Legal Privilege or Act of Civil Disobedience?' (1987), 61, *Florida Bar Journal*, 11, 14.

12 Golder WE, 'War Resister's Sanctuary', *U.S. Catholic* (November 1972), 34.

Part II, that binary is in fact something of an illusion, for the two are largely complementary rather than anatagonistic. It is 'grassroots asylum', as practised by the Sanctuary Movement and the Sans-Papiers, that challenges the erection of ever stricter borders, the panapoly of border controls and legal processes for entry, the archipelago of detention centres and all the other degradations visited upon the refugee/migrant today.

5 The US Sanctuary Movement

Introduction

As mentioned in the Introduction to Part III, there is a long tradition of grassroots asylum in the United States, from the colonial era protection of regicides in New Haven through to the Underground Railroad and the sanctuary offered to Vietnam War draft-resisters. The impetus for the creation of the Sanctuary Movement came from the experiences of the rapidly growing numbers of people who were escaping from a particularly brutal set of conflicts in Central America in the early 1980s. In Guatemala and El Salvador, up to 1.5 million people were displaced, not to mention the many more who also had to flee their homes in Nicaragua and Honduras. Hundreds of thousands moved north into the United States.[1] Not only did these refugees have to suffer the trauma of the violence wrecking their home countries, but they found it almost impossible to gain asylum in the US. Statistics from the period demonstrate that Salvadorans had a less than 3% chance of being granted refugee status in the United States.[2] Although, it should be noted that those fleeing Nicaragua, which had a government hostile to the United States, were far more likely to get refugee status. Of course, this was in the context of a new institutional framework inaugurated by the 1980 Refugee Act. This is the basis of the argument put forward by Zucker and Zucker that refugee law itself was presenting an almost impenetrable wall for those seeking asylum.[3]

As was to become increasingly clear over the months and years following the introduction of the 1980 Refugee Act, in practice, the Immigration and Naturalization Service (INS) was routinely dismissing refugee claims from people fleeing regimes allied with the United States, while continuing to be more liberal

---

1 Crittenden A, *Sanctuary: A Story of American Conscience and the Law in Collision* (Weidenfeld & Nicolson, 1988), xvi.
2 Zucker NL and Zucker NF, *Desperate Crossings: Seeking Refuge in America* (ME Sharpe, 1996), 85.
3 Ibid 89.

in granting refugee status to those arriving from Communist countries. In the year following passage of the Act, just two Salvadorans were granted refugee status by the US government, while 154 claims were rejected. The year after, in 1982, 61 Salvadorans were given asylum, 994 were rejected and a backlog of 22,314 was awaiting a decision.[4] The politics of asylum were being obscured behind the legal 'objectivity' of the new system inaugurated by the 1980 Act.

In the summer of 1980, a particularly grisly event alerted faith groups, lawyers and other activists in Tucson, Arizona, to the problem. A group of twenty-seven Salvadorans were discovered in the Arizona desert attempting to cross into the United States, with half of them dead and the rest very close to death. Over the next 2 years, as a city very close to the border, the sight of refugees, often in states of great distress, being picked up and deported by the Border Patrol became a regular occurance. The direct impetus for the birth of the Sanctuary Movement came from a chance encounter, when a local rancher picked up a refugee hitchhiker heading north from the Mexican border.[5] When their car was pulled over, the refugee was promptly arrested and hurriedly deported. News spread of this incident, and soon a loose network of Quakers and others in Tucson were secretly hosting Central Americans in their homes, to protect them from arrest, detention and deportation. As spaces were rapidly filling up, Jim Corbett, who had been the instigator for this *ad hoc* form of grassroots asylum, then asked John Fife, pastor of Southside Presbyterian Church, to help out.[6] Fife, after consulting others in the church, agreed. Southside Church decided to give sanctuary to refugees in late 1981. A studio apartment had been fitted out at the back of the church, and refugees would stay there or in the Sunday school rooms.

According to Fife, it was Corbett who initially convinced him to break from a purely legalistic approach to helping the refugees, on the basis that the first principle was to adapt to the needs of the refugees rather than following legal rules. Whereas Southside Church had hitherto only housed refugees who had been bonded out of detention, Corbett asked Fife if they would also put up undocumented refugees, such as those he was already accommodating in his own house.[7] Once Southside had begun housing undocumented refugees in the church, Fife took to introducing new arrivals at the Sunday service and telling their stories, and each time challenging the congregation: 'Your government says that these people are illegal aliens. It is your civic duty when you know about their status to turn them in to INS. What do you think the faith requires of you?' After the services, members of the congregation would often take the refugees home for dinner, and subsequently invite them to continue their sanctuary in

---

4 Crittenden (n 1), 98.
5 Details of what followed can be found in Ibid 28–31.
6 Bau I, *This Ground is Holy: Church Sanctuary and Central American Refugees* (Paulist Press, 1985), 11.
7 'Conspiracy of Compassion', *Sojourners* (March 1985), 16–17.

their homes. Soon members of the congregation were going even further, by transporting refugees who had illegally crossed the border up to Tucson.[8] At this stage, no distinction was being made between 'legal' and 'illegal' refugees.

Corbett had begun organising to help refugees over the border with a collective of goat-herders that he was part of, who knew the border area well, and places where people could cross over safely from Mexico. The number of people involved in this 'border work' expanded into the Tucson refugee support group (Trsg), with hundreds of local residents involved in helping refugees get across the border and hosting them in their homes.[9] Following a trip by Corbett to Mexico in late 1981, one final strand of what would become the Sanctuary Movement was put in place. He discovered that many churches in Chiapas just over the border from Guatemala were already giving sanctuary to refugees from there and El Salvador, involving the offer of housing and food, finding jobs and assisting them to get past checkpoints. During this visit, the groundwork was laid for the stretch of 'underground railroad' from Chiapas up to the Mexican-US border.[10] Later this was joined up with a network of churches and private houses throughout the United States too.

After almost a year of this semi-clandestine activity, members of Southside Presbyterian Church recalled the ancient practice of church sanctuary, and it was suggested that they go public. Their aim was to highlight the plight of the refugees, and to call on others to join them in providing sanctuary for Central American refugees.[11] It was also clear that the Border Patrol were now aware of their activities, and it was felt that by going public they could pre-empt any allegations that they were nothing more than people-smugglers.[12]

But before making a final decision on a public declaration, the church council studied the history of sanctuary and the existing law on assisting refugees.[13] As part of this study, law professors from the University of Arizona were invited to brief them on the possible consequences of setting up a sanctuary. It was confirmed that there was no legal basis in the United States for church sanctuary.

---

8 Ibid 17; Tomsho R, *The American Sanctuary Movement* (Texas Monthly Press, 1987), 25.
9 The Trsg gave their group a lowercase acronym to symbolise the non-hierarchical nature of their group organisation.
10 Davidson M, *Convictions of the Heart: Jim Corbett and the Sanctuary Movement* (University of Arizona Press, 1988), 62–63. For a moving and evocative description, along with photographs, of the conditions in El Salvador and the experiences of refugees moving across the border through Mexico and into the United States assisted by the underground railroad and the sanctuary movement, see Dale Maharidge and Michael Williamson (photos), 'Escape from El Salvador', The Sacramento Bee, a five-part series that ran from 26 to 30 August 1984.
11 Cunningham H, *God and Caesar at the Rio Grande: Sanctuary and the Politics of Religion* (University of Minnesota Press, 1995), 31.
12 Smith C, *Resisting Reagan: The U.S. Central America Peace Movement* (University of Chicago, 1996), 66.
13 Crittenden (n 1), 66.

They would be liable for sentences of up to 5 years in jail and a $2,000 fine for harbouring illegal aliens. Yet, in spite of this, the council recommended that the church declare sanctuary. When put to the whole congregation in January 1982, it was endorsed by fifty-nine of them, with just two voting against and four abstaining. In his presentation to the congregation in favour of sanctuary, Fife had quoted the Old Testament injunctions to provide sanctuary.[14] At first, the offering of sanctuary was based on the Augustinian mode, with Fife declaring: 'We do not check Green Cards at the door; we meet people's needs. We will provide hospitality at this church to anyone who needs it'.[15] At the beginning, therefore, it was about 'hospitality' and human need and not law or legal definitions.

Birth of a movement

On 24 March 1982, on a cold sunny morning in Tucson, Arizona, Southside Presbyterian Church publically declared itself as a sanctuary. For the occasion, the front of this small, shabby Anglo-Latino church was draped with two huge banners. The first read '*La Migra No Profana El Sanctuario*' (INS, Don't Profane the Sanctuary) and the second read '*Este es El Sanctuario de Dios Para Los Oprimidos de Centro America*' (This is a Sanctuary of God for the Oppressed of Central America). It was clear from the beginning that the Sanctuary Movement had a 'profound identification with [the] ancient tradition of sanctuary'.[16] When asked 3 years later, 'how the Sanctuary Movement got started', Jim Corbett replied: 'You'll have to consult Exodus on that'.[17] It is also clear from the slogans chosen for this public declaration that they saw sanctuary as not universal but directed at the 'oppressed'. It was therefore very much a political statement. In their contemporary account of the movement, Renny Golden and Michael McConnell, two leading activists from Chicago, reference antiquity, medieval canon and English law and the Underground Railroad, as part of the sanctuary tradition that informed movement for Central American refugees.[18] Later on, adherence to that tradition was underlined in an annual 'Freedom Seder' in Tucson that became a calendar event for the Sanctuary Movement. This was hosted by the

14 Ibid 58.
15 Quoted in Ibid 57. See also Coutin SB, *The Culture of Protest: Religious Activism and the U.S. Sanctuary Movement* (Westview Press, 1993), 29.
16 Bau (n 6), 124.
17 'Conspiracy of Compassion', Sojourners (March 1985), 15. This article, a joint interview with Jim Corbett, John Fife, Stacy Merkt and Phil Willis-Conger, provides a detailed description from leading participants about the origins of the movement. Elsewhere, the mainstream media also made the same links with the tradition of sanctuary stretching back to antiquity, e.g. 'Offered Sanctuary: Scores of U.S. Churches Take In Illegal Aliens Who Flee Guatemala and El Salvador', *Wall Street Journal* (21 June 1984), 26.
18 Golden R and McConnell M, *Sanctuary: The New Underground Railroad* (Orbis Books, 1986), 15.

Temple Emanu-El for the refugees as 'a remembrance of Passover that weaves the present experience of refugees and sanctuary congregations into an awareness of more than three millennia of exile, oppression, and liberation'.[19]

In front of the banners sat a group of people around a table, ready to address the press. Rev. John Fife, the pastor of Southside Presbyterian Church, chaired the proceedings. He said that his congregation had decided 'after Bible study, prayer and agonizing reflection that they could not remain faithful to the God of the Exodus and prophets and do anything less. It was for us a question of faith'.[20] At the beginning of the Sanctuary Movement, there was no talk of upholding the supposed principles of refugee law. Indeed, on the same day as making their public declaration of sanctuary, Southside Church sent a letter to the US Attorney General, in which they stated:

> We are writing to inform you that Southside United Presbyterian Church will publically violate the Immigration Nationality Act 274(a). We have declared the Church as a 'sanctuary' for undocumented refugees. The current administration of U.S. law prohibits us from sheltering these refugees of Central America. Therefore, we believe that administration of the law to be immoral as well as illegal.[21]

There is a curious, and apparently contradictory, aspect to this statement. On the one hand, it makes it quite clear that the church is knowingly intending to break the law, yet at the same time accuses the government of acting illegally. The precise nature of the government's illegal act is left unspecified. But it does suggest already that the nascent movement was attempting to seek some legal legitimacy for their actions, even while declaring themselves to be acting outside the law.

The INS undercover agent who attended the public declaration reported to his superiors: 'It seems that this movement is more political than religious but that a ploy is going to be Border Patrol "baiting" by that group in order to demonstrate to the public that the US government via it's [*sic*] jack-booted Gestapo Border Patrol Agents think nothing of breaking down the doors of their churches to drag Jesus Christ out to be tortured and murdered. I believe that all political implications should be considered before any further action is taken toward this group'.[22] Even allowing for the crude and hyperbolic nature of this report, it is evident that indeed the movement's aim was political, that it was largely formed by people who had long histories of involvement in anti-war,

---

19 Corbett J, *Goatwalking* (Penguin, 1992), 157.
20 Quoted in Allitt P, *Religion in America since 1945: A History* (Columbia University Press, 2003), 176.
21 Letter to US Attorney General William French Smith from Southside Presbyterian Church, 23 March 1982, quoted in *Basta!* (January 1985), 25 (*Basta!* was the semi-regular newsletter of the Chicago Religious Task Force on Central America).
22 Quoted in Cunningham (n 11), 33–34.

trade union and other left-wing movements and were therefore predisposed to be hostile to the Reagan administration, and sympathetic to the refugees escaping the regimes of US allies in the Cold War. At this very early stage, Corbett, who would later take an aggressively legalistic stance against the more 'political' wing of the movement, could describe the role of sanctuary as part of a political strategy to defeat US imperialism in Central America, and as such sets up sanctuary against the sovereign order:

> The military regimes of El Salvador, Guatemala, and a number of other Latin American countries are simply the middle managers of U.S. domination . . . military terrorism as practiced by the national security state is *the* political instrument for maintaining established patterns of ownership and rule in Latin America. The terror pursues Salvadoran and Guatemalan refugees up through Mexico and into the U.S., where they are hunted down, hidden from public awareness, and shipped back by the tens of thousands. Both here and there, it is the same terror and a single process. We here in the U.S. are in the best position to stop it.[23]

Following the public declaration on March 24, Southside was inundated with requests from refugees. Fife recalled, 'We discovered refugees we didn't even know existed in Tucson, let alone all along the border'.[24] Thus, public sanctuary enabled the hidden refugees and the community to connect. David Matas comments: 'The public declaration of sanctuary . . . [made] the source of help visible, it also made the problems refugees face visible . . . Publicity also meant making sanctuary a mass movement'.[25] Thus, going public was itself a political act. There was also a moral imperative in making sanctuary public: 'Publicity was a proclamation that they were doing what they believed to be right. Secrecy meant silence not only about their own activities but also about the violations of human rights they were trying to prevent'.[26] In any case, the huge and swift growth in the demands on the Tucson activists led them to seek out allies who could help share the burden and develop and coordinate the movement across the country. And this is when the Chicago Religious Task Force on Central America (CRTFCA) became involved.

Chicago Religious Task Force on Central America

The CRTFCA had been founded in January 1981 in response to the rape and murder of four US nuns by right wing paramilitaries in El Salvador, around the same time that sanctuary was getting off the ground in Tucson. It had been set

---

23 Undated [1982?] letter from Jim Corbett (GSSC).
24 Tomsho (n 8), 87.
25 Matas D, *The Sanctuary Trial* (University of Manitoba, 1989), 49.
26 Ibid.

up by a group of political activists based in a variety of local churches in Chicago. Their aims included raising awareness of the conditions of that war and of the dictatorships being imposed on the people of Central America, opposing the US government's support for repressive regimes in the region, and building solidarity for Central Americans both in their countries and for those who had fled as refugees to the United States. In the autumn of 1982, as the numbers of refugees arriving across the border snowballed and the existing sanctuary activists in Arizona struggled to cope, Corbett and Fife approached the CRTFCA for help in assisting the refugees and in establishing a nationwide network of sanctuaries. The CRTFCA agreed, and almost immediately Wellington Avenue Church of Christ in Chicago declared itself a sanctuary.[27] The CRTFCA took on the role of national coordinator of sanctuary and within 2 years helped set up additional sanctuaries across the United States, including churches, synagogues and Quaker groups.[28] The CRTFCA's Statement of Faith made clear the way in which they saw sanctuary as one part of drawing out political connections between various sources of injustice:

> The sanctuary movement seeks to uncover and name the connections between the U.S. government and the Salvadoran death squads, and the connection between U.S. business interests and the denial of human and economic rights of the vast majority of people. We believe that to stop short of this is to betray the Central American people and the refugees we now harbor.[29]

The CRTFCA 'refined the concept of public sanctuary, in which church-sponsored refugees agreed to tell their story to the public over and over again'.[30] This emphasis on getting refugees to speak publically gave them a voice as well as a more active role in sanctuary, and created a human story that allowed others to identify with them. The CRTFCA outlined the basis of their engagement with the Sanctuary Movement on the basis of political mobilisation, and incorporated the issue of the refugees within a broader political context that gave rise to the causes of their flight in the first place:

> If we are able to keep the clear focus in the sanctuary project that the most important part of the refugee support work is to end U.S. aid to El Salvador and Guatemala so that we stop creating more refugees and that the refugees in the USA can return to their homeland, then all of our direct action and legislative action can be seen as a part of the refugee support work; i.e., a part of the sanctuary project.[31]

---

27 Crittenden (n 1), 88.
28 Ibid 90.
29 Quoted in Allitt (n 20), 177–178.
30 Crittenden (n 1), 90.
31 'Working Paper: Sanctuary Project as CRTF Central Organizing Tool', nd [1983?] (CRTFCAR), 4.

They also attempted to ground their theology within an avowedly political stance:

> From the earliest times, sanctuary has had a deeply religeo-political signifi-
> cance. It is a recognition of the moral limits of a civil order and the ultimacy
> of the divine claim on human allegiance . . . sanctuary is a faithful response
> to the liberating God who calls us into solidarity with the oppressed.[32]

Christian Smith describes the impact of the CRTFCA joining the movement:

> The movement's identity began to evolve. Sanctuary began as a movement
> of hospitality that aimed to provide for the humanitarian needs of vulnerable
> refugees. But Sanctuary quickly became more than that. It grew into a
> *political* movement that sought to end the human oppression generated by
> the U.S.-sponsored war in Central America . . . heightened grassroots political
> awareness and the spread of Sanctuary fuelled each other.[33]

While it is certainly true that the CRTFCA injected a militant attitude into the nascent movement, as has already been made clear the movement was political at its inception. Smith, writing in 1996, is refracting his analysis back through a damaging split in the movement, in which the activists based in Tucson would later accuse the CRTFCA of politicising sanctuary. This will be discussed in greater detail later. However, at the outset, everyone seemed to be on the same page in conceptualising sanctuary as having a political edge. Corbett's early view has already been quoted above. Also, in a section on sanctuary as part of a guide for activists involved in assisting refugees from Central America, written in late 1982 and jointly prepared by the CRTFCA and the Tucson Ecumenical Council (TEC), the political aspect of sanctuary is again made quite clear:

> Sanctuary offers a concrete and direct way to challenge the inhuman policy
> of the U.S. government in Central America and of the INS, as well as pro-
> viding a direct service to the refugees created as a result of these policies.[34]

The Movement grows

During their first year, Southside alone organised sanctuary for an astonishing 1,600 refugees.[35] Although just six churches in total had declared sanctuary on

32 'Historical and Theological Basis for Sanctuary', undated [1982/early 1983?], unsigned
typed mimeographed document (CRFTCA).
33 Smith (n 12), 69.
34 *Seeking Safe Haven: A Congregational Guide to Helping Central American Refugees in the
United States* (American Friends Service Committee, Church World Service Immigration
and Refugee Program, Inter-Religious Task Force on El Salvador and Central America,
and Lutheran Immigration and Refugee Service, 1982), 64.
35 Smith (n 12), 68; Bau (n 6), 12.

March 24, the movement spread rapidly. Wellington Avenue Church in Chicago declared itself a sanctuary in July 1982. It had previously given sanctuary to protestors fleeing the police riot during the Democratic Convention in 1968.[36] A further eighty-five churches in Chicago publically supported Wellington Avenue Church's declaration.[37] In total, by the end of 1982, 15 churches had declared sanctuary, with another 150 churches supporting refugees in various ways, such as raising money, providing food, clothes, etc.[38] In addition to the public declarations, the underground railroad developed, linking together churches, private homes and other spaces all the way from the Mexico-Guatemala border north across the US-Mexico border and then throughout the United States and up into Canada.[39] The mass media took an interest in the growing movement, culminating in December when CBS's *60 Minutes* broadcast a report on the movement to millions of viewers. By the end of 1982, the Sanctuary Movement was 'by any measure . . . tiny. But it was beginning to irritate the colossal United States government'.[40] According to the CRFTCA's newsletter, *Basta!*, by early 1983, around 20,000 people had been involved 'in open defiance of U.S. immigration law'.[41] And by the end of that year, some 1,000 congregations had publically supported the Sanctuary Movement, and a new sanctuary was being set up at a rate of at least one each week. More than 20,000 copies of the CRTFCA's handbook had been distributed, running into its fourth printing in less than a year.[42]

At the end of February 1983, less than a year after the public declaration, the TEC agreed that its employees could engage in actively assisting refugees to reach sanctuary churches. In effect, the Tucson churches were endorsing and paying for refugees to be smuggled illegally across the border. Indeed, border crossings soon became a major aspect of the movement's activities. This alone was a brave act, and one which directly challenged sovereign control over migration and asylum. It was, therefore, also the aspect of the movement that most antagonised the state authorities, and would form the basis of prosecutions of leading activists over the coming years.

By 1984, the number of sanctuaries had mushroomed to around 3,000. In addition to churches of various denominations, these included synagogues, Trappist monasteries, private homes in Nebraska, farms in Iowa and Native American reservations.[43] The number of public sanctuaries – those that made

---

36 Tomsho (n 8), 86.
37 Matas (n 25), ix.
38 Crittenden (n 1), 100.
39 Ibid 79.
40 Ibid 100.
41 *Basta!* (February 1983), 1.
42 *Basta!* (December 1983), 2.
43 Golden and McConnell (n 18), 52–53. In relation to the recent history of Native Americans and sanctuary, it is worth noting here that even before the birth of the Sanctuary Movement, there were some examples of sanctuary on reservations being used as part of resistance against the federal government, e.g. 'Dennis Banks at the Six Nations', Pacifica Radio (January 1983), Sound Recording, Library of Congress, RYA 3947.

public declarations to the media and openly mobilised support – had grown to 45, with a further 600 'co-conspiring' congregations providing various levels of support, such as raising money or supplying food, clothing, etc.[44] Yarnold suggests that the actual number of sanctuaries might have been higher than that reported, as some churches may have not wanted to be seen to be linked to the wider movement.[45] The movement also had an influence internationally, generalising the issue of sanctuary beyond the specific circumstances of Central America. Activists in Britain, Norway, Holland, France, Belgium, Switzerland, Italy, West Germany and Australia were inspired by the movement in the United States in their own efforts to offer sanctuary to asylum-seekers and other irregular migrants from various parts of the world.[46]

All the major Protestant denominations in the United States, except for the Evangelicals, endorsed sanctuary, and many Catholic bishops had also endorsed it.[47] Indeed, the Archbishop of Milwaukee, Rembert Weakland, gave sanctuary to eight Salvadoran refugees in his official residence.[48] The Union of American Hebrew Congregations and the Central Confederation of American Rabbis also came out in support of the movement.[49] The profile of sanctuary was such that it found a resonance in some surprising places. For example, life prisoners at Rahway State Prison in New Jersey, who had watched TV news footage of a family arriving at sanctuary at Rutgers University Chapel, managed to organise for a truckload of toys that they had been tasked with repairing to be donated to refugee children living in sanctuary.[50] At its height, the Sanctuary Movement's network extended to thirty-four states, including conservative areas such as the Deep South and parts of the Midwest.[51] From 1980 to 1991, almost 1 million

---

44 Crittenden (n 1), 139–140.
45 Yarnold BM, *Refugees without Refuge: Formation and Failed Implementation of U.S. Political Asylum Policy in the 1980's* (University Press of America, 1990), 211.
46 Ferris EG, 'The Churches, Refugees, and Politics' in Gil Loescher and Laila Monahan (eds), *Refugees and International Relations* (OUP, 1989), 172; Lippert RK, *Sanctuary, Sovereignty, Sacrifice: Canadian Sanctuary Incidents, Power, and Law* (UBC Press, 2005), 4.
47 Davidson (n 10), 84.
48 Allitt (n 20), 177.
49 Lorentzen R, *Women in the Sanctuary Movement* (Temple University, 1991), 29.
50 Golden and McConnell (n 18), 134.
51 Lorentzen (n 49), 14. Evidence of the movement's implantation in the Deep South can be found in 'Guatemalan credits life to sanctuary movement', *Baton Rouge Morning Advocate* (8 June 1985), 10A. In the CRFTCA archive, there are letters from farmers in remote parts of the country and close to the Canadian border offering assistance in hiding and transporting refugees as part of the underground railroad, e.g. letters from Anne and Eric Nordell, and Dora Marin to the CRFTCA in 1984 (CRFTCA). In one district in Ohio which had voted Republican solidly for the previous 40 years, there were four churches offering sanctuary to refugees who had entered the country illegally. Most of these had no history as activist churches. Indeed, one of them had censured a previous pastor for marching with Martin Luther King in the early 1960s. 'Offered Sanctuary: Scores of U.S. Churches Take In Illegal Aliens Who Flee Guatemala and El Salvador', *Wall Street Journal* (21 June 1984), 26.

refugees from Central America entered the United States, most of them illegally.[52] It is likely that a significant number of those were either directly or indirectly helped by the Sanctuary Movement. Thus, it would not be an exaggeration to say that the impact and spread of the Sanctuary Movement has few equals in US history, and that it posed a very real challenge for the government at the time. The INS archive suggests that they took the threat of the Sanctuary Movement seriously, with regular memoranda discussing the issue and the circulation of various news stories reporting on the movement. For example, at the end of 1985, in the midst of the high-profile trial of leading sanctuary activists taking place in Arizona, the INS distributed a detailed refutation of the movement to every newspaper in the western United States – except for Arizona, so as not to prejudice the trial there.[53] The scale of the challenge provoked the INS into making panicked claims that the movement was acting as a 'Trojan Horse' for communist agitation, and was responsible for the possible infiltration of 'drug dealers, burglars and other assorted undesirables'.[54]

Another aspect of the movement that was developed was the concept of 'sanctuary cities'. During the Vietnam War, Berkeley City Council had passed a resolution to this effect, but it had not been replicated elsewhere. But as part of the Sanctuary Movement during the 1980s, more than fifty cities in the United States passed 'sanctuary city' legislation that prohibited any municipal resources or employees from being used to enforce federal immigration laws. Some went even further by barring all municipal employees from enquiring as to someone's citizenship status.[55] As Jean McDonald points out: 'These changes in municipal policy were not simply "granted" by municipalities; rather, these transformations were hard-won by (im)migrants, refugees and their allies through research, networking, advocacy and political action'.[56] This is an example of what McDonald calls 'regularization from below',[57] but can also be included as a form of 'grassroots asylum'. She then explains some of the practical effects of this movement:

> [It enables] a higher quality of life for all members of our city's communities. This movement does this by disrupting immigration laws that seek to create legal distinctions between human beings in crude attempts to reframe certain groups of people as having less or no access to political, legal or social rights.[58]

52 Guzder D, *Divine Rebels: American Christian Activists for Social Justice* (Lawrence Hill, 2011), 101; Lorentzen (n 49), 11.
53 Memorandum WRPIO 7110/2.1-C, 22 November 1985 (INSA).
54 INS News Release, 'INS Warns of Los Angeles Sanctuary Proposal Impacts', 26 November 1985 (INSA) 1, 4.
55 McDonald J, 'Building a sanctuary city: municipal migrant rights in the city of Toronto' in Peter Nyers and Kim Rygiel (eds), *Citizenship, Migrant Activism and the Politics of Movement* (Routledge, 2012), 131.
56 Ibid 131.
57 Ibid 139.
58 Ibid 143.

This represented a gesture towards realising Badiou's slogan: 'everyone here is from here'.[59] But more immediately, it avowedly challenges the legal categorisations that distinguish refugees from other migrants, 'genuine' versus 'false' refugees, etc. As Todd Howland and Richard Garcia note in their survey of the sanctuary city declarations, 45% of them explicitly stated that city services would be provided to refugees 'regardless of how the federal government classifies them'.[60] In those cases, it is clear that at least some attempt was being made to challenge the legal categorisation of refugees. For the others, not making this point explicit at least preserved some ambiguity on the question.

The practice of sanctuary

As already mentioned above, 'border work' began in a rather informal way with a co-operative of goat-herders, who knew the border well, assisting refugees to cross. But over time, this became a much more central part of the movement's work with many other activists in the border states of Arizona and Texas taking part. It also became more dangerous as a cat-and-mouse game developed between the activists and the Border Patrol. Indeed, the later trials of members of the Sanctuary Movement were based on charges relating to these illegal border crossings. Members of the Sanctuary Movement would travel just over the border into Mexico for a pre-arranged meeting with groups of refugees seeking help. They would be given instructions on where to cross the border, usually a bit of fence that was easily navigable (i.e. broken or easily climbed) and which was at certain times out of view of the Border Patrol. The refugees might also be given information about churches or private homes over the border to which they could seek further help or sanctuary. Often they would then be transported onwards to sanctuary in Tucson or elsewhere in the United States.

As Corbett perceived it, the real problem for Central Americans fleeing violence was that, at the US border, the Mexican informal, church-based system of protection and transportation collapsed. What was required was a 'border ministry' – a strategy of action that would safely move Central Americans into the United States where they could contact a lawyer and apply for asylum. In an open letter to fellow Quakers written in July 1981, Corbett detailed treatment of Central Americans by the INS and began to formulate a theology of an 'underground railroad', based on the notion of hospitality to strangers and incorporating elements of Latin American liberation theology, particularly the concept of *comunidades de base*. Corbett's letter also contained possibly the first reference in the movement's history to 'sanctuary'. In typical Quaker fashion, he treated sanctuary not as a historical and legal institution but as a community activity

59 Hallward P, 'Badiou's politics: Equality and justice' (2002), *Culture Machine*, 4.
60 Howland T and Garcia R, 'The Refugee Crisis and the Law: The "City Sanctuary" Response' in Ved P Nanda (ed), *Refugee Law and Policy: International and U.S. Responses* (Greenwood Press, 1989), 192.

(what he referred to as a church) whose members are gathered around a commitment to (or 'solidarity' with) the dispossessed and the poor.[61]

A further element to border work was added following the opening up of a legal loophole. In 1984, a sanctuary activist in Texas, Stacey Lynn Merkt, was arrested, charged and convicted of transporting illegal aliens. The Fifth Circuit Court of Appeals reversed her conviction on the grounds claimed by her lawyers that she was taking them to get legal assistance on making a claim for asylum. Their ruling stated: 'By definition, a person intending to assist an alien in obtaining legal status is not acting "in furtherance of" the alien's illegal presence in this country'.[62] The Fifth Circuit's judgement opened the way to a clever strategy used by the Tucson activists. Before all border runs, the Trsg would send a letter to the INS informing them that they were assisting asylum claimants to get legal advice on making those claims. On a number of occasions, the Border Patrol had to release sanctuary activists caught transporting refugees from the border once they were shown copies of these letters.[63] However, this tactic proved controversial with fellow activists in the movement, as it led towards a greater collaboration with the law enforcement agencies. Indeed, as we shall see, the logic of this practice led some activists to quite openly see themselves as an adjunct to the INS. In any case, this loophole was closed by the Immigration Reform and Control Act 1986, which made it an offence to assist aliens to enter by any other method than inspection at a port of entry.[64]

Once the refugees were assisted over the border, the next stage in the work of sanctuary was arranging a place for them to stay. Most of the refugees who were helped into the United States chose to live anonymously in the cities. But around one in twenty of them were prepared to go into 'public sanctuary'. Those who chose the latter were coached by Sister Darlene Nicgorski into how to deliver their testimonies and to appear at press conferences. Nicgorski was a nun who had lived and worked with displaced people in Guatemala for a number of years, spoke fluent Spanish and had since become involved with the Sanctuary Movement in Arizona. The refugees were then matched up with a church that was willing to receive them and were sent there, via the underground railroad of homes and churches.[65] The refugees were often difficult for the sanctuary churches to accommodate: many of them were traumatised, some were alcoholic and some of the men displayed chauvinistic behaviour. Many churches requested refugees 'the way they might select a new pet dog': there were requests for refugees who were non-smokers or vegetarians, those who were 'Indians' or Salvadorans, with older children or younger ones or none at all. One church requested a refugee

61 Cunningham (n 11), 27.
62 *United States v. Merkt*, 764 F.2d 266 (5th Cir, 18 June 1985), quoted in Corbett (n 19), 173.
63 Corbett (n 19), 175–176.
64 Ibid 178.
65 Crittenden (n 1), 119.

with carpentry skills.[66] So for many of the churches – especially those in more conservative, prosperous areas – a patronising, charitable attitude, along with many of the prejudices of 'good' versus 'bad' refugees, remained. Corbett's response to those sanctuaries that complained about the refugees being too rough around the edges was apt and to the point: 'We never promised we would send them the Holy Family, only the people'.[67]

While many churches engaged in long and anguished discussions before deciding to offer sanctuary, which was then inaugurated with a press conference or some other public demonstration, in some cases, sanctuary occurred on an almost *ad hoc* basis, and with no fanfare at all. In one such case, a church received a request by a priest in the local Hispanic community to take in a family of refugees. Without time for formal consultation, the family was brought over that same night and was welcomed by members of the congregation. Those members of the church who were there then proceeded to gather various things for the family such as clothes and food from others in the community. And because there was concern about the possible attitudes of the more conservative members of the church, the sanctuary activists did not reveal to the whole congregation the fact that the family did not have legal status.[68] Indeed the decisions by churches and synagogues on whether or not to offer sanctuary led to splits and people leaving one church or temple for another, depending on their beliefs over the issue.[69] Churches and synagogues that endorsed sanctuary tended to have less hierarchical structures than others, much more like 'base community' (*comunidad de base*) churches.[70] In this way, a political 'dissensus' cut across faith lines.

Testimonies

All the refugees who chose to take 'public sanctuary', and even many of the ones who did not, were encouraged to deliver testimonies on their experiences, in particular on the causes of their flight. These testimonies were delivered to congregations, those that had already given sanctuary and those who were considering it. The testimonies also featured prominently in press conferences and other public declarations of sanctuary. The purpose was two-fold: first, to educate people about the realities of events in Central America that were too often obscured by the government and the mainstream media, and second, to help persuade more congregations and individuals to get involved in sanctuary. Without a doubt, the testimonies were often powerful, and did much to drive the movement forward.[71] One sanctuary activist recalled:

---

66 Ibid 120.
67 Quoted in Golden and McConnell (n 18), 55.
68 Lorentzen (n 49), 62–64.
69 Ibid 29–30.
70 Ibid 32.
71 Westerman W, 'Central American refugee testimonies and performed life histories in the Sanctuary Movement' in Rina Benmayor and Andor Skotnes (eds), *Migration*

The Sanctuary refugees actually brought the war in Central America *here* to the U.S. The refugees told their dreadful stories . . . This human contact helped move anyone with a conscience, even people not previously politicized, to become active. This helped escalate the movement.[72]

Christian Smith illustrates how for many activists the testimonies were absolutely central as a tool for mobilizing people. Even translators brought in who had little interest in politics became activists after being exposed to the refugees and their stories.[73] One Salvadoran refugee commented: 'Once these people listen to us, I believe that they are not going to be the same anymore'.[74]

William Westerman was able to identify six discrete sections of the standard testimony: '(1) introduction and background, (2) life and activity in the home country, (3) persecution, (4) escape, (5) exile,and (6) analysis and call to action'.[75] But for the refugees to be able to engage many of their audience of North Americans, the testimony had to push narratives evoking sympathy rather than politics: 'That meant concentrating on human, anecdotal narrative and removing political commentary that could be construed as inflammatory or accusatory',[76] for political testimony could be experienced by North American audiences as 'threatening'.[77] For Westerman, testimony was a way of turning the refugees into something more than abstractions through a four-fold process: (1) by speaking as a political act in criticising the injustice that forced them to flee, (2) by attempting to turn their religious beliefs into a platform for action, (3) by 'creat[ing] solidarity between the refugees' and their listeners and (4) by enabling the refugees to turn a traumatic event into a tool for galvanizing themselves and others into action to attempt to right the injustice.[78] Westerman expands on this: 'Testimony is about people rising from a condition of being victims, objects of history, and taking charge of their history, becoming subjects, actors in it. History no longer makes them; they make it, write it, speak it'.[79] Renny Golden and Michael McConnell express succinctly the effect of the refugees' testimony as public witness: 'Sanctuary, at its best, has not been a place to hide in, but a platform to speak out from'.[80]

However, the refugees would often get tired of giving their testimonies repeatedly at church after church, and would withdraw from it after a while.

---

and Identity: International Yearbook of Oral History and Life Stories, Volume III (OUP, 1994), 170.

72 Smith (n 12), 152.
73 Ibid.
74 Quoted in Westerman (n 71), 169.
75 Ibid 170.
76 Ibid 171.
77 Ibid 179.
78 Ibid 176.
79 Ibid 177.
80 Quoted in Jean R and Isaac E, 'The Sanctuary Movement and the Jews', *Midstream* (May 1986), 8.

Many also felt a disconnection between what they were describing and the response they received. One refugee explained: 'Commonly we talk to 30 or 50 people. Almost every time, we feel like we are living again what we are telling. For us it is telling the life. We think there is going to be great impact, but then people are really quiet'.[81] Crittenden also provides an insightful critique of the testimonies, or more particularly of what was expected of them by many in the movement:

> The refugees headed for public sanctuary not only had to be fairly stable and adaptable but had to be able to speak effectively before an audience and with the press . . . Above all, they had to have a 'good story', one that described the horrors of life in their country in a politically sophisticated, persuasive way . . . In many ways, then, the screening of refugees for public sanctuary – as distinct from the prior screening for assistance into the United States – became a mirror image of the government's screening of aliens for admission into the United States.[82]

Testimony thus has a dual aspect: it enabled refugees to speak for themselves and it also required them to perform for and be judged by others.

The pull towards law

In the very earliest days of sanctuary in Tucson, sanctuary activists took little notice of the legal definition of a refugee. The letter sent by Fife to the US Attorney General just before the public declaration in March 1982 referred to their intention to 'publically violate' the law. Reflecting on the Sanctuary Movement, some 20 years after its demise, Fife described its origins:

> When we started hearing stories from these refugees, I thought, 'Hey, we can't just sit here and do nothing . . . We can't just let our Central American brothers and sisters die.' So, we started meeting them in Mexico and walking them through the desert into this country and giving them a place to stay. We didn't even really care much about the authorities, although they sure cared a lot about us.[83]

Just like some of Corbett's own comments early on in the movement, there was no care given to distinguishing between 'genuine' and 'bogus' refugees, nor any apparent concern to uphold the law. According to Fife, the origins of ditching

---

81 Tomsho (n 8), 37–38.
82 Crittenden (n 1), 120.
83 Rose A, *Showdown in the Sonoran Desert: Religion, Law, and the Immigration Controversy* (OUP, 2012), 29.

the language of civil disobedience and law-breaking lay in a phone call he received early on from a human rights lawyer who told them:

> You are doing more harm to human rights and refugee law than anyone else I know. Listen carefully! You are not doing civil disobedience. Civil disobedience is [publically] violating a bad law, and assuming the consequences, in order to change an unjust law. We don't want to change U.S. refugee law. It conforms to international standards. The problem is that the government is violating our own refugee law. The government is doing civil disobedience.[84]

The extent to which this one phone call was decisive is debatable. In my view, as I discuss in greater detail below, the more general pressures towards establishing a legitimate basis, as commonly understood, for sanctuary, coupled with the damaging effect on morale of a series of prosecutions in 1984/1985, were the most important influences in this respect. Indeed, around the same time as this phone call, following a threat by the local prosecutor, there was a feeling that, if the activists were going to be arrested, they would be better able to defend themselves if they could show they were only helping those who, according to law, had a right to asylum. However, the logic implicit in this lawyer's advice, and the belief in the inherent rightness of refugee law would, within a relatively short time, lead many of the activists in Tucson and elsewhere to perform the law on refugees, rather than resist it, as they had done hitherto.

One member of the Sanctuary Movement in Tucson recalled the effect of this shift in focus, namely that through her work in the movement, she had learnt 'the difference between a refugee and a "refugee". Before, I'd thought of a refugee as someone who is seeking shelter, but after working with the Central Americans, I became aware that it's a legal status'.[85] According to Crittenden, Corbett had not engaged in screening the refugees at first, for he was not interested in 'hair-splitting' between those who were fleeing because of persecution or from war conditions in general. Corbett had, of course, pioneered the practice of assisting refugees to cross the border illegally.[86]

However, beginning in 1983, a screening process was put in place. This involved sanctuary activists travelling to where the refugees were waiting in Mexico and interviewing them there in the manner of officials adjudicating asylum claims. They would then return to Tucson and the group would discuss the case and decide whether or not they would be given sanctuary.[87] Some of

---

84 Quoted in Ibid 30.
85 Quoted in Bibler Coutin S, 'Enacting law through social practice: sanctuary as a form of resistance' in Mindie Lazarus-Black and Susan F Hirsch (eds), *Contested States: Law, Hegemony and Resistance* (Routledge, 1994), 287.
86 Matas (n 25), 47.
87 Crittenden (n 1), 119.

the tests appeared somewhat oblique. One, for example, involved asking the refugees if they would be prepared to spend up to a year in jail in the United States, which was the penalty if they were caught crossing the border illegally. If they answered 'yes', they were deemed to be genuinely afraid of returning to their home countries, and thus possessed a well-founded fear of persecution. However, if they demurred and instead said that they would be prepared to return to their countries and try to cross at another time, then they were not considered to be genuine refugees.[88] Thus, rather than cleaving to the Augustinian approach with which they began, they were instead adopting the practices decreed by the law of 397 and criticised by Augustine – of, effectively, turning the custodians of sanctuary into its inquisitors. Of course the key point is that, had a legal definition not been current at the time, both in terms of the 1951 Convention and the 1980 Refugee Act, it is doubtful that Corbett and others in Tucson would have used such practices at all, for there would have been no legal yardstick by which to ascertain the quality of the refugees. This is but the most obvious example of how refugee law serves to undermine the practice of sanctuary.

The hold of legal ideas and, in particular, of the legal category of refugee was evident not just in Tucson but elsewhere too. For example, one church in the Midwest spent 13 months in discussion before finally deciding to become a sanctuary. The details of how agreement was reached and on what basis are revealing of the kinds of discussions that would have taken place across the movement. A member of the committee, tasked with coming up with a draft statement, said: 'I can only support a program which is truly interested in helping others. I cannot support a program which uses the church to make a political statement'.[89] The first draft, therefore, stated that the church took no position on the US government's policy on Central America, and that all people had the right to live free from torture and persecution. However, it also concluded with the following: 'We also believe that as Christians we cannot turn our back on those who have come to us for protection from brutality. Acting on those beliefs, we at The Church of the Covenant[90] will give sanctuary to any refugee from persecution *whether or not they are termed so by the United States government*'. The committee, after a 'tense discussion', insisted that the drafter change the statement and the final sentence was altered to, 'Acting on these beliefs, we at The Church of the Covenant will give sanctuary *to any refugee who comes to us in need*'.[91] In a curious way, the second draft was both softer and harder in its departure from law. On the one hand, the explicit reference to ignoring the decision of the government on whether someone was a refugee or not was dropped. Yet, on the other hand, the broadening of the concept of a refugee from someone fleeing

---

88 Ibid 123.
89 Slater NG, 'A case study of offering hospitality: choosing to be a sanctuary church' in Nelle G Slater (ed), *Tensions between Citizenship and Discipleship: A Case Study* (Pilgrim Press, 1989), 5.
90 This name is a pseudonym.
91 Slater (n 90), 5–6.

'persecution' to one in 'need' is a break from the legal definition of the refugee. It is not clear what precisely the argument was in the committee over the draft rewrite or to what extent they were aware of the legal definition of the refugee. In any case, later on, due to pressure from the more conservative members of the committee, a document entitled 'Refugee Issue' was drawn up, which began by stating the Christian duty to help the oppressed and those in need, but also included two clauses re-stating the law in relation to the 1980 Refugee Act and the 1951 Convention. It also claims sanctuary as something that is part of the 'Judeo-Christian tradition and is recognized in common law'.[92] When this resolution was put before the congregation, those opposed argued: 'With all due respect to the moral and human rights issues involved in the question of "sanctuary" for refugees from El Salvador and Guatemala, it must be pointed out that these refugees are considered illegal aliens by the immigration authorities and the State Department'.[93] Eventually, the congregation voted by 151 to 91 in favour of the resolution and to offer sanctuary.[94] Walter Brueggemann identifies the apoliticism that underpinned these discussions:

> The decision of the Church of the Covenant to act as a sanctuary was a bold act of evangelical obedience and compassion . . . But it was also understood in a way that tended to preclude any political interpretation. The capacity to embrace a religious act and preclude a political understanding embodies a certain sense of biblical authority.[95]

What becomes apparent in these discussions is a tension between a more open theological approach and a more restrictive legal one. The Gordian Knot could have been cut through a more political understanding of sanctuary, such as that taken by the CRTFCA, but instead an attempt was made to somehow see legitimacy flowing from Judeo-Christian theology, common law and international refugee law together. But as we have seen, these streams each have, in fact, very distinct and in some cases antagonistic relationships to one another.

The tendency towards an apolitical humanitarian approach could also reinforce notions of the refugee subject as passive victim. For example, at Dumbarton United Methodist Church in Washington, DC, America Sosa, who was well known among the refugees as a leading activist for their rights, was welcomed into the church and spent three nights there as a symbolic act before moving into a private home. Subsequently, she was able to move to her own apartment in a predominantly Hispanic area of DC, with the congregation paying her a subsidy of $800 per month to live on. However, it soon became clear that Sosa 'was not

---

92 Ibid 11–13.
93 Ibid 14–15.
94 Ibid 17.
95 Brueggemann W, 'Textuality in the church' in Nelle G Slater (ed), *Tensions between Citizenship and Discipleship: A Case Study* (Pilgrim Press, 1989), 48.

interested in getting a job or supporting herself'. Instead, she was insistent upon continuing her activism as a member of a Salvadoran organisation called COMADRES, which involved travelling around the United States agitating for people to pressure the Salvadoran government to stop the war and to respect human rights. This apparently caused concern among the congregation: 'She was thus far more than a refugee the church had expected to shelter'. Only 'after much soul searching and with some misgivings, the congregation decided to continue its support [for her]'.[96] In other words, they were happy to support her as a charitable case, but not to assist her in maintaining her political commitments, her political subjectivity. It is telling that they believed she was 'far more than a refugee', i.e. they were not prepared for a person more multi-dimensional than that: a fully-rounded human being.

The split in the Movement

The emerging split within the Sanctuary Movement between its 'Tucson' and 'Chicago' wings became apparent very early on. In 1983, the TEC wrote to the CRTFCA: 'We provide sanctuary to the persecuted, regardless of the political origins of their persecution or of their usefulness in promoting preconceived purposes'.[97] The CRTFCA responded:

> You reduce the multidimensional process of solidarity to apolitical human-itarian band-aids rather than expanding it to include all that comes from choosing the side of the oppressed ... During the rise of the Third Reich, Dietrich Bonhoeffer said that the church must of course bind up the victims being crushed beneath the wheel, but there comes a time when the church must be the stick put in the spokes to stop the wheel from crushing the people.[98]

And indeed, the movement not only helped the refugees but also did much to raise awareness of the US government's own culpability in causing refugees to flee in the first place. As such, for many in the movement, this was important in asserting a duty of the United States in taking in the refugees, as much as it was a right of the refugees themselves. Similar claims, in a much different context, will be evident in the case of the Sans-Papiers, discussed in the next chapter.

Golden and McConnell, partisans of the 'Chicago' wing of the movement, identify the split between Tucson and Chicago as basically that of 'charity or liberation'.[99] Others have described the split as between 'a national grassroots

---

96 Stevens F, 'Irresistible visions' in Jane Donovan (ed), *Many Witnesses: A History of Dumbarton United Methodist Church 1772–1990* (Dumbarton United Methodist Church, 1998), 421.
97 Davidson (n 10), 82.
98 Ibid 83.
99 Golden and McConnell (n 18), 177.

resettlement effort, and a national network of antiwar activists'.[100] Robin Lorentzen, on the other hand, based on her extensive interviews with activists involved in the movement, downplays the divide between 'political' and 'humanitarian' factions:

> While the actual differences between the Tucson and Chicago movements are arguable, each of the two orientations does appear to have character-ized the movement at different times. In its natural history the political tended to become its end; the humanitarian, its means. As one woman noted, 'At first people just wanted to help those refugees here. After a while, they began bringing them in clandestinely.' Perhaps initially an expressly humanitarian act, sanctuary became more intentionally political in response to government and media attention. The movement's growing politicization refutes the notion that participants had either a humanitarian or a political orientation exclusively.[101]

What Lorentzen has identified is the way in which sooner or later, sanctuary, by coming up against the law, would become more self-evidently political. Perhaps another way of understanding the split is as one between people who recognised this and embraced the political and by doing so recognised the primacy of politics over law, and those who feared that politics would somehow contaminate the humanitarian aims of the movement. The latter view sought recourse in a paradigm that offered the same kind of universalising and objective approach as humanitarianism: law. As such, I think the split can be seen overall as one involving a divergence between legal and political ways of thinking.

The Sanctuary Movement on trial

On 10 January 1985, a Federal Grand Jury indicted sixteen Sanctuary Movement activists, including John Fife, Jim Corbett and Darlene Nicgorski. In addition, on the same day, raids were carried out across the country and sixty refugees who had been assisted by the movement were arrested as unindicted co-conspirators.[102] The accused were charged with a variety of offences under the Immigration and Nationality Act 1952, including assisting aliens to enter the country, transporting aliens, 'concealing, harbouring or shielding aliens' and encouraging aliens to enter the country illegally.[103] They were all also charged with conspiracy. The ensuing trial, which became known as the Sanctuary Trial, began in October 1985 and ended 7 months later. There had been smaller-scale prosecutions of individual activists the year before, in Texas and Arizona, but this trial was on an

---

100 Lorentzen (n 49), 16.
101 Ibid 55.
102 Matas (n 25), 51.
103 Ibid 67.

altogether bigger scale and became a *cause célèbre*, with its proceedings reported nationally and internationally.

Immediately following the indictments, the defendants put out a collective statement:

> After the Second World War, our government committed itself by law never again to expel or return refugees to any country where they would face persecution . . . Consequently, providing sanctuary for refugees is not an act of civil disobedience. Rather, the need to provide sanctuary for refugees demonstrates that, in its violations of human rights both here and abroad, the present administration lacks legitimacy.[104]

Their position follows three steps. First, law, and refugee law in particular, guarantees the right of asylum to refugees. Second, sanctuary is necessary as that right has been denied by the US government. Therefore, third, it is the US government, rather than the Sanctuary Movement, that is acting illegally and thus lacks legitimacy. The starting point is erroneous for, as we have seen, there is no right of asylum in law that is vested in refugees themselves. It also relies on a typically romanticised view of international refugee law. Further, the defendants hold to the line that assisting people to cross an international border into the United States by evading the authorities is not an illegal act, when in fact it violates the pre-eminent right of sovereign powers to determine who can or cannot enter its territory. More specifically, it was in most cases certainly a violation of the Immigration and Nationality Act 1952. The more general point was made by the judge in the Sanctuary Trial in relation to an ironic twist that occurred during pre-trial hearings. Following the kidnapping of one of the Salvadoran President's daughters, his family was flown to the United States on a specially chartered plane to be given asylum. When this was raised in court by the defence as an example of the gross inconsistency in how asylum was being granted, the judge replied that there were 'powers reserved . . . to the political branch' that were not exercisable by individuals.[105] The final point in the defendants' collective statement, however, is correct insofar as the Sanctuary Movement had successfully begun to rival the government in terms of legitimacy in relation to the right of providing sanctuary for Central American refugees. However, on the question of legality, the government had certainly the far stronger case. Helping people to cross the border, by evading the authorities was quite clearly illegal. Moreover, the available evidence suggests that the driving factor in the movement's legitimacy was not its adherence or otherwise to legality, but rather its moral and political stance. Consistently in press conferences, liturgical celebrations of sanctuary, the public testimonies of refugees, media

104   Corbett (n 19), 169–170.
105   Cited in Crittenden (n 1), 243–244.

reports, etc., members of the movement stressed not legal but moral, theological and political justification for their actions.

Yet, in spite of having a strong legal case, the government was clearly wary that a jury would acquit out of sympathy for the refugees and support for the sanctuary activists. So, a motion submitted by the prosecution that all discussion of religious or ethical justification for sanctuary should be prohibited was accepted by the judge. Further, the judge decreed that all mentions of words such as 'refugee' should be avoided, with 'aliens' the preferred nomenclature. The defence lawyers, partly as a result of these sorts of restrictions, but also as part of a conscious strategy, made a largely technical defence, and decided that none of the accused should testify on their own behalf.

David Matas, a Canadian lawyer specialising in refugee and immigration cases, wrote a detailed report and analysis of the trial on behalf of the International Commission of Jurists. On the one hand, Matas blames the weak defence strategy on the unjust restrictions placed upon them by the court, which had left the lawyers with practically no other strategic option.[106] Yet, on the other hand, it is hard to escape the impression that Matas feels that an alternative way of presenting the defence should at least have been attempted. So while Matas acknowledges the restrictions on the defence, he also writes:

> There was a choice being offered in the Sanctuary Trial . . . It was a choice to the Sanctuary Movement. It was the choice, not of ignoring refugees or asserting United States government legitimacy, but rather of the Movement ignoring itself or asserting its own legitimacy. The Movement chose to ignore itself, argue reasonable doubt, rather than assert its own legitimacy in the face of the court's rulings.[107]

The emphasis on choice leaves one with the unavoidable impression that, for all the excuses one could make for the defence in the circumstances – and there is no doubt that they were difficult and complex – Matas clearly believes that an alternative political defence was not only possible but necessary. The linking thread between this failed strategy, which led to all but one of the defendants being convicted, and aspects such as the screening procedures applied to refugees at the Mexican border, was a misplaced faith in the law. The fallout from the trial was a large degree of demoralisation and disorientation, which further pulled many sanctuary activists to the law, at the expense of sanctuary and the refugees themselves.

'Trial Trauma'

Six months after the end of the trial, the CRTFCA, in an internal discussion document, declared the movement to be 'comatose', as a result of lack of momentum

---

106   Matas (n 25), 118.
107   Ibid 120.

and failure to significantly alter government policy.[108] They further suggested that the trial was a turning point in applying conservative pressure on the movement. In particular, they identified a problem with the strategy pursued in the courtroom:

> The crowds in the courtroom were well-behaved, not challenging. The defendants were polite in the courtroom, not risking contempt. The lawyers, while contemptuous at times, usually were that way [only] when the jury was out of the room. Neither lawyers nor defendants could decide whether they wanted to pursue a straight criminal trial or a political trial . . . They provided no militant model and we are still suffering the results of that.[109]

Even though the defendants issued statements of defiance following the verdicts, it quickly became apparent that the impact of the trial had been to push sections of the Sanctuary Movement further in the direction of adopting legal procedures and criteria. One leading commentator on the movement writes:

> [T]hose returning from the [Sanctuary] trial had been profoundly influenced by court arguments and wished to implement procedures that would underscore the 'legality' of Sanctuary work. Among these was the adoption of the United Nations High Commissioner for Refugees (UNHCR) guidelines regarding refugee determination.[110]

This led to tensions even within Trsg, resulting eventually in a split and the formation of the *El Puente* (The Bridge) group, which allied itself with the CRTFCA network. They continued to use the legal definition of refugee as contained in the 1980 Act, but they refused to use the criteria relating to the amount of time they had spent in Mexico and they did not insist that the refugees make a formal asylum claim, both of which had become conditions for sanctuary imposed by Tsrg.[111] Kathe Padilla, one of those who joined *El Puente*, has given a sharp and vivid account of the increasingly slavish adherence to the law that afflicted the movement in Tucson following the trial:

> In the beginning, it was rules about how far can you go to the fence, can you cross this way. Do this or that. There were those types of rules around the work . . . Then it started when we presented cases. And a pattern began to emerge to me and to other people, that there was a high degree of caution. I can tell you some things about people who were turned down by

---

108   'State of the Movement' (draft), January 1987, CRTFCA Discussion Document (CRTFCAR), 1
109   Ibid 2.
110   Cunningham (n 11), 168.
111   Ibid 173.

Trsg that really shows that this is true. I called it 'trial trauma'. It looked to me that you had to be a perfect case of a refugee to be passed by Trsg. And there were certain people who came up finally where I said, 'I am sorry. I'm not going to have this person's life on my head. And I am going to help this person.' So I say that due to this trauma of the trial, perhaps, that Trsg became more strict than either the U.S. or Canadian governments.[112]

A member of Trsg also admitted that, 'after the indictments, border workers adopted a more restrictive definition of "refugee" '.[113] Even prior to the major trial, a number of people in Trsg, including some who eventually left to join *El Puente*, were unhappy about the idea of the strategy of the Merkt letters to INS and the insistence on the refugees making a formal asylum claim, as they believed that it 'placed too much faith in the INS'.[114] A Trsg statement regarding refugee assistance, written just 4 months after the trial ended (19 November 1986), confirmed that they had by this time adopted very strict criteria for helping refugees, along the lines of refugee law. This document asserts that 'in spite of the ... dangers' many refugees were able to find refuge in Mexico, and that although they had to put up with the 'abject poverty endemic to Mexico' they were no longer victims of violence or persecution. Therefore, 'even *legitimate* refugees' may have only been coming to the US for 'primarily economic reasons'.[115] Many activists, including many of the refugees already in sanctuary, were outraged at what they saw as a discriminatory approach to those seeking sanctuary who were temporarily settled in Mexico and that, as a result, the Trsg were 'turning away legitimate refugees'.[116]

Nomophilia

The extent of the pull towards legality can be gauged from some of the prolific letters and articles put out at the time by Corbett. As well as having significant and deserved authority within the movement as one of its founders, he also effectively acted as a spokesperson for the 'Tucson' view on sanctuary. Having previously accepted the illegality of the practices of sanctuary, and having said repeatedly that abiding or remaining constrained by the law 'trains us to live with atrocity', he ended up making statements that with little substantive amendment could have been made by representatives of the INS or the government. He criticises those 'who no longer care whether [or not] those they bring [across the border] are refugees'. The failure to make such a distinction serves to 'erode

---

112 El Puente member interviewed in Ibid 168–169.
113 Bibler Coutin (n 15), 36.
114 Cunningham (n 11), 169.
115 Quoted in Ibid 169–170 (emphasis added).
116 Ibid 170.

rather than promote the international rule of human rights law'.[117] Elsewhere he quotes the Reagan administration official, Elliott Abrams, approvingly when the latter said: 'Legally and morally, the distinction between economic migrants and political refugees matters greatly. The United States is legally obligated and morally bound to protect refugees but not to accept for permanent residence every illegal immigrant who reaches our shores'[118] Corbett himself then stresses the importance of 'the distinction between refugees and illegal immigrants' so as to ensure 'refugee law's relevance to the practice of sanctuary'.[119] What Corbett has done here is to move from a tactical adherence to law to establishing a principle that sanctuary belongs within the framework of refugee law, not as a challenge to it.

Around the same time, Corbett claimed that only 10% of those then arriving from El Salvador and Guatemala were genuine refugees, most instead being merely people fleeing generalised violence.[120] Moreover, he claimed that most of those arriving were coming 'primarily because their country's economy is in shambles', i.e. they are economic migrants rather than refugees. As such: 'A shrinking minority of Central Americans arriving at the border now clears the Tucson refugee support group's screening procedures'.[121] He concluded by setting up the classic notion of the rule of law as a free society holding its government to account.[122] Therefore, he argued that 'the practice of sanctuary requires accountability to the legal order'.[123] From this general comment, Corbett went on to lay out the basis on which sanctuary should be offered to refugees. The refugee had to fit the narrow criteria of refugee law, the INS must always be informed when they were brought across the border, and the INS must be regularly informed of the status of the refugees, e.g. how many applications for asylum had been made, who had emigrated to or sought asylum in another country, who had fallen out of contact. In short, sanctuary was to become an adjunct to the INS.

In an extraordinary letter, written as trial proceedings were just getting underway in Phoenix, Corbett, on behalf of the Tsrg, sought joint work with the INS in processing asylum applications. There he wrote:

> We recognize that there are also valid administrative concerns about the potential abuse of asylum procedures, so all of us need to explore ways

117   Corbett J, 'Sanctuary and Revolutionary Struggle', 21–23 November, 1986, typed mimeographed document (GSSC), 2.
118   *Los Angeles Times* (17 January 1985).
119   Corbett J, 'The State, the Law, and the Sanctuary Covenant', undated typed mimeographed document (FUMCOG), 1.
120   Corbett, 'Revolutionary Struggle' (n 87), 2.
121   Ibid 3.
122   Ibid 6.
123   Corbett J, 'A Covenant for Sanctuary Services on the Border – Preliminary Discussion Draft', 12 December 1986, typed mimeographed document (GSSC), 1.

to assure that only those who are truly in need of asylum would be encouraged to apply if affirmative filing were possible at ports of entry. But if we work together on some of these problems we might find some practicable solutions.[124]

The INS responded by agreeing to a meeting in Phoenix – although it is not clear if this ever actually took place – and challenging Corbett's assertion that INS officers were acting in violation of the law at the Mexican border.[125] Replying to this letter, Corbett then made the concrete suggestion of informing INS each time sanctuary activists assisted someone over the border, so as to comply with the law as laid down in the 5th Circuit Court's ruling on Stacy Merckt's appeal. Although he spent several pages detailing abusive acts by INS officers, he also offered suggestions on how sanctuary activists could avoid being 'frivolous and opportunistic in our use of the asylum process'. This included a commitment to making the legal process of asylum work, and most perniciously focussing on those 'most [in] need' rather than those who were 'using refugee laws to delay deportation'. The aim of sanctuary was therefore to become focussed on the following precept: 'making the system work must take priority over playing the odds'.[126] In this extraordinary exchange, Corbett would have sanctuary not only commit itself to the law on admitting refugees but would help police the border by excluding from sanctuary those alleged to be duping the system.

The end of Sanctuary

Just as the movement had mushroomed over a short period, so its decline was equally swift following the debacle of the Sanctuary Trial. By the close of 1986, public sanctuary had fizzled out, as most refugees did not want to take the risk of legal prosecution. So this part of the movement subsequently focused mainly on getting legal representation for refugees for their asylum claims and for helping those who wished to return to resettle in their home towns and villages.[127] Certainly, by spring 1987, the Trsg was acting effectively as a legal support group rather than as sanctuary *per se*. Although they were still assisting refugees to cross the border illicitly, they were scrupulous about notifying the INS on each occasion before doing so. Moreover, as is clear from a document produced in July 1987, Trsg was subordinating its operations and tactics to legal advice from attorneys.[128]

124 Letter from Jim Corbett to Delia Combs, Assistant Commissioner, INS, 23 June 1985 (GSSC).
125 Letter from Delia Combs, Assistant Commissioner, INS to Jim Corbett, 29 July 1985 (GSSC).
126 Letter from Jim Corbett to Delia B Combs, Assistant Commissioner, INS, 13 August 1985 (GSSC).
127 Crittenden (n 1), 345.
128 'Annual Report on Trsg Sanctuary Services', 4 July 1987, typed mimeographed document (FUMCOG) 2.

In late 1987/early 1988, a questionnaire sent to 380 sanctuaries received only 37 replies, and of these, only 20 had a refugee in sanctuary and only 11 stated a willingness to take in a new refugee, suggesting perhaps the extent of the movement's decline by then.[129]

Yet, at the same time, some sanctuary groups were not only continuing their activities in response to new waves of refugees but were also deepening their understanding of forced migration and radicalising their critique of the legal categories in place. A 1987 report from various border groups states that while the numbers of refugees, particularly from El Salvador and Guatemala, were somewhat reduced, there was a significant increase in the numbers coming from Nicaragua and Honduras. In answer to the question of whether or not refugees were being directed towards applying for asylum, the Rio Grande Defense Committee in Texas answered in the negative for, 'To do so would mean that [the refugees] would be arrested immediately'.[130] The San Diego Interfaith Task Force reported that while applying for asylum was an option put to the refugees, and they were offered support in accessing legal advice for that, on the other hand 'During the last year no asylum cases have been filed from San Diego, mainly due to the nearly impossible chance of success: 0% before appeal, and little on appeal'.[131] The Rio Grande Defense Committee demonstrated the extent to which some in the movement had deepened their critique of refugee law and its effects in demarcating 'refugees' from 'illegal aliens':

> Congregations also need to remember that some of the most desperate cases needing help are not people who would qualify under the strict UN convention [*sic*] definitions. This is especially true for women who have left their kids back home. People's 'economic' woes are a real driving force in making life decisions. Some people will walk through fire to feed their children. Are we in any way responsible for the prolonged violence and misery in their countries? . . . It's past time to be deprecating one kind of immigrant because they're 'only economic'. By giving what is perceived as preferential treatment and attention to one small part of the undocumented population, we could be seen as trying to divide the [Latino] community, and as ignoring the plight of the majority of the undocumented, possibly the most oppressed group there is. By explaining what makes someone a refugee, we should not internalize INS regulations and sound as though we justify the way INS treats the rest of the undocumented.[132]

In a more low-key manner, the El Paso group make a similar point: 'We operate as a house of hospitality for the homeless poor. We deal with people on

---

129   National Sanctuary Defense Fund (NSDF) Board Memo, 2 February 1988 (GSSC).
130   'Border Task Force Report', National Sanctuary Communications Council (NSCC), 1987, typed mimeographed document (CRFTCA), 2.
131   Ibid 3.
132   Ibid 4.

an individual basis and try to deal with their individual needs. Each person tends to have a very different personal situation. We tend not to draw distinctions between nationalities'.[133] However, the combination of the now more or less complete split in the movement, demoralisation and fear following the convictions in the trial, and the almost complete subsuming of the Tucson activists into a legal paradigm rendered such insights moot as the movement came to an end.

What should be reasonably clear so far is the manner in which the Sanctuary Movement attempted to recreate an essential element of the sanctuary tradition: creating spaces beyond the reach of the law and sovereign power. What should also be very evident is the way in which norms derived from the quite different paradigm of refugee law compromised a significant part of the movement in this respect, in their recreating of some of the practices of refugee law within sanctuary such as screening and judging against a spurious set of criteria. Yet, another aspect, briefly touched upon in relation to the case of America Sosa, and which is closely tied to the acceptance of the limits of the legal paradigm, is the depoliticising of the refugee subject. For the remainder of this chapter, I will focus more critically on the following three questions in relation to the context of the Sanctuary Movement: (1) How the movement (re)configured the refugee subject in ways that both challenged and reinforced legal paradigms; (2) the role of law in closing down rather than opening up a space of asylum and; (3) the depoliticising of asylum by law.

Sanctuary subjects: activists or victims

Susan Bibler Coutin argues that the Central Americans who were given sanctuary 'were in a contested state of being', i.e. they were challenging their identification as 'illegal aliens' and asserting that they were in fact refugees who deserved asylum, and yet they did this by entering the country illegally, thus appropriating the right to declare what is or is not an illegal act or being.[134] There is certainly some truth to this claim. Indeed, the preparedness of so many of the refugees to tell their stories publically, in testimony to churches or through media appearances, is evidence of this. Activists from the more militantly political wing of the movement saw sanctuary as more than simply a relationship between paternalistic Anglos and needy Latinos. For example, Golden and McConnell describe the movement in the following terms:

> Sanctuary is not merely a safe place to hide in but a prophetic platform to speak out from. It is a strategy of action, a plan of struggle. It is a stipulation in the covenant relationship between God and the faithful, and between the faithful and their neighbours.[135]

---

133 Ibid 5.
134 Bibler Coutin (n 86), 283.
135 Golden and McConnell (n 18), 15.

By the same token, the testimony of Anna, a refugee from Guatemala, also demonstrates the kind of agency that refugees brought to the Sanctuary Movement:

> I made the decision to come [to the United States] because sanctuary was going to help us and because we wanted to keep helping our people by talking to the North American people about the reality of our country.[136]

It was also the case that often the refugees were entirely cognisant and in control of their role within the movement. During one sanctuary conference, the refugees insisted that the primary aim of the movement had to be stopping the US involvement in Central America. One of them, Linda from El Salvador, said: 'We want to go back home. We want El Salvador and Guatemala to be sanctuaries'.[137] This was a sentiment echoed by many other refugees too. So for them, sanctuary and politics were inextricably, and understandably, linked. Such was the case with America Sosa. As we saw earlier, in her relationship to her sanctuary church she refused to play the role of being just a refugee, a victim who needed supporting. Instead, she chose to use sanctuary as a 'platform to speak out from'.[138] And this caused tensions between her and the members of the congregation providing her with sanctuary. Indeed, that whole relationship of 'providers' and 'receivers' often lent an unpleasant paternalistic element to sanctuary. One example of this was a church announcing the arrival of refugees to take sanctuary: '*Our* refugees are coming?'[139] There was at least one recorded case where a family of refugees felt compelled to leave their sanctuary because of this kind of attitude.[140] A number of churches placed bans on the consumption of alcohol, supervised phone calls to relatives in Central America to control phone bills and other seemingly petty restrictions were put in place.[141] For sure, there were examples of severely traumatised individuals having trouble adjusting, and many sanctuaries were operating on tight budgets. However, these types of rules tend to suggest that the refugees were seen in general as wayward adolescents, rather than adults who had already shown sufficient wherewithal to

---

136 Ibid 34.
137 Ibid 165.
138 It is worth noting a similar point made by an American GI who took sanctuary to resist involvement in the Vietnam War: 'I chose sanctuary so I could make a stand, so I could tell people how servicemen feel about the war'. Foley MS, 'Sanctuary! A bridge between civilian and GI protest against the Vietnam War' in Marilyn B Young and Robert Buzzanco (eds), *A Companion to the Vietnam War* (Blackwell Publishers, 2002), 425.
139 Letter to members of the congregation of First United Methodist Church of Germantown from Virginia Klipstein, 27 July 1984 (FUMCOG) [emphasis added].
140 'Sanctuary Refugees Plan to Leave Burlington', *Burlington Free Press* (2 March 1986).
141 See, e.g, 'The Sanctuary Program at Southside United Presbyterian Church, Tucson, Arizona', 6 July 1982, typed mimeographed document (CRTFCAR).

escape brutal conditions and make a 1,000-mile overland journey to a country in which many of them did not yet speak the language.

Randy Lippert, in a highly sophisticated and insightful investigation, explores how paternalism developed in the context of the Canadian Sanctuary Movement that grew out of its US equivalent during the 1980s. He describes the first public declaration of sanctuary in Canada for 'Raphael', which took place at St. Andrew's United Church in Montreal in December 1983:

> Raphael had become the object of sovereign power . . . this was an instance, as Raphael's protectors put it, of 'God's law coming before the government's.' Authorized by this and other 'higher' laws, here a sovereign power began to flow from a much older wellspring of local church and community and then to surge through channels of mass media to become a torrent of spectacle sufficient to attract onlookers, including political authorities in high places.[142]

Lippert goes on to cite Foucault's description of 'pastoral power', arguing that 'Raphael became the object of this power and transformed into a needful, silenced "sheep" cared for and watched over by sacrificing "shepherds" '.[143] And yet this 'spectacle', as Lippert refers to it, was successful. A few hours after the public declaration, the government announced that all deportations to Guatemala would be suspended and that, in spite of breaking immigration laws themselves, the sanctuary activists would not be prosecuted. The price of success here was that the refugee had to perform the role of victim, to be helped by the active subjects of pastoral power. On another occasion, a sanctuary activist complained that a new group of refugees were 'much more radical, less conciliatory, and politically much more savvy'. As a result of these characteristics, they were told to leave sanctuary.[144] When another refugee in sanctuary left one night and decided to go underground, as her case seemed to be going nowhere and she feared the consequences, the response of one of the sanctuary providers was:

> I felt a little ripped off . . . We were preparing to have them here for [the] long term . . . We were prepared to do that . . . She decided that no, I don't want to do that, I don't want to wait, let's get out of here . . . That was a little disappointment.[145]

But is this a problem in the relationship between the refugee and the sanctuary providers inherent to sanctuary historically, or just to this particular manifestation of it? This is a difficult question to answer because details of the sanctuary subject

---

142 Lippert (n 46), 1–2.
143 Ibid 2.
144 Ibid 136.
145 Ibid 137.

in the medieval period appear sketchy at best; in antiquity, the contours become even more obscured. Instead, most of the historical evidence that we have relates to the question of the space of sanctuary rather than to the individuals who benefitted from it. One possibility, of course, is that the relative absence of information about the sanctuary-seekers of old is due to their lack of importance as subjects worth commenting upon. However, I think the key point was that the biopolitical paradigm was far less prominent then, and as such the question of sanctuary was not primarily one that concerned the qualities or otherwise of the person in sanctuary. There were often certain rituals and oaths that had to be performed in order to be granted sanctuary, but these appear to have been mostly perfunctory and routine. It was, instead, the sacredness of space, or the intercession of saints or gods, or their earthly representatives, that were of central importance. It is, of course, true that in his last works, Foucault identified a biopolitical paradigm reaching back into antiquity based on care of the self and of men's souls.[146] This notion certainly played a part in the tradition of church sanctuary, as its origins lay in the belief that people guilty of crimes could still seek salvation within the church, both as an institution and as a bounded consecrated space. Nevertheless, I have found very little in my research to suggest that the kind of meticulous and perverse construction of a refugee subject that has been pervasive in modernity, and especially in the era of refugee law, existed in earlier times. Aspects of it appear from time to time: the law of 397, which forced priests to judge sanctuary subjects as to the truth of their religious faith, and the canon law's *casus excepti* are obvious examples. But it was never generalised to anything like the extent that it has become today, with the hegemony of law and the advent of refugee law specifically. The problem, therefore, that Lippert identifies is, I think, specific to the attempt to resurrect sanctuary in the contemporary context, one in which largely, if not solely, through the law the refugee is conceived of as a mere victim, a symptom of disorder, a problem to be managed.

Central to Lippert's analysis is that 'sanctuary is not alien to rationality, sovereign power, and notions of law typically associated with the nation-state but is instead constituted by them'.[147] Sanctuary is, in fact, 'saturated with legal discourse'.[148] Therefore, sanctuary does not represent 'a majestic and eternal conflict' between church and state, rather it is 'a short-lived tension between two historical rationalities of government: the liberal and the pastoral'.[149] While Lippert's analysis is a necessary corrective to the often romanticised picture of sanctuary drawn by commentators and the activists involved, I think his judgement here is overly blunt and ignores many of the tensions that were present and,

---

146   Foucault M, *The Use of Pleasure: The History of Sexuality, Volume II* (Robert Hurley tr, Penguin, 1992); Foucault M, *The Care of the Self: The History of Sexuality, Volume III* (Robert Hurley tr, Penguin, 1990).

147   Lippert (n 46), 14.

148   Ibid 20.

149   Ibid 14–15.

indeed, opened up by sanctuary historically and in the context of the recent movements. First, as the historical evidence strongly suggests, sanctuary has in fact been a concept repeatedly in conflict with law and sovereign power. Insofar as Lippert correctly identifies a leading tendency in the practice of the modern Sanctuary Movement, I think he covers over the tensions between that tendency and those who represented the more militant and political wing of the movement. Moreover, many of the refugees themselves were able to use sanctuary as a means to engage in political struggle over the causes of their migration and the terms on which they could seek asylum in North America. The problem of paternalism was in fact addressed head-on in the CRTFCA newsletter *Basta!*, in which, among other things, the right of the refugees to nurture and maintain their own culture, and not be expected to assimilate into that of North America, is emphasised. In that issue, one refugee in sanctuary, Carmen Monico, is quoted as saying: 'We are not only receiving, but we are giving, we are active participants'.[150] In the case of at least one church, the family given sanctuary felt the need to express, by way of a letter to the sanctuary committee of the church, their feelings of resentment at the unbalanced relationship between them and their hosts, between 'we, the refugees and you the North Americans at home, with all the comfort and confidence that this confers on you, we the helped and you the helpers'.[151] Two years earlier, *Basta!* published a series of contributions from various refugees in sanctuary, almost all of whom argued for the movement to be more political, to be more open in taking sides against the dictatorships at home and the US government policy of intervention in the region. One of them, Linda, writes:

> Sanctuary is an answer for Salvadorans and Guatemalans because they recognize that we are political refugees and that gives us the opportunity to talk to U.S. people so that they may learn what life for us, Salvadorans, means in terms of: the reasons we had to leave our country; the repression of the government against the Salvadoran people; the reasons why our people are fighting; the consequences of U.S. aid to El Salvador; *the capacity and right we have to decide our own future*.[152]

There were also many cases of refugees seeking sanctuary who would then later become leading activists, and who would then encourage and support others to move up from Mexico and gain sanctuary in the United States.[153] In short, it would be a denial of the refugees' agency to ignore the fact of their own

150 Malcolm M, 'Overcoming Paternalism in the Sanctuary Movement', *Basta!* (March 1987), 23.
151 Letter from 'Joel' and 'Gabriella', June 1987 (FUMCOG).
152 Statement of 'Linda' in sanctuary in Tabernacle Church, Philadelphia, *Basta!* (January 1985), 16 [emphasis added].
153 'Guatemalan Credits Life to Sanctuary Movement', *Baton Rouge Morning Advocate* (8 June 1985), 10A.

frequent attempts to challenge the pastoral or paternalistic tendency in the movement that Lippert correctly identifies.

Judith McDaniel offers a view of these tensions from the perspective of a sanctuary activist. She suggests that the meaning of sanctuary lay fundamentally in the way in which it forced those who were living in relatively safe and prosperous countries to challenge their own prejudices, and to experience some of the precarity and risk that is the everyday reality of the refugee.[154] In other words, sanctuary *can* force the hosts to reflect on their own unacknowledged privileges. Cunningham, too, describes how the illegality of sanctuary could destabilise established subjects of sovereign power:

> Participation in Sanctuary often resulted in a reorientation of identities in which traditionally aligned memberships (that of family, church, and nation) were reconstituted. Because of the underground nature of Sanctuary activism, one of the principle kinds of identity to undergo change in Sanctuary was the relationship of the individual to the state.[155]

The politics of sanctuary cut across faith lines, leading to splits within congregations, and people switching between churches. It also led to many Americans who were active in the movement questioning their previously held faith in the government and law. For example, one American sanctuary activist described how:

> Once you become aware of oppression in one part of the world, you can make connections in your own back yard. You start seeing it all over. You just become a more critical person.[156]

Even subjectivities based on already existing modes of resistance were troubled and reconstituted in the course of the movement. At a national sanctuary conference in 1987, a group of North American women expressed their feeling of being dominated by fellow male activists, and therefore proposed that the national steering committee be made up of half women and half men. The Central American women opposed this, with various of them arguing, 'No we won't do it, no gender parity'; 'the only thing that counts is *el pueblo*'; 'we don't care how many women and men – we can work together'; 'whoever has resources should be the basis of participation'; 'we're not into this – this is your struggle', etc.[157] Thus, a clash developed between working and middle class, between socialism and feminism, between class and identity politics. One female activist

---

154 McDaniel J, *Sanctuary: A Journey* (Firebrand Books, 1987), 144.
155 Cunningham H, 'Sanctuary and sovereignty: church and state along the U.S.–Mexico border' (1998), 40, *Journal of Church and State*, 371, 382.
156 Lorentzen (n 49), 125.
157 Ibid 88.

described sanctuary as 'moving beyond' feminism.[158] Another expressed how a certain realisation of the nature of the struggle from the point of view of the refugees set in:

> I think when you're fighting for your life, engaged in life/death situations in a revolution, gender differences break down ... They'd look at our demands as a lot of white middle-class foolishness.[159]

And indeed some of this 'middle-class foolishness' came to the fore when a group of sanctuary activists went to visit Central America. Staying in a youth hostel in Nicaragua, a few of them started complaining about sanitary conditions and the lack of access to the 'five basic food groups'. One of the women in the group puts it bluntly: 'What started out as a gender split became an ideological split surrounding reality versus romance. You romanticize "blessed are the poor, blessed are the hungry", but you get there and it's fucking hard to be poor and hungry and listen to stories of killing'.[160] Lorentzen comments:

> Women's class-conscious approach may determine whether they 'work for' or 'stand with' the refugees – a critical distinction between the two orientations. To avoid patronizing those they hope to help, they must give up their own cultural models of organizing and become receptive to the refugees' models.[161]

There are elements here of Jacques Derrida's concept of 'hospitality', of an unconditional opening, in which one allows the self to be transformed by the other.[162] The notion of hospitality is indeed one we have encountered a number of times over the course of this book, from St. Augustine onwards, albeit in slightly varied forms. It could perhaps be argued, therefore, that a recurrent feature of sanctuary is not so much a reaffirmation of pastoral power, but instead a blurring of the lines between shepherd and sheep. Lippert himself refers to one instance when a conflict arose between sanctuary providers and the refugees when the latter wanted to engage in a hunger strike, thus breaking a rule set by the former that prohibited such actions in sanctuary. The response from the sanctuary providers was unyielding. As Lippert notes:

> The prospect of a hunger strike by migrants in sanctuary, the severe threat that such acts posed to migrants' very lives, constituted resistance to the ideal of passive, obedient, pastoral objects in need of others' life-affirming

---

158 Ibid 180.
159 Ibid 89.
160 Ibid 111.
161 Ibid 115.
162 Derrida J and Dufourmantelle A, *Of Hospitality* (Rachel Bowlby tr, Stanford University Press, 2000), 25.

care and guidance *and* resistance to the overlapping exercise of other sovereign powers that demanded 'bare life'.[163]

There were of course objective difficulties to be overcome. For example, 90% of the refugees were *campesinos* who were often unaccustomed to urban life even in their own countries, never mind in a country as different as the United States where they did not speak the language. This, together with an often poor level of Spanish among the hosts, led to tensions and unexpressed resentment. During a meeting of sanctuary activists in Madison, Wisconsin, the hosts and the refugees held separate meetings to discuss issues and then came together in a plenary. There the refugees felt confident enough to raise many issues, such as their feeling of being infantilised and not being allowed enough independence and autonomy by the sanctuary providers.[164] The point is that, while paternalism and established tropes of rescuer asylum providers and refugee victims persisted, sanctuary opened up a space in which those notions could be challenged and undermined, not least by the refugees themselves.

Sanctuary, law and legitimacy

The starting point in assessing the legal compatibility of sanctuary in the United States in the 1980s is to state clearly that no such right existed. To claim that there were spaces, whether religious or secular, which existed beyond the reach of law had no legal basis. The lawyers consulted by Southside Church in the run-up to the first public declaration of sanctuary made that clear.[165] Indeed, the question of sanctuary had been directly addressed 14 years previously by the US Supreme Court in the case of *Warden, Maryland Penitentiary v. Hayden* [1967].[166]

---

163 Lippert (n 46), 86. It is striking how the same dynamic played itself out between the refugees/migrants and their supporters in the Sans-Papiers movement in relation to the tactic of the hunger strike, e.g. Siméant J, *La cause des sans-papiers* (Presses de Sciences Po, 1998); Blin T, *L' Invention des sans-papiers: Essai sur la démocratie à l'épreuve du faible* (Presses Universitaires de France, 2010). The use of the hunger strike as a means by which the Sans-Papiers could retain or take back control of their struggle and their identities is discussed further in the next chapter.

164 Golden and McConnell (n 18), 55.

165 A legal memorandum prepared for the TEC a few weeks before the public declaration at Southside in March 1982 made it quite clear that offering sanctuary, i.e. harbouring aliens who had not been formally admitted at the border, was illegal. Indeed, the charges that were eventually brought against sanctuary activists in the Arizona trial were those cited in this memo. [Legal Memorandum, 9 March 1982, reproduced in *Sanctuary: A Justice Ministry* (Chicago Religious Task Force on Central America, 1986), 29–33.]

166 *Warden, Maryland Penitentiary v. Hayden*, 387 US 294 (1967). The case dealt with the question of the right of the police to enter a private home to make a search based on suspicion without an arrest warrant. The majority of the court held in certain circumstances this was permitted. Justice Douglas' comments were part of his dissenting opinion to this decision.

In *obiter* comments, Justice William Douglas made clear that the traditional notion of sanctuary had no place in societies operating under the rule of law:

> The right of privacy protected by the Fourth Amendment relates in part of course to the precincts of the home or office. But it does not make them sanctuaries where the law can never reach. There are such places in the world. A mosque in Fez, Morocco, that I have visited, is by custom a sanctuary where any refugee may hide, safe from police intrusion. We have no sanctuaries here.[167]

Note how he infers that sanctuary only belongs in backward undeveloped countries, a theme that chimes with the prejudices that pervade the modern historiography of ancient sanctuary as discussed in Part I. Following Justice Douglas, the Northern California District Director of INS, David Ilchert, correctly stated the law when he wrote: 'Some churches have supported ecclesiastical sanctuary, but there is no such legal entity . . .'[168] Moreover, since the right of church sanctuary was expunged from canon law in 1983, 'any force it adds to the current sanctuary movement's legal arguments are derived only from its moral force rather than from any concrete legal principle or precedent'.[169]

Therefore, the effectiveness of the Sanctuary Movement, such as it was, rested largely on shifting the political discourse in such a way as to create a space between itself and sovereign law. It was for this reason that although the government knew about the activities of the Sanctuary Movement in detail almost from the beginning, they held off from applying the full force of the law for several years. Leon Ring, chief of Border Patrol in Tucson, understood the dynamics and adjusted his strategy accordingly:

> This underground railroad – or the various church groups – wanted publicity. They were baiting us to overreact. Therefore, we have deliberately been very low-key. Certain arrests could have taken place if we had wanted to, but we felt that the government would end up looking ridiculous, especially as far as going into church property – anything where the ethics involved would be questioned.[170]

This policy of non-enforcement, necessitated by a political reality that it did not control, effectively 'created a twentieth-century sanctuary privilege in America', one that existed in spite of the law, not because of it.[171]

The more radical political wing of the movement around the CRTFCA was fairly consistent and clear on the essential conflict between sanctuary and law.

---

167 Ibid, per Justice Douglas' dissenting opinion.
168 Bau (n 6), 88.
169 Ibid 92.
170 Ibid 89.
171 Ibid.

Perhaps the most militant exposition of the Christian opposition of sanctuary to law in the Sanctuary Movement is given by Golden and McConnell. They point out how slavery and segregation were once legal and are now illegal, and that, moreover, it was 'protest and resistance' that changed those laws:

> Those in power want to elevate national law to ultimate or sacred status, but that is simply idolatry. Laws are not sacred, justice is. We worship God, not Caesar or the president.[172]

In the month when the federal government came down on the movement with mass arrests, raids and indictments, the following appeared in a January 1985 editorial of *Basta!*:

> Sanctuary by its very nature breaks the law and/or current implementation of law. All of us in the Sanctuary Movement have chosen to break the law, not as an end in itself, but to defend the powerless, the Central Americans in the U.S. and those still in their homelands.[173]

The tension between sanctuary and law was also not lost on a leading judge, John T. Noonan, when he wrote:

> Sanctuary is shocking to the secular mind. How can there be any place within the confines of a nation that the law does not operate? How can religion claim a privilege to say it is beyond the law? How can the law stultify itself by acknowledging that in certain places the law ceases to hold sway?[174]

In a reference to the nineteenth-century Underground Railroad, Noonan goes on to write: 'Here sanctuary was not incorporated into the law to limit the law but operated in bold defiance of the law'.[175] Barbara Yarnold, a sympathetic commentator on the Sanctuary Movement, described it as something which 'at its core, [is] an illegal attempt to bypass the legal structures of U.S. immigration law'.[176] Even if some in the movement believed that they were abiding by the spirit and the letter of refugee law, by taking the decisions on entry into the country and the granting of refugee status into their own hands, they were coming into direct conflict with sovereign right, a point that was emphasised by the prosecution in the Sanctuary Trial.

At the outset, the Sanctuary Movement activists, feeling their way around the problems faced by the refugees, understandably sought to explore every avenue

172   Golden and McConnell (n 18), 134.
173   Cunningham (n 11), 40.
174   Forward by John T. Noonan, Bau (n 6), 2.
175   Ibid 3.
176   Yarnold (n 45), 200.

within the law before breaking it. Defending the movement from criticisms that they were reckless law-breakers, Fife said: 'So if you hear from the INS that what those church people ought to do is try to work within the law first, we did it. And we did it with as much energy and imagination and creativity as we could'.[177] Among other things, this involved assisting the refugees with asylum claims and bailing them out of detention. Gary MacEoin, reflecting back on the origins of the movement, would say: 'We began with an absolute belief in the system, a belief in the integrity of the system'.[178] The power of the ruling ideology, particularly as expressed within legal frameworks, will mean that the vast majority of people moving into a position of resistance will begin in the same place as that described by Fife and MacEoin, with a belief in the law's capacity to deliver at least some justice. What is troubling is how the 'Tucson' faction began with illusions in law, then in the face of its pernicious role in negating asylum adopted a position of resistance to law, only to end up playing a role as adjunct to the laws and enforcement agencies that had provoked them into action in the first place. The desperation on the part of some in the movement to maintain legitimacy by reference to the law ended up reinforcing the law's demand that the refugee prove their legitimacy as true refugees. And it was this logic that led sections of the movement to replicate the practices of law in screening and policing refugees at the border. As Tom Gerety notes: '[T]he sanctuary movement has learned its law quickly, and almost too well. Its legalism seems more thorough, more elaborate, and more urgent than its circumstances require'.[179] Gerety suggests a reason for this:

> 'He became what he beheld,' wrote Blake. Peaceable movements like sanctuary may turn to legalism because everywhere, in their struggles, legalism is what they encounter. They become like the judges and prosecutors they behold.[180]

Gerety goes on to argue that in every dissenting movement, the point at which dissent crosses the line to resist the law is crucial, as it requires the confidence to say: 'I will not only criticize the law, I will disobey it'.[181] What is perhaps most dispiriting about a large portion of the Sanctuary Movement is that it crossed that line with much courage and determination, only to end up retreating back over it again.

Early on, after the initial realisation of the limits of the law, there was a healthy attitude to working outside the law. At the time and since, in numerous accounts

177 Fife quoted in 'Conspiracy of Compassion', *Sojourners* (March 1985), 16.
178 Cunningham (n 11), 28.
179 Gerety T, 'Sanctuary: a comment on the ironic relation between law and morality' in David A Martin (ed), *Refugee Law in the 1980s: The Ninth Sokol Colloquium on International Law* (Martinus Nijhoff, 1986), 167–168.
180 Ibid 171.
181 Ibid.

of the movement, Jim Corbett has been portrayed as the leading voice in arguing against politicising sanctuary, and for defending the existing legal framework of refugee law and a commitment to working within it. Certainly, from a period shortly before the Sanctuary Trial and onwards, Corbett played this role. But this was not always the case. In 1982, just a couple of months after the public declaration of sanctuary at Southside Church, he acknowledged that giving sanctuary breached US law, specifically the ban on harbouring illegal aliens under s274 of the 1952 Immigration and Naturalization Act. But he goes on to write that when the state prohibits assisting people 'fleeing from oppression', then 'passive protest merely trains us (and any who may look to us for guidance) to live with atrocity'.[182] Around the same time, he could also write: 'The oppressed are often betrayed by clergy and congregations who give primary allegiance to the law and order of established powers . . .'.[183] And elsewhere, he remarked: '[J]ust as the refugees are outlawed, hunted down, and imprisoned, if we choose to serve them in spirit and truth, we will also be outlawed'.[184] Thus, there was an acknowledgment by Corbett of being forced outside of the law in pursuit of justice. And this was a view held throughout the movement at its early stages and for some time afterwards. When Luther Place Memorial Church in Washington, DC, declared itself a public sanctuary in March 1983, they included in the liturgy for the occasion references to Jesus breaking the laws of the Pharisees and of Caesar.[185] The pastor of another sanctuary church in Philadelphia announced to the press: 'We're violating a law that in our judgement is unjust and immoral. We're doing this openly'.[186] Dick Simpson, head of the outreach committee of Wellington Avenue Church in Chicago, which was one of the original churches to declare sanctuary in March 1982, was equally emphatic: 'We are breaking the laws of our government because of a higher moral law . . . the need to save the lives and protect the liberty of these refugees'.[187] And echoing an Augustinian approach to hospitality, The Revd Stephen Lynch, pastor of a sanctuary church in Brooklyn, could say:

> There may be the law of immigration law, but there's the law of God . . . Our job is to give hospitality and fulfil the law of God and that requires us to receive anyone with hospitality, especially the poor person who has no

---

182 'Will You Join in Making Your Church a Sanctuary for Refugees', 31 May 1982, typed mimeographed document (CRTFCAR). This document is unsigned, although it is written in Corbett's distinctive style, and the correspondence address listed is his home address.
183 Bau (n 6), 14.
184 Golden and McConnell (n 18), 59.
185 'Liturgy for an Ecumenical Service of Public Sanctuary', 24 March 1983, typed mimeographed document (LPMC), 5.
186 The Revd Ted Loder, quoted in 'Church Will Defy Feds, Shelter Refugees', *Germantown Courier* (30 May 1984), 1.
187 'Church offers Refugees Sanctuary', *Chicago Sun Times* (25 July 1982).

other recourse. God doesn't recognize legal and illegal; the frontiers aren't God's frontiers.[188]

For many in the campus element of the Sanctuary Movement, such as those involved in the first campus sanctuary at University of California–Riverside, breaking the law was an essential component as they grew to understand that 'while support work can be legal, harbouring refugees legally is an impossibility'. Moreover, they recognised that there was a 'legalistic perspective that existed not just without but also within the movement' which served to hold it back by seeking compromise with the system and the law. And yet for this conservative element within their ranks, this legalistic concern 'evaporated as people began to better understand our efforts'.[189] As late as November 1984, Fife could say at a sanctuary meeting:

> We have no middle ground between collaboration with the U.S. betrayal of faith and resistance to that betrayal. We cannot do both. If we choose to stand with the oppressed, then we will have to run the risks of doing certain acts which our government considers illegal . . . But I remind you, law-abiding protests only train us to live with atrocity.[190]

The only person pushing the legal position at this meeting was A. Bates Butler III, a lawyer from Tucson, and soon to be one of the attorneys representing the defendants in the Arizona trial.[191]

Perhaps the reason that Corbett and others in Tucson increasingly cleaved to the legal framework had more to do with maintaining a certain level of legitimacy. This pull became greater following the verdict in the Sanctuary Trial. Corbett would later complain that politicising sanctuary played into the hands of the government's attempts to delegitimise the movement.[192] He had direct experience of this early on, after he had written: 'When the government itself sponsors the torture of entire peoples and then makes it a felony to shelter those seeking refuge, law-abiding protest merely trains us to live with atrocity'.[193] This was widely quoted by both many in the movement and by the government and INS. As in the quote from Fife above, that last phrase became almost a mantra. Corbett later claimed that this had in fact been a 'carelessly constructed sentence'.[194] Instead, he was only trying to make the point that helping

---

188   Moreno S, 'A Refuge Outside the Law', *Sunday Newsday* (24 July 1983).
189   Duran L, 'Campus Sanctuary', *Nuestra Cosa* (Winter 1985).
190   'Future Directions of Sanctuary Movement Discussed at Presbyterian Consultation', typed minutes of consultation meeting, Pacific Palisades, California, 26–28 November 1984 (FUMCOG), 7.
191   Ibid 8–9.
192   Corbett (n 19), 161.
193   Ibid 164.
194   Ibid, footnote.

refugees had to be more than a symbolic act. It is hard to accept that gloss on his original statement, particularly as he and others used the same formulation repeatedly.[195] Again, it was perhaps his concern with the question of maintaining legitimacy that led him to backtrack. As he himself said, he rued the fact that the quote was used repeatedly by the government to delegitimise him and the movement.[196]

However, it seems to me as if the period from early 1984 through to 1985, when the first prosecutions of sanctuary activists began and leading up to the climactic Sanctuary Trial in Arizona, marked a change, which saw the Tucson group seeking increasingly to situate their acts within a legal framework. And it was this development that, more than anything else, fomented the split in the movement. According to the CRFTCA, in April 1984, in response to the first arrests of various sanctuary workers, members of the Tucson group urged that the Sanctuary Movement refrain from stating that they have a 'willingness to break the law but instead say that we are law-abiding and in fulfilment of the law'.[197] They go on to argue that:

> The concern about reprisals if the sanctuary movement we publically [*sic*] state its intentions is a tactical matter. It represents a new development within the sanctuary movement and a change in the position of Tucson. Tucson originally agreed with us that our public position would express a willingness to break laws, while clearly showing that the government is illegally interpreting the U.S. Refugee Act and U.N. Protocol Accords as Refugees [*sic*].[198]

There were two problems with this idea of maintaining legitimacy. First, it did not protect them either from the law itself – most of those who were placed on trial adhered to the more legalistic wing of the movement. Second, by following the steps of refugee law, they transferred the onus of being 'legitimate' from themselves back onto the refugees. This grew out of the mistaken belief that refugee law provided a genuine space for most of those coming from El Salvador or Guatemala to make a successful claim for asylum. But even adopting a faithful

---

195   For example, Corbett J, 'Preliminary Statement Concerning Salvadoran Refugees', National Council of Churches of Christ Witness to Immigration, typed mimeographed document, 28–30 January 1982 (CRTFCAR); 'Will You Join in Making Your Church a Sanctuary for Refugees', 31 May 1982, typed mimeographed document (CRTFCAR); comments by Fife J, 'Future Directions of Sanctuary Movement Discussed at Presbyterian Consultation', typed minutes of consultation meeting, Pacific Palisades, California, 26–28 November 1984 (FUMCOG), 7.

196   Corbett (n 19), 164.

197   'Some Considerations on Direction for the Sanctuary Movement', *Basta!* (January 1985), 24.

198   Ibid 24–25.

reading of refugee law excludes most asylum-seekers.[199] The recent passing of the 1980 Refugee Act, as we saw in Chapter 4, had been largely based on a desire by the government to restrict asylum on the basis of the limited definition found in international law. An anti-immigration pressure group, the Federation for American Immigration Reform (FAIR), made clear in publicity attacking the Sanctuary Movement that they supported the 1980 Refugee Act on the basis that it limited asylum only 'to those who would be singled out for persecution in their home countries'.[200] In a coolly and, in legal terms, soundly argued demolition of the movement's claim to legality, an associate general counsel with the INS and a law student at the Catholic University in Washington, DC, write: 'The Refugee Act of 1980 did not create an entitlement to asylum; it created a right to petition for asylum'.[201] And they conclude: 'Today's sanctuary movement should be recognized for what it is, an act of civil disobedience, rather than a legal principle'.[202]

In their propaganda battle with the Sanctuary Movement, representatives of the government were in fact able to deploy the legal argument to some effect. The INS used the 1951 Convention precisely to delegitimise the refugees, pointing out that, just because they came from war-torn countries, they 'are not considered to be legitimate asylum applicants unless they can substantiate individual persecution', and their claim fails if they cannot show that 'they were in no more jeopardy than others in El Salvador'.[203] Elliott Abrams, at that time the assistant secretary of State for Human Rights and Humanitarian Affairs, described the refugees from Central America thus:

> They come here for a very good reason. They come here for a better life. They come here for better jobs, but that doesn't entitle them to asylum. Asylum is a very special thing which we give to people who can prove that they have a well-founded fear of persecution.[204]

A few years later, a spokesperson for the State Department attempted to refute some of the claims of the Sanctuary Movement in a letter to the *New York Times*:

> It is not enough for the applicant to state that he faces the same conditions that every other citizen faces. [Under the terms of the 1980 Refugee Act we

---

199 Behrman S, 'Accidents, Agency and Asylum: Constructing the Refugee Subject' (2014), 25, *Law and Critique*, 249.

200 FAIR Legislative Bulletin, 'Extended Voluntary Departure (EVD) for Salvadorans S.377/H.R. 822', in FAIR Sanctuary Information Packet (INSA).

201 Walsh JH and O'Neil ME, 'Sanctuary: A Legal Privilege or Act of Civil Disobedience?' (1987), 61, *Florida Bar Journal*, 11, 15.

202 Ibid 16.

203 Ezell H (Western Regional Commissioner), 'A Realistic View of the Sanctuary Movement', typed manuscript, nd (INSA), 5.

204 60 Minutes, CBS (12 December 1982).

ask] Why are you different from everyone else in your country? How have you been singled out, threatened, imprisoned, tortured, harassed?[205]

Moreover, the then deputy general counsel for the INS echoed these statements and expounded in great detail on the various elements of refugee law to show why most of the Central Americans arriving were not eligible for asylum.[206] And in a set-piece debate on the Sanctuary Movement between the director of INS, Alan C. Nelson, and William Sloane Coffin, Nelson was able to hide behind a legal-bureaucratic justification for the refusal to grant asylum:

> It is not up to me, or Reverend Coffin or sanctuary movement leaders to determine who is a refugee or who is entitled to asylum in the United States. We have a system to make that determination.[207]

Elsewhere, in response to the argument that the US government was deliberately frustrating the asylum applications of people fleeing right-wing regimes, Nelson pointed out that decisions on asylum were not vested solely in government agents but could be taken through a long and complex appeals process, and thus to accept this criticism, one had to also accept a large-scale 'organized conspiracy'.[208] One cannot completely discount the impact that the government has over the asylum process if they publically insist that a certain country is not persecuting its citizens, and such a bias does not require a conspiracy, rather it is how policy and ideology can percolate into 'common sense' assumptions, e.g. that claims of persecution from a certain country are likely to be spurious. However, the real issue here, one that was obscured by the Sanctuary Movement's reliance upon the legal definition of a refugee, is that it is precisely the legal definition that acts as the conduit for closing the door on asylum for so many people. Therefore, in principle, it does not matter how many appeals there are, or how many decision-makers are involved, once the reference point by which the refugee is measured is 'objective' and 'universal'.

In his debate with Coffin, Nelson emphasises that the burden of proof rests with the asylum-seeker and the need for the applicant to prove individual persecution. Coffin's response begins by explicitly relegating the 'legal questions surrounding sanctuary' to the background, in favour of the 'moral, political and

205 'Letter from Laura Dietrich', *New York Times* (2 October 1985) A26. The same point is made by right-wing critics of the Sanctuary Movement, e.g. 'The Sanctuary Movement: Revolution Walking across Our Border', *West Watch* (April/May 1985), 6.

206 Schmidt PW, 'Refuge in the United States: The Sanctuary Movement Should Use the Legal System' (1986), 15, *Hofstra Law Review*, 79.

207 Nelson AC and Coffin WS, 'A Debate on Sanctuary' (1985), 7, *Church & State Abroad*, 1, 2.

208 Cited in Francis ST, *Smuggling Revolution: The Sanctuary Movement in America* (Capital Research Center, 1986), 39.

historical aspects of the sanctuary movement'.[209] He rejects the distinction between economic and political refugees, and acknowledges criticism from Nelson that the Sanctuary Movement did not accord with many aspects of its traditional practice during the Middle Ages, while championing the innovative aspects of the movement such as involving the re-assertion of the refugees as active political subjects:

> [It] is quite right to say that that this is not standard sanctuary. The sanctuary movement has added features. The churches and synagogues provide food, shelter, clothing *and* a common platform on which both Central and North Americans can stand together to decry the deportation of innocent Salvadorans and Guatemalans.[210]

And yet, Coffin quickly finds himself bending towards the law. The starting point is again the notion that refugee law contains within it some essential element of protection. And so he pleads that the INS 'administer the law according to humanitarian and legal concerns instead of on the basis of foreign policy considerations'.[211] From trumpeting the political aspect of the movement, Coffin calls forth the law as a shield to the political aims of the state. Moreover, he gives further ground when he champions the use of screening refugees at the border. When challenged by Nelson and others on why the movement is better qualified than the INS to carry out such procedures, he ends up arguing that it takes time to establish whether the 'claimant's story is plausible', and that it is necessary to protect against the 'embarrassment' of having a 'phoney' in sanctuary.[212] And here it becomes almost impossible to draw a distinction between this position and that of government officials when they say: 'There is no such thing as a "self-appointed refugee". Each person who seeks the protection of the United States must *apply* for asylum, and each application is examined on a case-by-case basis'.[213]

The Sanctuary Movement as border control

Lippert correctly identifies a significant lack in most sanctuary scholarship, namely the failure to recognise the extent to which the US Sanctuary Movement adopted the framework of the legal refugee determination process through their own selection procedures for admitting refugees into sanctuary.[214] And yet this aspect was central both to the Tucson faction's claim to legitimacy and to the eventual

---

209 Nelson and Coffin (n 207), 4.
210 Ibid 4–5 (emphasis in original).
211 Ibid 5.
212 Ibid 8.
213 Contribution by Elliott Abrams to 'Sanctuary and the Sanctuary Movement: A Symposium', *This World* (Spring/Summer 1985).
214 Lippert (n 46), 70.

split in the movement. The logical endpoint of cleaving to legal legitimacy was for that part of the movement to perceive themselves as, effectively, adjuncts to border control. As Zucker and Zucker note, the Sanctuary Movement 'came to function as a kind of shadow image of the government's refugee programs, screening Central Americans, determining the validity of their claims of persecution, and offering them resettlement assistance'.[215] The fact that both economic collapse and political persecution were factors in Central America at the time 'enabled the United States to respond inequitably to the refugees. Following its own dictates, the United States could choose to close one eye and look only through the other'.[216] Of course, this was only possible because in law, there is a distinction between refugees and economic migrants. But as one commentator argues: 'If buses are burned, bridges are blown up and people cannot go to work or school, or if the political turmoil interferes with the means to earn a living, it becomes impossible to disentangle political from economic reasons for migrating'.[217] But the critical point about the break from the legal paradigm which is predicated on sitting in judgment on the refugee is very well expressed by one of the leading activists in the Sanctuary Movement, who was also one of the defendants in the Tucson trial, Darlene Nicgorski: 'And when all is said and done, I would rather be judged for having helped a refugee than for having defined what one is'.[218]

Bibler Coutin writes that by 'manipulating the notions and practices' of immigration law the Sanctuary Movement were able to 'legitimize their work and, in the process, to create novel notions of citizenship, legal identity, and law'.[219] The Sanctuary Movement both 'invoked and redefined' the discourse around immigration in the United States. The latter was achieved by assisting refugees to cross the border to safety and shelter and by giving them a platform to have their stories told. Yet the former was done by forcing the refugees to have their stories judged by members of the movement, and through reinforcing the legal categories of refugee and non-refugee.[220] Bibler Coutin identifies how merely shifting authority for implementing the law from the state to the 'community' does not obviate the power relations involved:

> By assuming the authority to interpret law, Sanctuary workers created hierarchies between themselves and Central Americans . . . [the testimonies provided to the Sanctuary workers either just before or just after their entry

---

215   Zucker and Zucker (n 2), 82.
216   Ibid.
217   Cecilia Menjívar, quoted in Ibid. A similar point is also made in Loescher G, *Beyond Charity: International Cooperation and the Global Refugee Crisis* (OUP, 1993), 6.
218   Quoted in García MC, ' "Dangerous Times Call for Risky Responses": Latino Immigration and Sanctuary, 1981–2001' in Gastón Espinosa, Virgilio Elizondo and Jesse Miranda (eds), *Latino Religions and Civic Activism in the United States* (OUP, 2005), 166.
219   Bibler Coutin (n 15), 107.
220   Ibid 108.

into the U.S.] subjected Central Americans to the scrutiny of Sanctuary workers who would define these immigrants' legal identities and use this knowledge to fuel volunteers own activism. The Sanctuary movement's oppositional legal practices thus demonstrate the difficulty of drawing on the law's potential for resistance without simultaneously invoking its capacity to oppress.[221]

Indeed, as one sanctuary activist in Tucson said with pride: 'We are better at separating political refugees from economic refugees than the INS is!'[222]

In spite of this, Bibler Coutin argues that it would have been a mistake for the movement to reject a discourse based on law, as 'it would have abandoned a powerful source of legitimacy and allowed authorities to define the movement's legal significance'.[223] But as I have argued above, holding on to the discourse of law inevitably meant facilitating the continued suspicion of the legitimacy of refugee claims via the screening process, adopting a managerial approach towards the refugees and disabling the defence in court. Moreover, it can be reasonably questioned whether or not the movement's legitimacy was really founded upon its adoption of legal categories and practices. It seems to me that the combination of increased awareness of the brutal conditions in El Salvador and Guatemala, the US government's role in propping up the regimes there and the visible plight of the refugee arrivals had far greater weight.

Bibler Coutin herself appears unable to reconcile her sophisticated understanding of how legal paradigms reinforce power relationships at the expense of refugees, while at the same time claiming that somehow the operation of the law at a community level can change the nature of that relationship. She argues, therefore, that in taking on the task of enacting law, the sanctuary activists 'continually constituted Central Americans as refugees' as opposed to economic migrants.[224] This is not strictly true, as they judged many as being non-refugees, and thus refused to help them cross the border. In any case, while this process labelled many more Central Americans as refugees than the INS were prepared to do, it did not involve 'manipulating the notions and practices' of law, nor did it 'create novel notions of citizenship, legal identity, and law'.[225] Instead, it served to reinforce existing categories of refugees and illegal aliens, passing judgement on those seeking asylum according to those categories. Corbett would write, for example: 'concerning the screening, placement, and protection of Central American refugees . . . *the sanctuary network is an emergency alternative to the INS . . .*'.[226] While one can argue that the very act of private citizens

---

221   Bibler Coutin (n 86), 283.
222   Ibid 293.
223   Bibler Coutin (n 15), 108.
224   Quoted in Ibid 111.
225   Ibid 107.
226   *National Lawyers Guild's Central American Refugee Defense Fund Newsletter*, 6 June 1986 (GSSC) [emphasis added].

appropriating for themselves the right to decide on the legal status of immigrants was itself a radical reimagining of law,[227] equally it can be perceived as symptomatic of how the ideological hegemony of law has reached even into resistance to it.

The testimonies of some of the border workers give us a sense of how adhering to the legal standard of a refugee in practice, while reconciling this with their religious or ethical beliefs, often caused a real crisis of conscience. One border worker in Tucson expressed her unease with maintaining fealty to the legal distinction between a refugee and an economic migrant:

> By adhering to Trsg standards, we're playing a role in trying to change refugee law . . . [But] what do you do when an economic refugee comes to you and says their children are dying? They're just as dead whether they're economic or political.[228]

Another Tucson activist, Marty Shelton-Jenck, recalled a Trsg meeting in which there was apparently an irreconcilable dispute over whether a refugee family seeking help were really refugees or economic migrants, with Shelton-Jenck himself opposed to helping them. However, someone suggested that they take a break to pray and sit in silence for 5 minutes, after which the entire group immediately agreed to help the family over the border and into sanctuary. According to Shelton-Jenck, 'That time of silence gave everybody a moment to really think where their hearts and minds really were'.[229] Another way of looking at this tale is that, once they stepped back from an obsession with the legal definition, they were able to go with their instincts and their hearts. Sometimes, of course, the conflict would resolve itself for activists in favour of the law. A Tucson border worker describes how she went to the border to meet what she thought was going to be a group of seven refugees. Instead, there were twenty-five, including starving mothers with their babies. 'And for me, it was a dilemma between the 1980 Refugee Act and Matthew 25. Matthew 25 called me to help all those who are in need'. On deciding that they did not fit the legal definition of a refugee, they instead gave them some food, but refused to help them cross the border. 'Crossing them wouldn't help the goal of sanctuary'.[230] What that goal was, she does not say.

In spite of some radical statements that he would later disavow, Corbett's nomophilia was to become increasingly evident over time. After the movement had wound itself down, he wrote:

> All of us sometimes and some of us most times must be coerced into civility. All of us in civil society need police protection from one another. And, for

227 Bibler Coutin (n 15), 109.
228 Ibid 114.
229 'Marty Shelton-Jenck interviewed' in Elna L Otter and Dorothy F Pine (eds), *The Sanctuary Experience: Voices of the Community* (Aventine Press, 2004), 307–308.
230 Bibler Coutin (n 15), 115.

a nation-state to exist at all, governmental organization must maintain the national borders by repelling attackers, and excluding unauthorized aliens.[231]

He argues for seeing a distinction between obeying the government (often bad) and obeying the law (good). He sees wisdom in the Founding Fathers, and proposes Blackstone's *Commentaries* as a civilizing tool along with the Bible.[232] Corbett was the son of a land-owning lawyer, and in recalling disputes during his childhood between his dad and their neighbours over land and water rights, Corbett asserts: 'Outside the law, there can be neither justice nor rights'.[233] So, certainly for one of the leading figures in the movement, adopting legal categories and processes became not mere exigency but a good in itself. It is important, however, to recognise that, as well as being central to setting up the screening procedures, he had also pioneered helping refugees to cross the border illegally, and with much hard work and courage had been instrumental in laying the tracks of the 'underground railroad' from the Mexico/Guatemala border up to the United States. But, of course, the movement was not simply a tool of Corbett's, a notion, which to his credit, he consistently disavowed. The point is that the sorts of ideas that he expresses are the common sense of society, and they were and are pervasive in relation to refugees. What Corbett clearly expresses are the prejudices that have been inculcated into society over many years by the ideology of law, which have come to dominate the field of asylum and which ended up compromising the practice of the Sanctuary Movement.

Lippert identifies the 'refugee's ascendency throughout the twentieth-century as an object of government' through the growth of state control over borders, immigration and refugee asylum.[234] In the Canadian context, he identifies this development with the country's signing up in 1969 to the 1951 Refugee Convention and the 1967 Protocol. Crucially, it was a factor of the incorporation into the 'governmental domain' of the determination as to who is and who is not a refugee.[235] As I have argued, the same process was at work in the 1980 Refugee Act in the United States. By the 1980s, the hegemony of the legal refugee determination process acted as an impetus for the creation of sanctuaries. And yet, the hegemonic growth of law in relation to the refugee was also felt in sanctuaries by their 'heavy reliance' on legal representation and following the legal process.[236] One of the effects of the growing juridical basis of refugee admittance has been that refugee determination has been moved out of the political sphere into one managed by a 'non-political' body that 'governs at a distance', a dominant feature of 'advanced liberalism'.[237] Another writer on

231 Corbett (n 19), 88.
232 Ibid.
233 Ibid 90.
234 Lippert (n 46), 43.
235 Ibid 44.
236 Ibid 49.
237 Ibid 56.

Canadian sanctuary, Jean McDonald, reflects on the movement there, and in doing so makes a trenchant critique of its reliance on existing legal categories which is apt in the US context too:

> If proponents of the sanctuary movement do not oppose the categorization of people into deserving versus undeserving immigrants and refugees, the offering of sanctuary will not pose a substantial challenge to the immigration system. Instead, sanctuary becomes a space where 'mistakes' can be corrected and the legitimacy of the immigration system upheld, albeit indirectly.[238]

Law and the depoliticising of sanctuary

One of the arguments for seeking the sort of legitimacy discussed earlier in this chapter was that it was a key element in spreading the movement beyond the usual suspects of radical activists on the coasts and into the US heartland of small conservative towns. But on a number of levels, there could be a price paid for accommodating to this conservatism. Karen Lebacqz points out how the discourse used in one particular Midwestern church departed in a crucial way from that of much of the rest of the movement. Where others talked of sanctuary as solidarity, here 'Themes of *need*, *hurt* and *help*' were consistent. The paternalism of the congregation was epitomized for Lebacqz by one member who talked of 'our Christian duty to show compassion for the needs of others who are less fortunate'.[239] Lebacqz suggests that the view of members of the church was that they 'saw the refugees as victims but declined to "hold them up and parade them around" for political purposes . . . [to avoid] using their plight to raise political questions'.[240] However, there is a big gap between *using* refugees for political purposes and *enabling* them to be political actors themselves. As we saw above, for many of the refugees, sanctuary was precisely a means for them to remain or become again political subjects. Although the refugees who were candidates for sanctuary at the church Lebacqz discusses were, according to the associate minister, 'vote gifts . . . had good stories . . . were likable people . . . pretty verbal', it was decided not to introduce them to the congregation until just a couple of weeks before the vote. The reason for this was so that the congregation would 'vote on the question, not on the specific *people*'. In this, the church was very different from CRTFCA, for whom it was indeed all about the people.[241] Moreover, there is more than a hint of a patronising attitude to the refugees when valorising them as 'vote gifts'. This is the sort of subject that belongs to a

---

238 McDonald J, 'Citizenship, illegality, and sanctuary' in Vijay Agnew (ed), *Interrogating Race and Racism* (University of Toronto Press, 2007), 123.

239 Lebacqz K, 'Paul Revere and the Holiday Inn: a case study in hospitality' in Nelle G Slater (ed), *Tensions between Citizenship and Discipleship: A Case Study* (Pilgrim Press, 1989), 113.

240 Ibid 114.

241 Ibid 116–117.

charitable or humanitarian paradigm where our sympathy is engaged due to their saintly suffering, rather than solidarity based on their active engagement in resistance. In contrast to this approach, Golden and McConnell describe the concept of 'conscientization':

> a process of critical reflection at deeper and deeper levels about how human beings live and die in this world. It invariably destroys old assumptions and breaks down mythologies that no longer explain reality because of new information . . . Encountering refugees, their story, and a more intensive study of the history and present reality of Central America have shaken the dominant worldview of many in the religious community.[242]

The process of 'conscientization' led sanctuary activists to radicalise, first by questioning the United States' involvement in Central America, and then the imperialist ideology that informed it.[243] In response to those in the movement who argued not to be political for fear of alienating those more conservative elements within the churches and wider society, a Salvadoran Baptist minister, Marta Benavides, said: 'Our people can't wait for your religious community to be converted. We are dying. We are at war. And whether you acknowledge it or not, you too are at war and must choose sides'.[244] And in answer to the argument that it was important to retain the legitimacy of working within the law and of not being 'political', Nicgorski wrote in *Basta!*: 'We cannot "legitimate" our involvement with refugees – it is impossible. As we begin to walk with them, some of the marginalization, oppression, and repression will come to us'.[245] It is these sorts of positions that foster an understanding of sanctuary as politics rather than humanitarianism or legal interpretation, as dissensus rather than 'legitimacy', as solidarity rather than charity.

In practice, the growing determination of the Tucson group to eschew open politics in favour of a strict adherence to the legal definition of a refugee led to some perverse decisions. At one point, a refugee who had been a member of Organización Democrática Nacionalista (ORDEN), a notorious right-wing death squad in El Salvador, was helped by Corbett and given sanctuary. This understandably offended many in the movement, especially those refugees in sanctuary who had fled the terror inflicted by ORDEN. Corbett's defence was that this woman, along with other members of ORDEN, was suffering persecution and was thus legally a refugee.[246] Issues around these sorts of refugees were an additional factor in the split among the Tucson activists that led to the creation of *El Puente*. One activist described why she agreed with Corbett's argument:

242   Golden and McConnell (n 18), 135.
243   Ibid 149.
244   Ibid 171.
245   *Basta!* (January 1985), 23.
246   Davidson (n 10), 131.

[My] position in the end was that some of them were children and babies, and that the humane thing to do in those circumstances is to help. Because what I realized is that for me, sanctuary isn't political. It isn't Left or Right, it isn't black or white, but instead there's a lot of gray.[247]

One can certainly understand the humanitarian impulse when members of death squads turned up in desperation with their young children. But the question then is: why not the same attitude when faced with 'children and babies' of economic refugees? It seems to me that one could argue for sanctuary on the sort of Augustinian basis of hospitality to all seeking protection and assistance, or one can recognise a political element that does make distinctions, albeit ones that are based on an honesty regarding one's subjective position and respect for the active subject position of the refugee. The problem with sanctuary relying on legal categories is that it neither opens itself out to all nor does it operate as a space in which refugees can (re)establish themselves as political subjects.

Conclusion

By claiming space beyond the reach of, and resistant to, sovereign power in which people could seek a place of safety, the US Sanctuary Movement had its roots in the long tradition of asylum discussed in Part I. The movement and its law-breaking aspect were not preconceived but arose out of the needs of the Central American refugees. Thus, it was not law-breaking for its own sake, but a practical realisation that sanctuary could not exist in any meaningful way without confronting the law. The retreat of those in Tucson, along with their supporters, into a legalist position was an attempt to somehow theorise and legitimise what they were doing by reference to an apparently benign refugee law. But as we have seen in Part II, refugee law is anything but benign, either in its construction of the refugee subject or in how it treats forced migrants. The failure to recognise that led to a category mistake by those sanctuary activists, which further led them to perform some of the more offensive practices of refugee law such as screening, categorising and controlling refugees according to a narrow definition given by law. In short, while they did much to assist many who would otherwise not have been able to successfully cross the border and get protection, at the same time they reinforced many of the underlying premises which had led to the plight of the refugees at the border in the first place. Thus, when the movement came to an end, those paradigms and premises appeared as stable as they had ever been. Moreover, by rejecting a political approach to sanctuary, they missed the opportunity, created by those who did adopt a more political stance, to open up the space previously closed down by law, in which the refugees could themselves become active subjects in the movement.

247   Bibler Coutin (n 15), 115.

Earlier, I cited Zucker and Zucker's point that refugees confronted the 'wall' of 'refugee law . . . and the definition on which it is based'.[248] We can say that the Sanctuary Movement found themselves too up against that same wall. But instead of attempting to break it down, much of the movement ended up accepting it as an acceptable or even a positive boundary. By the early 1990s, leading figures in the CRTFCA were looking back on the Sanctuary Movement as a missed opportunity. One of them, Darlene Gramena, felt that the trial had been the turning point:

> It scared people. The movement was on a path but was slowed down by the trial, by the people on trial who took it personal as opposed to public.' She felt that the way in which the defendants proceeded at the trial, by following the rules of the court and engaging their own lawyers, really undermined the unity of the movement . . . 'We had greater hopes of [sanctuary] being a social movement and digging deeper. Instead it was one mile wide and only one inch deep.[249]

Guzder suggests that the decision to consciously wind down the movement in 1991 was evidence of 'remaining myopically focused on Central American refugees', rather than drawing the wider lessons about law and sovereignty. As a result, the movement 'never harnessed its true potential to radically reform immigration policy'.[250] Some churches, however, saw sanctuary as not specific to Central Americans, or even to refugees in general. For example, the University Lutheran Chapel in Berkeley, California, originally offered sanctuary to Vietnam draft-resisters and deserters in 1971, then again for Central American refugees in 1982, for US military personnel who refused to be deployed to Honduras in 1988 and, later still, for those being deployed to the Persian Gulf in late 1990.[251] But this, alas, was a rare exception rather than the rule. Guzder argues that it was the failure of the movement to generalise in such a way that 'created a window' for President Bill Clinton in 1996 to sign into law two bills that substantially increased the scope for deporting immigrants including refugees.[252] From this point onwards, attacks on migrants increased, culminating in the construction of the border fence, and a massive deportation programme that has run through the administrations of George W. Bush, Barack Obama and most recently Donald Trump.

The New Sanctuary Movement was set up in 2007, as a response to these attacks. However, they explicitly rejected breaking the law. Instead, they aimed

---

248 Zucker and Zucker (n 2), 89.
249 Hobbs HH, *City Hall Goes Abroad: The Foreign Policy of Local Politics* (Sage, 1994), 101.
250 Guzder (n 52), 117.
251 'Sanctuary: Resolution of University Lutheran Chapel', revised and reaffirmed 25 November 1990, typed mimeographed document (GSSC).
252 Guzder (n 52), 117.

merely to 'provide a public witness' and to help only those whose case is 'viable under current law'.[253] In the same year when an undocumented migrant, under a deportation order, took sanctuary in a church in Simi Valley, California, the protests were not supportive but xenophobic. On a weekly basis, assorted anti-immigration activists, including some neo-Nazis, demonstrated outside with signs such as 'Unchecked immigration, a wildfire that will consume our nation. Stop the invasion'.[254] The umbrella group that organised the protests, Save Our State, put out a press release which, among other things, attacked: 'Liliana [who had taken sanctuary], the corrupt church, and the Simi Valley government [as] symbols of the *lawless invasion* and terrorism of our nation'.[255] Once again, foreswearing contestation with law did not protect either the movement or, more importantly, the migrants from being constructed as 'illegals'. At the time of writing, a new invigorated sanctuary movement appears slowly to be reconfiguring itself in response to one of the highest ever rates of deportations in the United States, and the violent nativism that has risen along with the presidency of Donald Trump. Because this nascent movement is confronting a phenomenon involving, in addition to refugees, irregular economic migrants – for which there is not even a legal regime claiming humanitarian status, as is the case for refugees – there appears to be a much clearer understanding of the need to confront the law. Indeed, as is demonstrated in a news report on Southside Church in Tucson restarting its sanctuary activity as part of this movement, almost all reference to a legal justification for sanctuary is eschewed.[256] It remains to be seen how far the movement will develop and in what directions it will do so, given the rise of a far-right nativism that reaches into the White House. In particular, it will be critical to see whether or not the Trump administration succeeds in its stated aim of stamping out one of the lasting gains of the Sanctuary Movement, the Sanctuary Cities.

The limits of 'sanctuary legalism' are well drawn out by Gerety when he writes:

> I am struck by the irony of sanctuary legalism. A self-consciously religious and moral movement finds its preferred style of argument in law. Even the substance of its arguments comes mostly from law . . . it is the imagination of law – of better law – that restrains and inspires the radical dissenter.[257]

---

253 Rademacher N, 'Sanctuary Movement' in Patrick J Hayes (ed), *The Making of Modern Immigration: An Encyclopedia of People and Ideas* (ABC-CLIO, 2012), 677.

254 Daniel B, *Neighbor: Christian Encounters with 'Illegal' Immigration* (Westminster John Knox Press, 2010), 119.

255 Quoted in Ibid 120 (emphasis added).

256 'Mexican Claiming Sanctuary in Church Seeks Amnesty', *Daily Mail* (27 October 2014), www.dailymail.co.uk/wires/ap/article-2810286/Mexican-claiming-sanctuary-church-seeks-amnesty.html; 'The fight for immigration reform in Arizona', MSNBC (28 October 2014), www.msnbc.com/all-in/watch/the-fight-for-immigration-reform-349235267957, accessed 27 January 2015.

257 Gerety (n 254), 174.

Chloé Bregnard Ecoffey, writing within the Swiss context, offers a theological refutation of this nomophiliac tendency. She criticises Christian theologians in Switzerland who have attacked the draconian laws against refugees by arguing that upholding the principle of asylum means a reaffirmation of law and sovereign order, in much the same manner as Corbett did in the US Sanctuary Movement. Ecoffey offers an alternative theological view of the subject that draws heavily on Agamben's call to decouple life from law:

> [T]he notion of Human Rights is not biblical, for liberty or life are *gifts* and not *rights*. And this means that human dignity as a gift from God has to be respected *at all costs*, there is no pragmatic or security argument to be opposed. Moreover, if life is a gift from God and belongs to him, it can no longer be linked with law nor be the subject of biopolitics.[258]

The failure of the Sanctuary Movement was the failure to recognise the need to break this link between sanctuary and law.

---

258 Ecoffey CB, 'Asylum in Switzerland: a Challenge for the Church' (Masters Thesis, University of Manchester, 2007), 29.

6 The Sans-Papiers

Introduction

The Sans-Papiers of France have been the subject of much commentary relating to how they have troubled notions of citizenship, nation and belonging. Of particular interest has been a strand of first-hand testimony by leading participants, including a number of the Sans-Papiers themselves, as well as supporters including priests of churches where they have taken sanctuary. There are also archives that are available online, which often make fascinating reading for the ebbs and flows of the movement. Many of these resources are drawn upon in this chapter. However, what has been relatively little explored is the attitude of the Sans-Papiers towards the law, both in terms of its operations and its categories. This question is critical because of the ways in which the Sans-Papiers have consistently challenged and undermined the distinctions between labour migrants and refugees, between legality and illegality of status. In this chapter, I attempt to address these issues by further developing certain themes that should now be clearly evident: that the aim and practice of refugee law has been to restrict and control the refugee subject; that a specific mechanism of this control can be found in how law in general, and refugee law in particular, is predicated on segmenting migrants into categories that have the effect of imposing artificial subjectivities onto them; and that by resisting the legal paradigm, a form of 'grassroots asylum' based on recreating spaces beyond the law and remaking the refugee/migrant subject can be realised.

Like the Sanctuary Movement, the Sans-Papiers of France have claimed spaces, in particular churches, in order to raise the demand for their right to remain in France, and to protect themselves against threats of deportation by the state authorities. France, of course, like the United States, is a secular state. Yet, even more than the United States, the ideology of *laïcité* creates a far greater distance between church and state than in the United States.[1] While the US Sanctuary Movement did extend beyond churches and other places of worship to secular

---

1 For some illuminating discussion of this concept and how it has developed in twentieth-century France, see Scot J-P, *L'Etat chez lui, l'Eglise chez elle: comprendre la loi de 1905* (Seuil, 2005); Willaime J-P, '1905 et la pratique d'une laïcité de reconnaissance sociale des religions' (2005), 129, *Archives de sciences sociales des religions*, 67.

spaces, these were relatively marginal to the movement, which remained religiously focussed. The Sans-Papiers, by contrast, have been far more eclectic in their choice of spaces, having occupied theatres, disused depots, workplaces and trade union offices, in addition to churches. In the case of the Sans-Papiers, sanctuary took on a much clearer political aspect than in the United States, where the Sanctuary Movement was anchored much more in theological precepts. There are other important distinctions to be drawn, notably that the Sans-Papiers were led by the refugee/migrants themselves whereas their US counterpart was led by church members and other activists. The Sans-Papiers have raised demands that more clearly challenge legal paradigms, yet at the same time they have found themselves pulled towards accepting legal categories and processes. This tension has led to similar splits to that of the Sanctuary Movement, between those who cleave more towards the law and those who seek to challenge it. It must also be acknowledged that the Sans-Papiers never achieved a sustained mass mobilisation on the scale of the Sanctuary Movement; its core of activists was much smaller. Yet, arguably, the Sans-Papiers achieved a greater shift in terms of discourse, and recognition of the place of migrants within French society. In short, the approach of the Sans-Papiers to sanctuary, both in terms of spaces and how they should be used, and to law and its subject, presents us with an interesting counterpoint to the US Sanctuary Movement in terms of reconstructing sanctuary in the present as what I have been calling 'grassroots asylum'.

Johanna Siméant, who has written one of the seminal works on the Sans-Papiers, laments that immigrants are considered only on the basis of their socioeconomic significance, 'devoid of any political meaning', and rarely do studies of immigrants reflect their capacity for 'collective action initiated "by immigrants for immigrants"'.[2] One of the great achievements of the Sans-Papiers has been to spawn not only a movement but also a literature that is forced to address this capacity of refugees/migrants to speak for themselves. Indeed, this chapter draws heavily on a number of published testimonies from leading figures and other activists within the movement, none of which have been translated into English, as well as archival documents such as unpublished communications, communiqués and polemical pieces written at the height of the struggles. As such, I hope to round off this book by demonstrating how refugees/migrants generally can and should be at the forefront of resistance to a legal framework that seeks to divide migrants into artificial categories. Moreover, the Sans-Papiers offer an important complementary example to the US Sanctuary Movement, of how grassroots asylum can be conceived of as an alternative to a state-based legal regime that judges each individual migrant on their supposed value or worth, either as refugees or as other types of migrants. Just like the Sanctuary Movement, this effort was fraught with tensions and contradictions; the Sans-Papiers at various points both challenge assumptions about what makes a 'good' refugee or migrant, but at other times, they adopt some of these frameworks in order to assert their

2 Siméant J, *La cause des sans-papiers* (Presses de Sciences Po, 1998), 30.

rights. So, on the one hand, there are many claims based not so much on the character of the Sans-Papiers themselves, but instead on the duties owed to them by France, either because they have come from former French colonies or have a history of fighting on France's behalf in wars, or having provided much needed labour in France's extraordinary economic recovery and development in the decades following World War II. On the other hand, these claims can also serve to reinforce notions of the deserving migrant, focussing on the productive 'Sans-Papier worker'[3], or similarly of the good 'neo-liberal subject'.[4]

It is important to point out that the Sans-Papiers include a broad range of immigrants, and not just refugees. What they have in common is that for one reason or another they have been denied official documents regularising their residence in France. Many are straightforward asylum-seekers who have failed the legal test for refugee status, or who straddle the artificial, and legally constructed, dividing line between refugees and economic migrants. One of the defining features of the movement has been precisely to resist the categorisations imposed upon them by law, and indeed the premise that each of them must prove their individual case in law. This aspect is evident in the key slogan raised by the movement: '*Papiers pour tous*'. As such, whereas much of the Sanctuary Movement was taken up with questions as to whether or not people fell within the specific legal category of a refugee, among the Sans-Papiers, they were much more resistant to these types of delineations. However, as we shall see, this often became an issue for their supporters. Of course, some might argue that the conditions being faced by those fleeing Central America in the 1980s were far more acute than those faced by the Sans-Papiers. It is true that for most of the Sans-Papiers, they were not fleeing brutal war zones. Instead, they have mostly come from countries where political violence was often present, as in the case of Senegal in the 1980s and 1990s, or governed by autocratic regimes such as Mali, Vietnam and Cambodia. Moreover, what they all had in common was that they came from countries where poverty was rife, and economic necessity was a major factor in driving people to migrate. Equally, a great many of those who fled Central America were not themselves the targets of direct persecution, but were instead seeking to escape generalised violence and impoverishment caused by the civil wars. The key point is that, while the specific conditions were different for the migrants in France and the United States, they were certainly mostly forced in nature. It is only because of the legal categories imposed upon them that they appear more distinct than they actually are. Indeed, in the published chronicle of the struggle of the Loiret collective of Sans-Papiers, most of the testimonies given by those who had asylum applications rejected explain that they had been denied asylum because they could not prove

3   Nicholls WJ, 'Making Undocumented Immigrants into a Legitimate Political Subject: Theoretical Observations from the United States and France' (2013), 30, *Theory, Culture & Society*, 82.

4   McNevin A, 'Political Belonging in a Neo-Liberal Era: The Struggle of the Sans-Papiers' (2006), 10, *Citizenship Studies*, 135.

persecution.[5] Ababacar Diop, one of the leading figures in the movement, when it took off in the mid-1990s, rejected the distinction between economic migrants and political refugees largely based on his own experience. He describes his decision to come to France from Senegal both because he had been involved in political activity against a repressive government and because he wished to pursue life opportunities that were not available back home.[6]

One issue, which became much sharper and thus more contested than with the Sanctuary Movement, was the relative autonomy of the refugees/migrants *vis-à-vis* their supporters. One critical difference in the formation of the two movements was that in the United States example, it was founded by those *giving* sanctuary to the refugees, whereas in France, it was the refugees/migrants who took the initiative, and thus were able to shape and lead the movement from the outset. This eventually led to tensions between the Sans-Papiers and their supporters, with the latter including many seasoned activists who were used to leading movements themselves on behalf of others. Importantly, these tensions and splits, just as with the Sanctuary Movement, often took the form of conflicting approaches to legal categories, and of the strategic attitude to be adopted towards the law.

With the Sans-Papiers, these questions became framed within two rival demands. The first, and the one that emerged at the height of the struggle in mid-1996, was encapsulated in the slogan already mentioned above: 'papers for all'. The radical implication of this demand was that it denied to the state the right of deciding who could stay and who could not, or put another way, who could be allowed full membership of the community and who must remain excluded, or at the very least semi-detached from wider society. In essence, the demand is a concrete example of Badiou's epigram, 'everyone here is from here'.[7] In contrast to this, two rival demands were formulated, both of which accepted the logic that it was ultimately the state and the law that retain ultimate discretion over the question of who is allowed to remain and who must leave. One demand was that counterposed by some elements of the state and the more liberal supporters of the Sans-Papiers, which was that every claim had to be judged on a case-by-case basis. The other demand, which eventually became the mainstream of the Sans-Papiers, was that of 'papers for those who make a request for them'. Superficially, this is the same as 'papers for all'. However, it placed the Sans-Papiers in a subservient relationship to the law in two respects. First, it reinforced the primacy of the state in making the decision: the request had to be made, and it would be for the state to decide. Second, in reality, it also placed the Sans-Papiers in a potential Catch-22 situation. In order to gain the legal right to stay in France, they had to make themselves known to the authorities, and because the authorities could then retain the right to reject the applications,

---

5   Collectif des Sans-Papiers du Loiret, *Sans papiers, tu vis pas* (L'Harmattan, 2000).
6   Diop A, *Dans la peau d'un sans-papiers* (Seuil, 1997), 38–39.
7   Hallward P, 'Badiou's Politics: Equality and Justice' (2002), *Culture Machine*, 4.

the Sans-Papiers were endangering their ability to live unmolested by the state. Arguments over the different positions became, as with the Sanctuary Movement, fraught and likewise the question of law became a fault line which arguably served to weaken the movement. At the same time, resistance to the law opened up questions and possibilities for how forced migrants and their right to remain could be reimagined outside the strictures of the law.

Closely tied to the issue of belonging, was that of the collective identity of the Sans-Papiers. Indeed, solely at the level of how to refer to them, or how they referred to themselves, became of paramount importance. The shift from the previously dominant label of *clandestins* to Sans-Papiers was itself a major element in the assertion of their collective identity on their own terms; at various times, they also referred to themselves as 'Africans' and 'refugees'. The adoption and rejection of these various terms was in itself a type of reckoning with the imposition of legal categories, or rather their exclusion from them, notably that of 'refugee'.

Who are the Sans-Papiers?

Bénédicte Goussault describes the Sans-Papiers as being defined principally by their historic exclusion from the political realm, although they have long played a crucial role within the economic sphere as a supply of cheap labour, from the labour shortages post-1945 onwards.[8] The origins of the movement of the Sans-Papiers lie in the dramatic shift in migration policy by the French government in the early 1970s. Following almost three decades of unprecedented economic growth – the so-called *trente glorieuses* – the French economy, along with the rest of the Western world, suffered a severe recession exacerbated by the 'oil shock' of 1973. The period of economic growth had been largely facilitated by large numbers of immigrant workers, including people seeking asylum from Eastern Europe, Portugal and Turkey and increasingly from former French colonies such as Algeria and Vietnam.

On 2 November 1945, the Provisional Government of the French Republic, which had the task of rebuilding the French state and preparing for a new constitution, issued a piece of executive legislation that has been the key legal instrument of post-war immigration policy ever since.[9] It instituted a complex and detailed categorisation of visas along with the various methods of gaining admittance into the country. The ordinance also effectively gave the government the right to control immigration based on economic and demographic needs.[10] For example, the creation of a national *Office d'Immigration* centralised in government hands decision-making on who could be allowed in for work purposes,

---

8　Goussault B, *Paroles de sans-papiers* (Les Éditions de L'Atelier, 1999), 14.
9　*Ordonnance du 2 novembre 1945 relative aux conditions d'entrée et de séjour en France des étrangers et portant création de l'Office national d'immigration.*
10　Hargreaves AG, *Immigration, 'Race' and Ethnicity in Contemporary France* (Routledge, 1995), 178.

whereas previously this could be done by private enterprises. Initially, many immigrants evaded the requirements contained in the legislation and the government responded harshly. Already by June of the following year, the French government was carrying out raids and expelling undocumented migrants from the country.[11] Yet, this strictness in application of the law was swiftly abandoned as it became clear that economic recovery and growth were dependent on this flow of new workers.[12] Around the same time as the ordinance was enacted, leading demographers in France were arguing that the country needed more than 5 million immigrants in order to deal with the labour shortage and to rebuild the international power and status of France.[13] As such, by the 1960s, the vast majority of undocumented workers were being regularised only after they had already settled and found work.[14] As one writer describes it, this was a period during which government policy was 'regularisation *a posteriori*'.[15] At the same time, as discussed in Chapter 4, the French government moved swiftly to incorporate the 1951 Refugee Convention into domestic law, and by so doing, began to more strictly control access to refugee status, and to control the movements of asylum-seekers in general. In any case, from an immigrant population of 1.7 million in 1946, by 1975, that number had risen to 3.7 million.

By the end of the 1960s, racism towards increasing numbers of non-white immigrants and early indicators of the slowing down of the economy brought an end to an effective open-door policy. The initial targets were non-Europeans such as Moroccans and Turks, who saw regularisation rates slump.[16] With the sudden economic deterioration in the early 1970s, national governments, including the French, slammed the door on what had hitherto been a relaxed approach to immigration. The immediate consequence was to render the position of migrant workers more precarious, and thus subject to super-exploitation. The sociologist, Emmanuel Terray, has described this as *délocalisation sur place*, in which rather than employers having to move production abroad to get cheaper labour, the production of undocumented migrants by the state enables such processes to take place at home.[17] Furthermore, pressures in the developing

---

11 Abdallah MH, *J'y suis! J'y reste!: Les luttes de l'immigration en France depuis les années soixante* (Éditions Reflex, 2000), 8–9.

12 Hargreaves (10), 177–180; Boutang YM, Garson J-P and Silberman R, *Économie politique des migrations clandestines de main-d'œuvre: Comparaisons internationales et exemple* (Publisud, 1986).

13 Cohen R, 'Citizens, Denizens and Helots: The Politics of International Migration Flows in the Post-War World' (1989), 21, *Hitotsubashi Journal of Social Studies*, 153.

14 Abdallah (n 11), 9.

15 Laacher S, *Mythologie du Sans-papiers* (Le Cavalier bleu editions, 2009), 14.

16 Abdallah (n 11), 10–11.

17 Terray E, 'Le travail des étrangers en situation irrégulièr ou la délocalisation sur place' in Étienne Balibar, Monique Chemillier-Gendreau, Jacqueline Costa-Lascoux and Emmanuel Terray (eds), *Sans-Papiers: l'archaïsme fatal* (Éditions La Découverte et Syros, 1999). For more on how the Sans-Papiers have been subjects of a strategy for producing cheap labour, see François A, 'Capitalisme et sans-papiers' in Antoine Pickels (ed), *À la lumière des sans-papiers* (Complexe, 2001).

world caused by structural poverty and civil conflict were leading to increased emigration, and the French economy continued to rely on a steady flow of immigrant workers. So, while immigration continued, it became a much more tortuous process for the migrants themselves as a result of the new restrictions imposed upon them. As such, there was a rapid increase in the numbers of undocumented or irregular migrants and refugees.

The legal turning point in French policy towards immigrants was a sharp one. In 1972, the Minister of the Interior and the Minister of Employment together issued two government decrees – commonly known by the names of the two ministers as the *circulaires Marcellin-Fontanet* – which made it compulsory for all foreign workers to apply for residency and work permits. In addition, the circular placed limits on the numbers of foreign workers who could obtain these papers. Two years later, a further government decree suspended all new arrivals of immigrant workers.[18] The term 'Sans-Papiers' originates in late 1972 and 1973 as a result of the rapid increase in undocumented migrant workers created by these decrees.[19] Since that time, there have been a series of struggles for recognition and rights by migrants and asylum-seekers, including Tunisians and Moroccans who agitated against the original imposition of border controls in 1972–1975, Turkish refugees in 1980, and rejected asylum-seekers in 1991–1992. Often the resistance took the form of hunger strikes, the first of which was carried out by eighteen Sans-Papiers at a church in Valence in South-East France in December 1972, and which quickly multiplied across France in the following months.[20] In an important symbolic action, the priests of Valence refused to carry out Christmas mass in solidarity with the Sans-Papiers on hunger strike.[21] The government backed down in this instance and regularised some 50,000 Sans-Papiers. At the same time, a rash of strikes and occupations took place across the country by undocumented workers seeking better conditions, protections at work and regularisation of status. The government again relented somewhat in June 1973, by allowing for some *ex post facto* regularisations, based on certain criteria. On the one hand, this led to some 35,000 regularisations over the next 4 months. On the other hand, it diffused the movement by creating an impetus for the Sans-Papiers to move away from collective struggles towards working on their individual claims for regularisation. This was to become a common tactic of the government in the following decades, as we shall see below. Another hunger strike, this time by Turkish refugees in 1980 led to more than 3,000 regularisations; huge demonstrations and the coming to power of a left government led to 130,000 being given papers in 1982, and in 1991, protests led to the regularisation of 17,000 refugees whose asylum claim had

---

18 *Circulaire du 5 juillet 1974 "relative à la suspension de l'immigration des travailleurs".*
19 Siméant (n 2), 181; see also Abdallah (n 11), 32–40, for a good description of these early movements of Sans-Papiers during the 1970s.
20 Abdallah (n 11), 35.
21 *Désobéir avec les sans-papiers* (Éditions le passage clandestin, 2009), 14.

been denied.[22] In short, while legal restrictions on immigration and the granting of refugee status became more oppressive, autonomous social movements achieved a measure of success in overcoming these obstacles and establishing a right to stay in France.

The Sans-Papiers were often able to find support among those other groups within French society who were, like them, politically marginalised such as the far left, and those within a milieu of social or cultural avant-gardism. What they shared in common was that, 'the immigrant activists had at the beginning of the movement been politically formed within organisations of the far left, they were young and politicised, often students and for that reason had real intellectual and political resources'.[23] Moreover, by keying into pre-existing groups and networks of activists, they had a political space within which to raise their demands.[24] In the case of activists in Dev Yol (a Turkish group involved in the 1980 hunger strikes), their aim was not really about getting documentation per se, rather their mobilisation had much more substantial political aims. As one of those activists said, 'We had the idea: we are proletarian revolutionary communists. What the fuck do we want with papers? There needs to be a revolution in Turkey, we need to fight for the Turkish workers, to teach the Turkish workers'.[25] While this was, of course, a very particular aspect of their struggle, their refusal of the offer of individual regularisation, insisting instead on being granted papers collectively, was to become an important theme in the movement as it developed from the mid-1990s onwards.[26] At the same time, the tension between collective mobilisation and being forced through individualised legal processes, which had hobbled the movement in the mid-1970s, has been a recurring motif of the struggles of the Sans-Papiers over the decades. The demand, *'papiers pour tous'*, that became a rallying cry once the movement achieved its major breakthrough in 1996, clearly cut against the attempt to box refugees/migrants into making purely individual claims.

The Sans-Papiers as a self-conscious movement with staying power really emerged in the mid-1990s. The background to this was increasing hostility towards people seeking asylum, from politicians of both the left and the right. It was at this time that the Socialist Prime Minister Michel Rocard came out with his notorious phrase, 'we cannot accommodate all the misery of the world'. With the return to power of the right in 1986, draconian anti-immigrant laws were passed – known as the *lois Pasqua*, after the hard-line Interior Minister who pushed them through. They excluded undocumented migrants from access to welfare and other social provisions, and enabled local prefects to order their

---

22 Laacher (n 15), 15.
23 Siméant (n 2), 76.
24 Ibid 94.
25 Quoted in Ibid 84.
26 Ibid 342.

immediate deportation.[27] This was part of a policy announced by Charles Pasqua to aim for 'zero immigration'. As part of that aim, a further law restricting the right to gain or have papers renewed was passed in 1993.[28] In the early 1990s, increased numbers of asylum-seekers had their claims for refugee status denied.[29] Many of these people were thus forced to live precariously without papers, and therefore often suffered from super-exploitation at work. Indeed, many of those who would be part of igniting the Sans-Papiers movement in 1996 were precisely those whose asylum claims had been rejected and who had been denied regularisation by other means.[30] Beyond rejected asylum-seekers, there were also many other migrants who, although they had entered the country legally, had subsequently been rendered undocumented through the loss of a job, thus entailing the loss of residency rights, or the refusal of a renewal of their residency papers by the local prefecture.

The 'irruption' of the Sans-Papiers movement in 1996 extended the field of support quite considerably, beyond that enjoyed by earlier struggles.[31] Siméant argues that this can be at least partly explained by certain peculiarities and confluences that were present, such as the huge publicity accompanying the break in and expulsion by the French riot police, the *Compagnies Républicains de Sécurité* (CRS) at the church of Saint-Bernard, which the Sans-Papiers had occupied in the summer of 1996; a reaction against some of the more offensive anti-immigrant measures of the right-wing government at the time, and the prosecution of Jacqueline Deltombe, a French citizen, in early 1997 for giving shelter to undocumented migrants in her home;[32] all important aspects that are discussed in detail below. Others, such as Thierry Blin, have identified a political weakness in this set of circumstances.[33] While support was broader, against a background of the retreat of the left post-1991, and the rise of a more de-politicised humanitarianism, the movement that emerged in 1996 lacked some of the sharpness of the politics of earlier struggles.[34] In essence, the position of weakness experienced by the Sans-Papiers in the mid-1990s, that is their lack of significant political and social resources, meant that they were forced to rely more on 'symbolic resources' of political action; these include things like the hunger strike and the insistence on being labelled 'Sans-Papiers' rather than

---

27 *Loi no 86–1025 du 9 septembre 1986 relative aux conditions d'entrée et de séjour des étrangers en France.*
28 *Loi no 93–1027 du 24 août 1993 relative à la maîtrise de l'immigration et aux conditions d'entrée, d'accueil et de séjour des étrangers en France.*
29 Whereas 78% of applications for asylum had been granted in 1981, by 1991, this figure had dropped to 20%. Figures cited in Blin T, *L'Invention des sans-papiers: Essai sur la démocratie à l'épreuve du faible* (Presses Universitaires de France, 2010), 64.
30 Abdallah (n 11), 79.
31 Siméant (n 2), 161.
32 Siméant (n 2), 210–211.
33 *Thierry Blin Les sans-papiers de Saint-Bernard: Mouvement social et action organisé* (L'Harmattan, 2005); Blin (n 29).
34 Blin (n 29), 120–121.

'clandestins'.[35] While on the one hand, movements of the Sans-Papiers benefitted from the existence of an extra-parliamentary and radical left in the 1970s especially, it was far more disorientating for the movement when faced with a left government as in 1991–1992 and following the elections in June 1997. Yet, I tend to agree more with Siméant that: 'Support for the Sans-Papiers, implies more generally a related claim to illegalism ... as a discourse involving the defense of undocumented immigrants is one that opens the way to a more radical challenge to the statist order'.[36] This does not mean that the challenge posed by the Sans-Papiers *necessarily* takes this form; indeed, as we shall see, there were many ways in which the claims of the Sans-Papiers *could* be framed in such a way that reinforced the statist order. Alain Morice seeks to explain the contribution of the Sans-Papiers within the then prevailing political context. He writes of the consensus that had settled in France across the political spectrum over the previous two decades that controls on immigration were both just and necessary:

> But the current movement of the Sans-Papiers, with their iconoclastic motto of 'regularisation for all', have arrived opportunely to disturb this consensus and shake up a collective conscience which has been accustomed for a long time to find it natural to claim the right to limit the movements of the inhabitants of this planet in their movements and to persecute those who flout these limits.[37]

The key point, though, is that the demand that the state accept and ensure a place for all is itself a challenge to the idea that decisions over who belongs within the community is ultimately one that resides with the state. In that sense, and in common with the Sanctuary Movement, we can accurately describe the Sans-Papiers as a form of 'grassroots asylum'.[38] This is ultimately the movement's radical edge, and one that opens the way to a reimaging of asylum not dependent on law and the state.

There were some important differences in the struggles of 1996, compared to earlier ones, which have been critical in raising the profile of the Sans-Papiers far beyond that of the previous two decades. These include the public nature of the protests, the scandalousness of occupying churches and the way in which the movement began to challenge aspects of their identity foisted upon them by French society and the legal categories that framed their 'illegality'. A further important difference from earlier struggles was that the actions coalesced into an organised movement, one that produced its own permanent structures, whereas in previous years, they had been focussed on very specific immediate aims, or

---

35 Blin (n 33), 91–104.
36 Siméant (n 2), 189–90.
37 Morice A, 'Migrants: libre circulation et lutte contre la précarité' in *Sans-Papiers: Chroniques d'un Mouvement* (Éditions Reflex/Agence IM'média, 1997), 90.
38 Behrman S, 'Accidents, Agency and Asylum: Constructing the Refugee Subject' (2014), 25, *Law and Critique*, 249.

around specific groups of migrants. This practical move was partly tied to a new political outlook that looked beyond the immediate demands for regularisation of their status and the right to stay in France, towards larger questions of belonging, of the rights to movement and of duties owed by France to the immigrant communities and the countries that they had come from. As such, the previously marginalised and invisible groups that made up the movement achieved a re-assertion of themselves as active subjects. Up until this moment, they had been constructed in the public mind not as Sans-Papiers but as *clandestins*; illegal, hidden, a threat. The change in nomenclature that took place in 1996 was thus part of their success, a gain that has remained in place until today.

While much of the discussion that follows focusses on the events of 1996, and the immediate aftermath, the Sans-Papiers have remained a fixture in the French consciousness and political life ever since. As we shall see, there have been moments when the movement has experienced sharp splits, demoralisation and disorientation. Yet it has endured and morphed over different stages, as occupations spread over other parts of the country in the late 1990s and early 2000s, and revived significantly and in new directions following the occupation of trade union offices in Paris and a series of workplaces strikes in 2008. In the United States, the Sanctuary Movement has experienced something of a revival in recent years, but it was effectively in abeyance for two decades from around 1991 onwards. Two key differences, in my opinion, account for the relative staying power of the Sans-Papiers: their relative autonomy in relation to their supporters and that they developed a more generalised critique of the law and its categories than was the case with the Sanctuary Movement. Both these aspects are themes that are developed below.

The occupations of 1996

The major turning point for the Sans-Papiers, the moment when they achieved national (and indeed international) prominence and became a cohesive movement, was the series of occupations that took place during the spring and summer of 1996. A group of undocumented migrants living together in so-called *foyers*, social housing specifically for migrant workers, decided that a gesture was necessary to raise awareness of their plight and to assert their demands for regularisation of their legal status and better protections of their rights at work. The previous year the right had returned to power, promising a hard line on 'illegal immigration'. Yet, very quickly the government had been weakened by a series of strikes in the winter of 1995–1996 against changes to labour laws. As such, the political situation was opportune in presenting a clear 'enemy' in government, yet one that was potentially vulnerable to political resistance. In addition, they were also inspired by the example of the asylum-seekers who had gone on hunger strike 5 years earlier, and succeeded in winning regularisation of their status.[39] After a couple of days' discussion among a relatively small

---

39 Diop (n 6), 71.

group, they contacted other Sans-Papiers and agreed to occupy the church of Saint-Ambroise in eastern Paris on March 18. The decision to choose that church was purely practical, as it was the easiest in Paris to reach from the *foyer* at Montreuil where most of them were living.[40] On the day, around 300 Sans-Papiers entered the church and announced their presence along with their demands via a press release.

The majority of those who launched the initial occupation at Saint-Ambroise were rejected asylum-seekers.[41] The rest were made up of people whose residency permits had expired, or who had otherwise not been able to regularise their status. Many activists and supporters of the movement have been anxious to stress that, for the most part, Sans-Papiers have not entered the country illegally – they had the necessary papers to do so, or went through the proper process of an asylum claim – but instead their status has been changed while living in France, thus rendering them undocumented *sur place*, so to speak. While this may be true, it is also clearly the case that the fact that they had continued to work and live in France without permits was a clear violation of the ordinance of 2 November 1945, which as we recall, explicitly vested sole authority for granting such rights of entry and work to the state.

The Archbishop of Paris, Cardinal Lustiger, denounced the occupation of Saint-Ambroise as a 'manipulation'. Interviewed on national TV, he expressed disbelief that a group of people, most of whom, according to him, could not speak French, and who included over a hundred women and young children, had the wherewithal to organise the occupation without being directed by some political organisation.[42] This casual racism is also marked by a common view of refugees/migrants, that denies their potential for political agency. Lustiger gave his implicit authorisation to the police to evacuate the church, which was in fact carried out just 4 days after the occupation began, and was done with the co-operation of the priest of the church.[43] The fact of occupying a church within the capital city in a deeply Catholic society, coupled with the swift and brutal expulsion by the forces of the state, did much to raise the profile of the Sans-Papiers and their demands. Rather than disperse and disappear, the 'Sans-Papiers of Saint-Ambroise' stayed together and over the next few months successively occupied a theatre (with the consent and support of its director Ariane Mnouchkine), a disused railway depot and other spaces. Finally, on June 28, they entered and occupied the church of Saint-Bernard in northern Paris. This time they had the support of the priest, Henri Coindé, and a much higher public profile and public support than they had in March.

40 Cissé M, *Parole de sans-papiers* (La Dispute, 1999), 19. *Sans-Papiers: Chroniques d'un movement* (Éditions Reflexe/Agence IM'média, Paris, 1997), 15.
41 Diop (n 6), 152.
42 *Chroniques d'un movement* (n 40), 16.
43 Abdallah (n 11), 82; Simonnot D, 'Le souvenir de Saint-Bernard', Libération, 3 September 2002, available at www.liberation.fr/france/2002/09/03/le-souvenir-de-saint-bernard_414222. For a visceral first-hand account of the eviction, see Sané M, *'Sorti de l'ombre'*, *Journal d'un Sans-papiers* (Le Temps des Cerises, 1996), 45–46.

Within the various occupations, decisions were taken collectively, and people were delegated to perform tasks by general consent rather than formal elections. A 'general assembly of families' within the occupation took all strategic decisions. The assembly then elected delegates, who were themselves always recallable, to act as representatives with supporting organisations and others.[44] Very quickly, following the occupation of Saint-Bernard, dozens of other Sans-Papier collectives were set up elsewhere around Paris and in the rest of the country, often occupying churches or other spaces. These local collectives then in turn grouped together on a regional basis so as to negotiate with prefectures over getting papers on a case-by-case basis, and also collaborated at the national level to coordinate their demands with the government. On July 20, at the height of the struggles of that year, a national coordination of Sans-Papiers collectives was established.[45] As such, the Sans-Papiers developed from the ground up, maintaining local autonomy, while also establishing links of support. During the occupation at Saint-Bernard, many different actions and tactics were deployed: hunger strikes, assistance with revising individual applications for regularisation, demonstrations, public meetings, etc. For almost 2 months, the occupation of Saint-Bernard further raised the profile of the Sans-Papiers, both nationally and internationally, and was critical in solidifying their struggle into a movement with widespread support. By the end of August, one opinion poll was showing that 46% of French people were supporting the Sans-Papiers, with just 36% opposed to their campaign,[46] whereas another at the same time put support for them as high as 53%.[47]

Indeed, as Mogniss H. Abdallah describes, by the summer, the movement had managed to discredit the government's 'zero immigration' policy, and instead had begun opening up the question of free movement in the context of globalisation and the free movement of goods around the world, as well as foregrounding issues over the exploitation of the Global South by the Global North.[48] This point was most forcefully argued by Cissé:

> The issue of immigration . . . is a larger one . . . of the relationship between the countries of the north and those of the south. And I would go further, and speak of Third World debt. I tell myself that all is linked, the whole repressive apparatus that has existed in France for the past 20 years to control the flow of migration, not only in France but also in Europe. The fact

---

44 Abdallah (n 11), 84.
45 At this meeting, there were fourteen collectives of Sans-Papiers represented from thirteen different departments across France, which gives an indication of the rapid development of the movement over the course of just 4 months. *Coordination nationale des collectifs de sans-papiers*, 'Communiqué', 20 July 1996, available at www.bok.net/pajol/com-med.html.
46 Blin (n 29), 100.
47 Abdallah (n 11), 83.
48 Ibid 86.

that Europe has become a fortress and has barricaded itself against those who are coming from the South is not by chance but is something that appears as a result of a globalised economic policy ... It is the [Global North] that dictates policies in our countries and now that ... the crisis is taking place [in the Global North], they barricade themselves off and no longer want us.[49]

Étienne Balibar, inspired by the example of the Sans-Papiers, has written of the need to decouple citizenship from nationality, in favour of a 'right to the city' which deposes the 'hierarchy of rights of movement'.[50] As such, the Sans-Papiers have opened up a challenge not just to the specific restrictions imposed by this or that law but also the global socio-economic order that has created the system of borders and border controls.[51]

What had begun in March with a core of people who were largely from Francophone West Africa now also brought in other groups, notably Chinese and Turkish undocumented migrants who had been hitherto marginalised even among those who had fought for immigrant rights until that time.[52] The Sans-Papiers also reached out, and found a response, from other groups of 'sans', such as the unemployed, and the homeless (*sans-emploi, sans-logis*), thus building bridges across the immigrant/citizen divide while developing a class-conscious basis for their struggle, which in turn 'led new strategies for critiquing and transforming existing regimes of citizenship'.[53] This development was also critical in their conscious remaking of their identities, as will be discussed further below.

At 7:30 am on Friday, August 23, more than 1,000 police officers raided Saint-Bernard and forcibly removed the Sans-Papiers and their supporters from the church.[54] The operation was carried out brutally, with people being dragged out on the floor. The racism of the police, and indeed of the whole operation,

---

49 'Entretien avec Madjiguène Cissé', 14 August 1996, available at www.bok.net/pajol/madjiguene.html.
50 Balibar E, 'Le droit de cite ou l'apartheid' in Étienne Balibar, Monique Chemillier-Gendreau, Jacqueline Costa-Lascoux and Emmanuel Terray (eds), *Sans-Papiers: l'archaïsme fatal* (Éditions La Découverte et Syros, 1999), 112.
51 Behrman S, 'On the Creation and Accommodation of the Misery of the World: The Case of the Sans-Papiers' (2017), 49, *Refugee Watch*, 26.
52 Abdallah (n 11), 88. Of particular note, was the formation of the 'Troisième Collectif', comprising more than thirty different nationalities, the greatest number of whom were Chinese refugees. *Chroniques d'un movement* (n 40), 26–28.
53 Milner N, 'Sanctuary sans-frontières: social movements and solidarity in post-war Northern France' in Randy K Lippert and Sean Rehaag (eds), *Sanctuary Practices in International Perspectives: Migration, Citizenship and Social Movements* (Routledge, 2013), 66; Akin S, 'Sans-papiers: une denomination dans cinq quotidiens nationaux de mars à août 1996' (1999), 60 *Mots* 59, 73.
54 The details of what happened during this and the ensuing days is given in email circulars by the Sans-Papiers sent at the time. These communications have been archived online and are available at www.bok.net/pajol/zpajol/z8-25-00.html.

was evident in the fact that the people caught in the church were segregated between blacks and whites, with the former arrested on suspicion of being undocumented migrants. The irony was that while a number of people who were either French citizens or had papers were detained solely because they were black, several Sans-Papiers who were white were left free to go. Those arrested were immediately taken to a detention centre, and the following day, fifty-seven of them were put onto a military plane and deported back to Senegal. Indeed, the reason a military plane was used was because a week earlier, six trade unions at Air France had announced their refusal to co-operate with deportations of the Sans-Papiers.[55] Yet, in a remarkable act of international solidarity, at Dakar airport, workers there refused to help the military flight disembark those who had been summarily deported.[56] On the day of the evacuation of the church, between 10,000 and 25,000 people were mobilised on a demonstration that made its way to the detention centre at Vincennes where the Sans-Papiers were being held. Almost as much as the occupation itself, the manner of its ending only served to further raise the profile of the Sans-Papiers and their demands, and to arouse public sympathy for their cause. In contrast, as we saw, the US authorities were much more conscious that a heavy handed approach would cause such a reaction, and thus they refrained from violent incursions into sanctuary churches. The point is that the idea of church sanctuary evidently still has resonance, even in our modern secular societies.

Far from petering out, the evacuation from Saint-Bernard proved to be merely a staging post in a much longer struggle. Demonstrations, petitions and further local occupations continued into 1997. An event that particularly shocked French society, and further galvanised the movement was the arrest and prosecution of Jacqueline Deltombe. A French citizen, she was arrested, tried and convicted in January 1997, for having allowed an undocumented migrant to live in her apartment. Specifically, she was found to have been in breach of Article 21 of the ordonnance of 2 November 1945, as amended by Charles Pasqua in 1993, which made it a criminal offence to in anyway aid or provide shelter to someone entering or residing in the country illegally.[57] The 'crime' carried a possible sentence of up to 5 years in prison and a fine of 200,000 francs. Deltombe's conviction led to an outpouring of protests, culminating in a march in Paris of more than 100,000 people. By the end of the year, while her conviction was upheld by the Court of Appeal, no punishment was imposed, which suggests that the movement had been somewhat successful on her behalf.

The government sought to further repress solidarity actions by proposing a new law, which made it a duty of French nationals to report to the authorities whenever they hosted a non-EU national in their homes. Local authorities would

---

55 Email circular, 17 August 1996, available at www.bok.net/pajol/zpajol/z8-20-00. html.

56 Abdallah (n 11), 87.

57 *Loi no 93–1027 du 24 août 1993 relative à la maîtrise de l'immigration et aux conditions d'entrée, d'accueil et de séjour des étrangers en France.*

then have the right to inspect the papers of those who were staying as guests to check whether or not their papers remained in order. In response, a group of filmmakers published a petition in the national newspapers, stating that they had hosted undocumented immigrants in their homes, and calling on other French nationals to do likewise and disobey the new law.[58] This petition quickly gathered around 120,000 signatures, and on 22 February 1997, more than 100,000 people demonstrated in Paris against the new law. However, the bill was passed in April,[59] although it was quickly repealed a few months later with the return of the left to power.

Deltombe's case, and the massive support she received, is but one example of the solidarity shown towards the Sans-Papiers by individuals and groups within French society. Indeed, this is a strong point of comparison with the Sanctuary Movement, much of whose strength was derived from the preparedness of citizens, who were relatively protected by the law, and by their more secure place within the community to act in effective solidarity with refugees. There was significant practical solidarity by the priest Coindé at Saint-Bernard, by trade unions, Ariane Mnouchkine, who allowed the Sans-Papiers to occupy her theatre La Cartoucherie following the expulsion from Saint-Ambroise, and many other individuals and organisations. Of course, what this demonstrates is that, as in the United States, it is possible to activate society in support of the rights of migrants and refugees through collective action that challenges the law. In contrast, legal processes force the migrant/refugee to make their claims away from the public sphere, in individualised ways that render them far more vulnerable.

Solidarity sometimes took on innovative and curious forms. In 1998, a collective of Sans-Papiers and their supporters was formed at Orléans. Early on this included some 56 Sans-Papiers and 174 sponsors (*parrains* and *marraines*). The collective organised for those who had been denied papers on the basis of the available legal criteria to be twinned with local people for shelter and other forms of assistance. On the one hand, the idea of sponsors was a direct challenge to the legal prohibition on aiding or assisting those whose status was irregular.[60] On the other hand, there were elements of the sponsorship scheme which did suggest a paternalistic attitude. So, for example, the terms used for the sponsors (*parrain/marrain*) and the Sans-Papiers they assisted (*filleul*) mean 'godparent' and 'godchild'. Goussault notes that the practice of Sans-Papiers having a *parrain* is a symbolic re-enactment of the *parrainage républicain*, a secular form of baptism inaugurated during the French Revolution, which suggests an attempt to frame support for the Sans-Papiers within traditional republican values,[61] although the collective itself preferred the analogy of a lawyer or union rep.[62]

---

58 Published in *Le Monde and Libération* on 12 February 1997.
59 *Loi no 97–396 du 24 avril 1997 portant diverses dispositions relatives à l'immigration*.
60 *Collectif des Sans-Papiers du Loiret* (n 5), 6
61 Goussault (n 8), 54, footnote 1.
62 *Collectif des Sans-Papiers du Loiret* (n 5), 119.

Seizing church sanctuary

One of the major problems identified in the discussion of the US Sanctuary Movement in the last chapter was the often passive role of the refugees themselves. It was a key feature of that movement that it was the churches, and their congregations, who decided to grant sanctuary, while it was often the role of the refugees to present themselves as sympathetic and deserving through their testimonies, so as to convince the churches to take them in. In the case of the Sans-Papiers, the roles were reversed. Here the refugees/migrants took the initiative in occupying spaces of sanctuary; the priests, congregations and proprietors of spaces were instead presented with a *fait accompli*. For some of the Sans-Papiers, their occupation was in fact the first occasion they had ever set foot in a church,[63] suggesting the opportunistic nature of the choice of a church as a place of sanctuary. Indeed, many of the Sans-Papiers were Muslims. This fact then, of course, raises the question as to why they chose a church in the first place, rather than a mosque or other space. One commentator suggests that in a country where the majority were Christian, the church offered a credible space from which to confront the authorities.[64] It also suggests, perhaps, that the long tradition of church sanctuary still retains a hold over the collective imagination, long after it has ceased to carry any formal legal basis.

Just as in the United States, in France, there was no basis for recognising a legal right of sanctuary in churches. Indeed, secular republican values are perhaps more ingrained in France than in the United States. The 1905 law that inaugurated the modern concept of *laïcité* even went so far as to turn almost all churches into state property.[65] Whereas in the United States, jurisprudence simply states that church space is not exempt from the reach of the law,[66] in France, church space is in fact directly under the control of the state. Yet, still the notion of the church as a space outside the law persists. As a letter from the Council of Christian Churches, issued at the height of the occupations in the summer of 1996, puts it: 'We ask ourselves the question: in a secular society, have churches become the only sanctuaries to which those who wish to proclaim their distress can seek refuge?'[67] This raises a similar claim to that of the Sanctuary Movement, that the collective memory of churches as spaces beyond the realm of the law still holds a purchase in contemporary society, regardless of the legal status. Yet, the Sans-Papiers, unlike their US counterparts, would end up taking sanctuary in a much more varied range of spaces than just churches. The essential point is that in a world in which law and the state have colonised space, thus ending the

---

63 Sambou A, Davy J and Gispert H, *Chroniques des Sans-Papiers* (Éditions Syllepse, 2008), 12.
64 Véziane de Vezins, quoted in Blin (n 29), 92.
65 Article 12, *Loi du 9 décembre 1905 concernant la séparation des Églises et de l'Etat*.
66 *Warden, Maryland Penitentiary v. Hayden*, 387 US 294 (1967).
67 Quoted in Coindé H, *Curé des sans-papiers: Journal de Saint-Bernard* (Éditions du Cerf, 1997), 35.

sanctuaries and asylums of old, it has become of critical importance for refugees/migrants seeking to resist exclusion and deportation to seize and remake spaces that at least stake a claim to exist outside the law. Moreover, the belief that a theological approach to sanctuary exists in opposition to the law is suggested in an exchange between Henri Coindé, the priest at Saint-Bernard, during a chance meeting with one of the police officers who was involved in the violent evacuation of the Sans-Papiers from his church. The police officer asked Coindé for forgiveness for his actions, to which he replied that the two of them operated on the basis of two fundamentally different logics: 'You are within that of order and the application of the law. Me, I am within that of the Gospel. These two logics are sometimes in contradiction'.[68]

Having occupied the church of Saint-Ambroise, against the hostility of the national and local church authorities, with their occupation of Saint-Bernard in the summer, they had an ally in that church's priest, Coindé. He has published extracts from his diary at the time that provides testimony that is both contemporaneous and, as distinct from most of the other published testimonies of the movement, comes from someone who was not himself a Sans-Papier. Coindé recounts the words of one leading Sans-Papier on the day they arrived at Saint-Bernard: 'We, the Africans, have decided ourselves on this occupation. No-one can speak in our name. It is us who decide on our actions. Father . . . we are asking for your protection: give us asylum'.[69] In this assertion, there is a strong sense of autonomy expressed, and also a clear assertion that church sanctuary is being demanded, while also relying on a somewhat traditional and slightly submissive request for asylum from the church. Nonetheless, as leading supporters of the movement put it, the very fact of the occupations and the hunger strikes was 'testament to their determination to escape from conditions of irregularity'.[70]

At one point, a press release was issued by the bishops of France which among other things stated the following:

> Christians refuse in principle to choose between good and bad migrants, between illegals and legals (*clandestins et réguliers*), between citizens provided with papers and others without papers (*sans papiers*). Whatever they are, they are our brothers and sisters in humanity.[71]

This is a clear refutation of legal categories, and carries echoes of St. Augustine's call for sanctuary to be open to all, as discussed in Chapter 1. However, there was resistance from many within the hierarchy of the Church to the Sans-Papiers.

---

68 Ibid 113.
69 Ibid 16.
70 'Adresse au gouvernement', 15 June 1996, available at www.bok.net/pajol/commed.html.
71 Sambou et al. (n 63), 231–232.

In March 1996, Cardinal Lustiger had denounced the occupation of Saint-Ambroise, and supported the eviction carried out by the police. During another occupation by Sans-Papiers, more than a decade later at the church of Saint-Paul de Massy in Essonne, the bishop informed them that he had called on the authorities to evict them from the church because: 'A church is and must remain a place solely for prayer'.[72] A debate thus opened up about the proper place of the church: should it remain a sacred space in the sense of being divorced from wider society or should it reflect the social issues that surround it? For example, in response to the letter from the bishop calling for the expulsion of the Sans-Papiers at Saint-Paul de Massy, the collective organised a petition in their support. One signatory, signing himself as a 'Catholic believer' (*croyant catholique*), wrote: 'if use of the church remains open to the parish community, then the presence of the Sans-Papiers does honour to the church. It is the best testimonial to the love of God for the poor . . .'.[73]

Of course, at the same time, church sanctuary is conceived of as somehow outside of the sovereign order that surrounds it. The point is that from that perspective, it is not a space necessarily of withdrawal, but of resistance. In other words, it is not about separation but about antagonising and challenging the sovereign order. This brings the contemporary space of the church much closer to the significance it held in the pre-modern period, where, it was a site of resistance to the secular rule of emperors and kings. The attitude of the Sans-Papiers towards the Church was fundamentally one based on an assumed right of sanctuary within its walls, perhaps covered with a patina of deference to its sacrality. For many in the Church, they held firm to the theological rejection of legal categories and the belief that the space of the church should exist beyond the reach of the sovereign order. Between them, they effectively recreated the historical form of sanctuary/asylum.

Remaking identities

As we saw with the Sanctuary Movement, there was a tension between playing into and challenging aspects of an imposed subjectivity: as victims in need of humanitarian assistance, or as political activists with a voice of their own. In addition, and related to those issues of identity, there was the question of whether an appeal to humanitarianism or a claim rooted in the political dynamics of wars in Central America, and the United States' role in relation to them, was the appropriate framework for asserting the right of sanctuary. These tensions were replicated among the Sans-Papiers, although with the refugee/migrants themselves much more at the heart of shaping the debates. In the case of the Sans-Papiers, there has been an ambivalent relationship to the universal subject. On the one hand, they have often relied upon a classic claim to universal human

---

72 Ibid 199.
73 Ibid 220.

rights; on the other hand, they have also self-identified on the basis of particularity, e.g. based on France's colonial past in their countries of origin, and their shared fate with the French working class. The very first task, though, just as with the Central American refugees, was the need to emerge from an enforced position of being hidden from wider society, certainly in terms of asserting themselves as active subjects.

In the initial discussions in the occupation at Saint-Ambroise, many of the Sans-Papiers expressed the problem that they 'lacked an identity' as a collective, but also in the sense of not being recognised as having a legal status, of being hidden.[74] Until then, the undocumented had been commonly referred to in media and political discourse as *clandestins*, which denotes them as hidden or passive subjects. As well as the obvious translation of 'clandestine/hidden', the word is perhaps more accurately rendered in English as 'illegal' in the context in which it has been used in France.[75] Yet so pervasive was this epithet that one of the first statements issued by the Sans-Papiers was entitled *Le SOS des clandestins de Saint-Ambroise*.[76]

One of the founders of the movement, Madjiguène Cissé, who emerged as perhaps the most eloquent spokespersons of the movement, was clear about why rejection of *clandestin* was critical in asserting their arrival on the political scene:

> The word '*clandestin*' contains a pejorative connotation of the pariah, implying also a parasite. A *clandestin* is someone invisible, who hides, who probably has something to hide, who could be dangerous. However, we are there, clearly visible, and we intend to remain so.[77]

A communiqué issued by female Sans-Papiers on 9 May 1996 made a similar claim when it declared: 'We are not *clandestins* for we have been in France for many years and we *chose to live here*'.[78] They go on to demand the 'right of free movement for everyone' and 'refugee status for everyone'.[79] This is a direct challenge to the right of the state to decide on categorisations of immigrants and indeed of any form of control over movement into the country. Here there is an added element to the construction of their identities as active subjects – their choice to be in France. Another of the leading figures, Ababacar Diop, writes of how effecting this change of nomenclature was also part of escaping the legal framework that forced them into the shadows:

74 Diop (n 6), 28.
75 Raissiguier C, *Reinventing the Republic: Gender, Migration, and Citizenship in France* (Stanford University Press, 2010), xi.
76 Diop (n 6), 76.
77 Cissé (n 40), 78.
78 Quoted in Diop (n 6), 134 [emphasis added].
79 Ibid.

We had chosen a new form of struggle and decided to come out into the open to point the finger at the extreme situations caused by the laws themselves. We wanted to force the French to see, to open their eyes. We wanted to demonstrate that we had no fear of repression. We no longer wanted to live in the shadow cast by the laws.[80]

Again, note the stress on choice and will; there was a clear determination on the part of the Sans-Papiers to assert their agency. Thus, they were rejecting both the notion that they were hidden or underground, and also the Rocardian idea of a wave of misery simply pushed towards the shores of France. In the words of Anne McNevin, this shift in terminology was an 'explicit rejection of the language and image of illegality in favour of the language and image of entitlement'.[81] It is a rejection of categories and an assertion of the right to stay by the migrants themselves. In other words, rejecting the label of illegality necessarily entailed a rejection of the legal distinctions between refugee and migrant, between undocumented and documented. By the time that they issued their manifesto in January 1997, the Sans-Papiers were adamant: 'We are not *clandestins*. We have emerged into the open'.[82]

The shift towards the nomenclature of Sans-Papiers – a term that is both less pejorative and more indicative of their actual situation to that of *clandestins* – was thus a major part of the reconfiguration of their identities as a collective within the public sphere, but importantly also as an active and present one.[83] Moreover, the very fact that the Sans-Papiers were refusing to be hidden, and instead presenting themselves as 'active agents in their own political futures', was itself a challenge to established norms regarding the place of the migrant within the 'host' society.[84] By contrast, the *clandestin*, because of their exclusion from the public space, was perceived as a danger to the social and political equilibrium of society.[85] By insisting on a collective identity framed by themselves, it communicated a sense of their own power, and projected to the wider public the image of active subjects engaging in a classic form of political protest. As Catherine Raissiguier writes:

The Sans-Papiers' choice of a public and collective display of their presence on French territory is the first, and probably most important, element of the movement's strategy. The Sans-Papiers creatively appropriated, transformed,

---

80 Ibid 76.
81 McNevin (n 4), 143.
82 'Le texte du manifeste des sans-papiers', *Libération*, 25 February 1997, available at www.bok.net/pajol/film.html.
83 Laacher (n 15), 20–21.
84 McNevin A, *Contesting Citizenship: Irregular Migrants and New Frontiers of the Political* (Columbia University Press, 2011), 112.
85 Laacher (n 15), 23.

and politicised the (in)visible, precarious, and nomadic character of their lived experiences. They refused to be turned into outlaws and illegal immigrants. In the process, they were able to do two contradictory things: bring themselves back into and unsettle the logic of the human rights discourse at the core of the French republican model, and position themselves as subjects under French law while critiquing the inner workings of the law itself.[86]

An important aspect alluded to here by Raissiguier is that their claims and the manner in which they made them crossed the legal barrier between refugees and migrants. While the majority of the Sans-Papiers were rejected asylum-seekers, they also included a great many who had entered the country as labour migrants, and who had for various reasons been rendered undocumented by changes to their status, or the loss of a job.[87] Yet they refused to accept the distinction between economic and human rights criteria as applied to the two groups. Instead, all of them asserted their right to full residency rights within France. I discuss the transgressing of legal categories further below, but it is worth noting here how the very fact of asserting collective identity *necessarily* leads to a challenge to the law, by rejecting any distinction among themselves as to the reasons for their migration or their lack of papers.

The adoption of the term 'Sans-Papiers' was therefore critical in demonstrating a resistance to being subjected to existing legal categories. It is not entirely clear the process by which the term 'Sans-Papiers' replaced that of '*clandestins*', but there was certainly a concerted effort among the occupiers to relabel themselves, from the beginning.[88] For a time, they referred to themselves as the 'Africans of Saint-Ambroise', and indeed they were frequently referred to simply as 'the Africans' by their supporters and in the media too. This label was quickly rendered obsolete as the movement began to encompass many non-African Sans-Papiers. Yet at other times, in the first stages of the occupation, they referred to themselves as the 'Refugees of Saint-Ambroise'.[89] Later on during the occupation of Saint-Bernard, the priest Coindé, who was supportive of the Sans-Papiers, raised objections to the use of the term

---

86 Raissiguier (n 75), 20.
87 Diop (n 6), 152.
88 The now classic text on how labels, particularly that of 'refugee', have been artificially constructed is Zetter R, 'Labelling Refugees: Forming and Transforming a Bureaucratic Identity' (1991), 4, *Journal of Refugee Studies*, 39. Zetter revisited this theme some years later, in which he highlighted the ways in which labelling had been taken out of the hands of NGOs and others and exclusively imposed by state institutions; see Zetter R, 'More Labels, Fewer Refugees: Remaking the Refugee Label in an Era of Globalization' (2007), 20, *Journal of Refugee Studies*, 172. In this context, the achievement of the Sans-Papiers in wrestling back some control over the labelling of refugees/migrants is more clearly evident.
89 A communiqué issued in April was issued under this name. See Diop (n 6), 106.

'refugee' to describe themselves. First, he argued, 'in a juridical sense, you are not refugees'. Second, 'except for the rejected asylum seekers, you are legally in France. It is the changes to the law that have placed you outside the law'.[90] A similar logic was applied at the same time by one leading supporter of the movement, the retired Admiral Antoine Sanguinetti, when he argued that: 'None amongst them is an illegal immigrant (*un clandestin*)'.[91] Both Coindé and Sanguinetti were without doubt trying to be sympathetic, but there are echoes here of the advice given by a lawyer to John Fife in the early stages of the Sanctuary Movement, to rely upon an assumed claim to legality, rather than challenging the legal/illegal bifurcation imposed on immigrants.[92] While they were correct up to a point in their assertions, they all played into the hands of their respective governments, by accepting the idea that the law can and should decide on who is or is not a refugee, or on who should be allowed into the country. In any case, in June 1996, the occupiers relabelled themselves as the 'Sans-Papiers of Saint-Bernard', and it appears that from this point onwards the term stuck.

Therefore, the term Sans-Papiers was born out of an attempt to both break free from legal categories, and to some extent to respect them. Yet it is important to emphasise that the identity as Sans-Papiers did fundamentally undermine imposed legal categories. Rather than being failed asylum-seekers, immigrant workers or visa-overstayers, the simple fact of being without official recognition as a rights-bearing subject was what united them. Moreover, it formed the basis of a demand – *Papiers pour tous!* – that refused to allow the state to choose who should or should not be granted to 'the right to have rights' within French society.[93] It was also a rebuke to those supporters and others who sought to impose their own views as to who among the Sans-Papiers was most deserving. In response to activist groups like *SOS Racism* who focussed only on the rights of families split apart because of the vagaries of French law, Cissé retorted: 'Some people claim the right to family life. We claim the right to live *tout court!*'[94] Moreover, as Bonaventure Kagné has written, the term 'Sans-Papiers' has no legal foundation as a category, but serves instead a political purpose to unify the many different individuals and groups, irrespective of how or why they entered the country, but who have in common exclusion from official sanction to reside and work.[95] As well as gesturing towards an alliance with those French citizens

90 Coindé (n 67), 32.
91 'Transcript of interview with Amiral Sanguinetti, Journal de 13h sur France-Inter', 7 August 1996, available at www.bok.net/pajol/amiral.html.
92 Rose A, *Showdown in the Sonoran Desert: Religion, Law, and the Immigration Controversy* (OUP, 2012), 30.
93 Arendt H, *The Origins of Totalitarianism* (Schocken, 2004), 296.
94 Quoted in Abdallah (n 11), 83.
95 Kagné B, 'Sans-Papiers en Belgique' in Antoine Pickels (ed), *À la lumière des sans-papiers* (Complexe, 2001), 42–43.

without housing and work, the prefix 'sans' was a clear echo of the haloed *sans-culottes*, the poor of Paris who initiated the French Revolution.[96] In other words, the nomenclature unites by ignoring the juridical categories into which each Sans-Papier is placed, or excluded from, by the state, and instead frames their status in ways that suggest exclusion and belonging on a socio-economic basis. This aspect, of remaking their identities along class lines, is discussed further below.

The question of autonomy

One of the critical issues faced by the Sans-Papiers from the beginning, and which has continued to play an important role in shaping the movement ever since, has been the desire to maintain autonomy over their own struggle. As we saw with the Sanctuary Movement, lack of autonomy was a weak point that often risked framing sanctuary within a similar paradigm to that of international refugee law, where refugees are the objects rather than the subjects of asylum. In the case of the Sans-Papiers, because they had taken the initiative in launching the movement, they were in a relatively strong position to lead it from the beginning. In addition, taking the leading position in their own struggle was a means of rupturing the common view of refugees/migrants (especially non-white ones) as incapable of, or unworthy of, political agency. But quickly, traditional forms of leadership threatened to assert themselves. These took shape in a committee of mediators made up of the great and good to act as negotiators with the government, and attempts by various supporting organisations such as NGOs, political groups, trade unions, etc., to impose their will upon the movement. Diop describes how initially the occupation seemed to be dominated by various supporting organisations such as *Group d'information et de soutien des immigrés* (GISTI), *SOS-Racisme* and *Droits devant!!*, rather than by the Sans-Papiers themselves: 'We were not the masters of the movement'.[97]

Yet, the Sans-Papiers were clear in demanding their autonomy and their refusal to work under the direction of even well-intentioned others. Cissé has described the initial struggle to retain control of the movement when established organisations, who 'were used to acting as the relay between immigrants in struggle and the authorities, and therefore more or less to manage the struggle', came to help the Sans-Papiers.[98] To prevent this, the Sans-Papiers held regular general meetings in the various sites of their occupation, and elected their own delegates

96 Keïta M, 'Le roi mage de Saint-Bernard était une princesse mandingue' in *Sans-Papiers: Chroniques d'un movement* (Editions Reflexe et Agence Im'média, Paris, 1997), 25.

97 Diop (n 6), 76.

98 Cissé M, *The Sans-Papiers: The New Movement of Asylum Seekers and Immigrants Without Papers in France—A Woman Draws the First Lessons* (Crossroads Books, 1997), 2–3.

so that they retained ongoing control over the movement. At one of the first meetings attended by Cissé, she insisted that it was up to the Sans-Papiers themselves to direct their meetings, while the supporting associations had to each nominate just one representative to attend them.[99] Allies of the Sans-Papiers therefore ended up 'working in conjunction with and under the leadership of the Sans-Papiers themselves'.[100] One member of GISTI, an NGO that campaigns for the rights of immigrants and for the principle of free movement across borders, was moved to say:

> It's quite extraordinary to see how the [antiracist] organizations – mine included – were taken aback by the fact that foreigners were taking the liberty to actually speak about their own issues and to organize their own fight . . . Foreigners gained power in their relationship to the allies. Before, they used to be allied to those who *defended* them . . . by troubling business as usual they troubled the nature of that relationship.[101]

A similar insistence on the autonomy and leadership of the Sans-Papiers, and a similar dynamic in their relations with supporting organisations, has been a key feature of the movement in the ensuing decades.[102] Perhaps the most militant example of the desire for autonomy and for ensuring that the movement remained led by the Sans-Papiers themselves is that provided by the collective CSP19 in Paris. Their rules stipulated that elected officers of the collective had to be Sans-Papiers, and if they achieved regularisation, then they would have to immediately step down and an election held for their successor.[103]

A critical aspect of maintaining autonomy over their struggle was deciding for themselves the terms of their claims, and what would be an acceptable outcome.[104] For instance, on the first demonstration called by the Sans-Papiers in March 1996, they resisted demands by certain left parties and NGOs to drop the call for 'papers for all immigrants', in spite of the decision by these organisations to boycott the protest as a result.[105] In addition, the Sans-Papiers resolutely opposed settlements that would grant papers to some but not others, based on the notion of deserving/undeserving migrants or good/bad cases. When negotiations with the government were first opened, the demand was that everyone involved in the

---

99   Diop (n 6), 96.
100   Raissiguier (n 75), 22–23.
101   Quoted in Raissiguier (n 75), 23.
102   Sambou et al. (n 63), 8. The Loiret collective also operated on the basis of collective decision-making and autonomy for the Sans-Papiers themselves. Collectif des Sans-Papiers du Loiret (n 5), 78–79.
103   Diallo M, Fofana V and Genz L, *Hier colonisés, aujourd'hui exploités, demain regularisés: Les journées de la Coordination 75 des Sans-Papiers* (Fage, 2010), 19.
104   Diop (n 6), 78; Abdallah (n 11), 83.
105   *Chroniques d'un mouvement* (n 40), 17.

occupation had to have their situation regularised, everyone's 'fate had to be linked to all the others'.[106] As we shall see, the question of autonomy and of how their claims were formulated became inextricably linked.

Le Collège des Médiateurs

In the days following their expulsion from the church of Saint-Ambroise in March 1996, the government refused to engage directly with the Sans-Papiers. In response, a group of leading figures in French society sympathetic to their cause put themselves forward as mediators between the movement and the government. These included academics, former resistance fighters, lawyers, diplomats, etc.[107] The Sans-Papiers agreed to the setting up of what became known as the *Collège des médiateurs*, and formally endorsed their role as negotiators.[108] At one level, the mediators represent a revival of the idea of intercession, as practised by the church in the context of medieval sanctuary.[109] At another level, they represented a potential re-assertion of traditional forms of political leadership, in which refugees and migrants are spoken for rather than speaking for themselves. However, the very fact that the mediators were chosen by the Sans-Papiers made them subordinate to the movement. The Sans-Papiers were clear that while the mediators could represent their views, they could not speak for them.[110]

Yet tensions quickly developed between the mediators and the Sans-Papiers. On the one hand, the mediators made a call for the government to 'open the way to a complete renewal of immigration and asylum policy' on a more generous and humanitarian basis.[111] On the other hand, at the outset, the mediators were keen to try and limit regularisation to certain categories that they felt were 'justified'.[112] They were clear from the beginning that they only sought regularisation 'within the boundaries of the French law',[113] which included the following ten criteria:

---

106 Diop (n 6), 78.
107 A full list of the mediators can be found at www.bok.net/pajol/college.html# membres.
108 For a critical view of the composition and role of the collège, see Blin (n 33), 35–46.
109 de Martin PTD, *Le Droit d'Asile* (Librarie du Recueil Sirey, 1939), 158, 161; Helmholz RH, *The Ius Commune in England: Four Studies* (OUP, 2001), 28; Shoemaker K, *Sanctuary and Crime in the Middle Ages 400–1500* (Fordham University Press, 2011), 22, 69.
110 'Entretien avec Ababacar Diop', 7 August 1996, available at www.bok.net/pajol/ababacar.html.
111 'Adresse au gouvernement', 15 June 1996, available at www.bok.net/pajol/appel.html.
112 Letter of 29 April 1996: 'Dix critères pour la régularisation', available at www.bok.net/pajol/com-med.html.
113 Statement of the College of Mediators, quoted in Raissiguier (n 75), 22.

(1) Parents of children with French nationality
(2) Common-law partners of French citizens
(3) Partners or children of immigrants with papers
(4) Parent of a child born in France
(5) Rejected asylum-seekers who entered France before 1993
(6) Those with a close relative resident in France
(7) Those who if returned to their country of origin would have medical treatment for a serious illness interrupted
(8) Where return would expose them to 'serious risks'
(9) Students in the middle of their studies
(10) People who were well integrated into French society, yet without a residency permit.

The first thing to note is that once again, we are presented with categories of deserving migrants, thus implying that the rest are undeserving. This is exactly the same paradigm used by the law of 397 in the late Roman Empire, of the medieval *casus excepti* and of the various elements of Article 1 of the 1951 Refugee Convention. The categories put forward by the mediators, although seemingly broad in scope, in fact betray certain prejudices. First, at least half of them (the last especially) privilege those who already have links with France. That final criterion makes this bias clear. The others have a broadly humanitarian bent – non-return to 'serious risks' could be interpreted as simply upholding the legal right of non-refoulement. The cut-off date of 1993 for people denied refugee status appears somewhat arbitrary, although presumably because they would, by this time, have been resident in France for at least 3 years, and would thus have been considered to have established sufficient ties and were 'well integrated' into French society. Single people, and those whose lives were particularly precarious because they had no familial support or regular work, which accounted for a significant number of the Sans-Papiers, were not covered by these criteria.[114] Moreover, the categories are suffused with value judgements about who is and is not deserving of being granted a legal status. Presumably those not covered were considered by the mediators to be fair game for deportation, or at least being maintained in a legal limbo in France.

It was on the basis of these categories that the government agreed to negotiate and accept the demand for at least revisiting claims on a case-by-case basis. Yet such a framework went against the collective solidarity of the Sans-Papiers expressed in their slogan 'papers for all'. At a meeting involving delegates of the Sans-Papiers, NGOs and the police, the representative of GISTI defended the compromises agreed by the mediators on the grounds that selective regularisation was being offered based on criteria that 'did not fall from the sky'

---

114   In a survey carried out of 227 Sans-Papiers who occupied Saint-Bernard, 45% were single people with no other ties to France. Figures cited in Blin (n 29), 151.

but were grounded in international and domestic law.[115] At this same meeting, the Director-General of the Paris police stated bluntly, 'France cannot accommodate all the ills of the world . . .' (*La France ne peut pas accueillir tous les malades du monde*), which of course is an almost exact repetition of Rocard's notorious phrase.[116] Thus, from every side, the Sans-Papiers were facing demands to accept the imposed categories of the law. While, on the whole, the Sans-Papiers held firm, it appears that at times they were ready to accept these categories, at least as the basis for further negotiations with the government.[117] Indeed, in the first instance, the ten criteria suggested by the mediators were in fact endorsed by the group that had carried out the initial occupation at Saint-Ambroise.[118]

However, when it became clear towards the end of June that the large numbers of Sans-Papiers who were not getting permission from the authorities for a re-examination of their dossiers, the mediators were moved to call for a 'profound review' of government policy in relation to immigrants, as the current state of the law produced 'unacceptable human conditions'.[119] But around the same time, they were only calling on the government to grant papers to those according to basic human rights norms, workplace legislation and international legal obligations.[120] Moreover, at least one of the mediators accepted the premise that 'illegal immigration' had to be fought, if only by trying to warn people in Africa that coming to France illegally would place them in sub-standard working and living conditions.[121] In short, while the intentions of the mediators may have been humanitarian and sympathetic, by remaining wedded to legal categories and legal norms, they threatened to betray the essential claims of the Sans-Papiers that everyone had a right to be regularised and to be guaranteed residence in France. It was left to a group of women Sans-Papiers to re-assert the original demands, when they occupied the town hall of the eighteenth Arrondisment on June 25: 'We do not want one just person regularised . . . We want everyone at the same time'.[122]

The value of migrants under the regularisation program agreed between the mediators and the government was presented in humanitarian and republican terms: namely in the interests of maintaining family unity and ensuring residency rights to those children born on French soil, and by extension to their immediate family. But excluded were those who were in polygamous marriages, who had

---

115 Diop (n 6), 126.
116 Ibid 127.
117 See, e.g., the Communiqué issued on 20 July 1996 by the Coordination nationale des collectifs de sans-papiers, available at www.bok.net/pajol/com-med.html.
118 *Chroniques d'un mouvement* (n 40), 17.
119 Statement of 26 June 1996, 'Inquiétudes sur les résultats', available at www.bok.net/pajol/com-med.html.
120 'Adresse au gouvernement', 15 June 1996, available at www.bok.net/pajol/com-med.html.
121 'Transcript of interview with Amiral Sanguinetti, Journal de 13h sur France-Inter', 7 August 1996, available at www.bok.net/pajol/amiral.html.
122 *Chroniques d'un mouvement* (n 40), 18.

been convicted of crimes and who did not have any dependent family. For those who would be regularised, work permits had to be renewed on an annual basis. However, renewal applications had to be submitted at least 2 months prior to their expiration, and on average, it took 3 months to do all the necessary things to prepare the application. As Cissé notes, in effect this meant that there were only 7 months a year in which normal life could be lived without having to worry about one's status.[123] The point being that for migrant workers to be allowed to remain in the country, they would be maintained in an indefinite state of precarity.

Diop describes how with the intervention of the mediators the phrases 'good dossiers' and 'bad dossiers' were introduced.[124] In other words, a distinction was being made between those who could produce sufficient proof that they fit into a recognised legal category and those who could not do so. The mediators believed, therefore, that they could not sit with government ministers and insist that everyone was granted papers.[125] Instead, the dossiers would have to be considered on a case-by-case basis. The Sans-Papiers, however, were adamant that:

> each dossier was also, was most importantly a person; that the dossiers indefensible according to the law, or those that were more difficult to defend than the others, were in spite of that not indefensible according to justice. One cannot always judge a person in terms of the law; there comes a time when the laws themselves have to be judged, in the name of the person themselves, of their real-life situation.[126]

Once again the conflict was between notions of sanctuary and belonging tied solely to law, or according to much broader ideas of justice.

The mediators effectively wound up their work in the summer of 1997, declaring that their role would continue as that of 'accompaniment, vigilance, and putting forward proposals'.[127] Their view was that the new left government's promises to suspend deportation and to review claims on a case-by-case basis had largely achieved the aims set out by the mediators a year earlier. However, this was far from being a settlement that fulfilled the aims of the Sans-Papiers themselves, namely a minimum of regularising the status of all undocumented migrants in France. While the mediators had no doubt given the movement a certain sense of legitimacy and profile at a critical moment in the struggle, and while they clearly believed in a more humane approach to the treatment of immigrants, ultimately they felt themselves bound to the law, specifically to the

---

123 Cissé (n 40), 155.
124 Diop (n 6), 113.
125 Email circular, 1 August 1996, available at www.bok.net/pajol/zpajol/z8-06-00. html.
126 Diop (n 6), 114.
127 Communiqué of 18 June 1997: 'Le rôle des médiateurs', available at www.bok.net/ pajol/com-med.html.

paradigm of categories of deserving and undeserving refugees/migrants. As such, they could not but end up antagonistic to the demands of the Sans-Papiers for universal regularisation. In the final analysis, for the mediators, the rule of law took precedence over the opening of sanctuary.

Strategies of the movement: legal versus political?

However, for some, it was possible to square the circle of law and politics in asserting the Sans-Papiers' demands. GISTI, in a pamphlet issued in support of the Sans-Papiers, describe their aim as not merely to 'agitate in favour of equal treatment between French people and foreigners, but also to promote the rule of law (*l'état de droit*)'.[128] Just like many of the Tucson activists in the Sanctuary Movement, GISTI insisted that the claims of refugees/migrants find their guarantor in law. The pamphlet goes on to pose the key question, 'How can a right be "reclaimed" when it is at the same time confronted with an administration which, at the outset, has placed one in a position of weakness?'[129] The answer will depend on the specific circumstances found in each case, yet it is 'essential that one never abandons one's rights'.[130] The central argument of GISTI is that political mobilisation can give force to the legal claims, particularly when it comes to drawing in support from citizens and other organisations. For example, in 1991, refused asylum-seekers agitated within the major trade union federations of which they were members and won them to a position in favour of regularisation.[131] Nonetheless, ultimately, GISTI argue that, 'The juridical tool is more than ever an indispensable lever'.[132] It is not clear exactly why they believe this, but the logic appears to be the standard progressivist idea that political agitation can and must feed into legal structures so as to effect lasting change. In some instances, this may well be true, but in the case of sanctuary/asylum, as this book has attempted to show, the opposite appears to be true. At each point that sanctuary/asylum becomes codified in law, it loses its essential characteristics of a space open to all, to become instead part of the apparatus of control over the refugee/migrant. In any case, the supporters were more concerned about the legalities of the Sans-Papiers' actions than the Sans-Papiers themselves.[133] Part of the reason for this approach may have been due to the 'prudence liberals typically harbour towards obeying the law and their distrust of collective struggle, with its potential for social disorder'.[134]

---

128 *Sans-papiers mais pas sans droits* (GISTI, 2004), 1.
129 Ibid.
130 Ibid.
131 Ibid 55.
132 Ibid 1.
133 Cissé (n 40), 89.
134 Patsias C and Williams N, 'Religious sanctuary in France and Canada' in Randy K Lippert and Sean Rehaag (eds), *Sanctuary Practices in International Perspectives: Migration, Citizenship and Social Movements* (Routledge, 2013), 183.

It would be wrong, however, to assert that the Sans-Papiers, either as a whole or as various groups among them, made a rigid separation between legal and political strategies. Both were deployed. On the one hand, there has been a legal focus on getting the government and local prefects to review applications for asylum and residency permits on a case-by-case basis. For example, very soon after the occupation of Saint-Bernard began, they had set up a table in the front of the church to assist Sans-Papiers in putting together their dossiers, and after just 3 days, some 1,000 had been prepared.[135] On the other hand, the movement has stood resolutely behind demands that express a more collective and uncompromising approach that demands papers for all. Nonetheless, at points it became clear that the contradictions between the two approaches could not be resolved, and this then led to some bitter disputes about which strategy should take precedence, as is discussed in detail below.

Cissé identifies the central contestation between the Sans-Papiers and the succession of laws and administrative measures from governments of both left and right. One of the objectives in setting up a national coordination of the various Sans-Papiers collectives in the summer of 1996 was to open up the question of the legal apparatus that had been developed by successive governments since the early 1970s, to challenge the concept of 'managing the flow of migration'.[136] Society as a whole appeared to be divided between those who took the view that the problem was one of individual Sans-Papiers and their situation, while others saw the issue as crucially one of broader social questions; between those who saw the question as one of justice for the Sans-Papiers, and those who saw immigration as determined by the need to manage the flow of additions to the labour force; between those who focussed on the need to fortify Europe's borders against those from the Global South, and those who saw the world as one where questions of inequality and justice traverse those borders.[137] Cissé also criticised those in the movement who followed the logic of making applications on a case-by-case basis and who therefore effectively made a distinction between 'good' and 'bad' Sans-Papiers. Thus, accepting such a process could effectively fracture the movement.[138] Indeed, the collectives of Sans-Papiers often had to overcome initial divisions among themselves, e.g. over whether or not to include single people who often had a weak case for regularisation together with the families.[139] In short, the Sans-Papiers often had to struggle to resist divisions among themselves that were being imposed by the law. In this context, Cissé argues that the demand of 'papers for all' was both politically necessary and a concrete solution to a real problem. This slogan:

135   Cissé (n 40), 42.
136   'Entretien avec Madjiguène Cissé', 14 August 1996, available at www.bok.net/pajol/ madjiguene.html.
137   Cissé (n 40), 165.
138   Ibid 165, 173–174.
139   Ibid 169.

is political, [for] it is not enough to speak of humanitarianism: we are not victims of a natural disaster, we are not asking for favours, rather we are demanding our legitimate rights. How can we, under the pretext of preserving their wellbeing, reject or exclude people whose lives are threatened or who are fleeing miserable conditions? . . . [it] is about spreading the idea of the free movement of people across the planet.[140]

Here again the right of movement, a right belonging to all, is being asserted against the right of the state to control its border. Free movement across the planet is conceived of here as a universal human right. At a stroke, therefore, the demand of 'papers for all' again denies the distinction drawn between categories; there is no distinction between those fleeing violence or those fleeing conditions of deprivation, of refugee and migrant, good dossiers and bad dossiers, deserving and undeserving, genuine and bogus. It is important to note at this point that the refusal to accept legal categorisation, the assertion of a claim that challenges sovereign right is in essence an attempt to place political contestation above the standard human rights narrative that qualifies a right of movement with the right of the state and the 'host' society.[141]

In the midst of the occupations in the summer of 1996, the *Conseil d'État* was called upon by the government to rule on the claims of the Sans-Papiers. Among other things, the ruling made it quite clear that there was no such thing as a legal 'right to regularisation', as such claims had to be determined according to the criteria set out in law.[142] In essence, this reaffirmed the principle that claims could only be considered on a case-by-case basis. Yet, throughout the various episodes of the struggle of the Sans-Papiers, the refusal to allow the state to determine status on an individual basis had been a key demand. So, in 1980, Turkish hunger strikers refused the offer of individual regularisation by the French government, insisting on being granted papers collectively.[143] Similarly, when negotiations with the government were first opened in 1996, the demand of the Sans-Papiers was that everyone involved in the occupations had to have their situation regularised, everyone's 'fate had to be linked to all the others'.[144]

The government's response has been to use the law precisely as a means by which to drain the demands of the Sans-Papiers of any political content. For the

---

140 Ibid 181.
141 To take one example, in refugee law, one can demonstrate proof of persecution and fear of harm, yet be denied asylum on the basis that one is considered to be guilty of a serious crime either political or non-political, e.g. Article 1(F) Convention Relating to the Status of Refugees, 28 July 1951, United Nations, Treaty Series, vol 189.
142 *Assemblée générale (Section de l'intérieur)* No 359 622 – 22 août 1996 'Etrangers non ressortissants de l'Union européenne'.
143 Siméant (n 2), 342.
144 Diop (n 6), 78.

Sans-Papiers, the government's demand that they accept regularisation on a strict case-by-case basis was effectively an attempt to isolate individuals and thus break the movement.[145] As Raissiguier writes:

> The French government … tried to depoliticise the conflict by providing individual responses to what the Sans-Papiers themselves see as a collective problem. By their refusal of this case-by-case logic, the Sans-Papiers demanded that France address the structural location of thousands of undocumented postcolonial immigrants within its national boundaries.[146]

What Raissiguier is describing is a demand – to recognise deep historical duties owed by France to the Sans-Papiers – that cannot be contained within a legal framework. The post-colonial context is indeed one which was frequently referenced within the movement, and is discussed in detail towards the end of this chapter.

With a breakdown of communications between the government, the mediators and the Sans-Papiers in the summer of 1996, the Interior Minister, Jean-Louis Debré, declared, that while he was prepared to negotiate, it had to be on the basis of the law, thus rejected asylum-seekers, for example, would not be regularised: 'We have a law and it must be applied'.[147] This type of response echoes precisely that given by the authorities in the United States when confronted by the challenge of the Sanctuary Movement. The Sans-Papiers, however, rejected the insistence on working within a legal framework:

> Why employ the term "negotiations" when we have been talking about our real-life situations, our links of friendship, family, parenthood? We are not negotiating anything; we have only been saying to you that no law can be said to be perfect. We are not negotiating anything; we are only reclaiming unconditional respect for fundamental rights and the right to be human.[148]

The mediators fell on the side of the government on this question, arguing that the only justified and winnable strategy was based on a review of individual dossiers, and their confluence with legal categories. The outcome of this strategy, however, was that in June, the government had agreed to regularise just 48 of the 315 members of the collective that had carried out the original occupation at Saint-Ambroise.[149] By October 1997, some 100,000 dossiers had been submitted, but only 1,200 had been granted regularisation.[150] Not only was the legal strategy a betrayal of the wider questions being raised by the Sans-Papiers, it was in

---

145   Cissé (n 40), 174.
146   Raissiguier (n 75), 28.
147   *Sans Chroniques d'un movement* (n 40), 21–22.
148   Diop (n 6), 168.
149   Abdallah (n 11), 85.
150   Siméant (n 2), 219.

practical terms ineffective as well, thus undermining the major justification for following the legal route in the first place. Even if the mediators and some supporters could not recognise this fact, the Sans-Papiers did. In dealing with the issue of the rejection of dossiers by the authorities, the *Coordination 75 des Sans-Papiers*, an umbrella group for the various collectives in Paris, declared that ultimately the question of acceptance or rejection was a political question rather than an administrative or legal one: 'The struggle of the Sans-Papiers must be conducted with the aim of forcing [open the political aspect]'.[151] The key point being made here, and it is something repeated among many of the Sans-Papiers, is that a legal framework *per se*, never mind the particularly restrictive laws prevailing in France at the time, was incapable of recognising the full scope of the demands being made by the refugees/migrants, and the context that gave those demands legitimacy. As one activist group puts it in relation to the claim that a case-by-case process was more 'realistic and credible' than 'papers for all':

> If the putting together of a dossier is a concrete and necessary perspective for each Sans-Papiers – whose objective, *a priori*, is not the radical transformation of society but to be able to live normally – to focus the struggle on these "practical" bases could only, as events have shown, lead it into a dead end. By getting bogged down in juridical constraints, many activists forgot the political aspects.[152]

Just as with the Sanctuary Movement, it was an irony that many of the seasoned activists, moulded by years of political activism, were far more likely to be pulled towards the law than the refugees/migrants themselves. Perhaps, having experienced first-hand how the law traps them, the refugees/migrants understood too well the extreme limitations of the legal route?

In some cases, there were obvious tensions between the principle of universal regularisation, and the pressure when attempting to gain papers for a specific group taking part in the struggle. The chronicle of the struggle of the Loiret collective of Sans-Papiers provides an excellent case study in this respect. For example, it is acknowledged that with them, the demand had effectively evolved from 'Regularise all the Sans-Papiers' (*Règularisez tous les Sans-papiers*) to 'Regularise all the Sans-Papiers who request it' (*Règularisez tous les Sans-papiers qui en font la demande*) to 'Regularise the 154 Sans-Papiers who have requested it, and who can establish proof of good reasons to be regularised' (*Règularisez les 154 Sans-papiers qui en on fait la demande et pour lesquels nous pouvons prouver qu'ils ont de bonnes raisons d'être régularisés*).[153] As one member of the collective puts it: there was 'a confrontation between the idealistic conception

---

151 Diallo et al. (n 103), 351.
152 *Commission Immigration du Réseau No Pasaran, Des papiers pour toutes et tous!*, annex to *Abdallah* (n 11), 133.
153 *Collectif des Sans-Papiers du Loiret* (n 5), 120.

of Human Rights abolishing all borders . . . on the one hand, and on the other hand, the reality of the government and its laws'.[154] In the opinion of another activist, discussing a revision of the law that in some respects reversed some of the most egregious aspects of the Pasqua laws, but which, nevertheless, retained strict categories and made no commitment to regularise the status of those applying for papers: 'The Sans-papiers made concessions when they submitted their dossiers within the framework of the Chevènement circular. That was the biggest concession that the Sans-papiers movement made'.[155] Others saw no contradiction between taking a principled position against all border controls and papers for all, while at the same time accepting that once they joined the collective they were prepared to agitate for regularisation on the basis of the existing law.[156] The danger, in practice, was that individuals could get bogged down in making their applications, thus rendering them atomised and leaving them vulnerable to the demoralisation of rejection. Testimonies from several Sans-Papiers describe the isolation and demoralisation of having to submit to the legal process of regularisation, in which the collective struggle was absent and the force of law was most acute.[157]

Again, the Loiret collective provides a useful example of how seizing church sanctuary became a practically effective means to win regularisation. After initially organising public protests and making formal representations to the local prefecture, on 26 July 1998, around forty Sans-Papiers occupied the Orléans cathedral.[158] By September, the local prefect agreed to reconsider all the applications (*dossiers*) presented to him, except for eight of them, in exchange for the Sans-Papiers ending their occupation of the cathedral. The Sans-Papiers refused this offer, insisting that all of them had to be granted papers.[159] At one point in the drawn-out confrontation, the Interior Minister made it clear that respecting the 'rule of law' was paramount when considering the admissibility or not of the dossiers presented by the Sans-Papiers.[160] Yet by February 2000, 154 Sans-Papiers had joined the Loiret collective, of which 124 had gained regularisation during the campaign.[161] The point is that the political campaign was effective and determinative; collective struggle produced concrete gains for individuals, without having to resort to an individualised approach to regularisation. Indeed, whereas originally they had struggled to get forty regularisations, with the authorities not even willing to consider all of them in the first place, they were eventually able to win papers for more than three times that number.

---

154   Ibid 122.
155   Ibid 125.
156   Ibid 132.
157   Goussault (n 8), 95–96, 106.
158   *Collectif des Sans-Papiers du Loiret* (n 5), 11.
159   Ibid 13.
160   Ibid 19.
161   Ibid 23.

The key demand of 'papers for all' has remained a constant over the course of the movement.[162] The slogan was even taken up by groups of undocumented migrants in Spain beginning in 2001. That movement also began with the occupation of a church, Santa Maria del Pi in Barcelona.[163] During the 2007 occupation at Massy, a suburb of Paris, a Catholic charity approached the collective to submit a selection of the most sympathetic cases for regularisation as a way of not allowing them to be held back by the others. The collective responded that there was no question of 'separating the group: it is "506 gift packages or 0"'.[164] Cécile Frank argues that there was, however, a contradiction in the movement's use of the slogan, 'papers for all', for it suggests the abolition of borders, whereas the explicit aim of the movement was to seek residency permits from a national state on the basis of residing within its defined territory.[165] Although one could argue that the slogan does not necessarily imply the end of borders *per se* but simply the abolition of border controls, or at least any controls over who can and cannot reside within the territorial borders of the state. In that sense, while not challenging the existence of borders or the nation-state, the slogan does seek to undermine the monopoly of the state on deciding who can cross borders or remain within them.

The movement in decline

In June 1997, to mark the anniversary of the occupation of Saint-Bernard, a protest took place outside the town hall of the eighteenth Arrondissement, where the church was located. The demand was for a group of forty Sans-Papiers to be regularised. The Socialist mayor explained to them and their supporters that not everyone could be regularised, and made the now familiar counter-demand that decisions could only be made on a case-by-case basis. In response chants of 'Papers for all!' brought the meeting to a halt. The Sans-Papiers then decided to peacefully occupy the town hall. At this, one of the members of the *collège des médiateurs*, Stéphane Hessel, made an outburst demanding that the Sans-Papiers cease their protest, 'consider themselves lucky to be sponsored by elected officials' and to leave the town hall. The CRS was called in and the occupation was violently evacuated with several of the Sans-Papiers requiring hospital treatment.[166] What is significant in this incident is how the denial of the political claim – papers for all – was bound up with a loss of patience, both of the Sans-Papiers themselves

---

162 Sambou et al. (n 63), 15, 16.
163 Frank C, 'Le traitement politico-institutionnel du mouvement des sans-papiers à Barcelone: de la négociation à la répression' in Magali Boumaza and Philippe Hamman (eds), *Sociologie des mouvements de précaires: Espaces mobilisés et repertoires d'action* (L'Harmattan, 2007), 187, 188.
164 Sambou et al. (n 63), 228.
165 Frank (n 163), 188.
166 'Anniversaire de l'occupation de Saint-Bernard', 28 June 1997, available at www. bok.net/pajol/sanspap/anniv.html.

at being fobbed off with promises of a mere re-examination of their claims on a case-by-case basis, and of the supporters who resented the refusal of the Sans-Papiers to follow their lead. In sum, the uneasy alliance between a militant movement led by migrant/refugees and seasoned activists used to speaking for others, and the yoking together of political and legal strategies was beginning to break under pressure.

Autonomy and resisting the legal paradigm have been central to the growth and success of the movement; the undermining of these aspects is closely intertwined with the decline of the movement in the late 1990s. In the summer of 1997, with the return to power of the left, many Sans-Papiers and their supporters had their hopes raised. Yet, while the new government repealed some of the more egregious laws, and temporarily suspended deportations, the new Interior Minister, Jean-Pierre Chevènement, issued a new circular setting out six categories for regularisation: spouses of French citizens or immigrants with papers; parents of children born in France; those who had integrated well into French society; people whose asylum claims had been rejected, but where sending them back would violate the principle of non-refoulement; those with severe illnesses; and students.[167] Once again, while there is clearly a humanitarian bent to some of these categories, others simply restate existing legal obligations such as non-refoulement, and betray the overriding prejudice that only those who can prove that they have done enough to earn their place in French society will be accepted. Moreover, the Chevènement circular simply gave the right to local prefects to re-examine in exceptional circumstances the status of Sans-Papiers who fit within these categories. But nowhere did the circular refer to 'regularisation' as such.[168] Moreover, the policy of the new Socialist government, that reconsideration of the status of the Sans-Papiers could only be determined on a case-by-case basis, was a direct repudiation of the claim for universal regularisation of the Sans-Papiers.[169] Jacqueline Costa-Lascoux also describes the burden imposed on migrants/refugees in being forced to prove their place within one of the defined categories worthy of being regularised:

> [The Chevènement circular] on the regulation of undocumented migrants or, more precisely, on the 're-examination of the situation of certain categories of foreigners in an irregular situation' ... [is based on] distinguishing categories of populations (rather than situational criteria), requires written evidence and official documents ... often impossible to provide, not through the fault of the applicants, but as a result of the deficiencies of the administrations of the countries of origin (for civil status documents

---

167   *Circulaire du 24 juin 1997 relative au réexamen de la situation de certaines catégories d'étrangers en situation irrégulière.*

168   Cissé (n 40), 154.

169   Ibid.

in particular) and the forms of exploitation of which they have been the victims in France.[170]

Initially, the Sans-Papiers seemed to be united in rejecting this repackaging of familiar restrictions and categorisations. At a meeting bringing together representatives of all local Sans-Papier collectives, the Chevènement circular was rejected in favour of the demand of granting papers to all undocumented migrants, in addition to calling for a permanent halt to deportations and the facilitation of the return of those already deported.[171] On the closing date for applications for submitting claims for regularisation under the circular, 1 November 1997, 5,000 Sans-Papiers and their supporters marched in Paris with the slogan 'Papers for all'. A petition to the government with the same demand gathered 30,000 signatures.[172]

However, the movement was already beginning to lose its momentum, at least partly due to internal structural problems. First, a number of supporting organisations effectively withdrew from the movement because they resented the demand of the Sans-Papiers for complete autonomy. Second, the loose horizontal structure of the movement was acting as a block to further development. The spokesperson of one of the local collectives lamented that the national coordination was no longer able to organise national events and had become mainly a talking shop.[173] For the supporting organisations, it appears that a number of them believed that with the arrival to power of a Socialist government, the movement no longer needed to take such a confrontational stance. Some groups, such as *SOS Racisme*, for example, were closely linked to the party now in power.

Yet reliance on the Socialist government proved to be misplaced. While, as outlined above, new, somewhat broader criteria for regularisation were allowed, even if they were successful, this only entitled people to receive a 1-year renewable permit, rather than the more secure one of 10 years that had previously been on offer. Indeed, of the 143,500 applications for regularisation under the new law, just 81,000 were granted. There was a large variation in acceptance rates from one prefecture to another, and particular groups fared worse than others, e.g. single men and Turks had far lower acceptance rates than families and people from China.[174] The ability to provide the necessary proofs needed sometimes relied on luck. For example, one person was only able to prove that she had been continuously resident in France for the requisite period of time because she

---

170 Costa-Lascoux J, 'L'illusion de la maîtrise: la politique migratoire en trompe-l'oeil' in Étienne Balibar, Monique Chemillier-Gendreau, Jacqueline Costa-Lascoux and Emmanuel Terray (eds), *Sans-Papiers: l'archaïsme fatal* (Éditions La Découverte et Syros, 1999), 43.
171 Abdallah (n 11), 95–96.
172 Ibid 101–102.
173 Ibid 96–97.
174 Ibid 100.

had kept some postcards sent to her. Others had to rely on receipts for purchases that they still happened to have after several years. And, yet, according to the testimony of the Sans-Papiers, it depended on which prefecture you sent your dossier to as to whether the evidence contained within would be accepted or not.[175] In addition, the requirement that all of the Sans-Papiers submit their claims individually to the government 'came to seem more like a trap than an offer', as now some 60,000 of them whose claims had been rejected and were therefore subject to deportation had provided full details of their names and addresses to the state.[176] As such the increased focus on the legal route led to demoralisation.

Beginning in November 1997, a split developed within the national coordination of the collectives of Sans-Papiers. A newly defined demand had been agreed by the majority: rather than papers for all, regularisation for those who submitted a dossier. In addition, the demand for the repeal of the Chevènement circular had been dropped. The Paris collective refused to accept this new set of demands and maintained that of regularisation for all Sans-Papiers.[177] Political tensions over increasingly divergent strategies came to a head in early 1998. A botched attempt at occupying the church of Saint-Jean in Montmartre in March was the impetus behind the removal of Cissé and Salah Teiar from the national coordinating committee. The committee was then reconstituted to include not only Sans-Papiers but also the representatives of supporting organisations.[178] This was a blow to the maintenance of autonomy by the Sans-Papiers over the movement. According to Cissé and Teiar, neither of them, nor anyone else from the original collective of Saint-Bernard, were informed let alone invited to this meeting, and a member of one collective supportive of them was expelled from the meeting before the vote.[179] The newly constituted committee also called for a demonstration in May 1998; noticeably absent from its demands was that of 'Papiers pour tous', which had hitherto been ubiquitous.[180] Cissé and Teiar issued a detailed analysis of the problems besetting the movement in a letter sent to all the Sans-Papiers collectives, in which they concluded in bold terms: 'The fundamental question that is posed today is that of the autonomy of the

---

175 Goussault (n 8), 70–71.
176 Hayter T, *Open Borders: The Case against Immigration Controls* (Pluto, 2000), 145.
177 Cissé (n 40), 179.
178 Abdallah (n 11), 116.
179 'Lettre aux Collectifs de sans-papiers et aux organisations de soutien', 5 May 1998, available at www.bok.net/pajol/sanspap/coordination/madjiguene4.html. Their claim is borne out of the fact that the report of the meeting notes just thirteen attendees, with ten voting to remove Cissé and Teiar, and three abstaining. See 'Résolution de la coordination nationale des sans-papiers', 29 March 1998, available at www.bok.net/pajol/sanspap/coordination/co29-03-98.html.
180 'Résolution de la coordination nationale des sans-papiers', 29 March 1998, available at www.bok.net/pajol/sanspap/coordination/co29-03-98.html.

Sans-Papiers'.[181] Intimately connected to this loss of autonomy was also a pull towards the law, and away from the more political challenge to the segmentation of Sans-Papiers according to legal categories, and indeed a challenge to the legal paradigm itself.

In a similar manner to the Sanctuary Movement in the United States where activists split over whether to work more closely with or maintain implacable resistance to the authorities, the movement around the Sans-Papiers split between this new committee who sought to engage more with the government on practical measures, while the *Ile de France* collective and others sought to re-found the movement on the basis of continued opposition to the government's ongoing restrictive measures, and a commitment to keeping open the demands for free movement and regularisation for all migrants.[182] Those grouped around the *National Coordination des Sans-Papiers* had a leadership that included supporting organisations and Sans-Papiers, while other collectives retained an autonomous structure. According to Cissé and Teiar, in some of the collectives in which the Sans-Papiers did not have full autonomy, their ability to speak for themselves was being 'suffocated' by the increased dominance of the voices of the supporters and their organisations.[183] Indeed, they were keener to seek compromises and agreements with the new left government, on the basis of a demand of regularisation for all those who requested it, i.e. those who submitted a formal application. In particular, these compromises demoted the demand for universal regularisation, and according to Cissé and Teiar, generally retarded the movement's dynamism. And as the collectives thus lost their momentum, the supporters gained greater weight within the national coordination committee, at the expense of the Sans-Papiers and their autonomy.

By contrast, the autonomous collectives, the most high-profile of which was the *Ile de France*, but which also included the original collective that emerged from the occupation of Saint-Bernard, stuck with the demand of 'papers for all'. For them, the left government of Lionel Jospin and Jean-Pierre Chevènement was continuing with the basic framework of repressive immigration laws, such as short-term residency permits that perpetuated precarity, and continued deportations. As discussed above, in most cases having submitted formal applications for regularisation, individual Sans-Papiers were refused. However, because of the applications, they were now known to the authorities and were at risk of harassment and deportation. That was the sting in the tail of the demand for papers for those requesting it; it created a false hope, and effectively assisted the state in identifying and rounding up people for eventual deportation.

---

181 'Lettre aux Collectifs de sans-papiers et aux organisations de soutien', 5 May 1998, available at www.bok.net/pajol/sanspap/coordination/madjiguene4.html.

182 Abdallah (n 11), 116.

183 'Lettre aux Collectifs de sans-papiers et aux organisations de soutien', 5 May 1998, available at www.bok.net/pajol/sanspap/coordination/madjiguene4.html.

A *Collectif des papiers pour tous* (CDPT) was set up, precisely to oppose negotiations on a case-by-case basis, and to reject the sub-division of the Sans-Papiers into the various categories determined by the state.[184] The CDPT was made up of supporters, rather than Sans-Papiers themselves, but was formed precisely to resist those elements among supporting organisations that were attempting to pressure the Sans-Papiers into accepting limited regularisation on the basis of 'good dossiers'. However, at the same time, another activist group sympathetic to this outlook believed that the absence of the CDPT from the mainstream of the movement, and thus from meetings of the national collective together with supporting organisations, hindered the further development of the movement.[185] The CDPT in fact took a sectarian attitude to the rest of the movement, and eventually petered out. This was in Paris, but elsewhere in the country, there was better coordination between the Sans-Papiers collectives and supporting organisations. The drawback in the provinces was that the Sans-Papiers often felt more exposed and isolated than in the capital. As a result, they would often be less willing to be solely responsible for an autonomous collective, and would instead lean on those with papers and others to take a more public role, for fear of exposing themselves to the threat of arrest, detention and deportation. This was the case, for example, with the Loiret Sans-Papiers discussed above, where the somewhat paternalistic idea of *parrains* and *marrains* was developed. However, some supporting organisations did recognise the problem. One of them, the Réseau No Pasaran, were keen to stress: 'We cannot struggle in place of the people'.[186]

Remaking the refugee/migrant subject

One should not underestimate the extent of the position of weakness from which the Sans-Papiers emerged. For they had been systematically degraded for decades in political discourse as *clandestins*, as an amorphous 'misery' washed up on the shores of France, and placed in positions of precarity and super-exploitation through an apparatus of legal controls and barriers. From that to the place that they have occupied for the last 20 years, as a social force to be reckoned with, in which they have shifted the terms on which they are described, in how their place within society is understood, has been an enormous achievement, and it has been won largely through resistance to the legal categories and processes imposed upon them. Indeed, it was those legal categories and processes that largely led to their degraded place within society in the first place. As Freedman writes, the struggle of the Sans-Papiers represents:

> a key moment in the recent history of immigration in France [that] symbolized both the determination of the French state to refuse to grant

---

184   Réseau No Pasaran (n 152), 134. Details on the formation and outlook of the CDPT can be found in *Chroniques d'un movement* (n 40), 35–36.
185   Réseau No Pasaran (n 152), 135.
186   Ibid 137.

rights to those who were believed to be residing illegally on its territory and also to expel those illegal immigrants wherever possible, and at the same time the political mobilization both of the immigrant population and their French supporters to resist this categorization of illegality.[187]

Others, however, have pointed out certain limitations in how the Sans-Papiers have attempted to challenge imposed identities and subject categories. For example, Walter J. Nicholls has written about how their discourse 'stressed a direct tie to [France]'. As such, they have 'forged their subjecthood not by dis-identification and dissensus, but by identification, and asserting their valid place in the national consensus on citizenship'.[188] Rather than necessarily relying on specific legal categories, they instead attempt to 'conform to national categories and understandings of a good and moral person'.[189] This is certainly evident in a number of claims made by the Sans-Papiers, such as in their appeal to recognition in the 'land of human rights', and as productive workers contributing to the economy. Yet this argument underplays the manner in which the claim for 'papers for all' ruptures the 'national consensus on citizenship' in at least two ways. First, as a demand, it denies to the state and the host community the right of determining membership of the community, instead making such belonging a matter to be contested and negotiated between all sides on an equal basis. Second, insofar as a 'direct tie' to France is asserted, yes, this is often framed in similar terms of shared language, culture, integration into local communities, etc. But it is also sometimes framed in terms of a debt *owed* by France to the post-colonial subject, those who have come from countries formerly ruled by France, or which today are impoverished by the Global North, of which France is of course a part. As such, the right of belonging upsets the collective amnesia in France of the violence of its colonial past and cultural/economic dominance in the present. In short, from a position of extreme vulnerability and weakness, the Sans-Papiers have understandably relied on existing norms of citizenship and belonging, but they have also gone a long way towards challenging them. In what follows, I look at the various ways in which they have done this, which demonstrate both the limitations and the possibilities evident in how the Sans-Papiers have attempted to remake the refugee/migrant subject.

Humanity

The Sans-Papiers have tended to reframe their collective identity in a number of ways. The initial stage consisted of asserting their human rights, by appealing to the history of France as the 'land of human rights', and their demand to have

---

187 Freedman J, 'The French "Sans-Papiers" Movement: an unfinished struggle' in Wendy Pojmann (ed), *Migration and Activism in Europe since 1945* (Palgrave Macmillan, 2008), 81.
188 Nicholls (n 3), 91.
189 Ibid 92.

their rights to live and work in dignity respected.[190] As Cissé argued at the outset of their struggle:

> In France up till now our fate as immigrants was: either take part in the Republic's process of integration, or be deported like cattle ... We have made ourselves visible to say that we are here, to say that we are not in hiding (*clandestin*) but we're just human beings. We are here and we have been here a long time. We have been living and working in this country for many years and we pay our taxes. In the files (*dossiers*) of the Saint-Bernard people you will find wage slips, income tax declarations, old documents giving leave to stay ... the media no longer talks about people who are underground (*clandestins*), but of Sans-Papiers ... we are simply demanding the piece of paper which is our right, so that we can live decent lives.[191]

The tactic of the hunger strike, which was often deployed during church occupations, was part of asserting this claim, for it 'is the place at which an intervention at an humanitarian level can take place, which aims precisely to contest the statist monopoly over the attribution of the individual's status, by blurring the frontiers between the rights of nationals and those of "outsiders", and based on the dignity of human suffering'.[192] However, Thierry Blin's critical reading of the movement argues that too much of their strategy was focused around these sorts of constructs borrowed from a depoliticised, moralistic humanitarianism.[193] While some of these criticisms have merit, he nevertheless acknowledges that the Sans-Papiers were operating at a time when the 'political landscape has been repainted in the colours of morality, where we no longer speak of class struggle but of exclusion, of humanity'.[194] Yet we could see these types of claims as merely the first stage, as a means by which to emerge from a condition of, if you like, *clandestinité* to the field of engagement within society, to assert their visibility and their 'right to have rights'. Many of the Sans-Papiers indeed found their 'political apprenticeship' during the course of hunger strikes, and continued afterwards as dedicated activists.[195]

Beyond that, demands for 'papers for all', which implicitly equals freedom of movement, help problematize and radicalise certain human rights claims. In a pamphlet issued by the NGO *Mouvement Utopia*, they argue that:

> Migration is in fact only a reflection of the exercise of an ancestral freedom, that of coming and going. It is at the very heart of freedom in general. It is

---

190   'Le texte du manifeste des sans-papiers', *Libération*, 25 February 1997, available at www.bok.net/pajol/film.html.
191   Cissé (n 98), 5.
192   Siméant (n 2), 306.
193   Blin (n 29).
194   Blin (n 29), 142.
195   Siméant (n 2), 346.

a fundamental right of the person, and the right to migrate cannot come solely within the legislation of a state.[196]

They go on to reference Article 13 of the Universal Declaration of Human Rights, which describes the right of all to leave their country, and point out that there is no corresponding right to enter another country, thus rendering the right of dubious value. Therefore, by resisting the right of the state to determine such questions, the Sans-Papiers have both used human rights discourse and exploited its aporia. As Freedman writes:

> The Sans-Papiers are not staking their claims on the basis of belonging to a national community or on the basis of status citizenship but rather on the rights that "being here" affords them. The Sans-Papiers draw on a variety of legal discourses that offer them different rights at the local, national, and supranational levels. By unlinking citizenship from national belonging, the Sans-Papiers align themselves with current discussions that challenge the hegemony of the national-citizen coupling within liberal democratic societies. Finally, by focusing on the concrete ways in which discursive and material practices undermine the basic rights to which they are entitled, the Sans-Papiers help disrupt notions of abstract universalism that dominates French political parlance.[197]

Two key ways in which this abstract universalism has been disrupted has been through their claims as workers and post-colonial subjects.

Workers

The second stage in the remaking of their self-identity was as part of the working class. This was most simply expressed in the Sans-Papiers Manifesto issued in January 1997: 'We produce the wealth and we enrich France with our diversity'.[198] It is also important to recognise that the turn towards the trade unions took place at the moment when the mediators ended up refusing to break from the legal framework offered by the government in the summer of 1996. It can therefore be seen as moving away from a more liberal humanitarianism, as represented by the mediators and other supporters. This shift was part of a general strategy of linking up their struggle with other oppressed groups such as the unemployed, the homeless, etc. Part of this was simply good strategy, mostly it was about

---

196 *Mouvement Utopia, Sans-papiers? Pour lutter contre les idées recues* (Éditions Utopia, 2010), 26.

197 Raissiguier (n 75), 10.

198 'Le texte du manifeste des sans-papiers', *Libération*, 25 February 1997, available at www.bok.net/pajol/film.html; Judith Balso brings out the highly class-conscious nature of the Sans-Papiers in 'Au coeur du coeur de notre monde' in *Antoine Pickels À la lumière des sans-papiers* (Complexe, 2001).

solidarity, but Cissé also suggests that it was about breaking down the categor-isation of immigrants as a problem or category apart from the rest of society: 'When one is "specific", one remains within one's own corner, one is control-lable'.[199] As she writes elsewhere, the decision following the occupation of Saint-Bernard to hold all their press conferences in a trade union hall was intended 'to make people understand that we are not only foreigners, but that we're also workers, men and women who work in France'.[200] The curious paradox was that by self-identifying as part of the poor and the working class, they were attempting to be more universal – breaking down the barriers between immigrant and citizen, yet at the same more specific in terms of socio-economic relations. This dual aspect is evident in their initial call to the unions:

> We are issuing an urgent appeal to you for solidarity. Most of us have worked here for many years and have often taken part in struggles at our workplaces. You know that there are no differences between us, workers with or without papers . . . Our struggle is also that of French workers. If we win, then it will be a victory for all. If we lose, it will be a defeat for all.[201]

By engaging the support of the trade unions, the Sans-Papiers made their discourse precisely one of class struggle, i.e. by overcoming the usual playing off of the super-exploited undocumented migrant against the established workforce in danger of having their pay and conditions undercut by the former. The fact that the Sans-Papiers were able to forge strong links with the trade unions so effectively is a testament to precisely their engagement at the level of class solidarity. The emphasis on a 'shared social fate' between documented and undocumented workers drove a wedge through an argument that is frequently used to divide 'indigenous' workers from immigrants. As Anne McNevin writes:

> In a neoliberal environment in which market value increasingly determines the validity of one's social contribution, the Sans-Papiers' claims as workers provide a powerful form of leverage and a legitimising image that directly contradicts the right-wing assault on migrants in general as antisocial lawbreakers.[202]

Indeed, as Saïd Bouamama argues, the effects of neo-liberal globalisation in the 1980s and 1990s had necessitated the creation of a precarious workforce, of which undocumented migrants were an essential part.[203] Yet, at the same time,

---

199 Cissé (n 40), 220.
200 Cissé (n 98), 3.
201 Diop (n 6), 157–158.
202 McNevin (n 84), 110.
203 Bouamama S, 'Contribution au bilan: De la lutte des sans-papiers à partir de l'expérience Lillois' in *Sans-Papiers: Chroniques d'un movement* (Éditions Reflexe/ Agence IM'média, Paris, 1997), 54.

as McNevin and others have noted, there are inherent problems in adapting to the construct of the neo-liberal subject that privileges the economically 'productive' over those who are constructed as parasitical. This has perhaps become most evident in the past decade, as the Sans-Papiers have shifted their emphasis from occupations of public spaces to workplace occupations and strikes.

As a result of new laws passed in 2006 that made employers liable for reporting to the local prefectures on the legal status of their employees,[204] large numbers of undocumented workers were sacked. This led to a wave of strikes and occupations by undocumented workers, often including their documented co-workers as well.[205] At one level, this was simply a clever and effective tactic, because under French law, the strike suspended the contract, thus preventing them from being formally ended. Moreover, occupying a place of work, as opposed to a church or other public space, triggered a legal process, which granted certain rights to the occupiers. In essence, the police are only allowed to evict them if they are not company employees.[206] These strikes and occupations continued for several years, and eventually gave rise to a new identity: the Sans-Papiers worker.[207] But this bred new tensions, between the traditional collectives of Sans-Papiers, which had not identified themselves *solely* as workers, and the new Sans-Papiers workers who were exclusively being organized on the basis of their employment relationship and thus through the trade unions. When in April 2008 the collective *Coordination 75 des sans-papiers* (CSP 75) had their dossiers summarily refused by the Prefecture of Paris because they had not been submitted by a recognised intermediary such as a trade union, they responded by occupying the offices of their trade union, declaring their autonomy and calling for a national strike by Sans-Papiers.[208] When they were evicted from the *Confédération générale du travail* (CGT) offices, the CSP 75 occupied another building, declaring themselves the 'Minister for the Regularisation of All Sans-Papiers'. At the time of writing, they continue to be an active group, fighting to defend the rights of refugees caught up in the so-called 'Jungle' camp at Calais.[209]

The strikes eventually petered out in 2010, at least partly because the form in which they took, with the new category of 'Sans-Papier worker', ended up being exclusionary, and forcing through regularisation via exiting legal routes. As such, Barron et al. assert:

---

204 *Loi no 2006–911 du 24 juillet 2006 relative à l'immigration et à l'intégration.*
205 For a detailed chronology and analysis of these events, see Barron P, Bory A, Chauvin S, Jounin N and Tourette L, *'On bosse ici, on reste ici!' La grève des sans-papiers: une aventure inédite* (Éditions La Découverte, 2011).
206 Barron P, Bory A, Chauvin S, Jounin N and Tourette L, 'State Categories and Labour Protest: Migrant Workers and the Fight for Legal Status in France' (2016), 30, *Work, Employment and Society*, 631, 638.
207 Ibid 639.
208 Declaration by the Coordination 75 des sans-papiers in occupation, reproduced in Diallo et al. (n 103), 15.
209 See their website: www.ministere-de-la-regularisation-de-tous-les-sans-papiers.net/ joomla1.5/.

The 'Sans-Papier worker' has not merely been a discursive articulation emerging from the imagination of trade union officials; it was first and foremost the product of state processes, economic transformations and social practices.[210]

The point that Barron et al. make is that the 'Sans-Papier worker' was useful as a symbolic and thus as a political claim to a collective belonging within the wider working class, but once it became tied to legal categories, it allowed once again the state to determine the status of belonging.

Post-colonial subjects

The Sans-Papiers were acutely aware of the fact that their presence in France was directly linked to France's own past occupation of their countries. This was evident from the beginning of the struggle in 1996:

> Where do we come from, we Sans-Papiers of Saint-Bernard? It is a question we are often asked, and a pertinent one. We didn't immediately realize ourselves how relevant this question was. But as soon as we tried to carry out a "site inspection", the answer was very illuminating: We are all from former French colonies, most of us from West-African countries: Mali, Senegal, Guinea and Mauritania. But there are also among us several Maghreb people (Tunisians, Moroccans and Algerians); there is one man from Zaire and a couple who are Haitians. So, it's not an accident that we find ourselves in France.[211]

Although they have not staked their claims mainly on this basis, it has been a recurrent theme that punctures much of the arrogance and collective amnesia that is expressed in ideas of waves of human misery, and judging the deserving or undeserving nature of immigrant rights claims. Recent statements from the movement which highlight the reasons for their flight from their home countries assert their agency in ways which encompass all irregular migrants, whether economically productive or not, and ignores the boundaries of the usual discourses on forced migration which tend to place its subjects at the level of mere victims. Instead, they demand recognition on the basis of post-colonial forms of exploitation:

> [We] have chosen to leave Africa . . . we always decided to move . . . we want a possibility, we wanted to keep our future in our hands . . . we wanted to free ourselves from a system of exploitation which has no borders.[212]

---

210 Barron et al. (n 206), 643.
211 Cissé (n 98), 1.
212 Quoted in McNevin (n 84), 112.

McNevin emphasises the overcoming of victimhood evidenced by this statement when she writes: 'their starting point is recognition as active agents in their own political futures, both at the point of choosing to migrate and within the context of their migration destination'.[213] A book chronicling the 2-year long occupation of the CGT offices in 2008–2010 bears a title that makes the explicit link between the colonial past, the exploitation of the present and their demands: *Hier colonisés, aujourd'hui exploités, demain regularisés* ('yesterday colonised, today exploited, tomorrow regularised').[214]

At the same time, the Sans-Papiers are keen to reject notions of what Susan Marks has described as 'false contingency', whereby things that appear as if they were purely a result of choice and chance are in fact largely determined by pre-existing circumstances.[215] So while the Sans-Papiers have 'chosen' to come to France, which in turn presents a choice to the host community as to whether or not to accept them, in fact the historical experience of colonialism which is also linked to contemporary divisions of wealth between the Global North and the Global South, have both impelled the Sans-Papiers towards France, and likewise *require* of France a duty in accepting them. Pierre Bourdieu and Loïc Wacquant write that 'every migrant carries this repressed relation of power between states within himself or herself and unwittingly recapitulates and re-enacts it in her personal strategies and experiences'.[216] One must add, though, that the Sans-Papiers have indeed not only become fully aware of the reasons why they are in France but have also educated the French about this 'repressed relation of power'. Vincent Decroly punctures the collective amnesia, when he challenges us to consider whether ' "all the misery of the world" was something inevitable, a reality parachuted in from some unknown and particularly malicious heaven'.[217] A group of Sans-Papiers held in prison made the point even more forcefully, when they wrote a letter of solidarity with the hunger strikers at Saint-Bernard:

If they say that France cannot support all the misery of the world, they forget that Africa is not the whole world. Because France has a duty to Africans. It is they who have impoverished us, exploited us (slavery, wars, colonisation, forced labour, etc.) How many Africans were transported to be sold? How many Africans died for France in all of its wars? How many tonnes (in billions) of mineral resources have been from Africa to France for its reconstruction, its development?[218]

---

213 McNevin (n 84), 112–113.
214 Diallo et al. (n 103).
215 Marks S, 'False contingency' (2009), 62, *Current Legal Problems*, 1.
216 Bourdieu P and Wacquant L, 'The Organic Ethnologist of Algerian Migration' (2000), 1, *Ethnography*, 173, 175.
217 Decroly V, 'Le devoir d'asile' in Antoine Pickels (ed), *À la Lumière des Sans-Papiers* (Complex, 2001), 235.
218 Quoted in Coindé (n 67), 96.

This position was echoed in a declaration issued by the collective of worker-priests condemning the expulsion of the Sans-Papiers from Saint-Bernard:

> It is not just today or yesterday that we take into our hearts the particularly painful fate of those people from elsewhere – especially from the countries of Africa – and who we have sacrificed for our defence and whose resources we have looted for our own development.[219]

Although somewhat more ambiguous in how they put it, the mediators also identified the same debt owed to the Sans-Papiers: 'Forgetting the contribution of previous generations of foreigners to its prosperity and its defence . . . France ignores the duties owed to their children as because of their contribution to its defence, its economy and its culture'.[220]

It is here, in these types of contestation, that it becomes evident how the Sans-Papiers have posited forms of subjectivity that can rupture ideas of citizens and outsiders. In doing so, they have re-established a discourse of the political as 'dissensus', the conflict of opposing subjects immune from any kind of universalist consensus and re-asserting the place in society of those hitherto excluded.[221] Moreover, by establishing such a discourse, the Sans-Papiers have forced French society to acknowledge the complex circumstances that have led to their flight, whether it be poverty, persecution, ties to the former colonial master-country or accidental circumstances that have led to their irregular status. They have, in short, successfully subverted legally fictitious categories and notions of belonging, which had resulted in the denial of papers in the first place. Through their collective political struggles that have problematised the paradigm of legal and illegal immigration, and reconfigured their identities as forced migrants using a much more sophisticated, and true, narrative of themselves as active in shaping their conditions, yet constrained and impelled by circumstances not of their choosing. As Naomi Millner writes:

> Rather than being articulated through universal rights claims, asserting particular obligations on states and citizenship regimes, the act of solidarity with irregular migrants' claims to presence problematises the partiality of state citizenship categories.[222]

Law, as a means for judging on the basis of 'objective' categories and abstract rights, cannot accommodate the sort of claims that have been made on the basis of historic and present exploitation of individuals, communities and indeed whole

---

219   Quoted in Ibid 156.
220   'Adresse au gouvernement', 15 June 1996, available at www.bok.net/pajol/com-med.html.
221   Rancière J, *Disagreement: Politics and Philosophy* (University of Minnesota, 1999).
222   Milner (n 53), 66.

regions of the world; indeed, it obscures and denies such claims. Through seizing and using sanctuary as a platform to demand protection and their place in the societies of the Global North, the Sans-Papiers have gone a long way towards remaking the refugee/migrant subject, precisely in terms of recognising narratives that cannot be contained within the law.

Conclusion

Accompanying the Sans-Papiers, we are a long way from claims made according to legal categories and norms, and even further away from the specific distinction in law between a refugee and a migrant. However, one should not overstate the case; the Sans-Papiers have not achieved complete success in terms of winning regularisation for all, or of re-establishing sanctuary outside of the law. But they have won tens of thousands of them the right to stay and to live their lives with a dignity that they would otherwise have been denied. They have forced French society to at least re-examine the basis on which migrants and refugees are allowed into the country. Bouamama highlights a number of important achievements, of which I think three are critical.[223] First, the Sans-Papiers have created spaces in which they are able to emerge from hidden and precarious situations, and gain the strength to act collectively. Second, their struggle has overcome the divisions into different legal categories. And third, they have established their right and their ability to organise autonomously. Smaïn Laacher has argued that, by demanding their right to stay in France, in spite of the strict interpretation of the law, the Sans-Papiers have moved public discourse in France away from a terrain of law and 'cold juridical technicalities to registering the confrontation of opinions in the space of what is just and unjust, of justice and injustice'.[224] In a famous speech given in support of the Sans-Papiers in March 1997, Étienne Balibar eloquently expressed the debt owed to the Sans-Papiers for achieving this:

> We owe them for having broken through the communication barriers, for being seen and heard for what they are: not specters of delinquency and invasion, but workers and families, from here and there at the same time, with their particularisms and the universality of their condition as modern proletarians. They made facts, questions and even oppositions linked to the real problems of immigration circulate in public space, instead of the stereotypes held by dominant information monopolies ... We owe them for having shattered the pretentions of successive governments to play two games: on one side, "realism", administrative competence and political responsibility (regulating population flows, maintaining public order, assuring the "integration" of legal immigrants ...); on the other side, nationalist and

---

223 Bouamama (n 203), 56–57.
224 Laacher (n 15), 18.

electoral propaganda (creating scapegoats for insecurity, projecting the fear of mass poverty into the phantasmal space of identitarian conflicts). The Sans-Papiers have demonstrated that the regime of illegality wasn't reformed by the State, but actually created by it. They have shown that this production of illegality, destined for political manipulation, couldn't happen without constantly violating civil rights.[225]

In short, the Sans-Papiers have taught us to reject the artificial constructs of the 'legal' refugee/migrant which have come to hegemonise discourse over the past century, and which have erected ever higher barriers to those seeking refuge and/or a better life. But their demands go further, for they:

> constitute a heretical transgression, "sacrilege", of national frontiers. To demand equality of rights between nationals and foreigners, and even more between nationals and undocumented, is to question that which is at the very foundation of the power of the state: the monopoly over the designation of national status.[226]

Thus, 'with the Sans-Papiers, the institution of a closed . . .community becomes fragile, random, non-definitive'.[227] This is the complete opposite of the stable, fixed and exclusionary paradigm of citizens and immigrants that has been a foundation of the modern world, one that denies the space of asylum. The means by which the Sans-Papiers have achieved this, moreover, was inaugurated through the tradition of using spaces of sanctuary to resist law and the sovereign order. Refugee law and law as such could not have achieved this, and indeed, insofar as it played a role in their struggle, it was a negative one. Such spaces of sanctuary could not survive in the long term, for as we saw in Part I of this book, the legal statist order is predicated upon the insistence that such spaces must always be subsumed within it. Yet it does show that sanctuary as a form of grassroots asylum survives as a space from which to win protection and acceptance that would otherwise be excluded from the legal construct of the 'refugee' or other migrant categories, and presents a challenge to the statist monopoly over asylum.

---

225 Balibar E, 'What we owe to the Sans-Papiers' in Len Guenther and Cornelius Heesters (eds), *Social Insecurity* (Anansi, 2000), 42–43.
226 Siméant (n 2), 159.
227 Laacher (n 15), 22.

Conclusion to Part III

A common argument put up by advocates of the international refugee law regime is that it provides the last line of defence for the rights of refugees. But for the 1951 Refugee Convention, forced migrants would be subject to the capriciousness of sovereign power. Yet, the picture that emerges from our discussion of the Sanctuary Movement and the Sans-Papiers is somewhat different. From that perspective, this legal regime is at worst an exclusionary tool, and at best simply does not speak to the needs of people who have been forced to migrate due to forms of structural violence and inequality. The delineation of the refugee subject, by insisting on evidence of individualised forms of persecution, simply cannot accommodate those fleeing wars and economic deprivation.

For some, it might seem that people suffering persecution are more deserving of protection, of being granted a specific status as a 'refugee', than other forced migrants. The problem with this is two-fold. First, as has been evident in the last two chapters, particularly in relation to those who escaped Central America in the 1980s, making such a distinction is impossible in a great many cases. Political repression, generalised violence and poverty are often closely linked, and practically speaking people do not slot neatly into one form of suffering or another. To insist on the rigid difference between these categories is to reject the demands of migrant groups, like the Sans-Papiers, whose personal histories and needs cannot be contained within them. Second, even if you think that making a distinction between 'refugees' and other forced migrants is both possible and justified, it inevitably follows that every migrant, including the privileged group, must be forced through a legal process in which proof must be offered to justify their inclusion into the category of refugee. As some in the Sanctuary Movement used to joke, proving refugee status often required presenting a 'note from your dictator' as sufficient evidence of persecution. As we saw in Part II, refugee law was constructed specifically to place that evidential burden on the putative refugee. The Sanctuary Movement and the Sans-Papiers both arose as a necessary means to offer support to refugees/migrants who have found themselves caught in the net of this legal trawling operation.

The instinctive move to claim spaces of sanctuary was, in both cases, a form of resistance to the reach of sovereign power, in particular to the legal trap of categorisations. Notwithstanding the later mirroring of the legal form by some within the Sanctuary Movement, that was the initial response of the activists in Tucson, when they found desperate people being routinely rejected for refugee status. The Sans-Papiers were even clearer about formulating an identity that transcended legal distinctions between labour migrants, refugees, asylum-seekers, etc. For the US activists, the inspiration of the historic tradition of asylum was clearly evident; for the Sans-Papiers, this was less the case. However, what they had in common was a recognition that protection is necessarily founded upon spaces, not on a defined subject, or at least not a subject as confined within legal norms. Activists in the Sanctuary Movement were pulled into the orbit of law, to their own detriment. The Sans-Papiers created a greater distance from the law by developing their claims on a more political basis. In both cases, though, they achieved a measure of protection by acting outside of, and then in confrontation with the law.

These two movements provide an additional and critical lesson for us. It is both possible and necessary for migrant activists and their supporters to prioritise forms of grassroots asylum, rather than simply pursuing claims within the framework of refugee law. For those who think that the current political context makes such strategies impossible, one should reflect on the fact that these achievements were won at the height of Reaganism in the United States and a Gaullist hegemony in France. The strength of these movements was the alliance between the refugees/migrants and their supporters. As such, they demonstrated the potential to break down the ultimate form of legal categorisation, between citizens and non-citizens. In the case of the Sans-Papiers, and to a lesser extent the Sanctuary Movement, the re-establishment of refugees/migrants as active subjects has been of the utmost importance in rejecting the passivity and false identities imposed upon them by refugee law. To pose the question of whether this could have been achieved via a legal strategy, even on the best terms granted by refugee law, is to answer it. As such, the Sanctuary Movement and the Sans-Papiers suggest that grassroots asylum rather than refugee law is the way forward in restoring protection and agency for refugees/migrants. For the avoidance of doubt, this is not a call to simply ignore the potential of the law to achieve certain rights. But it is about recognising the extreme limitations of this path, and the potential for it to close down rather than open up a space of asylum.

The movements were effective at a practical level. Tens of thousands, perhaps hundreds of thousands, of refugees/migrants were able to successfully resist deportation or win regularisation of their status, who otherwise would not have done so if they had relied on the legal process. Thus, grassroots asylum is not merely about posing some impractical ideal. On the contrary, one could argue that relying on the refugee law regime itself is somewhat unrealistic for most refugees/migrants in terms of winning protection and the ability to live in dignity.

The movements also shifted the terms of the debate in their respective countries in ways that would have been impossible via the law itself. The critical point is that the legal process is by nature an individualised one, and thus somewhat hidden from public view. Grassroots asylum is by nature collective and relies on engagement on the socio-political plane. In spite of the hostile political context towards refugees/migrants in the United States in the early 1980s and in France in the mid-1990s, forms of grassroots asylum were able to prise open a space of contestability. In both cases, this required raising the question of migration in the context of their states' role in creating the conditions that led to movements of refugees/migrants in the first place. Thus, the focus becomes less a biopolitical concern over controlling their movements, and more a geo-political recognition of the causes of movement. Opening up these questions therefore increased the legitimacy of the claim to stay and to be legally regularised. Of course, the ultimate aim is to have legal rights recognised; but paradoxically, this could only be achieved by extending the parameters of the question beyond the law.

Conclusion

The aim of this book has been to challenge the standard narrative that explains the downfall of the refugee in recent decades as a function of the corruption of the international refugee law regime. Instead, I hope that I have managed to substantiate the argument that in fact, the crises faced by refugees today is immanent to the existence of the legal form, particularly when applied to the question of delineating the refugee subject, and determining the basis on which asylum is conceived of and offered. The route out of the degraded and abusive situation faced by most refugees today cannot therefore be reliant on appeals to states to more closely cleave to the 1951 Refugee Convention, or other aspects of refugee law. From the law of 397 in late imperial Rome to the canon lawyers' *casus excepti* through to the 1951 Convention, law has repeatedly sought to confine the notion of the deserving refugee subject within narrow and artificial limits. The key distinction between the categories of the pre-modern age and those of today is that the former at least began from a presumption of open access to asylum, whereas contemporary refugee law categories start from the presumption of a closed system of asylum, to which only privileged groups can gain access.

In contrast, by outlining the key elements of asylum as it had been practised in Ancient Greece, Rome, the early Church and medieval England, I was able to show how it was grounded in the idea of being antagonistic to law, or at the very least maintaining an arms-length relationship to it. In addition, I highlighted the key instances where law had attempted to regulate asylum, and showed from the hazy evidence of Solon's laws, through to the Tiberian reforms, the Roman laws of the late fourth century and mid-fifth century, the canon law's *casus excepti* and the Tudor Reformation how repeatedly the imposition of law compromised or destroyed asylum. It is important to stress that in all these instances, bar that of the Tudors, the law did not aim at outlawing asylum altogether, only to regulate and manage the practice. The point is that the historical record shows that, even on those terms, the effect of law is toxic for asylum, and for those who would seek protection within it. This suggests, therefore, that the key problem is not crude attempts at prohibition but rather a more insidious process of defining and constraining.

In Part II, I attempted to show that the primary concerns that drove the birth and development of modern refugee law were about managing and controlling the movements of forced migrants rather than concern for them. What emerged clearly from that discussion is a much less romantic and humanitarian impetus towards the development of international refugee law than is generally acknowledged today. Certainly, there appears little to suggest that the phenomena of refugee law, involving the ever-greater monitoring, measuring and controlling of the refugee subject by states, has much in common with asylum, predicated as it was on its distance from sovereign power. Therefore, not only does refugee law fail to maintain or protect the underlying basis of asylum, it goes in completely the opposite direction.

But this still leaves open the question as to whether this problem is simply due to bad laws, and perhaps some other legal configuration could be an improvement, or could succeed in framing asylum in a more positive way. However, law, by its nature, seeks to define and regulate in universal terms; anything that fits within that picture is legal and thus right or just, anything that exists beyond that field of vision is then illegal and lacking legitimacy. Whereas asylum has frequently been about contested spaces and notions of justice, law steps in claiming the final word. The theoretical basis for understanding the nature of law as outlined in the introduction to this book, drawing upon writers such as Foucault, Agamben, Pashukanis, Badiou and others, goes some way to unpacking why and how law operates in the way that it does. Moreover, the themes introduced there, of biopolitics, securitisation, depoliticisation and the creation of hollowed-out subjects, that are all immanent to, or intimately linked to law, go some way to understanding that law will always impact negatively upon asylum.

In Part III, all of the aspects described above become telescoped through the lens of the Sanctuary Movement and the Sans-Papiers, and their relationship to law. Here, we find attempts to recreate spaces beyond the reach of law, and to facilitate the reconfiguration of subjectivities away from the deadening ones imposed by law. These movements challenged the right of law to have the final judgement, and opened up a space, literally and figuratively, in which issues over border control, on who should be granted asylum, on the responsibilities of the host state for the causes of the refugees' flight, on the distinctions to be drawn between 'refugees' and 'migrants', or between 'deserving' and 'undeserving', along with many other questions, could be contested. But we also saw how the existence of refugee law, and of legal categories generally, compromised these movements too. According to the standard narrative that posits refugee law as primarily concerned with humanitarian protection, the passage of the 1980 Refugee Act should have aided the refugees from Central America and indeed the Sanctuary Movement. For the refugees, it was evident from the pronouncements of administration and INS officials that the bureaucratic procedures and the restrictive provisions contained in the Act, all lifted from the 1951 Convention, actually created a more effective means to bar access to asylum. For the sanctuary activists – at least, a good proportion of them – the effect of refugee law was to lull them into thinking that recourse to law was the solution to the refugees' predicament, rather than the mechanism that was denying them asylum in the first place. Similarly, with the Sans-Papiers, in spite of France's long-standing commitment to the 1951 Convention, it did not act as an effective shield against denial of asylum, or the threat of deportation. Indeed, the rigid separation of different classes of migrants, from the 1945 *ordonnance* on immigration through to the creation of 'eligibility certificates' based on Article 1A of the 1951 Convention, became the means by which to deny asylum, and to render forced migrants of all sorts vulnerable to exploitation and exclusion. The recourse to 'respect for the law' became the rallying cry of the state in resisting the claims of the Sans-Papiers, and of some supporters to reject the demand of 'papers for all'. In the United States, supporters of sanctuary ended up performing the law on refugees; in France, they ended up cleaving more to the logic of the state than to the claims of the refugees/migrants themselves. In both cases, the problem stemmed from the belief in the idea of good laws being badly implemented or ignored, rather than recognising that law itself was the problem.

Finally, I wish to pose the question as to what should be the attitude of refugees, other activists and lawyers to asylum and refugee law, based on what we have learnt in this book. First, an argument for open borders must be waged, for it is evident that the coming of refugee law as a form of protection only became seen as a necessity with the development of border controls, passports, visas, etc.[1] To those who think that such a proposition is utopian, it is worth recalling that the dismantling of border controls would simply restore the international order to something resembling a system that existed prior to World War I. Even more recently, although border controls existed in the 1950s and 1960s, states largely abstained from enforcing them. An open borders policy effectively operates among the states of the European Union. At the height of the Syrian refugee crisis in 2015, Germany suspended most border controls to take in several hundred thousand people in just a few weeks. While there has been a backlash against these recent events, it does show that if the political will is there, we are capable, with difficulties to be sure, of 'accommodating the misery of the world' without the need for stringent border checks and a contrived determination of who should be allowed entry. Moreover, as was highlighted by both the Sanctuary Movement and the Sans-Papiers, those of us in the Global North cannot ignore the contribution of our states to the misery that drives many in the world to migrate in the first place. Thus, a policy of open borders also represents a duty owed to the poor and dispossessed. Moreover, without border controls, all of the concerns to do with categorising and subjectivising the range of people who move across the world would become of little importance.

Nonetheless, it must be recognised that we may be a long way off from achieving a reopening of borders on a global scale. This then makes an orientation towards 'grassroots asylum', a necessary short-term measure. We must recognise

---

1   For a detailed and convincing argument for open borders, see Hayter T, *Open Borders: The Case against Immigration Controls* (Pluto, 2000).

the difficulties of creating and sustaining such practices in a world so hegemonised by sovereign power and the rule of law. Nonetheless, as the Sanctuary Movement and the Sans-Papiers have proved, it is at least possible to open up spaces in which to contest the terms of refugee reception and in which refugees, and migrants generally, can reclaim some of their political identity and agency. Thus, a meaningful practice of asylum today must be based on the following precepts. First, respect for the political agency of refugees/migrants must be paramount, and this means recognising their right to autonomy. Even the most well-meaning supporters, as we have seen, can be pulled towards adopting and performing the law; autonomy for refugees/migrants can act as an effective check on that tendency. Second, in the context of strict border controls, we must recognise that it will be up to us, communities of refugees/migrants and their supporters, to consider ways of establishing spaces of asylum, which are not reliant on the law, indeed which act as bases from where the law may be resisted. Third, asylum must be offered without discrimination, by deconstructing the contrived boundaries between refugee, IDP, economic migrant, etc. Often refugee advocates argue for a rigid division between asylum and general immigration law on the basis that asylum is about offering help to people in distress who should not be subject to ordinary border controls. But, as we have seen in this book, once such a distinction is drawn, then *all* migrants are forced to undergo the strictures of border control, where the refugee 'wheat' can be sorted from the immigrant 'chaff'. Further, we will simply be acting as adjuncts to the state in imposing such divisions. It is a fallacy of refugee law that we can, and should, make rigid distinctions between someone fleeing a war zone in order to find a better life and working conditions, a refugee and an economic migrant. Is there really a qualitative difference in the need for protection if one's life is threatened by a persecutor, starvation, climate change, lack of adequate medical care, etc.?[2] Moreover, by insisting on such distinctions, we end up placing a heavy burden of proof on forced migrants to establish their bona fides, and arrogantly assume our right to judge them.

But for all that, it would be wrong to take an abstentionist approach to refugee law, or to whatever legal rights might be beneficial to aiding the crossing of borders and enabling a right to stay and to enjoy as decent a life as possible. To do so would, in a world of border controls, simply abandon forced migrants completely to the capriciousness of sovereign power. Moreover, the conditions for establishing forms of 'grassroots asylum' may often be missing, or difficult to achieve. But there is a big difference between an opportunistic approach to law – to use and manipulate it as far as possible in the interests of forced migrants – and a romantic belief that it somehow contains within it the principle of asylum.

---

2   A detailed argument for conceiving people fleeing the effects of climate change as 'climate refugees' can be found in Chapter 2; Kent A and Behrman S, *Facilitating the Resettlement and Rights of Climate Refugees: An Argument for Developing Existing Principles and Practices* (Taylor and Francis, 2018).

Doing the latter involves a complete misunderstanding of the nature of both law and asylum, and it places one in a position of adjunct, rather than adversary, to sovereign power. The longer view of asylum and refugee law instead enables us to recognise the irreconcilable conflict between the two. For if asylum is to have any meaningful place in our society, then we – forced migrants, advocates, researchers, teachers, commentators, activists – must constantly assert its claim beyond the boundaries of law.

Bibliography

Archives

Atlanta Sanctuary Committee Papers, Swarthmore College Peace Collection, Swarthmore, PA (ASCP).

Chicago Religious Task Force on Central America Records, 1982–1992, Wisconsin Historical Society, Madison, WI (CRTFCAR).

First United Methodist Church of Germantown, Philadelphia, PA (FUMCOG).

Gustav Schultz Sanctuary Collection, Graduate Theological Union Archives, Berkeley, CA (GSSC).

Immigration and Naturalization Service Archives, History Library, United States Citizenship and Immigration Services, Washington, DC (INSA).

Luther Place Memorial Church, Washington, DC (LPMC).

Books and articles

American Friends Service Committee *Seeking Safe Haven: A Congregational Guide to Helping Central American Refugees in the United States* (American Friends Service Committee, Church World Service Immigration and Refugee Program, Inter-Religious Task Force on El Salvador and Central America, and Lutheran Immigration and Refugee Service, 1982).

Abdallah MH, *J'y suis! J'y reste!: Les luttes de l'immigration en France depuis les années soixante* (Éditions Reflex, 2000).

Abou-El Wafa A, *The Right to Asylum between Islamic Shari'ah and International Refugee Law: A Comparative Study* (UNHCR, 2009).

Adamic L, *America and the Refugee* (Public Affairs Committee, 1939).

Agamben G, 'We Refugees' (1995), 49, *Symposium*, 114.

—— *Homo Sacer: Sovereign Power and Bare Life* (Daniel Heller-Roazen tr, Stanford University Press, 1998).

—— 'In praise of profanation' in *Profanations* (Jeff Fort tr, Zone Books, 2007).

—— *De la très haute pauvreté: Règles et forme de vie* (Joël Gayraud tr, Bibliotèque Rivages, 2011).

Agier M, *On the Margins of the World: The Refugee Experience Today* (David Fernbach tr, Polity, 2008).

Akin S, 'Sans-papiers: une denomination dans cinq quotidiens nationaux de mars à août 1996' (1999), 60, *Mots*, 59.

Alleweldt R, 'Preamble to the 1951 Convention' in Andreas Zimmermann (ed), *The 1951 Convention Relating to the Status of Refugees and its 1967 Protocol: A Commentary* (OUP, 2011), 225–240.

Allitt P, *Religion in America since 1945: A History* (Columbia University Press, 2003).

Anker DE and Posner HP, 'The Forty Year Crisis: A Legislative History of the Refugee Act of 1980' (1981), 19, *San Diego Law Review*, 9.

Arendt H, *The Origins of Totalitarianism* (Schocken, 2004).

Arnaout GM, *Asylum in the Arab-Islamic Tradition* (UNHCR, 1987).

Augustine, *The City of God* (Henry Bettenson tr, Penguin, 1984).

Badiou A, *Ethics: An Essay on the Understanding of Evil* (Peter Hallward tr, Verso, 2001).

Baker JH, 'The English Law of Sanctuary' (1990), 2, *Ecclesiastical Law Journal*, 8.

Balibar E, 'Le droit de cite ou l'apartheid' in Étienne Balibar, Monique Chemillier-Gendreau, Jacqueline Costa-Lascoux and Emmanuel Terray (eds), *Sans-Papiers: l'archaisme fatal* (Éditions La Découverte et Syros, 1999), 89–116.

—— 'What we owe to the Sans-Papiers' in Len Guenther and Cornelius Heesters (eds), *Social Insecurity* (Anansi, 2000) 42–43.

Balogh E, *Political Refugees in Ancient Greece* (Witwatersrand University, 1943).

—— 'World Peace and the Refugee Problem' (1949), 75, *The Hague Academy of International Law*, 363.

Balso J, 'Au coeur du coeur de notre monde' in Antoine Pickels (ed), *À la lumière des sans-papiers* (Complexe, 2001) 197–206.

Barron P, Bory A, Chauvin S, Jounin N and Tourette L, *'On bosse ici, on reste ici!' La grève des sans-papiers: une aventure inédite* (Éditions La Découverte, 2011).

—— 'State Categories and Labour Protest: Migrant Workers and the Fight for Legal Status in France' (2016), 30, *Work, Employment and Society*, 631.

Barstad HM, 'The strange fear of the Bible: some reflections on the "Bibliophobia" in recent Israelite historiography' in Lester L Grabbe (ed), *Leading Captivity Captive: 'The Exile' as History and Ideology* (Sheffield Academic Press, 1998) 120–127.

Bassiouni MC, *International Extradition and World Public Order* (AW Sijthoff, 1974).

Bau I, *This Ground is Holy: Church Sanctuary and Central American Refugees* (Paulist Press, 1985).

Bauman Z, 'Who is Seeking Asylum – And from What?' (2005), 4, *Mediactive*, 90.

Beccaria C, 'On Crimes and Punishments' in Aaron Thomas (ed) *On Crimes and Punishments and Other Writings* (Aaron Thomas and Jeremy Parzen tr, University of Toronto, 2008) 1-113.

Behrman S, 'Accidents, Agency and Asylum: Constructing the Refugee Subject' (2014), 25, *Law and Critique*, 249.

—— 'Legal Subjectivity and the Refugee' (2014), 26, *International Journal of Refugee Law*, 1.

—— 'On the Creation and Accommodation of the Misery of the World: The Case of the Sans-Papiers' (2017), 49, *Refugee Watch*, 26.

Bellamy J, *Crime and Public Order in England in the Later Middle Ages* (Routledge and Kegan Paul, and University of Toronto, 1973).

Berman HJ, *Law and Revolution: The Formation of the Western Legal Tradition* (Harvard University, 1983).

—— *Faith and Order: The Reconciliation of Law and Religion* (William B Eerdmans Publishing, 2000).

Bevan V, *The Development of British Immigration Law* (Croom Helm, 1986).

Bianchi H, *Justice as Sanctuary: Toward a New System of Crime Control* (Indiana University, 1994).

Bibler Coutin S, *The Culture of Protest: Religious Activism and the U.S. Sanctuary Movement* (Westview Press, 1993).

—— 'Enacting law through social practice: sanctuary as a form of resistance' in Mindie Lazarus-Black and Susan F Hirsch (eds), *Contested States: Law, Hegemony and Resistance* (Routledge, 1994) 282–304.

Billheimer A, 'Naturalization in Athenian Law and Practice' (PhD Thesis, Princeton University, 1922).

Blin T, *Les sans-papiers de Saint-Bernard: Mouvement social et action organisé* (L'Harmattan, 2005).

—— *L' Invention des sans-papiers: Essai sur la démocratie à l'épreuve du faible* (Presses Universitaires de France, 2010).

Bolesta-Koziebrodzki L, *Le Droit d'asile* (AW Sythoff, 1962).

Bouamama S, 'Contribution au bilan: De la lutte des sans-papiers à partir de l'expérience Lillois' in *Sans-Papiers: Chroniques d'un movement* (Éditions Reflexe/Agence IM'média, Paris, 1997), 54–61.

Bourdieu P and Wacquant L, 'The Organic Ethnologist of Algerian Migration' (2000), 1, *Ethnography*, 173.

Boutang YM, Garson J-P, and Silberman R, *Économie politique des migrations clandestines de main-d'œuvre: Comparaisons internationales et exemple* (Publisud, 1986).

Bouvier J, *Bouvier's Law Dictionary: Volume II* (Francis Rawle ed, rev edn, Boston Book Co., 1897).

Brueggemann W, 'Textuality in the Church' in Nelle G Slater (ed), *Tensions between Citizenship and Discipleship: A Case Study* (Pilgrim Press, 1989), 24–41.

Bulmerinq A, *Das Asylrecht in seiner geschlichtlichen Entwicklung* (Martin Sandig, 1853).

Canefe N, 'The fragemented nature of the international refugee regime and its consequences: a comparative analysis of the applications of the 1951 Convention' in James C Simeon (ed), *Critical Issues in International Refugee Law: Strategies Towards Interpretative Harmony* (CUP, 2010) 174–210.

Carro JL, 'Sanctuary: The Resurgence of an Age-Old Right or a Dangerous Misinterpretation of an Abandoned Ancient Privilege?' (1986), 54, *University of Cincinnati Law Review*, 747.

Carroll RP, 'Exile! What exile? Deportation and the discourses of diaspora' in Lester L Grabbe (ed), *Leading Captivity Captive: 'The Exile' as History and Ideology* (Sheffield Academic Press, 1998) 62–79.

Chakrabarti S, 'Rights and Rhetoric: The Politics of Asylum and Human Rights Culture in the United Kingdom' (2005), 32, *Journal of Law and Society*, 131.

Chamberlain MD, 'The Mass Migration of Refugees and International Law' (1983), 7, *The Fletcher Forum of World Affairs*, 93.

Chicago Religious Task Force on Central America, *Sanctuary: A Justice Ministry* (Chicago Religious Task Force on Central America, 1986).

Chimni BS, 'From Resettlement to Involuntary Repatriation: Towards a Critical History of Durable Solutions to Refugee Problems' (2004), 23, *Refugee Survey Quarterly*, 55.

Cicero, *De Res Publica, De Legibus* (Clinton Walker Keyes tr, Heinemann, 1928).

—— *De Oratore: Volume One* (EW Sutton tr, Heinemann, 1942).

—— *Letters to Atticus: Volume One* (DR Shackleton Bailey tr, Harvard University, 1999).

Cissé M, *The Sans-Papiers: The New Movement of Asylum Seekers and Immigrants without Papers in France – A Woman Draws the First Lessons* (Crossroads Books, 1997).

—— *Parole de Sans-papiers* (La Dispute, 1999).

Cohen EE, ' "Whoring under contract": the legal context of prostitution in fourth-century Athens' in Virginia Hunter and Jonathan Edmondson (eds), *Law and Social Status in Classical Athens* (OUP, 2000) 113–148.

Cohen R, 'Citizens, Denizens and Helots: The Politics of International Migration Flows in the Post-War World' (1989), 21, *Hitotsubashi Journal of Social Studies*, 153.

Cohen S, *From the Jews to the Tamils: Britain's Mistreatment of Refugees* (South Manchester Law Centre, 1988).

Coindé H, *Curé des sans-papiers: Journal de Saint-Bernard* (Éditions du Cerf, 1997).

Collectif des Sans-Papiers du Loiret, *Sans papiers, tu vis pas* (L'Harmattan, 2000).

Corbett J, *Goatwalking* (Penguin, 1992).

Costa-Lascoux J, 'L'illusion de la maîtrise: la politique migratoire en trompe-l'oeil' in Étienne Balibar, Monique Chemillier-Gendreau, Jacqueline Costa-Lascoux and Emmanuel Terray (eds), *Sans-Papiers: l'archaïsme fatal* (Éditions La Découverte et Syros, 1999), 35–62.

Coursier H, 'Restauration du droit d'asile' (1950), 32, *Revue Internationale de la Croix-Rouge et Bulletin international des Sociétés de la Croix-Rouge*, 909.

Cox JC, *The Sanctuaries and Sanctuary Seekers of Mediaeval England* (George Allen & Sons, 1911).

Crawford C, 'Embassy Confrontations and Diplomatic Asylum' (2009), 18 December, Diplomat www.diplomatmagazine.com/index.php?option=com_content&view=article&id=161&Itemi, accessed 24 January 2015.

Crittenden A, *Sanctuary: A Story of American Conscience and the Law in Collision* (Weidenfeld & Nicolson, 1988).

Crook JA, *Law and Life of Rome* (Thames and Hudson, 1967).

Cunningham H, *God and Caesar at the Rio Grande: Sanctuary and the Politics of Religion* (University of Minnesota Press, 1995).

—— 'Sanctuary and sovereignty: church and state along the U.S.–Mexico border' (1998), 40, *Journal of Church and State*, 371.

Daniel B, *Neighbor: Christian Encounters with 'Illegal' Immigration* (Westminster John Knox Press, 2010).

Davidson M, *Convictions of the Heart: Jim Corbett and the Sanctuary Movement* (University of Arizona Press, 1988).

Decroly V, 'Le devoir d'asile' in Antoine Pickels (ed), *À la Lumière des Sans-Papiers* (Complex, 2001) 231- 238.

Dench E, *Romulus' Asylum: Roman Identities from the Age of Alexander to the Age of Hadrian* (OUP, 2005).

Derrida J and Dufourmantelle A, *Of Hospitality* (Rachel Bowlby tr, Stanford University Press, 2000).

Diallo M, Fofana V and Genz L, *Hier colonisés, aujourd'hui exploités, demain regularisés: Les journées de la Coordination 75 des Sans-Papiers* (Fage, 2010).

Dio C, *Dio's Roman History: Volume 5* (Earnest Cary tr, Heinemann, 1969).

Dionysius of Halicarnassus, *The Roman Antiquities of Dionysius of Halicarnassus: Volume One* (Earnest Cary tr, Heinemann, 1937).

Diop A, *Dans la peau d'un sans-papiers* (Seuil, 1997).

Ducloux A, *Ad ecclesiam confugere: Naissance du droit d'asile dans les églises* (De Boccard, 1994).

Ecoffey CB, 'Asylum in Switzerland: A Challenge for the Church' (Masters Thesis, University of Manchester, 2007).

Edelman B, *Ownership of the Image: Elements for a Marxist Theory of Law* (Elizabeth Kingdom tr, Routledge & Kegan Paul, 1979).

Einarsen T, 'Drafting history of the 1951 Convention and the 1967 Protocol' in Andreas Zimmermann (ed), *The 1951 Convention Relating to the Status of Refugees and its 1967 Protocol: A Commentary* (OUP, 2011) 37–74.

Elmadmad K, 'Asylum in Islam and Modern Refugee Law' (2008), 27, *Refugee Survey Quarterly*, 51.

Ferris EG, 'The churches, refugees, and politics' in Gil Loescher and Laila Monahan (eds), *Refugees and International Relations* (OUP, 1989) 159–177.

Field T, 'Biblical Influences on the Medieval and Early Modern English Law of Sanctuary' (1991), 2, *Ecclesiastical Law Journal*, 222.

Foley MS, 'Sanctuary! A bridge between civilian and GI protest against the Vietnam War' in Marilyn B YoFung and Robert Buzzanco (eds), *A Companion to the Vietnam War* (Blackwell Publishers, 2002), 416–433.

Foot P, *Immigration and Race in British Politics* (Penguin, 1965).

Foucault M, 'Nietzsche, genealogy, history' in DF Bouchard (ed), *Language, Counter-Memory, Practice: Selected Essays and Interviews* (Cornell University, 1977), 139–164.

—— *The Care of the Self: The History of Sexuality, Volume III* (Robert Hurley tr, Penguin, 1990).

—— *The Use of Pleasure: The History of Sexuality, Volume II* (Robert Hurley tr, Penguin, 1992).

—— 'Truth and juridical forms' in James D Faubion (ed), *Power: Essential Works of Foucault 1954–1984, Volume Three* (Robert Hurley tr, Penguin, 2002).

—— *Security, Territory, Population: Lectures at the Collège de France 1977–1978* (Graham Burchell tr, Palgrave Macmillan, 2007).

—— *The Birth of Biopolitics: Lectures at the Collège de France 1978–1979* (Graham Burchell tr, Picador, 2010).

Francis ST, *Smuggling Revolution: The Sanctuary Movement in America* (Capital Research Center, 1986).

François A, 'Capitalisme et sans-papiers' in Antoine Pickels (ed), *À la lumière des sans-papiers* (Complexe, 2001) 109–126.

Frank C, 'Le traitement politico-institutionnel du movement des sans-papiers à Barcelone: de la négociation à la répression' in Magali Boumaza and Philippe Hamman (eds), *Sociologie des mouvements de précaires: Espaces mobilises et repertoires d'action* (L'Harmattan, 2007) 185–210.

Freedman J, 'The French "Sans-Papiers" Movement: an unfinished struggle' in Wendy Pojmann (ed), *Migration and Activism in Europe since 1945* (Palgrave Macmillan, 2008), 81–98.

Fruchterman RL, 'Asylum: Theory and Practice' (1972), 26, *Judge Advocate General Journal*, 169.

García MC, ' "Dangerous times call for risky responses": Latino immigration and sanctuary, 1981–2001' in Gastón Espinosa, Virgilio Elizondo and Jesse Miranda (eds), *Latino Religions and Civic Activism in the United States* (OUP, 2005), 159–176.

Gerety T, 'Sanctuary: a comment on the ironic relation between law and morality' in David A Martin (ed), *Refugee Law in the 1980s: The Ninth Sokol Colloquium on International Law* (Martinus Nijhoff, 1986), 159–180.

Gil-Bazo MT, 'Asylum as a General Principle of International Law' (2015), 27, *International Journal of International Law*, 3.

GISTI, *Sans-papiers mais pas sans droits* (GISTI, 2004).

Glover D, *Literature, Immigration, and Diaspora in Fin-de-Siècle England: A Cultural History of the 1905 Aliens Act* (Cambridge University, 2012).

Golden R and McConnell M, *Sanctuary: The New Underground Railroad* (Orbis Books, 1986).

Goldsmith-Kasinsky R, *Refugees from Militarism: Draft-Age Americans in Canada* (Transaction Books, 1976).

Goodwin-Gill G, *International Law and the Movement of Persons between States* (OUP, 1978).

—— 'Refugee identity and protection's fading prospect' in Frances Nicholson and Patrick Twomey (eds), *Refugee Rights and Realities: Evolving International Concepts and Regimes* (Cambridge University, 1999), 220–252.

Goussault B, *Paroles de sans-papiers* (Les Éditions de L'Atelier, 1999).

Grahl-Madsen A, 'The European Tradition of Asylum and the Development of Refugee Law' (1966), 3, *Journal of Peace Research*, 278.

—— *The Status of Refugees in International Law: Volume One* (AW Sijthoff, 1966).

—— *The Status of Refugees in International Law: Volume Two* (AW Sijthoff, 1972).

—— *Territorial Asylum* (Almqvist & Wiksell, 1980).

Greig DW, 'The Protection of Refugees and Customary International Law' (1978), 8, *Australian Year Book of International Law*, 108.

Grotius H, *The Law of War and Peace* (Francis W Kelsey tr, Bobbs-Merrill, 1962).

Guzder D, *Divine Rebels: American Christian Activists for Social Justice* (Lawrence Hill, 2011).

Haagen P, 'Imprisonment for Debt in England and Wales' (PhD Thesis, Princeton University, 1986).

Hallie PP, *Lest Innocent Blood Be Shed: The Story of the Village of Le Chambon, and How Goodness Happened There* (Harper and Row, 1979).

Hallward P, 'Badiou's Politics: Equality and Justice' (2002), 4 *Culture Machine*.

Hargreaves AG, *Immigration, 'Race' and Ethnicity in Contemporary France* (Routledge, 1995).

Harrell-Bond B, *Imposing Aid: Emergency Assistance to Refugees* (OUP, 1986).

—— 'Camps: Literature Review' (1998), 2, *Forced Migration Review*, 22.

Harris J, *Law and Empire in Late Antiquity* (Cambridge University, 1999).

Hathaway JC, 'The Evolution of Refugee Status in International Law: 1920–1950' (1984), 33, *International and Comparative Law Quarterly*, 348.

—— 'A Reconsideration of the Underlying Premise of Refugee Law' (1990), 31, *Harvard International Law Journal*, 129.

—— 'Why Refugee Law Still Matters' (2007), 8, *Melbourne Journal of International Law*, 89.

Hayes DM, *Body and Sacred Space in Medieval Europe, 1100–1389* (Routledge, 2003).

Hayter T, *Open Borders: The Case against Immigration Controls* (Pluto, 2000).

Helmholz RH, *The Ius Commune in England: Four Studies* (OUP, 2001).

Hobbs HH, *City Hall Goes Abroad: The Foreign Policy of Local Politics* (Sage, 1994).

Holborn LW, 'The Legal Status of Political Refugees 1920–1938' (1938), 32, *American Journal of International Law*, 680.

—— *Refugees: A Problem of Our Time* (Scarecrow Press, 1975).

Howland T and Garcia R, 'The refugee crisis and the law: The "City Sanctuary" response' in Ved P Nanda (ed), *Refugee Law and Policy: International and U.S. Responses* (Greenwood Press, 1989), 185–200.

Hunt A and Wickham G, *Foucault and Law* (Pluto, 1994).

Hutchinson EP, *Legislative History of American Immigration Policy 1798–1965* (University of Pennsylvania, 1981).

Ives EW, 'Crime, sanctuary, and royal authority under Henry VIII: the exemplary sufferings of the savage family' in Morris S Arnold and others (eds), *On the Laws and Customs of England* (University of North Carolina, 1981), 296–320.

Jahn E, 'Developments in Refugee Law in the Framework of Regional Organisations outside Europe' (1966), 13, *Association for the Study of the World Refugee Problem Bulletin*, 75.

Jefferies J, *The U.K. Population: Past, Present and Future* (Office of National Statistics, 2005).

Jennings RY, 'Some International Law Aspects of the Refugee Question' (1939), 20, *British Year Book of International Law*, 98.

Joly D, 'A new asylum regime in Europe' in Frances Nicholson and Patrick Twomey (eds), *Refugee Rights and Realities: Evolving International Concepts and Regimes* (Cambridge University, 1999).

Jordan WC, 'A fresh look at medieval sanctuary' in Ruth Mazo Karras, Joel Kaye and E Ann Matter (eds), *Law and the Illicit in Medieval Europe* (University of Pennsylvania, 2008), 17–32.

Juvenal, *The Sixteen Satires* (Peter Green tr, 3rd edn, Penguin, 1998).

Kagné B, 'Sans-Papiers en Belgique' in Antoine Pickels (ed), *À la lumière des sans-papiers* (Complexe, 2001) 41–60.

Kantorowicz EH, *The King's Two Bodies: A Study in Mediaeval Political Theology* (Princeton University, 1957).

Kaplan C, *Questions of Travel: Postmodern Discourses of Displacement* (Duke University, 1996).

Karatani R, 'How History Separated Refugee and Migrant Regimes: In Search of Their Institutional Origins' (2005), 17, *International Journal of Refugee Law*, 517.

Kaufman PI, 'Henry VII and Sanctuary' (1984), 53, *Church History*, 465.

Keïta M, 'Le roi mage de Saint-Bernard était une princesse mandingue' in *Sans-Papiers: Chroniques d'un mouvement* (Editions Reflexe et Agence Im'média, Paris, 1997), 24–25.

Kent A and Behrman S, *Facilitating the Resettlement and Rights of Climate Refugees: An Argument for Developing Existing Principles and Practices* (Taylor and Francis, 2018).

Kershaw R and Pearsall M, *Immigrants and Aliens: A Guide to Sources on UK Immigration and Citizenship* (2nd edn, The National Archives, 2004).

Kirby LJ, 'Sanctuary: The Right of Asylum in the Corpus Iuris Canonici' (Masters Thesis, Catholic University of America, 1986).

Koulish R, *Immigration and American Democracy: Subverting the Rule of Law* (Routledge, 2010).

Krenz FE, 'The Refugee as a Subject of International Law' (1966), 15, *International and Comparative Law Quarterly*, 90.

Kurzban IJ, 'A Critical Analysis of Refugee Law' (1982), 36, *University of Miami Law Review*, 865.

Kushner T and Knox K, *Refugees in the Age of Genocide* (Frank Cass, 1999).

Laacher S, *Mythologie du Sans-papiers* (Le Cavalier bleu editions, 2009).

Lauwers M, 'Le cimetière dans le Moyen Age latin: Lieu sacré, saint et religieux' (1999), 54, *Annales*, 1047.

Lebacqz K, 'Paul Revere and the Holiday Inn: a case study in hospitality' in Nelle G Slater (ed), *Tensions between Citizenship and Discipleship: A Case Study* (Pilgrim Press, 1989), 110–127.

Lee E, 'A nation of immigrants and a gatekeeping nation: American immigration law and policy' in Reed Ueda (ed), *A Companion to American Immigration* (Blackwell Publishing, 2006), 5–35.

Le Roy Ladurie E, *Montaillou: Cathars and Catholics in a French Village 1294–1324* (Barbara Bray tr, Penguin, 1980).

Lippert RK, *Sanctuary, Sovereignty, Sacrifice: Canadian Sanctuary Incidents, Power, and Law* (UBC Press, 2005).

Livy, *The Early History of Rome* (Aubrey de Selincourt tr, Penguin, 1971).

—— *Rome and the Mediterranean* (Henry Bettenson tr, Penguin, 1976).

Loescher G, *Beyond Charity: International Cooperation and the Global Refugee Crisis* (OUP, 1993).

Loescher G and Scanlan JA, *Calculated Kindness: Refugees and America's Half-Open Door, 1945 to the Present* (The Free Press, 1986).

Logan WA, 'Criminal Law Sanctuaries' (2003), 38, *Harvard Civil Rights-Civil Liberties Law Review*, 321.

Lorentzen R, *Women in the Sanctuary Movement* (Temple University, 1991).

McAdam J, 'The Enduring Relevance of the 1951 Convention' (2017), 29, *International Journal of Refugee Law*, 1.

McDaniel J, *Sanctuary: A Journey* (Firebrand Books, 1987).

McDonald J, 'Citizenship, illegality, and sanctuary' in Vijay Agnew (ed), *Interrogating Race and Racism* (University of Toronto Press, 2007), 112–134.

—— 'Building a sanctuary city: municipal migrant rights in the city of Toronto' in Peter Nyers and Kim Rygiel (eds), *Citizenship, Migrant Activism and the Politics of Movement* (Routledge, 2012), 129–145.

McNevin A, 'Political Belonging in a Neo-Liberal Era: The Struggle of the Sans-Papiers' (2006), 10, *Citizenship Studies*, 135.

—— *Contesting Citizenship: Irregular Migrants and New Frontiers of the Political* (Columbia University Press, 2011).

Macrides RJ, 'Killing, Asylum, and the Law in Byzantium' (1988), 63, *Speculum*, 509.

McSheffrey S, 'Sanctuary and the Legal Topography of Pre-Reformation London' (2009), 27, *Law and History Review*, 483.

Malkki LH, 'Refugees and Exile: From "Refugee Studies" to the Natural Order of Things' (1995), 24, *Annual Review of Anthropology*, 495.

Marfleet P, *Refugees in a Global Era* (Palgrave Macmillan, 2006).

—— 'Understanding "Sanctuary": Faith and Traditions of Asylum' (2011), 24, *Journal of Refugee Studies*, 440.

Marks S, 'False Contingency' (2009), 62, *Current Legal Problems*, 1.

Marrus MR, *The Unwanted: European Refugees from the First World War through the Cold War* (Temple University, 2002).

Marx K, 'The communist manifesto' in Max Eastman (ed and tr), *Capital, The Communist Manifesto and Other Writings* (The Modern Library, 1959), 34–62.

—— 'On the Jewish Question' in *Early Writings* (Rodney Livingstone and Gregor Benton tr, Penguin, 1975).

Matas D, *The Sanctuary Trial* (University of Manitoba, 1989).

Mazzinghi, TJ de', *Sanctuaries* (Halden & Son, 1887).

Milligan CS, 'Ethical aspects of refugee issues and U.S. policy' in Ved P Nanda (ed), *Refugee Law and Policy: International and U.S. Responses* (Greenwood Press, 1989), 165–184.

Milner N, 'Sanctuary sans-frontières: social movements and solidarity in post-war Northern France' in Randy K Lippert and Sean Rehaag (eds), *Sanctuary Practices in International Perspectives: Migration, Citizenship and Social Movements* (Routledge, 2013), 57–70.

Mokgoro JY, 'Ubuntu, the Consitution and the Rights of Non-Citizens' (2010), 21, *Stellenbosch Law Review*, 221.

Moore JB, *A Digest of International Law: Volume II* (US Government Printing Office, 1906).

Morey JH, 'Plows, Laws, and Sanctuary in Medieval England and in the Wakefield "Mactacio Abel"' (1998), 95, *Studies in Philology*, 41.

Morgenstern F, 'The Right of Asylum' (1949), 26, *British Yearbook of International Law*, 327.

Morice A, 'Migrants: libre circulation et lutte contre la précarité' in *Sans-Papiers: Chroniques d'un Mouvement* (Éditions Reflex/Agence IM'média, 1997), 90–102.

Mouvement Utopia, Sans-papiers? Pour lutter contre les idées recues (Éditions Utopia, 2010).

Nelson AC and Coffin WS, 'A Debate on Sanctuary' (1985), 7, *Church & State Abroad*, 1.

Ngai MM, *Impossible Subjects: Illegal Aliens and the Making of Modern America* (Princeton University, 2004).

Nicholls WJ, 'Making Undocumented Immigrants into a Legitimate Political Subject: Theoretical Observations from the United States and France' (2013), 30, *Theory, Culture & Society*, 82.

Noiriel G, *Le creuset française: Histoire de l'immigration XIXe -XXe siècles* (Seuil, 1988).

—— *Réfugiés et sans-papiers: La République face au droit d'asile XIXe -XXe siècles* (Hachette, 1998).

OFPRA, *De la Grande guerre aux guerres sans nom: une histoire de l'OFPRA* (OFPRA, nd).

Ong Hing B, *Making and Remaking Asian America through Immigration Policy 1850–1990* (Stanford University, 1993).

Osterweis RG, *Three Centuries of New Haven* (Yale University, 1964).

Otter EL and Pine DF (eds), *The Sanctuary Experience: Voices of the Community* (Aventine Press, 2004).

Ourliac P, 'Les villages de la region toulousaine: au XIIe siécle' (1949), 4, *Annales*, 268.

Pashukanis EB, *Marxism and Law: A General Theory* (Barbara Einhorn tr, Pluto, 1989).

Patsias C and Williams N, 'Religious sanctuary in France and Canada' in Randy K Lippert and Sean Rehaag (eds), *Sanctuary Practices in International Perspectives: Migration, Citizenship and Social Movements* (Routledge, 2013).

Patterson C, *Pericles' Citizenship Law of 451–50 B.C.* (The Ayer Company, 1981).

Plaut WG, *Asylum: A Moral Dilemma* (Praeger, 1995).

Plutarch, *Plutarch's Lives* (John Langhorne and William Langhorne tr, William Tegg, 1862).

—— *The Rise and Fall of Athens* (Ian Scott-Kilvert tr, Penguin, 1960).

—— *Plutarch on Sparta* (Richard JA Talbert tr, Penguin, 1988).

Polybius, *The Histories: Volume Four* (WR Patton tr, Heinemann, 1925).

Ponty J, *L'immigration dans les textes: France, 1789–2002* (Belin, 2003).

Pope S, 'Sanctuary: The Legal Institution in England' (1987), 10, *University of Puget Sound Law Review*, 677.

Porter B, *The Refugee Question in Mid-Victorian Politics* (Cambridge University, 1979).

Price ME, *Rethinking Asylum: History, Purpose, Limits* (Cambridge Univesity, 2010).

Rademacher N, 'Sanctuary Movement' in Patrick J Hayes (ed), *The Making of Modern Immigration: An Encyclopedia of People and Ideas* (ABC-CLIO, 2012), 663–682.

Rancière J, *Disagreement: Politics and Philosophy* (University of Minnesota, 1999).

Raissiguier C, *Reinventing the Republic: Gender, Migration, and Citizenship in France* (Stanford University Press, 2010).

Renou X, *Désobéir avec les sans-papiers* (Éditions le passage clandestin, 2009).

Réville A, 'L' "Abjuratio Regni"' (1892), 50, *Revue Historique*, 1.

Reyerson KL, 'Flight from Prosecution: The Search for Religious Asylum in Medieval Montpellier' (1992), 17, *French Historical Studies*, 603.

Rigsby KJ, *Asylia: Territorial Inviolability in the Hellenistic World* (University of California, 1996).

Rose A, *Showdown in the Sonoran Desert: Religion, Law, and the Immigration Controversy* (OUP, 2012).

Rosenwein BH, *Negotiating Space: Power, Restraint, and the Privileges of Immunity in Early Medieval Europe* (Manchester University, 1999).

Ryan WC, 'The Historical Case for Sanctuary' (1987), 29, *Journal of Church and State*, 209

Sambou A, Davy J and Gispert H (eds), *Chroniques des Sans-Papiers* (Éditions Syllepse, 2008).

'Sanctuary – The Congregation as a Refuge', Report of the international workshop, held under the auspices of the Council of Churches in the Netherlands and the Human Rights Desk of the National Council of Christian Churches in the United States of America, 26–30 August 1986 (Kerk en Wereld, 1986).

Sané M, *'Sorti de l'ombre': Journal d'un Sans-papiers* (Le Temps des Cerises, 1996).

Sans-Papiers: Chroniques d'un mouvement (Éditions Reflexe/Agence IM'média, Paris, 1997).

Schoenholtz AI and Bernstein H, 'Improving Immigration Adjudications through Competent Counsel' (2008), 21, *Georgetown Journal of Legal Ethics*, 55.

Schuck PH, *Citizens, Strangers, and In-Betweens: Essays on Immigration and Citizenship* (Westview Press, 1998).

Schmahl S, 'Article 1B 1951 Convention' in Andreas Zimmermann (ed), *The 1951 Convention Relating to the Status of Refugees and its 1967 Protocol: A Commentary* (OUP, 2011) 467–480.

Schmidt PW, 'Refuge in the United States: The Sanctuary Movement Should Use the Legal System' (1986), 15, *Hofstra Law Review*, 79.

Scot J-P, *L'Etat chez lui, l'Eglise chez elle: comprendre la loi de 1905* (Seuil, 2005).

Scott MC, 'Asylia' in Roger S Bagnall and others (eds), *The Encyclopedia of Ancient History* (Wiley-Blackwell, 2012), 892–893.

Sexton JP, 'Saint's Law: Anglo-Saxon Sanctuary Protection in the Translatio et Meracula S. Swithuni' (2006), 23, *Florilegium*, 61.

Shah P, *Refugees, Race and the Legal Concept of Asylum in Britain* (Cavendish, 2000).

Shoemaker KB, 'Sanctuary Law: Changing Conceptions of Wrongdoing and Punishment in Medieval European Law' (PhD Thesis, University of California, Berkeley, 2001).

—— *Sanctuary and Crime in the Middle Ages 400–1500* (Fordham University Press, 2011).

Siebert WH, 'A Quaker Section of the Underground Railroad in Northern Ohio' (1930), 39, *Ohio Archaeological and Historical Quarterly*, 53.

—— *The Mysteries of Ohio's Underground Railroads* (Long's College Book Company, 1951).

—— *The Underground Railroad: From Slavery to Freedom: A Comprehensive History* (Dover Publications, 2006).

Silverman M, *Deconstructing the Nation: Immigration, Racism, and Citizenship in Modern France* (Routledge, 1992).

Siméant J, *La cause des sans-papiers* (Presses de Sciences Po, 1998).

Simpson AWB, 'The Laws of Ethelbert' in Morris S Arnold and others (eds), *On the Laws and Customs of England* (University of North Carolina, 1981), 3–17.

Simpson JH, *Refugees: Preliminary Report of a Survey* (Royal Institute of International Affairs, 1938).

—— 'The Refugee Problem' (1938), 17, *International Affairs*, 607.

Skran C, 'Historical development of international refugee law' in Andreas Zimmermann (ed), *The 1951 Convention Relating to the Status of Refugees and its 1967 Protocol: A Commentary* (OUP, 2011) 3–36.

Slater NG, 'A case study of offering hospitality: choosing to be a Sanctuary Church' in Nelle G Slater (ed), *Tensions between Citizenship and Discipleship: A Case Study* (Pilgrim Press, 1989), 3–21.

Smith C, *Resisting Reagan: The U.S. Central America Peace Movement* (University of Chicago, 1996).

Southern RW, *Western Society and the Church in the Middle Ages* (Penguin, 1970).

Stanley A, *Historical Memorials of Westminster Abbey* (John Murray, 1886).

Stevens D, *UK Law and Asylum Policy: Historical and Contemporary Perspectives* (Sweet & Maxwell, 2004).

Stevens F, 'Irresistible visions' in Jane Donovan (ed), *Many Witnesses: A History of Dumbarton United Methodist Church 1772–1990* (Dumbarton United Methodist Church, 1998), 415–437.

Stevens J, 'Prisons of the Stateless' (2006), 42, *New Left Review*, 53.

Tacitus MG, *The Annales of Imperial Rome* (Michael Grant tr, Penguin, 1973).

—— *Germania* (JB Rives tr, Clarendon Press, 1999).

Terray T, 'Le travail des étrangers en situation irrégulièr ou la délocalisation sur place' in Étienne Balibar, Monique Chemillier-Gendreau, Jacqueline Costa-Lascoux and Emmanuel Terray (eds), *Sans-Papiers: l'archaïsme fatal* (Éditions La Découverte et Syros, 1999), 9–34.

Thornberry C, *The Stranger at the Gate: A Study of the Law on Aliens and Commonwealth Citizens* (The Fabian Society, 1964).

Thornley ID, 'The Destruction of Sanctuary' in RW Seton-Watson (ed), *Tudor Studies* (Longmans, 1924), 182–207.

—— 'Sanctuary in Medieval London' (1932), 38, *Journal of the British Archaeological Association*, 293.

Thucydides, *History of the Peloponnesian War* (Rex Warner tr, Penguin, 1972).

Thurman WS, 'A Law of Justinian Concerning the Right of Asylum' (1969), 100, *Transactions of the American Philological Association*, 593.

Tiberghien F, *La protection des réfugiés en France* (2nd edn, Économica, 1988).

Tigar ME, *Law and the Rise of Capitalism* (Monthly Review Press, 2000).

Timbal Duclaux de Martin P, *Le Droit d'Asile* (Librarie du Recueil Sirey, 1939).

Tomsho R, *The American Sanctuary Movement* (Texas Monthly Press, 1987).

Trenholme N, 'The Right of Sanctuary in England: A Study in Institutional History' (1903), 1, *University of Missouri Studies*, 1.

Trotsky L, *My Life: An Attempt at an Autobiography* (Penguin, 1975).

Tuitt P, *False Images: The Law's Construction of the Refugee* (Pluto, 1996).

—— *Race, Law, Resistance* (Glasshouse, 2004)

—— 'Rethinking the refugee concept' in Frances Nicholson and Patrick Twomey (eds), *Refugee Rights and Realities: Evolving International Concepts and Regimes* (Cambridge University, 1999), 106–118.

Türk V and Nicholson F, 'Refugee protection in international law: an overall perspective' in Erika Feller, Volker Türk and Frances Nicholson (eds), *Refugee Protection in International Law: UNHCR's Global Consultations on International Protection* (Cambridge University, 2003), 3–45.

Vauchez A, Dobson B and Lapidge M (eds), *Encyclopedia of the Middle Ages: Volume Two* (James Clark & Co., 2000).

Verdirame G and Harrell-Bond B, *Rights in Exile: Janus-Faced Humanitarianism* (Berghahn, 2005).

Walsh JH and O'Neill ME, 'Sanctuary: A Legal Privilege or Act of Civil Disobedience?' (1987), 61, *Florida Bar Journal*, 11.

Watson A (tr), *The Digest of Justinian* (University of Pennsylvania, 1985).

Webber F, *Borderline Justice: The Fight for Refugee and Migrant Rights* (Pluto, 2012).

Weis P, 'The International Protection of Refugees' (1954), 48, *The American Journal of International Law*, 193.

—— *The Refugee Convention, 1951: The Travaux Préparatoires Analysed with a Commentary by Dr Paul Weiss* (Cambridge University, 1995).

West EH, 'The Right of Asylum in New Mexico in the Seventeenth and Eighteenth Centuries' (1928), 8, *Hispanic American Historical Review*, 357.

Westerman W, 'Central American refugee testimonies and performed life histories in the Sanctuary Movement' in Rina Benmayor and Andor Skotnes (eds), *Migration and Identity: International Yearbook of Oral History and Life Stories, Volume III* (OUP, 1994), 224–234.

Wihtol de Wenden C, *Les immigrés et la politique: cent cinquante ans d'évolution* (Presses de Sciences Po, 1988).

Willaime J-P, '1905 et la pratique d'une laïcité de reconnaissance sociale des religions' (2005), 129, *Archives de sciences sociales des religions*, 67.

Willigan JD, 'Sanctuary: A Communitarian Form of Counter-Culture' (1970), 25, *Union Seminary Quarterly Review*, 517.

Wolff C, *Jus Gentium Methodo Scientifica Petractatum: Volume Two* (Clarendon Press, 1934).

Yarnold BM, *Refugees without Refuge: Formation and Failed Implementation of U.S. Political Asylum Policy in the 1980's* (University Press of America, 1990).

Zetter R, 'Labelling Refugees: Forming and Transforming a Bureaucratic Identity' (1991), 4, *Journal of Refugee Studies*, 39.

—— 'More Labels, Fewer Refugees: Remaking the Refugee Label in an Era of Globalization' (2007), 20, *Journal of Refugee Studies*, 172.

Zimmermann A and Mahler C, 'Article 1 A, para. 2 1951 Convention' in Andreas Zimmermann (ed), *The 1951 Convention Relating to the Status of Refugees and its 1967 Protocol: A Commentary* (OUP, 2011) 281–466.

Zucker NL and Zucker NF, *Desperate Crossings: Seeking Refuge in America* (ME Sharpe, 1996).

Index